Standard Korean Grammar
for
Foreigners

About the authors

Jong Rok Kim is a professor of Korean linguistics at Handong University. He began his study of Korean language education at Kyungpook National University, where he received B.A., M.A. and Ph.D. in Korean linguistics.
He is author of the popular introductory textbook *Korean School Grammar and Grammar Education* and *Korean Verb Conjugation Dictionary for Foreigners*. He has held visiting professorships at The University of California, Irvine and University of Oxford.

Ji Eun Jung is a Korean language instructor at center for Korean Language and Culture, Hankuk University of Foreign Studies. She received a B.A. in English and international area studies from Handong University and an M.Ed. in teaching Korean language as a foreign language from Hankuk University of Foreign Studies. She has completed doctoral course in Korean language as a foreign language where she received M.Ed.

Erin Lee is a professional interpreter & translator. After completing her master's degree in HUFS GSIT, she has worked as an interpreter at Hana Daetoo Securities, Shinhan BNP Paribas Asset Management and Hyundai Heavy Industries. Some of the major dignitaries for whom she interpreted include Indian Prime Minister Narendra Modi and economist Marc Faber.

Standard Korean Grammar for Foreigners

Copyright © 2016 by Jong Rok Kim & Ji Eun Jung & Erin Lee
All rights reserved.

Published by Pagijong press
4, Cheonho-daero 16ga-gil, Dongdamun-gu, Seoul 02589, South Korea
Tel : 82-2-922-1192~3
Fax : 82-2-928-4683
www.pjbook.com
Printed in Seoul, Korea

ISBN 979-11-5848-070-7 (93710)

Standard Korean Grammar

for Foreigners

Jong Rok Kim & Ji Eun Jung & Erin Lee

Pagijong Press

Preface

The best feature of this book is that it explained Korean grammar easily, simply and systematically. Throughout this book, foreigners will learn Korean grammar in relatively short period time.

This book is an English version of *Standard Korean Grammar for Foreigners*(『외국인을 위한 표준 한국어 문법』, 2008, 박이정) published in Korean. I have revised many parts of Korean version including appendix, so this book will help foreigners learn Korean grammar more effectively.

This book will be a great help to a person who wants to be a Korean language teacher for foreigners. First of all, this book explains Korean grammar systematically. If you read this book, you will stand on top of a mountain called Korean grammar and will realize how to teach Korean grammar.

Before I wrote this book, I received a lot of help. First, I want to thank professor Sang Tae Lee who led me like parents. He not only guided me to major Korean grammar, but also taught me what the true education should be.

Especially I thank God. God lets me know my raison d'etre and the purpose of life. And he makes me lie down in green pastures and leads me beside quiet waters whenever I get tired of living and get down.

I also want to thank Ji Eun Jung and Erin Lee, they translated the Korean version of this book into English, and made this book richer. Without their help, it would have been difficult to publish this book.

Lastly, I would like to express my thank to Mr. Chan Ik Park, the CEO of Pagijong Publishing Company, for the opportunity to publish this manuscript and editorial team manager Gee Eun Kim for her neat editing.

January 2016
Jong Rok Kim

Contents

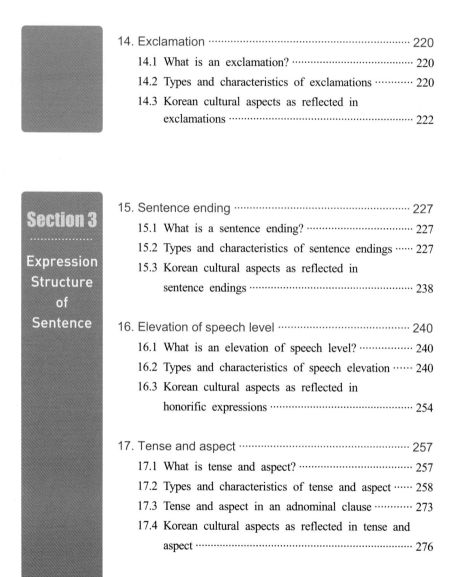

Section 3

················

Expression
Structure
of
Sentence

Section 4

Sentence
Extension

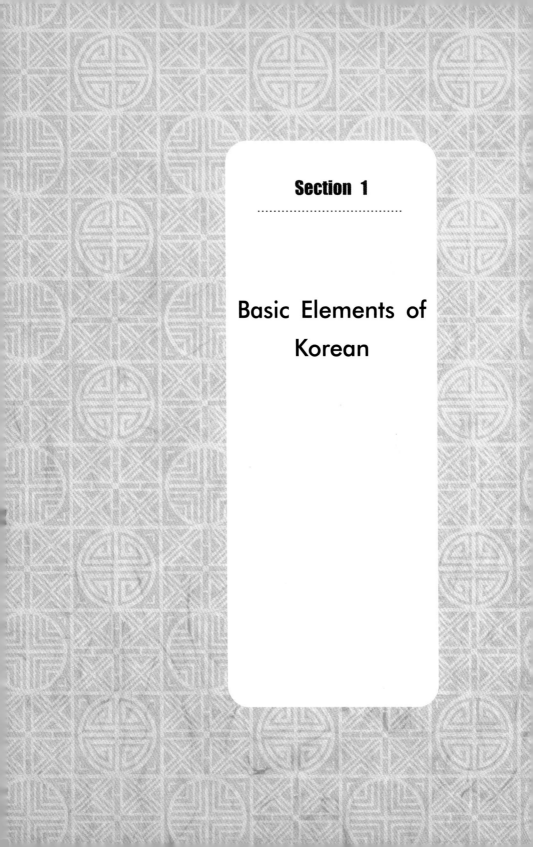

Section 1

Basic Elements of Korean

Standard Korean Grammar

for Foreigners

01 Vowel and consonant

1.1 What is a vowel and a consonant?

Every language in the world has consonants and vowels universally. However the number of consonants and vowels is different in many languages, and their own **phonetic values**(음가) are also different. Let us see Korean consonants and vowels, then.

- A **Vowel**(모음) is sound produced without blocking the airflow. Korean has 21 vowels.
- A **Consonant**(자음) is sound produced by completely blocking or so restricting the airflow. Korean has 19 consonants.

It is difficult for foreigners to study Korean pronunciation because there are many tensed and aspirated consonants, as well as several diphthongs. However, you will soon get used to Korean pronunciation easily through the understanding the characteristics of consonants and vowels according to the explanations of this book and repeating pronunciation many times.

1.2 Types and characteristics of vowels

Korean vowel has 10 **monophthongs**(단모음) and 11 **diphthongs**(이중모음). The monophthong is a vowel which is pronounced the same shape of tongue or lip from beginning to finish. For monothong, there are 'ㅏ, ㅓ, ㅗ, ㅜ, ㅡ, ㅣ, ㅐ, ㅔ, ㅚ and ㅟ'.

These **monophthongs**(단모음) can be classified into three categories, as follows: high vowels, mid vowels and low vowels according to tongue **height**(높이), front vowels and back vowels according to tongue **position**(위치), unrounded vowels and rounded vowels according to **shape**(모양) of lip during the pronunciation. The place where the 10 monophthongs are pronounced can be expressed in a chart as follows:

Backness / Height	Front		Back	
	Unrounded	Rounded	Unrounded	Rounded
High	ㅣ[i]	ㅟ[y]	ㅡ[ɨ]	ㅜ[u]
Mid	ㅔ[e]	ㅚ[ø]	ㅓ[ə]	ㅗ[o]
Low	ㅐ[ɛ]		ㅏ[a]	

Phonetic value and example of each **monophthong** is following below.

ㅏ[a]: 아버지 'a father'
ㅓ[ə]: 어머니 'a mother'
ㅗ[o]: 오리 'a duck'
ㅜ[u]: 우리 'we'
ㅡ[ɨ]: 음악 'music'
ㅣ[i]: 이름 'a name'
ㅐ[ɛ]: 애인 'a lover'
ㅔ[e]: 에너지 'energy'
ㅚ[ø]: 왼손 'the left hand'

ㅟ[y]: <u>위</u>로 'consolation'

The **diphthong**(이중모음) is a vowel which can be pronounced only through moving the tongue and changing the shape of lips during its articulation, and the sound is different from beginning to finish. The diphthongs are divided into two types: 'ㅑ, ㅕ, ㅛ, ㅠ, ㅒ, ㅖ, ㅘ, ㅝ, ㅙ and ㅞ' are rising diphthongs(상향 이중모음) and 'ㅢ' is a falling diphthong(하향 이중모음).

Phonetic value and example of each diphthong is following below.

ㅑ [ja]: <u>야</u>구 'baseball'
ㅕ [jə]: <u>여</u>름 'summer'
ㅛ[jo]: <u>요</u>금 'a charge'
ㅠ[ju]: <u>유</u>리 'glass'
ㅒ [jɛ]: <u>얘</u>기 'a talk'
ㅖ [je]: <u>예</u>의 'courtesy'
ㅘ[wa]: <u>왕</u> 'a king'
ㅝ [wə]: <u>원</u>숭이 'a monkey'
ㅙ[wɛ]: <u>왜</u> 'why'
ㅞ[we]: <u>웨</u>이트 'weight'
ㅢ[ij]: <u>의</u>사 'a doctor'

■ Pronunciation of diphthong '의'

As for the Article 1 of 'Hangul Orthography'(한글맞춤법), one should write the standard language following the grammar rules but according to its sounds. However in the case of diphthong '의', because Korean people does not pronounce it according to its phonetic value, conventionally pronounce as [ㅣ], another rule as below is prepared separately in Article 5 of 'Hangul Orthography'.

① When a consonant is in front of '의' the pronunciation of '의' becomes [의].
무늬[무니] 'a pattern'
띄어쓰기[띠어쓰기] 'spacing of the words'
희망[히망] 'hope'
유희[유히] 'amusement'

② When '의' is not the first syllable of word, it is pronounced as [의] or [ㅣ], and the particle '-의' is used, it is pronounced as [의] or [ㅔ].
주의[주의]/[주이] 'care'
협의[협의]/[협이] 'consultation'
의의[의의]/[의이] 'meaning'
서울의[서울의]/[서울에] 'of Seoul'
우리의[우리의]/[우리에] 'our'
고향의[고향의]/[고향에] 'of hometown'

■ Pronunciation of diphthong 'ㅖ'

According to Article 8 of Hangul Orthography, 'ㅖ' in '계, 례, 몌, 폐, 혜' spells 'ㅖ' even though there is a case that it is pronounced as [ㅔ]. It also indicates that Korean people pronounce it as [ㅔ], and this pronunciation is conventionally allowed.

계시다[계시다]/[게시다] 'to stay'   폐품[폐품]/[페품] 'waste articles'
혜택[혜택]/[헤택] 'benefit'   핑계[핑계]/[핑게] 'excuse'
사례[사례]/[사레] 'reward'   시계[시계]/[시게] 'a watch'

• Macron

The meaning of words is changed according to whether the vowel of the word is pronounced long or short.

ㅏ [a]: 밤[밤] 'night' ↔ 밤[밤:] 'chestnut'
ㅓ [ə]: 벌[벌] 'punishment' ↔ 벌[벌:] 'a bee'
ㅗ[o]: 동경[동경] 'Tokyo' ↔ 동경[동:경] 'yearning'
ㅜ[u]: 눈[눈] 'eye' ↔ 눈[눈:] 'snow'
ㅡ[ɨ]: 듣다[듣다] 'to hear' ↔ 듣다[듣:다] 'to drop'
ㅣ [i]: 이상[이상] 'more than' ↔ 이상[이:상] 'an ideal'
ㅑ [ja]: 양[양] 'a sheep' ↔ 양[양:] 'amount'
ㅕ [jə]: 연정[연정] 'combined government' ↔ 연정[연:정] 'tender passion'
ㅛ[yo]: 교감[교감] 'consensus' ↔ 교감[교:감] 'an assistant principal'
ㅠ[ju]: 유리[유리] 'glass' ↔ 유리[유:리] 'profitable'

However the length of vowel should be judged by its context which the word is used, because there is no special mark for **macron**(장단) of vowel.

Although the words with long vowel in first syllable like 밤[밤:] 'chestnut', 벌[벌:] 'a bee', 눈[눈:] 'snow', etc. are pronounced long, if some other words are put before the word, forming new words like 군밤[군밤] 'a roasted chestnut', 꿀벌[꿀벌] 'a honey bee', 함박눈[함방눈] 'large snow flakes', etc., the length of vowel are shortened.

• Tone

In Korean same sentence ending is often used for declarative, interrogative, imperative, propositive and exclamatory. In this case declarative, interrogative, imperative, propositive and exclamatory endings are classified by **tone**(억양), according to it, the sentence type is determined.

Declarative sentence: 학교 가.[→]
Interrogative sentence: 학교 가?[↗]
Imperative sentence: 학교 가.[↘]
Propositive sentence: 학교 가.[→↘]
Exclamatory sentence: 학교 가![→↗]

• Vowel harmony

Korean vowels can be classified into two types according to the characteristics of sounds. 'ㅏ, ㅑ, ㅗ, ㅛ, ㅐ and ㅚ' which called '**Yang vowel**(양성모음/**bright vowel**)' have nuance of 'light, positive, good, joyful and masculine'. However 'ㅓ, ㅕ, ㅜ, ㅠ, ㅔ and ㅟ' etc. which called '**Yin vowel**(음성모음/**dark vowel**)' have nuance of 'dark, negative, bad, sorrowful and feminine'.

Yang vowels tend to go together with following yang vowels, and yin vowels tend to go together with following yin vowels in making onomatopoeic or mimetic words and conjugate endings of verbs, and this is called **vowel harmony**(모음조화).

ㅏ-ㅏ-ㅏ-ㅏ ↔ ㅓ-ㅓ-ㅓ-ㅓ: 살랑살랑 ↔ 설렁설렁
ㅏ-ㅗ-ㅏ-ㅗ ↔ ㅓ-ㅜ-ㅓ-ㅜ: 알록달록 ↔ 얼룩덜룩
ㅗ-ㅏ-ㅗ-ㅏ ↔ ㅜ-ㅓ-ㅜ-ㅓ: 몰랑몰랑 ↔ 물렁물렁

ㅏ + '-아/아서/아라/아야/았다': 살다 'to live'
　　　　　　　　　　　　→ 살아/살아서/살아라/살아야/살았다
ㅓ + '-어/어서/어라/어야/었다': 먹다 'to eat'
　　　　　　　　　　　　→ 먹어/먹어서/먹어라/먹어야/먹었다

However vowel harmony is not an absolute rule any more, moreover in contemporary Korean this phenomenon is dying out.

깨다 'to wake up': 깨어/깨어서/깨어라/깨어야/깨었다

아름답다 'to be beautiful': 아름다워/아름다워서/아름다워라/아름다워야/
아름다웠다

1.3 Types and characteristics of consonants

Korean consonants can be classified into 5 ways according to the **place** (위치) of articulation, as follows: bilabial(양순음), alveolar(치순음), palatal(경구개음), velar(연구개음) and glottal(성문음) and they can also be classified according to the **manner**(방법) of articulation, as follows: plosive(파열음), fricative(파찰음), affricate(마찰음), nasal and liquid(유음). The classification can be expressed in a chart as follows:

Manner \ Place		Bilabial	Alveolar	Palatal	Velar	Glottal
Plosive	Relaxed	ㅂ[p]	ㄷ[t]		ㄱ[k]	
	Tensed	ㅃ[p']	ㄸ[t']		ㄲ[k']	
	Aspirated	ㅍ[pʰ]	ㅌ[tʰ]		ㅋ[kʰ']	
Fricative	Relaxed		ㅅ[s]			ㅎ[h]
	Tensed		ㅆ[s']			
Affricate	Relaxed			ㅈ[ʧ]		
	Tensed			ㅉ[ʧ']		
	Aspirated			ㅊ[ʧʰ]		
Nasal		ㅁ[m]	ㄴ[n]		ㅇ[ŋ]	
Liquid			ㄹ[r/l]			

The plosives, affricates and fricatives can be further subdivided into relaxed, tensed and aspirated sounds. The meaning of words can be changed according to consonant which is used. This is very different point in comparison with English.

The relaxed consonant as 'plain sound(예사소리)' is made softly and easily. The tensed consonant as 'tensed sound(된소리)' is made with tension in the muscles. The aspirated consonant as 'aspirated sound(거센소리)' is made rough with /h/ sound.

> ㄱ-ㄲ-ㅋ: 개다[kɛda] 'to fold up' – 깨다[k'ɛda] 'to break' –
> 캐다[kʰɛda] 'to dig'
> ㄷ-ㄸ-ㅌ: 달[tal] 'moon' – 딸[t'al] 'daughter' – 탈[tʰal] 'mask'
> ㅂ-ㅃ-ㅍ: 불[pul] 'fire' – 뿔[p'ul] 'horn' – 풀[pʰul] 'grass'
> ㅅ-ㅆ-Ø: 살[sal] 'flesh' – 쌀[s'al] 'rice'
> ㅈ-ㅉ-ㅊ: 자다[ʧada] 'to sleep' – 짜다[ʧ'ada] 'to be salty' – 차다[ʧʰada]
> 'to be cold'

There is no distinction between **voiced(유성)** and **voiceless consonant(무성)** in Korean. Therefore there is no meaning difference of such words even though the pronunciation is slightly different.

> 개다[kɛda/gɛda] ; 달[tal/dal] ; 불[pul/bul]

Phonetic value and example of each Korean consonant is following below.

> ㄱ[k]: 공기 'air' – ㄲ[k']: 꼬리 'a tail' – ㅋ[kʰ]: 코끼리 'an elephant'
> ㄷ[t]: 다리 'leg' – ㄸ[t']: 땅 'land' – ㅌ[tʰ]: 택시 'a taxi'
> ㅂ[p]: 바다 'sea' – ㅃ[p']: 뿌리 'root' ㅍ[pʰ]: 포도 'grape'
> ㅅ[s]: 사랑 'love' – ㅆ[s']: 쓰기 'writing'
> ㅈ[ʧ]: 자전거 'bicycle' – ㅉ[ʧ']: 짝사랑 'one-sided love' – ㅊ[ʧʰ]: 처음
> 'first time'
> ㄹ[r]: 라면 'instant noodle' – ㄹ[l]: 돌 'a stone'
> ㅁ[m]: 물 'water' – ㄴ[n]: 누나 'older sister' – ㅇ[ŋ]: 종교 'religion'
> ㅎ[h]: 한국 'Korea'

02 Writing system

2.1 Writing direction and letter

Most of old Korean books were written in vertical **direction**(방향) from top to bottom, and the lines were arranged from right to write. However, like English books, contemporary Korean books are written in horizontal direction from left to right, and the lines are arranged from top to bottom.

Two kinds of **letter**(문자) are used to write Korean: pure Korean words such as 사람 'a man', 집 'a house', 아버지 'a father' can be only written in Korean alphabet(Hangul in Korean), Chinese words such as 한국 'Korea', 학교 'a school', 자유 'freedom' can be written in both Korean alphabet and Chinese alphabet(Hanja in Korean).

- 한글(Korean alphabet): 집 'a house', 사람 'a man', 아버지 'a father', 얼굴 'a face', 마음 'mind', 믿음 'faith'
- 한자(Chinese alphabet): 韓國(한국) 'Korea', 學校(학교) 'a school', 冊(책) 'a book', 自由(자유) 'freedom', 生命 (생명) 'life'

2.2 Hangul

Korea has own alphabet, called Hangul(한글, Korean alphabet). It was created in 1,443 by King Se-Jong the Great. A book titled 『훈민정음』 (Hunmin Jeongeum) which contains principles of letter creation is handed down, and it is listed in UNESCO's Memory of the World Register.

Hangul is phonemic writing(음소문자) and can record every Korean. Hangul is not only easy to learn, but is the letter made based on scientific principles.

The consonant(자음) were created based on the shape of various articulatory organs(발음기관). For example, 'ㄱ' was created in the shape of blocking the soft palate (or ceiling) with tongue root, 'ㄴ' was created in the shape of touching the upper tooth-gum (or alveolar) with tongue blade (or tip), 'ㅁ' was created in the shape of the joined two lips, 'ㅅ' was created in the shape of the teeth, and 'ㅇ' was created in the shape of the throat. And the rest of the letters were created by adding a stroke to the above letters or a little changing: 'ㄲ, ㅋ' were created by adding a stroke to 'ㄱ', 'ㄷ, ㄸ, ㅌ' were added to 'ㄴ', 'ㅂ, ㅃ, ㅍ' were added to 'ㅁ', 'ㅆ ; ㅈ, ㅉ, ㅊ' were added to 'ㅅ', and 'ㅎ' was added to 'ㅇ'. And 'ㄹ' and 'ㅿ' were created by changing 'ㄴ' and 'ㅅ' little.

The vowels(모음) were created in the image of the sky(˙), land(ㅡ), and man(ㅣ) which are called basic three materials. The rest of the letters were created by putting together this three basic vowels like 'ㅣ+ ˙ → ㅏ' ; ' ˙ + ㅣ → ㅓ' ; ' ˙ + ㅡ → ㅗ' ; 'ㅡ+ ˙ → ㅜ'.

Korea adopted 'Hangul proclamation Day(한글날)' a national commemorative day. On that day is the day celebrating the creation and the proclamation of Hangul by King Se-Jong the Great. Hangul Day is celebrated on 9th October annually.

■ Disappeared letter 'ㅸ' and dialect

The phonetic value of 'ㅸ' which is used in the 15th century in Korea was 'voiced bilabial fricative' [β], and the trace of it remained in Gyeongsang dialect.

For example, if connective endings such as '-아/어서, -(으)니, -(으)며, -(으)면' are combined with 덥다 'to be hot', generally they become the forms of '더워서, 더우니, 더우며, 더우면'. In other words, because 덥다 is a irregular adjective ㅂ, 'ㅂ' is changed into 'ㅗ/ㅜ'.

However, in Gyeongsang dialect instead of changing 'ㅂ' into 'ㅗ/ㅜ', 'ㅂ' is pronounced the form of 'ㅸ' just like '더벙서, 더브니, 더벙면'. This is that the irregular verbs 덥다 is conjugated same way like regular verb.

Words like this are 굽다 'to roast', 눕다 'to lie down', 돕다 'to help', 줍다 'to pick up' ; 춥다 'to be cold', 밉다 'to be hateful', 무겁다 'to be heavy', 쉽다 'to be easy', etc.

2.3 Hanja

Korean and Chinese are very different languages. However, since there was no letter to write Korean sound until 1,443, **Hanja**(한자, Chinese alphabet) was borrowed and used for the Korean writing system. Hanja came to Korea in the 2nd~3rd century BC, and from then on, many words were borrowed from Chinese. Therefore 60 percent of Korean words are Chinese words and all of them can be written in Hanja, Chinese alphabet. However particles, verb endings and pure Korean words can not be written in Hanja.

Hanja is difficult to learn and write due the complexity of numerous strokes in Hanja. for this reason, Koreans rarely use Hanja words nowadays. However few newspapers and university textbooks still use some

Hanja words.

Most of Koreans learn about 1,800 Hanja words before graduating from high school, and the intellectuals of Korea know more than 1,800 Hanja words.

安寧(안녕)하십니까?
How are you?
제 이름은 金俊緖(김준서)입니다.
My name is Jun-Seo Kim.
저는 學校(학교)에서 韓國語(한국어)를 배우고 있습니다.
I am learning Korean at school.

03 Constitution of Syllable and Pronunciation

3.1 What is a syllable?

A **syllable**(음절) is the minimal unit of pronunciation. A vowel is necessary to create a syllable in Korean but consonant is dispensable. About 3,000 Korean syllables can be made with the combination of 'consonant + vowel + consonant'. This is the one of the greatest strength of Korean alphabet. It is possible to transcribe almost the whole phonetic value of other foreign languages with Korean alphabet.

3.2 Structure and types of syllable

3.2.1 Consisted of only [Vowel]

- 아이 'a child', 어머니 'a mother', 오늘 'today', 우유 'milk', 이야기 'a story', 애인 'a lover', 위 'a top', 외갓집 'one's mother's parents' home'
- 야구 'baseball', 여기 'here', 와글와글 'clamorous', 워낙 'so', 왜 'why', 예 'an example', 의지 'will'

The ' ㅇ ' at the beginning of a syllable does not have phonetic value. It is just used formally to make a syllable shape. In other words, this kind of syllables are consist of a vowel.

3.2.2 Consisted of [Vowel + Consonant]

- 악수 'a handshake', 얼음 'ice', 온도 'temperature', 웅덩이 'a puddle', 음악 'music', 입국 'entry', 왼손 'left hand', 윗니 'the upper teeth'
- 약속 'promise', 연인 'one's love', 용서 'forgiveness', 윷놀이 'playing yut', 월요일 'Monday', 완성 'completion'
- 앉다 'to sit', 없다 'to be nonexistent', 옳다 'to be right', 읊다 'to recite', 읽다 'to read', 있다 'to exist', 얇다 'to be thin'

3.2.3 Consisted of [Consonant + Vowel]

- 가다 'to go', 너 'you', 도깨비 'a goblin', 라디오 'a radio', 머리 'a head', 바람 'wind', 사진 'a photo', 자기 'oneself', 카메라 'a camera', 피아노 'a piano'
- 겨울 'winter', 교실 'a classroom', 뉴스 'news', 과거 'past', 뭐 'what', 동화 'a fairy tale', 지혜 'wisdom'

3.2.4 Consisted of [Consonant + Vowel + Consonant]

- 감기 'a cold', 넣다 'to put', 손 'a hand', 물 'water', 듣다 'to listen', 신문 'a newspaper', 색깔 'color', 벤치 'a bench', 괴물 'a monster'
- 현재 'present', 향기 'scent', 관광 'sightseeing', 권리 'right', 권투 'boxing', 된장 'soybean paste'

- 값 'price', 짧다 'to be short', 넓다 'to be wide', 밝다 'to be bright', 젊다 'to be young', 끓다 'to boil'

Two consonants can be used in the final position like 짧다 'to be short', 넓다 'to be wide'. However, only one of them is pronounced.

3.3 Pronunciation changes

3.3.1 Last letter representation

Last letter representation(음절의 끝소리 규칙) refers to the phenomenon which syllable-final consonants pronounced as one of seven consonants; ㄱ, ㄴ, ㄷ, ㄹ, ㅁ, ㅂ, ㅇ

① /ㄱ, ㄲ, ㅋ, ㄳ/ → [ㄱ]
밖[박], 닦다[닥따] ; 동녘[동녁], 부엌[부억] ; 몫[목], 뱃삯[밷싹]
② /ㄴ, ㄵ, ㄶ/ → [ㄴ]
앉다[안따], 얹다[언따] ; 많니?[만니], 점잖습니다[점잔씀니다]
③ /ㄷ, ㅅ, ㅆ, ㅈ, ㅊ, ㅌ, ㅎ/ → [ㄷ]
이웃[이욷] ; 있다[읻따] ; 늦잠[늗짬] ; 꽃[꼳] ; 끝[끋] ; 히읗[히읃]
④ /ㄹ, ㄼ, ㄻ, ㄽ, ㅌ, ㄾ, ㅀ/ → [ㄹ]
여덟[여덜] ; 외곬[외골] ; 핥니?[할니] ; 싫소[실쏘]
⑤ /ㅁ, ㄻ/ → [ㅁ]
삶[삼], 젊다[점따], 옮기다[옴기다]
⑥ /ㅂ, ㅍ, ㄿ, ㅄ/ → [ㅂ]
잎[입], 숲[숩] ; 읊다[읍따] ; 값[갑], 없다[업따]

If a syllable-final consonants followed by particles like '-이, -으로, -에서' or endings like '-으면, -으니까, -아/어서, -으며' beginning with a vowel, it is pronounced in original sound. The patchim, final consonant of syllable, is moved to next syllable and pronounced as the first sound of the following syllable.

꽃+이 → [꼬치] → 꽃이
사람+을 → [사라믈] → 사람을
서울+에서 → [서우레서] → 서울에서
잡+으니 → [자브니] → 잡으니
먹+어서 → [머거서] → 먹어서
앉+으면 → [안즈면] → 앉으면

3.3.2 Assimilation

When two neighboring phonemes come together, one resembles another and changed into similar or same phoneme. This is called **assimilation**(동화). The types of assimilation are nasalization, liquidization, palatalization, and tensification.

- When the nonnasal sounds 'ㄱ, ㄲ, ㅋ ; ㄷ, ㅌ ; ㄹ ; ㅂ, ㅍ ; ㅅ, ㅈ, ㅊ' meet a following nasal 'ㄴ' or 'ㅁ', it is pronounced as 'ㄴ[n], ㅁ[m] or ㅇ[ŋ]'. This phenomenon is **nasalization**(비음화).

① /ㄱ, ㄲ, ㅋ/ → [ㅇ]
국민[궁민] ; 깎는[깡는] ; 부엌문[부엉문]
② /ㄷ, ㅌ/ → [ㄴ]
듣는[든는], 묻는[문는] ; 곁눈질[견눈질] ; 끝나다[끈나다]
③ /ㄹ/ → [ㄴ]
대통령[대통녕], 중력[중녁], 결단력[결딴녁]
④ /ㅂ, ㅍ/ → [ㅁ]
톱날[톰날], 입말[임말] ; 앞문[암문], 높낮이[놈나지]
⑤ /ㅅ, ㅈ, ㅊ/ → [ㄴ]

덧니[던니], 잇몸[인몸] ; 젖니[전니], 찾는[찬는] ; 꽃말[꼰말]

- **Liquidization**(유음화) refers to the phenomenon that the nasal 'ㄴ' is pronounced as 'ㄹ' when it meets the liquid 'ㄹ' which is pronounced at the same place of articulation.

① /ㄴ–ㄹ/ → [ㄹㄹ]
  신라[실라], 난로[날로], 원래[월래], 한류[할류]
② /ㄹ–ㄴ/ → [ㄹㄹ]
  설날[설랄], 틀니[틀리], 달나라[달라라], 물난리[물랄리]
③ /ㅀ–ㄴ/ → [ㄹㄹ]
  앓는[알른], 뚫는[뚤른], 닳네[달레], 핥네[할레]

- **Palatalization**(구개음화) is the phenomenon that the dental 'ㄷ or ㅌ' is pronounced as the palatal 'ㅈ or ㅊ' when it meets a following 'ㅣ(i)' or 'ㅑ, ㅕ, ㅛ, ㅠ' starting with semi-vowel 'j'.

① /ㄷ/ → [ㅈ]
  굳이[구지], 맏이[마지], 미닫이[미다지], 해돋이[해도지]
② /ㅌ/ → [ㅊ]
  같이[가치], 붙이고[부치고], 샅샅이[산싸치], 피붙이[피부치]
③ /ㄷ–ㅎ/ → [ㅊ]
  갇히다[가치다], 닫히다[다치다], 묻히다[무치다]

- When two voiceless sounds come together, if the syllable-final sound of the preceding syllable is implosive 'ㄱ, ㄷ or ㅂ', and the following consonant is the sound which can be pronounced tense sound, the syllable-final sound is pronounced as 'ㄲ, ㄸ, ㅆ or ㅉ'. This is called **tensification**(경음화).

  The consonants 'ㄱ, ㄷ, ㅂ, ㅅ or ㅈ' after the verb stems which

has at the syllable-final position 'ㄴ or ㅁ' and adnominal ending '-(으)ㄹ' is pronounced as 'ㄲ, ㄸ, ㅃ or ㅉ'. The consonants 'ㄷ, ㅅ or ㅈ' after syllable-final 'ㄹ' of Sino-Korean words is pronounced as 'ㄸ, ㅃ or ㅉ'. These phenomena are also kinds of tensification.

① /ㄱ, ㄷ, ㅂ-ㄱ, ㄷ, ㅂ, ㅅ, ㅈ/ → [ㄲ, ㄸ, ㅃ, ㅆ, ㅉ]
   학교[학꾜], 껵다리[껵따리], 꽃병[꼳뼝], 젖소[젇쏘], 입장[입짱]
② /ㄴ, ㅁ-ㄱ, ㄷ, ㅂ, ㅅ, ㅈ/ → [ㄲ, ㄸ, ㅃ, ㅆ, ㅉ]
   안고[안꼬], 담지[담찌]
③ /ㄹ-ㄱ, ㄷ, ㅂ, ㅅ, ㅈ/ → [ㄲ, ㄸ, ㅃ, ㅆ, ㅉ]
   할 수[할 쑤], 갈등[갈뜽], 열정[열쩡], 할 바[할 빠]

3.3.3 Contraction and deletion

- **Contraction(축약)** is the phenomenon that two phonemes become one or two syllables pronounced as one. There are cases of **consonant contraction(자음탈락)** and **vowel contraction(모음탈락)**.

   When a preceding 'ㄱ, ㄷ, ㅂ or ㅈ' meets a following 'ㅎ', this contracts to 'ㅋ, ㅌ, ㅍ or ㅊ'. This phenomenon is **consonant contraction(자음축약)**. And **vowel contraction(모음축약)** is the phenomenon that when a preceding 'ㅏ, ㅓ, ㅗ, ㅜ or ㅣ' meets a following 'ㅣ, ㅡ, ㅗ or ㅜ' it contracts to 'ㅐ, ㅔ, ㅚ ; ㅑ, ㅕ, ㅛ, ㅠ ; ㅚ, ㅟ, ㅢ'.

① Consonant contraction
   좋고[조코], 많다[만타], 입학[이팍], 옳지[올치]
② Vowel contraction
   사이/새, 조이다/죄다, 주어라/줘라, 되었다/됐다

- When two contiguous phonemes come together, one disappears.

This is called **deletion**(탈락). There are cases of **consonant deletion** (자음탈락) and **vowel deletion**(모음탈락).

Deletions of syllable-initial ' ㄴ or ㄹ' of Sino-Korean words and syllable-final ' ㄹ or ㅎ' of compound words or verb stems are consonant deletions.

① /ㄴ, ㄹ/ → ∅
　*녀자/여자, *력사/역사
② /ㄹ/ → ∅
　*아들님/아드님, *불정/부정, *살니까/사니까, *둥글니까/둥그니까
③ /ㅎ/ → ∅
　좋으니[조으니], 많아서[마나서]

There are two types of vowel deletion. One is deletion of final-syllable '_' when it is placed before ' ㅓ'. The other is deleting final-syllable ' ㅏ, ㅓ' which is followed by ' ㅏ, ㅓ' ending.

① /ㅡ/ → ∅: *쓰어라/써라, *예쁘어서/예뻐서
② /ㅏ, ㅓ/ → ∅: *가아라/가라, *서어서/서서

3.3.4 Insertion 'ㅅ'

When a derivational or compound word is made in case of the first word ends with vowel, one of the three cases occur; voiceless 'ㄱ, ㄷ, ㅂ, ㅅ or ㅈ' of the following word is tensified. 'ㄴ' is added before the word-initial 'ㄴ or ㅁ' of second word, or 'ㄴㄴ' is added before the word-initial vowel. In these cases 'ㅅ' is inserted at the end of the leading word. These phenomena are called **insertion** 'ㅅ'(사잇소리 현상).

- The first word ends with a vowel and the word-initial consonant of the second word is tensified.

바다+가 → [바다까] → 바닷가 'beach'
코+등 → [코뜽] → 콧등 'the bridge of the nose'
귀+밥 → [귀빱] → 귓밥 'an earlobe'
배+사공 → [배싸공] → 뱃사공 'a boatman'
차+집 → [차찝] → 찻집 'a teahouse'

The following words show the same phenomenon.

나룻배 'a boat', 나뭇가지 'a bough', 냇가 'the side of a stream', 바닷가 'beach', 뱃길 'ship's course' 찻집 'a teahouse', 햇볕 'sunlight', 혓바늘 'sore on the tongue' ; 귓병 'ear trouble', 아랫방 'an outer-wing room', 전셋집 'a house for on a deposit money basis', 찻잔 'a teacup', 탯줄 'a umbilical cord', 텃세 'territorial imperative', 햇수 'years'

- The first word ends with a vowel and 'ㄴ' is added before the word-initial 'ㄴ or ㅁ' of the second word.

계+날 → [곈날] → 곗날 'the day which earns money for the mutual assistance society'
제사+날 → [제산날] → 제삿날 'a memorial ceremony day'
내+물 → [낸물] → 냇물 'stream'
이+몸 → [인몸] → 잇몸 'gums/the areas of firm, pink flesh inside one's mouth, which one's teeth grow out of'

The following words show the same phenomenon.

아랫니 'lower teeth', 멧나물 'seasoned roots of bindweed', 뱃놀이 'boating', 뒷머리 'back hair', 빗물 'rainwater', 아랫마을 'down town', 콧날 'bridge of nose', 텃마당 'the threshing ground of a community', 깻묵 'sesame dregs' ; 훗날 'the future', 양칫물 'gargling water', 툇마루 'verandah'

- The leading word ends with a vowel and 'ㄴㄴ' is added before the vowel of the following word.

나무+잎 → [나문닙] → 나뭇잎 'foliage'
뒤+일 → [뒨닐] → 뒷일 'aftermath'
아래+이 → [아랜니] → 아랫니 'lower teeth'

The following words show the same phenomenon.

베갯잇 'a pillowcase', 깻잎 'a sesame leaf', 댓잎 'a bamboo blade' ;
예삿일 'a commonplace event', 훗일 'future affairs'

Most phonological changes occur when the phonetic condition is given without exception, however, there are the cases that insertion 'ㅅ' does not occur even though the same condition is given.

소리+글자 → [소리글짜] → 소리글자 'a phonetic symbol'
노래+방 → [노래방] → 노래방 'karaoke'
노+스님 → [노스님] → 노스님 'an elderly Buddhist monk'
너구리+집 → [너구리집] → 너구리집 'a raccoon's house'

When the leading and the following words are both Sino-Korean words, even though the word-initial consonant of the following word is tensified, 'ㅅ' is not inserted.

외(外)+과(科) → [외꽈] → 외과/*윗과/*외꽈 'department of surgery'
효(效)+과(果) → [효꽈] → 효과/*횻과/*효꽈 'an effect'
주(株)+가(價) → [주까] → 주가/*줏가/*주까 'stock prices'
초(焦)+점(點) → [초쩜] → 초점/*촛점/*초쩜 'focus'
허(虛)+점(點) → [허쩜] → 허점/*헛점/*허쩜 'weak point'

However in cases of following Sino-Korean words '人' is inserted exceptionally.

고(庫)+간(間) → [고깐] → 곳간/*고간/*고깐 'a storeroom'
세(貰)+방(房) → [세빵] → 셋방/*세방/*세빵 'a rented room'
수(數)+자(字) → [수짜] → 숫자/*수자/*수짜 'a number'
차(車)+간(間) → [차깐] → 찻간/*차간/*차깐 'the inside of a car'
퇴(退)+간(間) → [퇴깐] → 툇간/*퇴간/*퇴깐 'an extend built by adding extra beams'
회(回)+수(數) → [회쑤] → 횟수/*회수/*회쑤 'number of times'

One step forward >>

■ insertion 'ㄴ'

According to the rule of standard pronunciation Article 29, when the leading word of a derivational or compound word ends with consonant and the following word starts with 'ㅣ, ㅑ, ㅕ, ㅛ or ㅠ', 'ㄴ' is inserted and pronounced as [냐, 녀, 뇨, 뉴]. However 'ㄴ' is not added in writing.

솜-이불 → [솜:니불]/*[솜이불] → 솜이불 'a cotton-wool comforter'
내복-약 → [내:봉냑]/*[내봉약] → 내복약 'an internal medicine'
색-연필 → [생년필]/*[색연필] → 색연필 'a colored pencil'
눈-요기 → [눈뇨기]/*[눈요기] → 눈요기 'visual pleasure'
식용-유 → [시굥뉴]/*[시굥유] → 식용유 'cooking oil'

Since insertion 'ㄴ' varies by individual pronunciation habits, there are many cases that the insertion 'ㄴ' does not occur in the same phonological environment.

육-이오 → *[육니오]/[유기오] → 육이오 (전쟁) 'the Korean War'
삼-일절 → *[삼닐쩔]/[사밀쩔] → 삼일절 'anniversary of the Samil Independence Movement'
송별-연 → *[송:별년]/[송:벼련] → 송별연 'a farewell dinner given for before one's departure'
등-용문 → *[등뇽문]/[등용문] → 등용문 'an opening to honors'

04 Sentence components and word order

4.1 What is a sentence?

A **sentence**(문장) is a composed of words and the unit of meaning that represents completed events and states. Thus a sentence, which is basically composed of a subject and an predicate, used when states an action or a state [a declarative sentence], asks a question [an interrogative sentence], gives a command [an imperative sentence], suggests that someone join something [a propositive sentence], or expresses feelings [an exclamatory sentence].

Korean sentences do not begin with a capital letter because there is no capital and small letter in Korean unlike English. However, it must put a period [.] at the end of a declarative, propositive and imperative sentence, a question mark [?] at the end of an interrogative sentence, or an exclamation mark [!] at the end of an exclamatory sentence.

Declarative sentence: 준서는 한국인입니다. Jun-Seo is a Korean.
Interrogative sentence: 준서는 한국인입니까? Is Jun-Seo a Korean?
Imperative sentence: 학교로 가십시오. Go to school.
Propositive sentence: 학교에 갑시다. Let's go to school.

Exclamatory sentence: 준서 씨, 멋있군요! Jun-Seo, you look neat.

4.2 Sentence components of Korean

The components of sentence, are subject, predicate, object, complement ; adnominal phrase, adverbial phrase ; independent words and others.

- **Subject**

A **subject**(주어) is an agent of incidents or conditions, and this sentence component corresponds to somebody or something in the sentences of 'Somebody does something(verb-sentence)', 'Something is some way(adjective-sentence)', 'Something is something(이다-sentence)'. '준서가, 이것이, 둘이서, 국회에서, 선생님께서' are the subjects in the sentences below. Subject particle '-가, -이, -서, -에서 ; -께서' is attached to the subjects.

> **준서가** 왔다.
> Jun-Seo came.
> 공원에 **사람들이** 많이 있다.
> There are many people in the park.
> 준서와 **둘이서** 산책을 갔었다.
> The two of us, I and Jun-Seo, took a walk with.
> 한국의 **국회에서** 북한을 돕기 위한 법률을 만들었다.
> Korea National Assembly made laws to help North Korea.
> **선생님께서** 나에게 질문을 하셨다.
> The teacher put a question to me.

■ The characteristic of subject in a Korean sentence

First, subjects are often omitted in a Korean sentence. In other words Korean people tend to omit most of situational elements like '나, 너, 지금, 여기', while talking and use '우리/우리의' more than '나/나의/내' when they must use the subject.

전에 한 번 뵌 적이 있는 것 같습니다.
→ I think I have seen you before.
죄송합니다. 성함이 뭐라고 하셨는지 잘 못 들었습니다.
→ I am sorry. I didn't get your name.
정말 기분이 좋군요!
→ Oh! How glad I am.
어디 보자. 10시 30분입니다.
→ <u>Let's</u> see. <u>It</u> is 10:30.
<u>우리</u> 아들은 고등학생입니다.
→ <u>My</u> son is <u>in high school</u>.

Second, a person is nominated for the subject in Korean sentences. In English things, incidents, events tend to be nominated for the subject, however, Korean does not except when emphasizes especially. It should be noted that specially in Korean concrete things, incidents, events, distance, time, day of the week, weight is nominated for the subject than using formal subject like English 'it'.

나는 <u>그 일</u> 때문에 뉴욕에 왔다.
→ [?]<u>그 일</u>이 나를 뉴욕에 데리고 왔다.
→ Business brought me to New York.
(<u>날씨가</u>) 더워요.
→ <u>It</u>'s hot.
<u>내일은</u> 일요일이다.
→ <u>It</u>'s Sunday tomorrow.
서울까지의 <u>거리가</u> 30마일이다.
→ <u>It</u>'s 30 miles to Seoul.

- Predicate

A **predicate**(서술어) is a description of an action, a state or a character, etc. This sentence component express following meanings in the sentence; to be some way, do something or be something in the sentences of 'Somebody does something(verb-sentence)', 'Something is some way(adjective-sentence)', 'Something is something(이다-sentence)'. '왔다, 비싸다, 책이다' are the predicates in the sentences below. Verb, adjective or '(noun+)이다' can be used as predicate.

> 준서가 서울에 **왔다**. / Jun-Seo came to Seoul.
> 이 휴대전화는 매우 **비싸다**. / This mobile phone is very expensive.
> 이것은 내 **책이다**. / This is my book.

- Object

An **object**(목적어) is the entry of an action that the predicate stands for, and this sentence component corresponds to 'something' in the sentence 'Somebody does something'. '노래를 and 책을' are the objects in the sentences below. Object particle '-을 or -를' is attached to the objects. And '부르다 and 사다' are transitive verbs that require an object.

> 민서가 **노래를** 부른다. / Min-Seo sings a song.
> 준서가 **책을** 샀다. / Jun-Seo bought a book.

- Complement

When a sentence which is only composed a subject and predicate cannot fully convey the meaning. A **complement**(보어) is used to complete the meaning of the sentence. In a sentence complement usually means, 'something' in the sentences like 'something becomes something' or 'something is not something'. In the given sentence bellow, '변호사가' and '한국 사람이' are the complement particle '-가 or -이' is attached to the complements.

준서는 **변호사가** 되었다. / Jun-Seo became a lawyer.
존은 한국 **사람이** 아니다. / John is not a Korean.

● Adnominal phrase

An **adnominal phrase**(관형어) is the word modifying a subject and an object, and located before them. Adnominal phrase corresponds to 'how' and 'does something/did/will do' in the sentences of 'something how' or 'person does something'. '준서의 and 서울에 간' are adnominal phrases in the sentences below. Adnominal particle '-의' or adnominal endings '-는, -(으)ㄴ, -(으)ㄹ' is attached to adnominal phrase. Adnominal, of course, is used as adnominal phrase like 새 'new'.

민서는 **준서의** 자전거를 빌렸다.
Min-Seo borrowed Jun-Seo's bicycle.
준서는 **서울에 간** 민서를 그리워한다.
Jun-Seo misses Min-Seo who went to Seoul.
민서는 **새** 책을 샀다.
Min-Seo bought new book.

Adnominal phrase is not imperatively necessary as sentence component for making basic sentence, because it only modifies imperatively necessary sentence component which comes after adnominal phrase. In other words, it is a optional sentence component. However, the meaning of sentence is more clear and precisely when the adnominal phrase is used.

- Adverbial phrase

An **adverbial phrase**(부사어) is placed before predicate and modifies it. An adverbial expresses the meaning of 'how or what' in a sentence. In the given sentences below, '꽃처럼 and 칼로' are the adverbial phrase and adverb, of course, is used as adverbial phrase like 빨리 'quickly'.

민서가 **꽃처럼** 아름답다. / Min-Seo looks as beautiful as a flower.
자동차가 **빨리** 달린다. / The car drives quickly.

Just like adnominal phrases adverbial phrases can be omitted because it is not imperatively necessary sentence component for making sentence. However, there are some cases sentences become ungrammatical it adverbial of omitted. This kind of adverbial phrase called an **essential adverbial phrase**(필수적 부사어). The essential adverbial phrase are determined based on the predicates. '다르다, 싸우다, 삼다, 살다' in the sentences below are the verbs that require adverbial phrase, therefore '수박과, 민서와, 아내로, 서울에' are the essential adverbial phrases.

사과는 모양이 **수박과** 다르다. / Apples differ from watermelons in shape.
준서는 어제 **민서와** 싸웠다. / Jun-Seo fought with Min-Seo yesterday.
준서는 민서를 **아내로** 삼았다. / Jun-Seo took Min-Seo to his wife.
민서는 **서울에** 살고 있다. / Min-Seo lives in Seoul.

- Independent words

A **independent word**(독립어) is the word that are unrelated to other sentence components, therefore it could be used independently. This sentence component corresponds to 'admiration', 'surprisal' or 'call' in the sentences. '민서야 and 신이시여' are the independent words in the sentences below. Independent words are placed at the very beginning of sentence. Vocative case particle '-아 or -야' is attached to independent words. Exclamations, are used as independent words like 와 'wow'.

민서야, 이리 오너라. / Min-Seo, come here.
신이시여, 저를 도와주소서. / God, help me.
와, 굉장하구나! / Wow, how marvelous!

4.3 Word order of Korean and basic sentence structure

About 6,000 languages are in the world, and these languages can be classified by which word order each language has. The word order in French, German, etc., including English, is usually SVO(subject-verb-object) type languages. On the other hand Japanese, Turkish, etc., including Korean, have SOV(subject-verb-object) word order type languages.

Subjects in the Korean sentences come at the beginning of, objects come after, and verbs are placed at the very end of the sentence. Of course, these components can be inverted for the special purpose a sentence.

- **[Sentence Form 1]: Subject(S)-Verb(V)**
강물이[subject] 흐른다[predicate].
A river flows.
준서가[subject] 학교에[adverbial phrase] 간다[predicate].
Jun-Seo goes to school.

- **[Sentence Form 2]: Subject(S)-Complement(C)-Verb(V)**
준서가[subject] 의사가[complement] 되었다[predicate].
Jun-Seo became a doctor.
고래는[subject] 동물이[complement] 아니다[predicate].

A Whale is not animals

- **[Sentence Form 3]: Subject(S)-Object(O)-Verb(V)**

준서가[subject] 빵을[object] 먹는다[predicate].

Jun-Seo eats bread.

준서가[subject] 민서를[object] 사랑한다[predicate].

Jun-Seo loves Min-Seo.

The biggest difference between Korean and English sentences is that verbs(predicates) come at the very end of sentence. Although verb(predicate) comes at the end of the sentence generally. However, as particles decide the function of the word in Korean it is relatively free to change the word order in order to emphasize or for other purposes.

빵을[object] 준서가[subject] 먹는다[predicate].

Jun-Seo eats bread.

Also, there is no change in word order when converting declarative sentences into interrogative. You only change a declarative ending into an interrogative ending and put question mark[?] at the back.

준서가[subject] 빵을[object] 먹느냐?[predicate-interrogative ending]

Does Jun-Seo eat bread?

준서가[subject] 민서를[object] 사랑하느냐?[predicate-interrogative ending]

Does Jun-Seo love Min-Seo?

- **[Sentence Form 4]: Subject(S)-Indirect Object(IO)-Direct Object (DO)-Verb(V)**

Unlike English, indirect object are essential adverbial phrase because adverb particles like '-에게, -께, -에' are placed after indirect objects in

Korean. **Essential adverbial phrase** and direct object can be inverted.

준서가[subject] 민서에게[essential adverbial phrase] 선물을[direct object]
주었다[predicate].
Jun-Seo gave Min-Seo a present.
선생님께서[subject] 책을[direct object] 준서에게[essential adverbial phrase]
사 주었다[predicate].
The teacher gave Jun-Seo a book

- **[Sentence Form 5]: Subject(S)-Object(O)-Complement(C)-Verb(V)**

Complements are essential adverbial phrase because an adverb particle
like '-(으)로' is placed after complements in Korean.

아버지께서[subject] 자기 아들을[object] 의사로[essential adverbial phrase]
만들었다[predicate].
The father made his son a doctor.

And there are many other kinds of sentences except sentence forms
above. A common characteristic is that subjects are placed at the very
front of the sentence and verbs at the very end of the sentence.

Different form English, particles are very much developed in Korean.
Korean is free word order language since particles show sentence component. This is very distinctive property of Korean language. The nuance
of sentences below can be little different but the meaning of them are
the same.

아버지께서[subject] 자기 아들을[object] 의사로[essential adverbial phrase]
만들었다[predicate].
The father made his son a doctor.

자기 아들을 **아버지께서** 의사로 만들었다.
자기 아들을 의사로 **아버지께서** 만들었다.
자기 아들을 의사로 만들었다 **아버지께서**.

만들었다 자기 아들을 아버지께서 의사로.
의사로 **만들었다** 아버지께서 자기 아들을.
자기 아들을 의사로 **만들었다** 아버지께서.

However in the above sentences the object '자기 아들을' and the essential adverbial phrase '의사로' cannot be inverted because the meaning of adverb particle '-(으)로' is changed 'result' to 'material' in the sentences above.

아버지께서 자기 아들을 **의사로** 만들었다. (-(으)로: result)
아버지께서 **의사로** 자기 아들을 만들었다. (-(으)로: material)

● [Sentence Form 6]: Topic-Comment

There is a sentence which consists of 'Topic-comment' structure in Korean. It is the analysis of a sentence in discourse level. It is the way of making a sentence that particular **topic**(주제) set forth and **comment**(평언), explanation of topic, placed after topic. Topic refers to a person or thing that is being talked about in the sentence and comment is supplementary explanation of 'a person or thing'.

In numerous instances, topic corresponds to 'subject'. However, they do not necessarily correspond. Topic particle '-은/는' is attached to the topic in the back while subject particle '-이/가' to the subject.

그 사람은[topic] ‖ 늘 진실만을 말한다[comment].
He always tells the truth.
토끼는[topic] ‖ 앞발이 짧다[comment]. / The rabbit's front paws are short.

존은[topic] ∥ 미국인이다[comment]. / John is an American.

■ Interpretation of multiple subjects sentence

Sometimes more than two subjects are used consecutively in one sentence in Korean, this sentence is called multiple subjects sentence.

그 선생님은 키가 대단히 크다.
The teacher is really tall.

Multiple subjects sentence is very unique phenomenon in Korean language. There are many interpretation of it.

First interpretation is that '그 선생님' is regarded as topic and '키가' as subject. However, it is still in question that how to call '딸이, 세 명이 ; 가방 값이, 만 원이' should be called in the sentences below.

그 사람은 딸이 세 명이 있다.
He has three daughters.
롯데백화점은 가방 값이 만 원이 싸다.
In Lotte department store, the bags are 10,000 won cheaper.

Second, is that '그 선생님' is regarded as main subject and '키가' as minor subject. However this is not persuasive because the words 'main subject' and 'minor subject' are ambiguous, moreover there is nothing to explain this sentence grammatically.

Third way is to see them as a relationship of whole and part. That is, semantically, '키는' is a one part of '그 선생님'. However, this way is not acceptable because '만 원' is not the part of '가방 값', and '가방 값' is not the part of '롯데백화점'.

Fourth, it is the way that even thought it looks like there are two subjects in the surface sentence, subject is one in the underlying sentence au fond. In other word, '그 선생님의 키가 대단히 크다' is the underlying sentence of the sentence above. And it is regarded that '그 선생님의' is changed to '선생님은' when draws it out to surface sentence.

4.4 place of modifier

Look at the place of modifier. Modifiers come after the modified words in English while modifiers come before the modified words in Korean. Modifiers include adnominal phrases which modify noun and adverbial phrases which modify verbs.

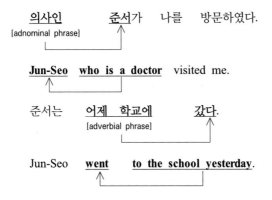

The position of adnominal phrase can not be changed as shown below.

의사인[adnominal phrase] 준서가 나를 방문하였다. (의사 = 준서)
*준서가 의사인[adnominal phrase] 나를 방문하였다. (의사 = 나)

However changing the position of adverbial phrase is free relatively.

어제 준서는 학교에 갔다.
준서는 **어제** 학교에 갔다.
준서는 학교에 **어제** 갔다.
준서는 학교에 갔다 **어제**.

4.5 Omission of subject and topic

In most languages, already noted information, speaker or listener is generally omitted. **Subjects** or **topics** are omitted very often in Korean. Specially it can be omitted when the meaning of sentence is clearly conveyed without subject of topic. This omitted component is mostly **old information**(구정보).

(**당신은**) 아주 부드러운 피부를 (**당신이**) 가지고 있는 것을 압니까?
Do **you** know that **you** have such smooth skin?

(**당신이**) 그렇게 생각하세요?
Do **you** think so?

예, (**그것은**) 비단같이 부드럽군요.
Yes, **it** feels like silk.

Usually, subject or topic in parenthesis in the sentences above is omitted. Because speaker and listener is decided in Korean normal discourse situation. In other words, it is thought that speaker and listener recognize normal discourse information.

Speaker and listener already recognize the information in discourse it is not ungrammatical to show subject or topic in parenthesis thought. However they are not used unless subject or topic is specially emphasized.

Impersonal pronouns 'it' does not exist in Korean.

Subject as well as other sentence components which speaker and listener know can be omitted. However, new information should not be omitted.

준서는 학교에 갔습니까? / Did Jun-Seo go to school?

예, 준서는 학교에 갔습니다. / Yes, Jun-Seo went to school.

예, (준서는) 학교에 갔습니다.
예, (준서는) (학교에) 갔습니다.
예, (준서는) (학교에) (갔습니다.)

Section 2

Words and Parts of Speech

Standard Korean Grammar
for Foreigners

05   **Noun**

5.1 What is a noun?

Noun(명사) is a word that indicates the name of person, things and places. Noun includes the concrete things such as '집(house), 사람(person), 나무(tree) and 물(water)' or abstract things such as '사랑(love), 평화(peace) and 정의(justice)' which expresses a concept.

Nouns can be classified into proper noun and common noun depending on usage. Nouns also can be divided into life-noun and non-life noun, depending on ability of expressing emotion and independent noun and dependent noun according to dependency.

5.2 Types and characteristics of nouns

5.2.1 Proper noun and common noun

Proper nouns(고유명사) refers to a unique entity such as the name for specific persons or things which exist only one.

한국 'Korea: the name of the country', 이순신 'Sun-Sin Lee: the name of the person', 백두산 'Baekdu Mountain: the name of the mountain', 한강 'Han River: the name of the river', 삼국사기 'The Chronicles of the Three States: the name of the book'

준서는 <u>서울</u>에 갑니다.
Jun-Seo goes to Seoul.
<u>세종</u> 임금님께서 <u>한글</u>을 만들었습니다.
King Se-Jong made Hangul.

Since singleness is a prerequisite for proper nouns, proper nouns can't be used together with an numeric adnominal such as 한 'one', 두 'two', 세 'three', 네 'four', a plural suffix such as '-들', an auxiliary particle '-마다' which means 'each' or an indicative adnominal such as 이 'this, here', 그 'that, there', 저 'that, over there'.

[*]<u>두 준서</u>가 뉴욕으로 유학을 갔다.
Two Jun-Seos went to New York to study.
[*]<u>서울의 **광화문들**</u>에 불이 났다.
There was a fire in Gwanghwamuns of Seoul.
[*]만나는 **준서마다** 도와달라고 부탁했다.
Every Jun-Seo I meet asked me to help.
[*]<u>그 **민서**</u>가 음악을 들으면서 한국어 공부를 하고 있다.
That Min-Seo was studying Korean with music.

Common nouns(보통명사) is a generic term depending item which exist more than one. Therefore plural suffix '-들' can be attached. '-들' can not come with **uncountable noun**(불가산명사), and abstract noun just like English.

책 'a book', 사람 'a person', 물 'water', 땅 'land', 사과 'an apple',

대통령 'a president', 국민 'a nation', 가족 'a family', 아버지 'a father',
정부 'a government'
사랑 'love', 결혼 'marriage', 가정 'a family', 행복 'happiness', 생활
'life', 평화 'peace', 정의 'justice', 선악 'good and evil', 영원 'eternity',
상징 'a symbol'

나는 **서점**에서 **책들**을 샀습니다.
I bought books at the bookstore.
호랑이들이 **구덩이**에 빠졌습니다.
Tigers fell into a hole.

5.2.2 Animate noun and in-animate noun

Animate nouns(유정명사) indicate a life that can reveal his emotion
externally like human being or an animal. Animate nouns can move by
theirselves therefore get along with a verb and can be used in combination
with an adverbial particle such as '-에게, -에게서, -(으)로서'.

여자 'a woman', 아버지 'a father', 세종대왕 'King Se-Jong', 장군 'a
general', 호랑이 'a tiger'

그 **여자**는 제 **여동생**에게 책을 사 주었습니다.
That woman bought a book for my sister.
저의 **어머니**는 새를 매우 좋아하셨습니다.
My mother liked a bird very much.
나는 **아버지**로서 네게 충고한다.
I advise you as a father.

In-animate nouns(무정명사) indicate a life which cannot reveal their
emotion exteriorly like a flower and a stone. In-animate nouns cannot
move by theirselves, so in-animate nouns usually get along with an

adjective. In-animate noun can be used in combination with an adverbial particle such as '-에, -에서, -(으)로써'.

> 진달래 'an azalea', 소나무 'a pine', 바다 'sea', 담배 'tobacco', 연필 'a pencil', 서울 'Seoul', 야구 'baseball', 에너지 'energy', 방송국 'a broadcasting station', 자동차 'a car'

> 준서는 **KBS**에서 아나운서로 근무하고 있다.
> Jun-Seo is working as an announcer at KBS.
> 인간은 <u>소리</u>의 <u>한계</u>를 글로써 극복했다.
> Human beings overcame the limitations of sound by writings.

5.2.3 Independent noun and dependent noun

Independent nouns(자립명사), which can be used alone without being modified by adnominal phrase, have a practical meaning.

> 배 'a ship', 동화 'a children's story', 신문 'a newspaper', 은혜 'a favor', 약속 'a promise', 사랑 'love', 형제 'brothers', 고래 'a whale', 비둘기 'a dove', 학교 'a school', 성적 'a record'

> <u>학생증</u> 좀 보여주시겠어요?
> May I see your student ID card, please?
> 어느 <u>대학</u>에 다니십니까?
> What university do you attend?

Dependent nouns(의존명사), must be modified by adnominal phrase to have a meaning. Dependent nouns can be divided into formal dependent nouns and measurable dependent nouns.

- formal dependent nouns:

것 'a thing, a possession'	수 'a means, possibility'
채 'just as it is/stands'	줄 'how to do, the fact that'
바 'a way, a thing'	따름 'only, just, merely, simply'
지 'from the time when'	척(하다) 'make-believe, pretense'
양(하다) 'set up for, pretend to'	체(하다) 'make-believe, pretense'
뻔(하다) 'almost nearly, come near'	
듯(하다) 'look like, seem'	
만큼 'an extent, a degree, a measure'	
대로 'as, directly'	
때문 'reason, because'	

- measurable dependent nouns:

분 'a personage'	마리 'the number of animals'
개 'a piece, a unit, an item'	권 'a volume, a book'
동 'the number of houses'	장 'a sheet of paper'
원 'a won'	송이 'a blossom, a clusters'
그루 'a plant, a tree'	벌 'a pair of, a suit of clothes'
대 'a smoke, a blow, an injection'	잔 'a cup, a glass'
번 'a time, a number'	년 'a year'
해 'a year'	달 'a month'
일 'a day'	시간 'a hour'
분 'a minute'	초 'a second'

당신은 한국말을 **매우 잘할** **수** 있습니다.

You can speak Korean very well.

커피 **한** **잔** 주시겠습니까?

Could you give me a cup of coffee?

There are other ways to classify Korean language. It can be divide into concrete or abstract noun, countable or uncountable noun and so on. However, this book does not further explain these classification since such divisions is not very useful explaining Korean grammar.

▪ Spacing(띄어쓰기) of the nouns

First, there should be a space between a dependent noun and a word prior to a dependent noun.

아는∨것이 힘이다.
Knowledge is power.
나도 할∨수 있다.
I can do it as well.

The word in each example below can be used as either dependent noun or particle. When the word used as dependent noun, there should be space between the word and other word before it. On the other hand, if it is used as a particle it should be attached word before it.

Dependent noun: 먹을∨만큼만 가져가거라.
　　　　　　　Take only as much as you can eat.
Particle: 나도 너만큼은 농구를 잘할 수 있다.
　　　　　I can play basketball as much as you.

Dependent noun: 아는∨대로만 말씀해 주세요.
　　　　　　　Tell me just as you know, please.
Particle: 이번 사건에 대해 나대로는 할 말이 많습니다.
　　　　　I have lots of things to say about this incident in my own way.

Dependent noun: 준서는 공부를 잘할∨**뿐만** 아니라 운동도 잘한다.

Jun-Seo excelled in sports as well as his studies.

Particle: 너**뿐만** 아니라 수많은 사람들이 서울에 구경을 왔다.

Not only you but also a great number of people came to see the sights of Seoul.

Second, there should be a space when a word connects two other words, or for words used in lists.

과장 겸 팀장 'a section chief and team leader', 열 내지 스무 개 'from 10 to 20', 학생 및 교사 'students and teachers', 청군 대 백군 'the blue team versus the white team', 밤 {또는, 혹은} 사과 'chestnuts or apples' ; 책상과 걸상 등 'desks and chairs, etc.', 서울, 부산, 대구 등지 'Seoul, Busan, Daegu, and the like', 사과, 배, 귤 등속 'apples, pears, mandarins, and the like'

Third, when writing Arabic numeral, there should be a comma[,] every thousand. Whereas there should be a space between every the ten thousands when you write by number.

십이억 삼천사백오십육만 칠천팔백구십팔 원 '1,234,567,898won'
12억 3456만 7898원 '1,234,567,898won'
1,234,567,898원 '1,234,567,898won'

It is possible to write as '십이억 삼천 사백 오십 육만 칠천 팔백 구십 팔 원' instead of '십이억 삼천사백오십육만 칠천팔백구십팔 원' yet it is too inconvenient to read because there is too many spaces. Additionally it is hard to know its meaning because it takes too much space to write.

Fourth, as '-(으)ㄴ/는데' is connective ending which has the meaning of 'explanation and confrontation', and they should be attached to word in front of it. However '-는 데' is a combination of adnominal ending '-는' and '데'. Which is a noun representing 'place, fact, or situation'. Therefore, It should be space between two words.

> Connective ending:
>
> 그는 어제 서울에 갔는데, 거기서 뜻밖에 고향 친구를 만났다.
> He went to Seoul yesterday, met hometown friends there unexpectedly.
> 준서는 비가 오는데(도) 소풍을 갔다.
> Jun-Seo went on a picnic despite the rain.
>
> Adnominal ending+noun:
>
> 나는 잠깐 들를∨데가 있으니까 조금만 기다려 줘.
> There's a place where I have to stop by, so please wait a moment.
> 제가 아는∨데까지만 말씀을 드리겠습니다.
> I'll just tell you what I know.
> 질서를 잘 유지하는∨데는 법이 꼭 필요하다.
> The laws are indispensable in order to maintain order.

5.3 Making a compound noun

There is a case that a new noun is created when a noun and another noun or root combine to create new noun. This is called a compound noun. The **compound nouns**(합성명사) can be classified into **equal compound nouns**(대등 합성명사), **subordinate compound nouns**(종속 합성명사) and **convergence compound nouns**(융합 합성명사) depending on how the 'meaning' are combined.

- Equal compound nouns:

논 'a rice paddy' + 밭 'a field' → 논밭 'rice paddies and dry fields'
남 'male' + 녀 'female' → 남녀 'male and female'
동 'the east' + 서 'the west' → 동서 'the east and the west'

- Subordinate compound nouns:

돌 'a baby's first birthday' + 잔치 'party' → 돌잔치 'the birthday party for one-year-old baby'

볶음 'pan-broiled/roasted food' + 밥 'boiled rice' → 볶음밥 'fried rice'

늦 'late' + 잠 'a sleep' → 늦잠 'oversleeping'

군 'roast' + 밤 'a chestnut' → 군밤 'a roast chestnut'

첫 'the first' + 사랑 'love' → 첫사랑 'one's first love'

새 'new' + 해 'a year' → 새해 'a new year'

- Convergence compound nouns:

춘 'spring' + 추 'autumn' → 춘추 'age'

검 'black' + 버섯 'mushroom' → 검버섯 'dark spot'

큰 'big' + 집 'house' → 큰집 'house of eldest brother'

Sometimes a new noun can be created by adding prefixes or suffixes to a noun. This is called a **derived noun**(파생명사).

- Prefix derived noun:

군– 'unnecessary' + 말 'a word' → 군말 'an unnecessary remark'

개– 'wild' + 살구 'an apricot' → 개살구 'a wild apricot'

날– 'raw' + 고기 'meat' → 날고기 'raw meat'

맨– 'bare' + 손 'a hand' → 맨손 'bare hands'

숫– 'pure' + 처녀 'a virgin' → 숫처녀 'an immaculate virgin'

풋– 'unripe' + 고추 'a hot pepper' → 풋고추 'an unripe hot pepper'

홀– 'single' + 아비 'a father' → 홀아비 'a widower'

- Suffix derived noun:

강 'a dog' + –아지 'young' → 강아지 'a puppy'

아버(지) 'a father' + –님 'respectful person' → 아버님 'one's father'

울 'to cry' + –보 'a person' → 울보 'a crybaby'

짜임 'being put together' + –새 'shape' → 짜임새 'structure'

낚시 'fishing' + –질 'the act of doing' → 낚시질 'angling'

눈 'an eye' + –치 → 눈치 'tact, sense'

5.4 Making a noun

- **Suffixes which mean 'person'**

Suffixes '-가(家), -사(士), -자(者), -원(員), -인(人), -장(長), -민(民), -부
(父, 夫, 婦), -쟁이, -장이' is attached to a noun in the back, meaning
'person' who does certain action.

- -가: 교육(education)-가→교육가(an educator), 음악(music)-가→음악가
  (a musician), 평론(a critique)-가→평론가(a critic), 소설(a novel)-
  가→소설가(a novelist), 조각(a sculpture)-가→조각가(an engraver)
- -사: 조종(pilot a plane)-사→조종사(a pilot), 변호(defense)-사→변호사
  (a lawyer), 의(the medical art)-사→의사(a doctor), 회계(accounts)-
  사→회계사(an accountant), 세무(taxation business)-사→세무사(a
  licensed tax accountant), 법무(judicial affairs)-사→법무사(a
  judicial scrivener), 목(a shepherd)-사→목사(a pastor)
- -자: 노동(labor)-자→노동자(a laborer), 경영(management)-자→경영자
  (a manager), 환(trouble)-자→환자(a patient), 생산(production)-자
  →생산자(a producer), 소비(consumption)-자→소비자(a consumer)
- -원: 회사(a company)-원→회사원(a company employe), 공무(public
  service)-원→공무원(public service personnel), 사무(clerical work)-
  원→사무원(a clerk), 교(teaching)-원→교원(a teacher), 선(a ship)-
  원→선원(a seaman)
- -인: 군(an army)-인→군인(a soldier), 죄(a crime)-인→죄인(a criminal),
  상공(commerce and industry)-인→상공인(a merchant and worker),
  (종)교(a religion)-인→(종)교인(a man of religion), 시(poetry)-인→
  시인(a poet)
- -장: 회(a society)-장→회장(the chairman), 사(a company)-장→사장(the
  president of a company), 원(a hospital, a college, etc.)-장→원장(a
  president, a director), 공장(a factory)-장→공장장(a plant manager),
  총(lead, head)-장→총장(the president), 시(a city)-장→시장(a
  mayor), 선(a ship)-장→선장(the captain of a ship)

-민: 농(farming)-민→농민(a farmer), 어(fishery)-민→어민(a fisherman), 시(a city)-민→시민(the citizens), 국(a nation)-민→국민(people)

-부: 신(God)-부→신부(the Reverend), 어(fishery)-부→어부(a fisherman), 농(farming)-부→농부(a farmer), 매(a sister)-부→매부(one's sister's husband), 질(a nephew)-부→질부(the wife of a nephew)

'-쟁이' means a person who has 'such personality or habit', while '-장이' means a person who has 'such technique as a vocation'.

-쟁이: 고집(obstinacy)-쟁이→고집쟁이(an obstinate person), 개구(be mischievous)-쟁이→개구쟁이(a mischievous boy), 허풍(a bluff)-쟁이→허풍쟁이(a bluffer), 거짓말(a lie)-쟁이→거짓말쟁이(a liar), 변덕(caprice)-쟁이→변덕쟁이(a capricious person), 무식(ignorance)-쟁이→무식쟁이(an ignorant man), 중매(matchmaking)-쟁이→중매쟁이(a matchmaker), 요술(jugglery)-쟁이→요술쟁이(a juggler)

-장이: 대장(a smith)-장이→대장장이(a smith), 토기(an earthenware)-장이→토기장이(an earthenware maker), 풍각(a musical instrument or a performance)-장이→풍각장이(a street singer)

In case of suffix '-이' is attached to a verb stem or an adverb, it means a 'person', an 'animal', 'that work' or 'that thing' which does it.

person: 홀쭉(to be lanky)-이→홀쭉이(a lanky person), 왼손(the left hand)-잡(to seize)-이→왼손잡이(a left-handed person), 식(a food)-충(an insect)-이→식충이(a glutton), 겨레(offspring of the same forefather)-붙(to stick)-이→겨레붙이(members of a people), 멍청(to be stupid)-이→멍청이(a fool), 촐랑(to act frivolously)-이→촐랑이(a frivolous person), 늦(to be late)-깎(to cut)-이→늦깎이(a late bloomer)

animal: 코(a nose)-길(to be long)-이→코끼리(an elephant), 기럭(the sound of wild geese)-이→기러기(a wild goose), 뻐꾹(cuc-

koo)–이→뻐꾸기(a cuckoo), 점(a dot)–박(to drive)–이→점
박이(a person with a birthmark)

that work: 꽃(a flower)–꽂(to arrange flowers)–이→꽃꽂이(flower arrange-
ment), 달(the moon)–맞(to meet)–이→달맞이(enjoying the
moon), 고래(a whale)–잡(to catch)–이→고래잡이(whale fishing), 윷(a Yut)–놀(to play)–이→윷놀이(a game of yut), 물
(water)–놀(to play)–이→물놀이(playing in the water), 가을
(autumn)–걷(to harvest)–이→가을걷이(autumn harvesting),
방패(a shield)–막(to block up)–이→방패막이(a protector)

that thing: 손톱(a fingernail)–깎(to cut)–이→손톱깎이(nail clippers), 떡
(a rice cake)–볶(to fry)–이→떡볶이(rice cakes in hot sauce),
손(a hand)–잡(to grip)–이→손잡이(a handle), 재(ashes)–떨(
to knock off)–이→재떨이(an ashtray), 목(neck)–걸(to hang)–
이→목걸이(a necklace), 바람(wind)–막(to protect)–이→바
람막이(windbreak)

- ## Noun suffixes '-(으)ㅁ' and '-기'

'-(으)ㅁ, -기' are derivation suffixes which create noun when they are
added to verb stem. Generally, the addition of '-(으)ㅁ' to verb stem
expresses 'stative' and 'close' sense. Where as '-기' addition expresses
'active' and 'open' sense. Comparing with English, '-(으)ㅁ' type is
similar to 'noun' while '-기' type is similar to 'gerund' in English.

얼다(to be ice): 얼–음 → 얼음(ice) / 얼–기 → 얼기(freezing)
믿다(to believe): 믿–음 → 믿음(faith/trust) / 믿–기 → 믿기(believing)
죽다(to die): 죽–음 → 죽음(death) / 죽–기 → 죽기(dying)
자다(to sleep): 자–ㅁ → 잠(sleep) / 자–기 → 자기(sleeping)
살다(to live): 살–ㅁ → 삶(life) / 살–기 → 살기(living)
뛰다(to jump): 뛰–ㅁ → 뜀(jump) / 뛰–기 → 뛰기(jumping)

Accordingly, noun of '-(으)ㅁ' type can't be modified by an adverb and neither can be used as a predicate in sentences because it does not have 'the nature of verb'. On the other hand, noun of '-기' type can be modified by and adverb and either can be used as a predicate because it has 'the nature of verb'.

준서는 물이 잘 얼기를 기다렸다.

Jun-Seo is waiting for the water to freeze well.

*준서는 물이 잘 얼음을 기다렸다.

5.5 Gender of a noun

Nouns in Korean does not have **gender**(성, 性). So there is no affix or ending to indicate male, female or neuter gender in Korean.

5.6 Articles which modifies a noun

Korean does not have **articles**(관사) in front of a noun. Therefore in Korean, there is no morpheme which corresponds to 'a, an, the' of English. However adnominals such as '그, 어떤' tend to correspond with 'article' in English.

5.7 Number of a noun

Number(수) indicate whether the noun is singular or plural. Singular refers to 'one' person, thing of animal, while plural refers to more than one. '-들' is added to back of the plural noun in Korean to indicate plurality. However '-들' is not generally added, of there is no particular intention to emphasize plural.

In English, when a subject of third person singular present, '-(e)s' is added to verb ending to indicate number. 'be' verb also changed its form according to subject. However such distinction does not exist in Korean.

사 'a person' → 사람들 'people' ; 동물 'an animal' → 동물들 'animals' ; 꽃 'a flower' → 꽃들 'flowers' ; 책 'a book' → 책들 'books' ; 집 'a house' → 집들 'houses' ; 차 'a car' → 차들 'cars'

그 사람은 차를 가지고 있다.
He has a car.
그 사람은 {차를/?*차들을} 많이 가지고 있다.
He has many {car/cars}

In addition, not only plural suffix '-들' is attached to noun base but also to ending of adverbs or verbs, indicating a subject is 'plural'. In this case, the subject is omitted generally.

어서들 오십시오. Welcome.
많이들 드십시오. Bon appetit.
잡아들 보십시오. Catch me.

5.8 Politeness of a noun

Politeness(높임) is can be expressed by attaching suffix '-님' to a specific noun in the back in Korean. The words to which suffix '-님'

is attached should be a noun meaning person or vocation respected by people in the society.

> 선생–님 'a teacher', 교수–님 'a professor', 총장–님 'the president', 사장
> –님 'the president of a company', 과장–님 'the chief of a section', 선장님
> 'the captain of a ship'
> 아버(지)–님 'a father' → 아버님, 어머(니)–님 'a mother' → 어머님,
> 형–님 'an older brother' → 형님, 누(나)–님 'an older sister' → 누님
> 아들–님 'a son' → 아드님, 딸–님 'a daughter' → 따님, 하늘–님 'heaven'
> → 하느님

There are words which implying politeness in its meaning, therefore '–님' can not be added to these words since they already indicate politeness itself.

> 밥 'boiled rice' → 진지, 이 'a tooth' → 치아, (이) 사람 'a person' →
> (이) 분, 이름 'a name' → 성함/존함, 술 'alcoholic drink' → 약주, 말
> 'word' → 말씀, 씨 'Mr'. → 님, 아주머니 'ma'am' → 사모님, 아내 'a
> wife' → 부인, 선생 'a teacher' → 스승/은사, 어른 'an elder' → 어르신,
> 집 'a house' → 댁, 생일 'a birthday' → 생신

Especially '말씀' can be used in order to show respect other person's saying and to lower one's own saying. Christians refer to biblical verse as '말씀' or '성경 말씀' to show respect for it.

5.9 Korean cultural aspects as reflected in nouns

In this section, nouns will be explained, focusing on expression of title in order to look into language habits of Korean. Korean people put their family name in front of first name. Most of family names consist of one syllable while first names consist of two syllables. However there are family name which consist of two syllables, as well as, first name which consist of one syllable.

family name	first name
김 Gim(Kim)	준서 Jun-Seo
박 Bak(Park/Pak)	지성 Ji-Seong
이 I(Lee/Yi)	순신 Sun-Sin
황보 Hwangbo	민서 Min-Seo
독고 Dokgo	준 Jun

Family name and first name should be written without any space between them like '김준서, 박지성, 이순신'. However when there is need to make distinction of family name and first name, a space can be added between family name and first name like '황보 민서, 독고 탁'.

In a English-speaking culture, people generally refer to other people with first name which indicate friendliness. However, Korean elders rarely call first name in everyday conversation. Particularly, it is very impolite to call someone older than speaker by his/her first name.

Instead of calling someone by his/her first name, people generally add 'title' of family name.

씨 'Mr.', 군 'young boy', 양 'young girl', 님 'respectful person', 선생 'Mr. or teacher', 사장 'Mr. or the head of shop', 여사 'woman'

In case the person is a public officer, it is good manner to attach the title. If you want to show more respect for him or her, you can attach '-님' to the title in the back.

대통령 'a president', 장관 'a minister', 사무관 'an assistant junior official', 서장 'the head', 관장 'a director', 원장 'a president, a director', 총장 'the president', 교수 'a professor', 사장 'the president of a company', 차장 'a vice-chief', 부장 'the head of a department', 과장 'the chief of a section', 계장 'a chief clerk'

For example, a person is called like '박 장관(님), 손 사무관(님), 석 총장(님), 정 원장(님), 김 박사(님), 김 교수(님), 이 선생(님), 서 사장(님)' and when the writing, there should be a space between family name and first name.

Additionally even if the person is younger than speaker, '-님' can be added like '정 원장님, 김 박사님, 이 선생님, 김 교수님' for a person who has higher position or is respected.

'-씨' can be added to full name or first name when referring to a person who is in same social position or status. However, it is important not to add '-씨' right after family name since it creates very impolite expression. Especially, this can never be used to someone who is older than speaker or someone in higher position.

김민준 씨, 어디 가세요?
Mr. Min-Jun Kim, where are you going?
민준 씨, 어디 가세요?
Min-Jun, where are you going?
김 씨, 어디 가세요?
Mr. Kim, where are you going?

'선생(님)' is sometimes attached to family name. In this case '선생(님)' is usually used for teacher, professor, doctor, lawyer, office clerk, musician, painter, critics or artist. Here '선생' literally means 'teacher' but could also refer to 'a person who has white collar job', or 'a person who made success in specific field' or 'a person who deserve a respect from other people'. Originally while it can mean 'a person who has white color job' or 'a person who made success in a specific field' or 'a person who deserve a respect by others a bit'.

김 선생님, 요즘 어떻게 지내십니까?
Mr. Kim how are you doing these days?

As for the person who runs his own business or a company, the word '사장' can be attached to family name in the back.

박 사장님은 취미가 무엇입니까?
What do you like to do when you're not working, president Park?

Also, it is common to use 군 'Mr.' for male and 양 'Miss' for female after family name when you call a student a person in such age like 김 군 'Mr. Kim', 박 양 'Miss Park'.

However children are generally called by their first names. In this case, vocative particle '-야' or '-아' is added to first name as '영수-야, 영희-야, 지성-아'. In order to show friendliness, a vocative particle is added only to the last letter of the first name as follows.

김민준 → 민준-아 → 준-아
박서연 → 서연-아 → 연-아
서민수 → 민수-야 → 수-야
김윤희 → 윤희-야 → 희-야

■ Classification of parts of speech in Korean

The word 'parts of speech' refer to classification of words based on specific rules. Generally, it is classified based on function, form and meaning.

First, classification by **function(기능)** means that parts of speech is classified by the role of word in the sentence. It is classified **substantives, inflectional words, modifying words, relational words** and **independence words**. Substantives include 'nouns, pronouns and numerals' and they have function as a subject in a sentence. Of course they can have the function of object, adverb and complement. Inflectional words includes 'verbs, adjectives and copula'. They have the function to describe subject in a sentence. Modifying words include 'adnominals and adverbs'. Adnominals modify substantive while adverbs modify inflectional words or other adverbs. Relational words include 'particles'. Particles have the function to make relationship between predicates and elements which precede it. The independences word include 'exclamations'. The exclamation is used independently from other elements in a sentence.

Second, classification by **form(형태)** means that parts of speech is classified according to whether there is a change in the form of word or not. Nouns, pronouns and numerals, adnominals, adverbs, exclamations, and particles are words whose form do not change where as verbs, adjectives, copula are words whose form change due to verbal conjunction.

Third, classification by **meaning(의미)** represents that parts of speech is classified according to the meaning of word. Noun is the word which expresses name of a person or a thing, pronoun is a word which substitutes for a noun or noun phrase. Numeral is the word which shows quantity or order. Verb is the word expressing movement. Adjective is a word showing the state of a person or a thing. Exclamation is the word expressing surprise, feeling, calling or answering of a speaker.

Adnominal modifies substantive and adverbs modified inflectional word. Particles are added to substantives in the back to add meaning to it, copula confirms the meaning of substantive. However we can't say they show the exact meaning even if they are the names classified according to its meaning.

To summarize it as follows:

Form	Function	Parts of speech (meaning)	Examples
Un-changeable word	Substantive	Noun	준서(Jun-Seo)가, 책(a book)이, 물(water)을, 가는 것(a thing)도
		Pronoun	그(he)가, 그녀(she)도, 누구(who)를, 무엇(what)이니?
		Numeral	하나(one)가, 둘(two)도, 첫째(the first)가, 제일(the first)이
	Modifying word	Adnominal	그(that) 사람, 새(new) 책, 갖은(all sorts of) 양념, 맨(most) 끝
		Adverb	매우(very) 맵다, 잘(well) 먹는다, 매일(every day) 기도한다
	Independence word	Exclamation	어머나(oh!), 하하(ha! ha!), 야호(Yoo-hoo!), 예(yes), 아니오(no), 글쎄(well)
	Relational word	Particle	달이(subject particle), 이야기를(object particle), 민서보다(adverbial particle), 형도(auxiliary particle), 친구야(vocative particle)
Changeable word	Inflectional word	Verb	가다(to go), 살다(to live), 먹다(to eat), 흐르다(to flow), 사람이다(to be), 있다(to exist)
		Adjective	길다(to be long), 아름답다(to be beautiful), 멀다(to be far), 다르다(to be different)
		Copula	책이다(to be), 책이냐? 책이고, 책이면, 책인 것 같다

06 Pronoun

6.1 What is a pronoun?

Pronoun(대명사) is a word that substitutes for a noun. There are two types of pronouns: personal pronouns that replace people and demonstrative pronouns that replace objects or locations. Demonstrative pronouns can be divided into material demonstrative pronouns and locational demonstrative pronouns.

Pronouns, which are sometimes accompanied with particles, can be used in the form of subject, object, complement, predicate, adnominal phrase, adverbial phrase, or independently. As in the case of '젊은 그대, *이 그들 ; 사랑스러운 당신, *그 당신 ; 자랑스러운 저들 ; *저 저들' pronouns can come with an adnominal phrase, but not with an adnominal.

6.2 Types and characteristics of pronouns

6.2.1 Personal pronoun

There are following **personal pronouns**(인칭대명사) in Korean. The biggest difference of Korean personal pronouns from English is that Korean pronouns are categorized into a plain, honorific and non-honorific level, which indicates the highly sophisticated level of honorific speech in Korean. It is very important to use the right honorific expressions in the right situation.

Person		Plain level	Honorific level	Non-honorific level
1st person	Singular	나/내	본인	저/제
	Plural	우리(들)		저희(들)
2nd person	Singular	너/네, 당신¹, 여보, 자기¹	어른, 어르신, 당신², 그대, 부인	자네 당신³
	Plural	너희(들)	어른들, 어르신들, 그대들, 여러분(들)	
3rd person	Singular	그, 그녀, 자기²	당신⁴	
	Plural	그들, 그녀들		

Personal pronouns indicate persons only, not animals, objects or ideas. 'It' in English indicates not only people but also children and animals, whereas there are no Korean personal pronouns equivalent to 'it'. Instead, Koreans call an animal by its name. As for children, '그 애, 그 아이, 그 어린애, 그 어린이' are generally used regardless of sex, even though '그, 그녀' are supposed to be used for boys and girls, respectively.

I took the book and put **it** on the shelf.
나는 책을 집어서, (그것을) 선반 위에 올려놓았다.

Where is a cat? / 고양이가 어디 있니?
It is in the garden.
({고양이/*그것/*그}는) 정원에 있어.

I heard the baby crying, so I brought **it** some milk.

나는 어린애가 우는 소리를 듣고, ({그 애/그/그녀/*그것}에게) 우유를 갖다
주었다.

Also, Koreans usually omit pronouns in their conversation if the speaker
and the listener are already aware of who they are talking about. However,
pronouns must be used in written language, or when emphasis needs to
be made. For example, in the sentences above, 'it' must be used to make
the sentence grammatically correct. In Korean however, it is more natural
to omit such phrases in the case of '그것, 고양이 ; 그 어린애, 그, 그녀'.

In addition, there are no possessive pronouns that are equivalent to
mine, yours, his, hers, ours, yours, theirs, etc. Thus, possessive pronouns
are expressed in the form of personal pronouns + 것, such as '나의 것,
너의 것, 그의 것, 그녀의 것 ; 우리(들)의 것, 그들의 것'.

- Special usage of personal pronouns

First, 당신[1] is used by married couples to respect the other half. 당신[2]
which is similar to 그대, is used to call others in a friendly way. However,
당신[3] is used in arguments to look down on, or sneer at the other. 당신[4]
refers to those who deserve level of elevation, such as one's parents or
teachers.

[당신[1]]
A: **당신**이 어제 등산을 가자고 했지요?
   You yesterday said that you wanted to go mountain climbing?
B: 맞아요. 이번 주 주말에 함께 등산을 가자고 **당신**에게 얘기를 했어요.
   That's right. I said that this weekend we should go mountain climbing
   together.

[당신[2]]
김 계장, **당신**과 함께 일하면 일이 잘된단 말이야.

Mr Kim, everything seems to go well when I'm working with you.
어때, 이번에도 함께 일해 보지 않겠나?
Well, why don't we work together again this time?

[당신³]
A: **당신**이 정말 이럴 수 있는 거야?
How could you do this to me?
B: 왜, **당신**이 나한테 잘해 봐. 내가 그렇게 하나.
Well, you should have done better.

[당신⁴]
할아버지, **당신**께서는 늘 "착하게 살아라."라고 말씀하셨다.
My grandfather always told us to be good.
그래서 우리 형제는 **당신**의 말씀대로 살려고 노력하고 있다.
So my siblings are trying to live by your words.

Second, 자기¹ is used by young lovers to call each other in a friendly way. However, it is hardly used by those aged 50 or higher, no matter how much they love each other.

A: **자기** 나 사랑해? / Darling, do you love me?
B: 그럼, 내가 **자기** 사랑하지 누굴 사랑하겠어.
　　Of course, who should I love other than you?
A: 그래요, 내겐 **자기**밖에 없어. / Yes, I have only you.

자기², a third person pronoun which re-indicates the aforementioned person, means 'the very person' or 'oneself'.

준서는 **자기**의 애인을 데리고 여행을 갔다.
Jun-Seo took his girlfriend with him on his journey.
민서는 항상 **자기** 관리가 철저하다.
Min-Seo is always self-controlled.

■ Special usage of 우리

First, Koreans generally use the 1st person plural pronoun '우리', instead of the 1st person singular pronoun '나', because Koreans had lived in a clan society for a long period of time. Therefore, referring oneself as a part of a group is natural for Korean. Using '나/내' is very awkward for Korean speakers, even though it is grammatically correct. If '나' has to be used in this situation instead of '우리', '나' will be given an emphasis.

{나의/?내} 아빠 'my daddy' → 우리 아빠
{나의/?내} 엄마 'my mama' → 우리 엄마
{나의/내} 아내 'my wife' → 우리 아내
{나의/내} 아이 'my child' → 우리 아이
{나의/내} 집 'my home' → 우리 집
{나의/내} 학교 'my school' → 우리 학교
{나의/?내} 나라 'my country' → 우리 나라

Second, '우리' is used when the speaker calls himself or someone related to him/herself.

{우리/?나의} 회사는 분위기가 매우 좋다.
(Our/my) Company has a good atmosphere.
{우리/?너} 함께 놀러 갈까?
Do (you/we) want to go on a trip?

Third, '우리' is used when the speaker tries to emphasize his/her side.

우리가 남이냐? / Aren't we on the same boat?
이번 시합에서는 우리 편이 이겼다. / We (our side) won this game.

● Case of personal pronouns

In English, personal pronouns change their form according to cases, such as subjective case, possessive case and objective case, including 'I, my, me ; you, your, you ; he, his, him ; she, her, her ; who, whose, whom'. However, Korean personal pronouns do not change according to the case(격). Instead, the personal pronoun is accompanied with a **case particle**(격조사) (e.g. 내(I)-가, 나(my)-의, 나(me)를 ; 너(you)-가, 너(your)-의, 너(you)-를 ; 그(he)-가, 그(his)-의, 그(him)-를 그녀(she)-가, 그녀(her)-의, 그녀(her)-를).

In the sentences below, '그' is used as subject, object and adnominal phrase, each of them accompanied with a subjective case '-가', objective case '-를' and adnominal case '-의'.

> Subjective case: 그가 한국 김치를 먹었다.
> > He ate Korean Kimchi.
> Objective case: 나는 그를 한국 음식점에서 만났다.
> > I met him in a Korean restaurant.
> Adnominal case: 그의 차가 음식점 앞에 있었다.
> > His car was in front of the restaurant.

6.2.2 Demonstrative pronoun

Demonstrative pronouns(지시대명사) have a certain semantic pattern according to the prefix (e.g. 이- 'this, here', 그- 'that, there', 저- 'that, over there, over there').

> 이-: close to the speaker
> 그-: close to the listener
> 저-: far from both the speaker and listener

Target of Indication	이-	그-	저-
Object	이것	그것	저것
Location	여기	거기	저기

A: 김민준 씨, 어느 것을 사시겠습니까?

　　Mr. Min-Jun Kim, which one would you like to buy?

B: 저는 <u>이것</u>을 사겠습니다.

　　I will buy this one.

A: <u>저것</u>은 어떻습니까?

　　How about that one?

B: <u>저것</u>은 별로 좋지 않은 것 같습니다.

　　I don't think that one is good.

김민준 씨, <u>그것</u> 좀 주시겠습니까?

Mr. Min-Jun Kim, could you give me that?

Instead of '이-, 그-, 저-', '요-, 고-, 조-' can be used to refer to something small, cute and lovely. However, they can also be derisive.

Also, Korean's demonstrative words can be in the form of 'adnominal(이/그/저) + noun, pronoun or adverb', which has a similar meaning to that of material demonstrative pronouns and locational demonstrative pronouns. For example, '여기' refers to the location of the speaker, while '거기' refers to the location of the listener, or a place where both the speaker and listener are aware of. '저기' indicates somewhere slightly far from the speaker and the listener.

Target of Indication	Parts of speech	이-	그-	저-
Location	Pronoun	이곳	그곳	저곳
Person	Pronoun	이분	그분	저분
		이놈	그놈	저놈
Person	Pronoun	이이	그이	저이
		이자	그자	저자
		이들	그들	저들
Time	Pronoun	이때	그때	저때/접때
Case	Pronoun	이번	그번	저번

Direction	Pronoun	이쪽	그쪽	저쪽
Direction	Adverb	이리	그리	저리
Method	Adverb	이렇게	그렇게	저렇게
Degree	Adverb	이리	그리	저리
		이렇게	그렇게	저렇게

6.2.3 Interrogative pronoun

Interrogative pronoun(의문대명사), which is used when the person, time, location, object, etc. to be demonstrated are not known in detail, is also referred to as **undesignated pronoun**(미지칭대명사). It acts as a subject, object, complement, adnominal phrase or adverbial phrase in a sentence.

Interrogative pronoun	Target
누구/누/뉘	Person
언제	Time
어디	Location
무엇/무어/뭐	Object

'누구' is generally used in its original form of '누구'. However, if it is combined with a subject particle '-가', it becomes '누구-가 → 누가'. If it is combined with an adnominal particle '-의', it becomes '누구-의 → 뉘'. Also, '누구' can be changed into '누구누구/*누구들' to refer to a multiple number of people, thus substituting the original plural form of '누구'.

아직 <u>누구누구</u>가 안 왔니? [↘]
Still who are not here?

고향에는 친구들 가운데 <u>누구누구</u>가 살고 있어? [↘]
In the hometown, among our friends, who are still living there?

'무엇' becomes '뭐가, 무어가' with subject particle '-가', or '뭘, 무얼' with object particle '-을'. '무엇' becomes '뭐야? 무어야?' with '-야', a particle for interrogation, confirmation and emphasis, and becomes '뭐라고' with '-(이)라고'.

<u>뭐가</u> 문제가 됩니까?
What is the problem?
지난 주말에 <u>무엇을/무얼/뭘</u> 했습니까? [↘]
Last weekend, what did you do?
그렇게 하는 이유가 <u>뭐야</u>?
Why are you doing that?
준서가 <u>뭐라고</u> 말하더냐?
What did Jun-Seo say?

In English, the interrogative comes at the beginning of every sentence. However, there is no certain place for interrogatives in Korean sentences. Interrogatives tend to be placed in the most important part of the question. Typically, an interrogative sentence shows rising intonation in the back, but a sentence with interrogative show lowing intonation.

6.2.4 Indefinite pronoun

Indefinite pronoun(부정대명사) is used when there is no specific person or object to indicate, or there is no need to do so. It is expressed as pronouns '아무, 누구' or adnominal '어떤'. It can act as subject, object, adnominal phrase and adverbial phrase in a sentence.

If the subject of a sentence is '아무도, 누구도', which is a combination of particle '-도' with '아무' and '누구', negative verbs act as predicates (e.g. '-지 아니하다, -지 못하다, 말다, 없다'), negating the overall sentence.

아직 **아무도** 회사에 출근하지 않았다.
Yet nobody has come to work.
이 문제는 **누구도** 풀지 못할 것이다.
Nobody will be able to solve this problem.
어느 **누구도** 그 프로그램의 시행에 동의하는 사람이 없을 것이다.
Nobody will agree with the implementation of the program.
아무도 여기에 오지 마라.
Nobody should come here.

If the subject of a sentence is '아무나, 누구나', which is a combination of '아무, 누구' with particle '-(이)나', positive verbs (e.g. '-아/어도 좋다, -아/어도 상관없다, -아/어도 괜찮다') become the predicate, making an declarative sentence.

아무나 여기에 들어와도 괜찮다.
Anyone can come here.
누구나 자유롭게 이야기해도 좋다.
Anyone can feel free to talk.

Adnominal '어떤' can become an indefinite pronoun in the form of '어떤 + noun-이/가/을/를/에', which means 'some kind of ~ ; a certain ~'. It is useful when there is no need to go into details or indicate something.

어떤 사람이 너를 만나러 왔더구나.
Someone had come to see you.

어떤 일이 있기는 있었던 모양이다.
There must have been something.
어떤 때는 참 쓸쓸하더라.
Sometimes I feel so lonely.
그 사람에 대해서 어떤 말이 있었지만 그는 상관하지 않더라.
There were some rumors about him/her, but he/she didn't care.
그 문제를 해결할 어떤 방법이 있을 것 같기는 하다.
I think there can be some solutions to the problem.

However, if '어떤 + {사람/분/것/데/때/방법/방향/말/일/사건}' is accompanied with particle '-도' in the place of subject, negative verbs (e.g. '-지 아니하다, -지 못하다, 없다, 말다') should become the predicate, making a completely negative sentence.

어떤 사람도 이곳에 들어오지 못하게 하세요.
Nobody should be allowed to come here.
어떤 말도 나는 듣지 않겠다.
I will not listen to anything.
이곳에서는 어떤 사건도 없었다.
Here, there were no events whatsoever.
이제부터 어떤 말도 하지 말자.
From now on, let's not say anything.

Moreover, if indefinite pronouns are used as subject in combination with '-(이)나', predicates should consist of positive verbs (e.g. '좋다, 상관 없다, 괜찮다') to make a completely positive sentence.

Also, if the aforementioned undesignated pronoun is in an declarative sentence, it will have an indefinite semantic function.

밖에 누군가 온 것 같습니다.
I think somebody is outside.

무엇이든지 잘 먹어야 건강합니다.
If you eat well, you can be healthy.
도움이 필요하시면 **언제**든 찾아오세요.
If you need help, please come any time.
김 선생은 **어디**를 가서도 전화를 받을 수 없어요.
Mr. Kim, wherever he is, cannot answer the phone.

Sometimes, even if interrogatives such as '누구, 무엇, 언제, 어디' are in an interrogative sentence, the sentence may have an indefinite semantic function. In this case, the tone is raised at the end of the sentence. The listener may answer by yes or no and then talk about his/her opinion.

A: **누구**를 기다리는 중입니까?[↗]
   Are you waiting for someone?
B: 예, 친구를 기다리고 있습니다.
   Yes, I am waiting for a friend.

A: **무엇**을 찾고 있습니까?[↗]
   Are you looking for something?
B: 아니오, 음악을 듣고 있습니다.
   No, I'm listening to music.

6.2.5 Reflexive pronoun

Reflexive pronoun(재귀대명사) is used in place of a noun to avoid repeating the subject. In Korean, there are various reflexive pronouns according to the person and level of respect.

Personal pronouns such as first person '나, 저 ; 우리, 저희들' and second person '너 ; 너희들' can be used repetitively.

내가 미국에 처음 갔을 때, 나를 알아보는 많은 사람을 만났다.
When I went to the US for the first time, I met a lot of people who recognized me.
네가 너의 인생을 성공적으로 살고 싶으면, 무엇보다 네가 정직해야 한다.
If you want to live a successful life, the most important thing is for you to be honest.

However, third person pronouns use '자기, 저, 자신, 자기 자신, 본인, 당신' instead of '그, 그녀', as reflexive pronouns. If '-들' is added to reflexive pronouns, reflexive pronouns become plural. In particular, '당신' acts as a honorific title for '자기'.

그는 아직 **자기** 이름도 쓸 줄 모른다.
He still doesn't know how to write his name.
그녀는 **저**밖에 모른다는 말을 아직도 듣고 있다.
She is still said to be self-centered.
어느 **누구**나 **자기 자신**을 먼저 사랑할 줄 알아야 한다.
Anyone should know how to love her/himself first.
그들은 아직도 **자기들**이 세계에서 가장 잘 산다고 생각한다.
They still believe that they are the wealthiest people in the world.
아버님, **당신**은 제게 가장 소중한 분이셨습니다.
Father, you were the most precious man to me.

6.2.6 Relative pronoun

In English, **relative pronouns**(관계대명사) are 'who, which, that, what', etc. However, there are no equivalents in Korean, as modifiers always come before the modified. As such, adnominal endings act as relative pronoun in Korean.

어제	서울–에	오–ㄴ	사람–은	존슨	씨–이다.
Yesterday	Seoul-at	arrive-**who**	man	Johnson	Mr.-is

The man who arrived at Seoul yesterday is Mr. Johnson.

그 여자–는	내–가	가장	좋아하–는	책–을	가지고 있다.
She	I	most	like-**that**	book	has

She has the book that I like the most.

6.3 Korean cultural aspects as reflected in pronouns

First, when addressing others, Koreans use '너' to those who aged the same or younger, '어른, 어르신' to those aged older, and 당신[3] to the other party with whom they are quarreling. However, '너, 어르신, 자네, 당신[3]' are not in frequent use unless the speaker wants to specify the hearer, as Koreans tend to omit the subject in actual conversations.

Second, strangely enough, Koreans tend to indicate the hearer by words that represent **location**(장소) or **direction**(방향) instead of the name of the person, during phone calls. The speakers name just the location or direction to address each other on the assumption that they know each other fairly well. These expressions are in widespread use in everyday conversations, when there is no need to specify the hearer, or when the speaker wants to indicate the hearer as one group.

A: 어디서 전화 왔다고 할까요?
   Who is this?
B: 예, **성북동**에서 전화 왔다고 전해 주시겠습니까?
   Yes, could you say that Seongbuk Dong called?

A: **그쪽**에서 먼저 의견을 말씀해 주세요.

Please give me your idea first.

B: 아니요, **이쪽**에서는 별로 말씀 드릴 게 없습니다.

No, we don't have much to say.

Third, the **name of the person's hometown** can sometimes indicate married women. '서울댁, 부산댁' below refer to married women who come from Seoul and Busan, respectively.

A: **서울댁**은 어디 갔습니까?

Where did Seoul-Daek go?

B: 네, 은행에 볼일이 있어서 잠깐 외출했습니다.

She will be outside for a while to sort out something at the bank.

A: **부산댁**은 참 정(情)도 많아요.

Busan-Daek is so warm-hearted.

B: 네, 그렇게 말씀해 주시니 고맙네요.

Thank you for saying so.

07 Numeral

7.1 What is a numeral?

Numeral(수사) is a word that indicates the number, amount and order of person or things. For numerals, there are cardinal numbers that indicate the number and amount, and ordinal numbers that indicate the order, and they each have a dual structure of Korean origin and Chinese origin.

Numerals can be used as components, such as subject, predicate, object, and complement, and except in special cases, it can not be modified by adnominal or adnominals like '*새 둘, *무슨 둘, *예쁜 하나'.

7.2 Types and characteristics of numerals

7.2.1 Cardinal numeral

Cardinal numeral(양수사) is used for indicating the number or amount of person or things. For cardinal numeral, there are Korean origin cardinal numeral and Chinese origin cardinal numeral.

Korean origin cardinal numeral		Chinese origin cardinal numeral
	0	영/零, 공/空
하나	1	일, 一
둘	2	이, 二
셋	3	삼, 三
넷	4	사, 四
다섯	5	오, 五
여섯	6	육, 六
일곱	7	칠, 七
여덟	8	팔, 八
아홉	9	구, 九
열	10	십, 十

From 11 to 19, numbers in the table above are attached at the end of '열' or '십' like '열하나, 열둘, 열셋, 열넷, 열다섯, 열여섯, 열일곱, 열여덟, 열아홉 ; 십일, 십이, 십삼, 십사, 십오, 십육, 십칠, 십팔, 십구'.

For numerals of ten units, Korean origin has a separate name, and '십' is added from '일(1)' to '구(9)', for Chinese origin. There are up to '99, 아흔아홉' of Korean origin cardinal numeral in contemporary Korean, and the above are only Chinese origin cardinal numerals.

Korean origin cardinal numeral		Chinese origin cardinal numeral
열	10	일십 or 십, 十
스물	20	이십, 二十
서른	30	삼십, 三十
마흔	40	사십, 四十
쉰	50	오십, 五十
예순	60	육십, 六十
일흔	70	칠십, 七十

여든	80	팔십, 八十
아흔	90	구십, 九十
	100	일백 or 백, 百

Just like ten units, units, such as hundred, thousand, ten thousand, and hundred thousand, etc. are attached from '일(1)' to '구(9)' in '백, 천, 만, 억, etc.' units as well.

hundred(100) units: 일백(100), 삼백(300), 구백(900)

thousand(1,000) units: 일천(1,000), 삼천(3,000), 구천(9,000)

ten thousand(10,000) units: 일만(10,000), 삼만(30,000), 구만(90,000) ; 십만(100,000), 삼십만(300,000), 구십만(900,000) ; 일백만(1,000,000), 삼백만(3,000,000), 구백만(9,000,000)

hundred thousand(100,000,000) units: 일억(100,000,000), 삼억(300,000,000), 구억(900,000,000) ; 십억(1,000,000,000), 삼십억(3,000,000,000), 구십억(9,000,000,000) ; 백억(10,000,000,000), 삼백억(30,000,000,000), 구백억(90,000,000,000) ; 천억(100,000,000,000), 삼천억(300,000,000,000), 구천억(900,000,000,000)

Unlike English, there are many ways of representing uncertain number, and these are called the **round number**(어림수).

한둘/한두(1 or 2), 두셋/두세(2 or 3), 서넛/서너(3 or 4), 너덧(4 or 5), 댓(5 more or less), 대여섯(5 or 6), 예닐곱(6 or 7), 일여덟(7 or 8), 여남은 (10~12)

There are many cases of Korean origin numeral that represent amount like '하나(1), 둘(2), 셋(3), 넷(4) ; 열하나(11), 열둘(12), 열셋(13), 열넷(14), 스물(20), etc.' modify the nouns the following, and here, these forms are changed into '한, 두, 세, 네 ; 열한, 열두, 열세, 열네, 스무', and parts of speech is changed from a numeral to an adnominal.

오늘 결석한 사람은 {한/두/세/네/스무} 명이다.

{One/Two/Three/Four/Twenty} was/were absent today.

그는 젖소 {열한/열두/열세/열네/백 스무} 마리를 키우고 있다.

He keeps {eleven/twelve/thirteen/fourteen/one hundred and twenty} milk cows.

However, in cases of the rest of other Korean origin adnominals, the forms are not changed, even though they modify the following nouns.

준서가 사과 {다섯/여섯/열/서른/아흔} 개를 사 왔다.

Jun-Seo bought {five/six/ten/thirty/ninety} apples.

나는 노트 {일곱/열여덟/스물아홉} 권을 가지고 있다.

I have {seven/eighteen/twenty nine} notebooks.

One step forward >>

■ Special use of round number

People often ask other people something by using round numbers, and the round number of a smaller number than the number they want is used here. In other word, Min-Seo uses not '네다섯' but '서너', when she wants to get four apples.

준서: 사과 몇 개 줄까? / How many apples do you want?
민서: 서너 개 주세요. / Give me three or four.

In contrast, they always have to give the round number of a bigger number when they are giving something. Min-Seo can give four or five, because Jun-Seo asked for four or five. However, Jun-Seo is asking for five in fact, so it is correct to give five always as it is the reality of Korean language.

준서: 사과 네다섯 개 주세요. / Give me four or five apples.
민서: 그래, 다섯 개 여기 있어. / Ok, here are five apples.

7.2.2 Ordinal numeral

Ordinal numeral(서수사) is used for indicating the order or class of person, things or works. For ordinal numeral, there are also Korean origin ordinal numeral and Chinese origin ordinal numeral.

Korean origin cardinal numeral		Chinese origin cardinal numeral
첫째	1	제일, 第一
둘째	2	제이, 第二
셋째	3	제삼, 第三
넷째	4	제사, 第四
다섯째	5	제오, 第五
여섯째	6	제육, 第六
일곱째	7	제칠, 第七
여덟째	8	제팔, 第八
아홉째	9	제구, 第九
열째	10	제십, 第十

Korean origin ordinal numerals are made by attaching suffix '-째' that has a meaning of 'order' to the cardinal numeral like '둘, 셋, 넷, etc.' However, for the 'first' case, it is created by putting '-째' to a prefix '첫' that has a meaning of 'first', not putting '-째' to '하나'. And Chinese origin ordinal numerals are made by putting '제-' that has a meaning of 'order' to a cardinal numeral.

For numbers above '십(10)', cardinal numerals in the table above are attached to '열' or '십' as shown below. However, forms of '열하나째(11), 열둘째(12), 스물째(20), etc.' are changed a little bit into '열한째, 열두째, 스무째'.

Korean origin: 열한째(11), 열두째(12), 열셋째(13), 열넷째(14), 열여섯째
(16), 열아홉째(19)
Chinese origin: 제십일/제11(11), 제십이/제12(12), 제십삼/제13(13), 제십
사/제14(14), 제십육/제16(16), 제십구/제19(19)

The rest of other ordinal numerals can be made in the same way like
'열째, 서른째, 마흔째 ; 제십, 제이십, 제삼십, 제사십' as above.
There are some ordinal numerals that represent round number.

한두째(1 or 2), 두세째(2 or 3), 두서너째(2~4), 서너째(3 or 4), 너덧째(4
or 5), 댓째(5 more or less), 대여섯째(5 or 6), 예닐곱째(6 or 7), 일여덟째(7
or 8), 여남은째(10~12)

When representing the number of times, it is expressed as 'Korean
origin cardinal numeral + 번째' by using a Korean origin '번'. However,
a number of ten units like '20, 30 and 40, etc.' are expressed in two
ways as 'Korean origin or Chinese origin cardinal numeral + 번째'.

첫 번째(1st), 두 번째(2nd), 세 번째(3rd), 네 번째(4th), 다섯 번째(5th),
일곱 번째(7th), 아홉 번째(9th), 열 번째(10th), 스물한 번째(21st), 서른두
번째(32nd) ; 스무 번째/이십 번째/20번째(20th), 서른 번째/삼십 번째/30번
째(30th), 마흔 번째/사십 번째/40번째(40th), 백 번째/100번째(100th), 일
천 번째/1,000번째(1,000th), 일만 번째/10,000번째(10,000th)

It is also expressed in 'Chinese origin cardinal numeral + 회' by using
a Chinese origin '회(回)'.

제1회(1st), 제2회(2nd), 제3회(3rd) ; 제10회(10th), 제20회(20th) ; 제100
회(100th), 제125회(125th)

Particular nouns are used for counting days. For it, there are also Korean origin and Chinese origin.

Korean origin cardinal numeral		Chinese origin cardinal numeral
하루	1	일일, 一日
이틀	2	이일, 二日
사흘	3	삼일, 三日
나흘	4	사일, 四日
닷새	5	오일, 五日
엿새	6	육일, 六日
이레	7	칠일, 七日
여드레	8	팔일, 八日
아흐레	9	구일, 九日
열흘	10	십일, 十日
보름	15	십오일, 十五日

7.3 Reading of Korean origin numeral and Chinese origin numeral

7.3.1 Nouns that only Korean origin numeral are usable

When counting things as below, Korean origin numeral and numeric adnominal are used. However from 백 'one hundred' only Chinese origin numeral is used, because there is not Korean origin numeral and numeric adnominal.

- Unit nouns for counting Korean origin things and animals: 벌, 켤레, 마리, 쌍

옷 {한/*일} 벌(a suit of clothes), 양복 {두/*이} 벌(two suits of clothes), 운동화 {세/*삼} 켤레(three pairs of sneakers), 돼지 {네/*사} 마리(four pigs), 닭 {다섯/*오} 마리(five chickens), 비둘기 {여섯/*육} 쌍(six pairs of doves)

- Unit nouns for counting Korean origin person: 분, 사람, 놈

신사 {한/*일} 분(one gentleman), 책을 읽는 {두/*이} 사람(two person reading the book), 도둑 {세/*삼} 놈(three thieves)

- Unit nouns for counting Chinese origin and English things: 대(臺), 개(個), 병(甁), 잔(盞), 컵(cup)

라디오 {한/*일} 대(one radio), 텔레비전 {두/*이} 대(two TVs), 에어컨 {세/*삼} 대(three air conditioners), 냉장고 {네/*사} 대(four refrigerators) ; 넥타이 {네/*사} 개(four neckties), 리본 {다섯/*오} 개(five ribbons), 파인애플 {여섯/*육} 개(six pineapples), 아보카도 {일곱/*칠} 개(seven avocados) ; 링거 {여덟/*팔} 병(eight bottles of IV) ; 커피 {아홉/*구} 잔(nine glasses of coffee) ; 맥주 {한/*일} 컵(one cup of beer)

- Unit nouns for counting Korean origin month: 달

1달: {한/*일} 달(one month), 2달: {두/*이} 달(two months), 5달: {다섯/*오} 달(five months), 8달: {여덟/*팔} 달(eight months), 9달: {아홉/*구} 달(nine months), 10달: {열/*십} 달(ten months), 12달: {열두/*십이} 달 (twelve months)

- Unit nouns for measuring o'clock and hour: 시, 시간

3시: {세/*삼} 시(three o'clock), 5시: {다섯/*오} 시(five o'clock), 6시: {여섯/*육} 시(six o'clock), 8시: {여덟/*팔} 시(eight o'clock), 10시: {열/*십} 시(ten o'clock), 12시: {열두/*십이} 시(twelve o'clock)

3시간: {세/*삼} 시간(three hours), 5시간: {다섯/*오} 시간(five hours), 6시간: {여섯/*육} 시간(six hours), 8시간: {여덟/*팔} 시간(eight hours), 10시간: {열/*십} 시간(ten hours), 12시간: {열두/*십이} 시간(twelve hours)

7.3.2 Nouns that only Chinese origin numeral are usable

- Unit nouns for counting Korean origin year, month and day: 년, 월, 일

1979년: {천 구백 칠십 구/*천 아홉백 일곱십 아홉}년, 1995년: {천 구백 구십 오/*천 아홉백 아홉십 다섯}년, 2008년: {이천 팔/*두천 여덟}년

3월: {삼/*세} 월(March), 5월: {오/*다섯} 월(May), 6월: {유/*육/*여섯} 월(June), 8월: {팔/*여덟} 월(August), 10월: {시/*십/*열} 월(October), 12월: {십이/*열두} 월(December)

3개월: {삼/*세} 개월(three months), 5개월: {오/*다섯} 개월(five months), 6개월: {육/*여섯} 개월(six months), 8개월: {팔/*여덟} 개월(eight months), 10개월: {십/*열} 개월(ten months), 12개월: {십이/*열두} 개월(twelve months)

3일: {삼/*세} 일(three days), 5일: {오/*다섯} 일(five days), 6일: {육/*여섯} 일(six days), 8일: {팔/*여덟} 일(eight days), 10일: {십/*열} 일(ten days), 12일: {십이/*열두} 일(twelve days)

- Unit nouns for counting Korean origin minute and second: 분, 초

3분: {삼/*세} 분(three minutes), 5분: {오/*다섯} 분(five minutes), 6분: {육/*여섯} 분(six minutes), 8분: {팔/*여덟} 분(eight minutes), 10분: {십/*열} 분(ten minutes), 15분: {십오/*열다섯} 분(fifteen minutes), 30분: {삼십/*서른} 분(thirty minutes), 45분: {사십오/*마흔다섯} 분(forty five minutes)

3초: {삼/*세} 초(three seconds), 5초: {오/*다섯} 초(five seconds), 6초: {육/*여섯} 초(six seconds), 8초: {팔/*여덟} 초(eight seconds), 10초: {십/*열} 초(ten seconds), 15초: {십오/*열다섯} 초(fifteen seconds), 30초: {삼십/*서른} 초(thirty seconds), 45초: {사십오/*마흔다섯} 초(forty five seconds)

- Unit nouns for measuring weight: 그램(g), 킬로그램(kg), 톤(t)

3g: {삼/*세} 그램, 5g: {오/*다섯} 그램, 6kg: {육/*여섯} 킬로그램, 8kg: {팔/*여덟} 킬로그램, 10t: {십/*열} 톤, 12t: {십이/*열두} 톤

- Unit nouns for measuring length and distance: 미터(m), 킬로미터(km), 리(里)

3m: {삼/*세} 미터, 5m: {오/*다섯} 미터, 6m: {육/*여섯} 미터, 8m: {팔/*여덟} 미터, 10m: {십/*열} 미터, 15m: {십오/*열다섯} 미터, 30m: {삼십/*서른} 미터, 45m: {사십오/*마흔다섯} 미터

3km: {삼/*세} 킬로미터, 5km: {오/*다섯} 킬로미터, 6km: {육/*여섯} 킬로미터, 8km: {팔/*여덟} 킬로미터, 10km: {십/*열} 킬로미터, 15km: {십오/*열다섯} 킬로미터, 30km: {삼십/*서른} 킬로미터, 45km: {사십오/*마흔다섯} 킬로미터

3리: {삼/*세} 리(three lis), 5리: {오/*다섯} 리(five lis), 6리: {육/*여섯} 리(six lis), 8리: {팔/*여덟} 리(eight lis), 10리: {십/*열} 리(ten lis), 15리: {십오/*열다섯} 리(fifteen lis), 30리: {삼십/*서른} 리(thirty lis), 45리: {사십오/*마흔다섯} 리(forty five lis)

- Unit nouns for counting Korean money: 원

3원: {삼/*세} 원(three won), 5원: {오/*다섯} 원(five won), 60원: {육십/*

예순} 원(sixty won), 800원: {팔백/*여덟백} 원(eight hundred won), 9,000
원: {구천/*아홉천} 원(nine thousand won)

7.3.3 Nouns that Korean origin numeral and Chinese origin numeral are both usable

* Unit nouns for measuring area: 평(坪)

3평: {세/삼}평(three pyeong), 5평: {다섯/오} 평(five pyeong), 9평: {아홉/구} 평(nine pyeong), 10평: {열/십} 평(ten pyeong), 15평: {열다섯/십오}평(fifteen pyeong), 20평: {스무/이십} 평(twenty pyeong), 80평: {여든/팔십} 평(eighty pyeong), 99평: {아흔아홉/구십구} 평(ninty nine pyeong)

* Unit nouns for counting Chinese origin person: 명(名), 구(具)

어린이 {한/일} 명(one child), 학생 {두/이} 명(two students), 의사 {세/삼}명(three doctors), 시체 {네/*사} 구(four corpses)

7.4 Korean cultural aspects as reflected in numerals

First, Korean people detest a number 4 traditionally. Because the pronunciation of 4 is [사, sa], and it sounds the same as a Sino-Korean 사(死) which means 'death'. Therefore, they tend to avoid adding 4 when numbering the 'car number, apartment number, patient's room number and an examinee's seat number' as much as possible.

Second, people very like a number 7 because it is a lucky number. This is of Korean people accepting the western civilization of westerners calling 7 as 'Lucky Seven' as it is.

Third, a number 3 is often used when playing games like 윷놀이 'playing Yut', 씨름 'Korean wrestling' and 줄다리기 'tug-of-war', etc. People always compete 3 times and winning 2 games out of 3 is considered as winning the game.

Fourth, a number 10 and multiples of 10 like '100, 1,000, 10,000' are considered as a 완전수 'complete number', so they are often taken as anniversaries. For example, in a Korean proverb, 열 번 찍어 안 넘어 가는 나무 없다 'there is no tree that will not fall by chopping it ten times', and 'ten times' here means 'so many times'. 백일잔치 '100th day celebration' is a birthday party that celebrates the 100th day since birth, and in 천 번, 만 번 설득해도 소용없다 'persuading thousand or ten thousand times is useless', 'thousand or ten thousand times' also means 'so many times'.

Fifth, typical Koreans consider 억(100,000,000) unit as a largest number, and 억대 부자 'a rich person of one hundred million' is used to represent 'very rich person'. 'Hundreds of millions' in 'talking hundreds of millions' also has a meaning of 'very much'.

08 Particle

8.1 What is a particle?

Particle(조사) comes after a word or clause to represent a certain relationship with another word in the sentence, or add a certain meaning to a word in the sentence. Particles include case particles, complementary particles and connective particles.

Particles cannot be used alone. Thus, they should always be attached to the end of a word. Also, the form of particles does not change wherever they are. Particles can be sometimes placed at the end of a connective ending of an adverb or predicate, and multiple particles can be used in conjunction with each other in a single sentence.

> 드레스를 입은 신부의 모습이 퍽도 아름답다.
> The bride in the wedding dress looks so beautiful.
> 한국 김치를 먹어는 보았다.
> I have eaten Kimchi before.
> 어제까지만 해도 날씨가 대단히 좋았다.
> The weather was amazing until yesterday.

8.2 Types and characteristics of particles

8.2.1 Case particle

Case particles(격조사) are affixed to the end of a word so that the word can play a certain role in the sentence. Case particles include subject particles, object particles, complement particles, adverbial particles, adnominal particles and vocative particles.

8.2.1.1 Subject particle

Subject particles(주격 조사), which include '-이/가, -께서, -에서, -서', make the preceding word the subject of the sentence.

Subject particle '-이' and '-가' have completely same functions, and are thus phonological allomorph. '-이' is used if the preceding word ends in a consonant, and '-가' is used if the previous word ends in a vowel. '-이' and '-가' have following usage:

First, they can describe an observable action or circumstance in a neutral manner.

> 바람이 분다. / It is windy.
> 준서가 학교에 갔다. / Jun-Seo went to school.

If the above sentences are negated, the subject of the negated sentence usually comes with '-은/는', rather than '-이/가'.

> 바람은 불지 않는다. / It is not windy.
> 준서가 학교에 가지 않았다. / Jun-Seo did not go to school.

Second, they can emphasize or point out certain things, animals or people in order to differentiate them from others.

> 서울에는 민서**가** 갔다. / It is Min-Seo who went to Seoul.
> 나는 준서**가** 보고 싶다. / I miss Jun-Seo [not anyone else].

If an interrogative pronoun is the subject of a sentence, '-이/가' must be attached thereto as a subject particle.

> **누가** 이것을 했습니까? / Who did this?
> **무엇이** 이 세상에서 가장 아름답습니까?
> What is the most beautiful thing in the world?

Subject particle '-께서' is for a respectable subject, such as teacher, grandfather, head of company or pastor. In such a sentence, the verb should be in honorific forms (e.g. 계시다 'to be', 드시다 'to eat', 돌아가시다 'to die') or combined with prefinal ending '-시-'.

> 저의 아버지**께서** 워싱턴에 가셨습니다. / My father went to Washington.
> 목사님**께서** 저를 위해 기도해 주셨습니다. / The pastor prayed for me.

Subject particle '-에서' has a very special function. '-에서' is originally an adverbial particle which is equivalent to 'to' or 'at', but it can function as a subject particle if attached after a certain organization, such as the National Assembly, government, school, company, gatherings, etc.

> 국회**에서** 호주제에 관한 법을 폐지하였다.
> The National Assembly abolished the patriarchal family system.
> 회사**에서** 연말에 상여금을 많이 주었다.
> The company gave a generous bonus at the end of the year.
> 참여연대**에서** 국가보안법을 없애는 운동을 하고 있다.
> People's Solidarity for Participatory Democracy is trying to abolish the

National Security Act.

'국회에서' above refers to 'the lawmakers at the National Assembly', '회사에서' to 'the CEO of the company' and '참여연대에서' to 'members of the People's Solidarity for Participatory Democracy'.

Subject particle '-서', which means '-이/가 함께' 'together with' is always used in the form of 'native numeral + -이 + -서'.

준서와 민서는 둘이서 손을 잡고 걸어갔다.
Jun-Seo and Min-Seo walked hand in hand.
유비, 관우, 장비 이렇게 셋이서 중국을 통일했다.
Liu Bei, Guan Yu and Zang Fei, the three of them united China.

8.2.1.2 Object particle

Object particles(목적격 조사) can be divided into direct object particles such as '-을/를/ㄹ' and indirect object particles such as '-에게'. They serve to make the preceding word the object of the sentence.

Direct object particles '-을/를/ㄹ' are phonological allomorph: in other words, they have a completely identical semantic function, just in different forms. Use '-을' if the preceding word ends in a consonant, '-를' if it ends in a vowel, and '-ㄹ' for condensed expressions that end in a vowel. Transitive verbs must be used after the object particle.

Direct object particle(직접 목적격 조사) '-을/를' has two types of usages as below:

First, it puts forward something that is directly affected by the action of predicates in a neutral manner.

준서가 책을 읽는다. / Jun-Seo is reading a book.
민서가 모자를 쓰고 있다. / Min-Seo is wearing a hat.

Second, it 'distinguishes' or 'emphasizes' a certain thing or situation. Here, it is possible to use intransitive verbs, mostly motional ones such as 가다 'to go', 오다 'to come', 다니다 'to go somewhere frequently', 걷다 'to walk', 건너다 'to cross', 들르다 'to stop by', 떠나다 'to leave', 출발하다 'to depart', 지나다 'to pass'.

> 왜 그가 약속 장소에 나오질 않았을까?
> Why did he fail to turn up?
> 어딜 그렇게 정신없이 가는 중이니?
> Where are you going in such a hurry?
> 그렇게 아픈데 병원에를 안 가겠다니 무슨 말이야?
> Are you insane to say that you are not going to see the doctor even though you are so sick?
> 준서는 약국엘 들러서 집으로 왔다.
> Jun-Seo dropped by a pharmacy on his way home.

'-을/를' is also used in the form of '… -을/를 … -을/를' to 'confine' the range of the preceding noun. It can be used in the form of '… -의 … -을/를'.

> 민서가 준서를 빰을 세 대를 때렸다.
> → 민서가 준서의 빰을 세 대를 때렸다.
> Min-Seo slapped Jun-Seo in the face three times.
>
> 이 바지를 통을 좀 줄여야겠다.
> → 이 바지의 통을 좀 줄여야겠다.
> I have to make this pair of trousers more narrow-legged.

Indirect object particle(간접 목적격 조사) '-에게' and '-에' make a certain sentence component an adverb, not object, which is decidedly different from English. '-에게' is attached to the end of animate nouns, and '-에'

to in-animate nouns. They are essential adverbs in Korean.

준서는 민서<u>에게</u> 선물을 사 주었다.
Jun-Seo bought Min-Seo a gift.
나는 오늘 뉴욕에 사는 친구<u>에게</u> 전화를 했다.
I called my friend in New York today.

민서는 꽃<u>에</u> 물을 주었다.
Min-Seo watered the flowers.
한국은 도움이 필요한 나라<u>에</u> 무상 원조를 많이 하고 있다.
Korea is giving lots of financial aid to the countries in need.

■ Case particles can function as auxiliary particles

First, subject particle '-이/가' can act as an auxiliary particle:

나는 너를 보고 싶다.
→ 나는 네가 보고 싶다. I want to see you.

나는 민서를 만나고 싶다.
→ 나는 민서가 만나고 싶다. I want to meet Min-Seo.

'보다, 만나다' are transitive verbs that require corresponding objects. Thus, '너를, 민서를' are objects, while '-을/를' is an object particle. Sometimes, subject particle '-이/가' is used instead of this object particle, in which the grammatical function of '-이/가' is to point out and emphasize '너, 민서' rather than the subject. Thus, they are indicative auxiliary particles rather than a subject particle.

Second, '-을/를' for essential adverbs can act as an auxiliary particle.

나는 준서<u>에게</u> 선물을 주었다.
→ 나는 준서를 선물을 주었다. I gave a present to Jun-Seo.

'주다' is a verb that requires a corresponding object and an essential adverbial phrase (indirect object). If '준서에게' is changed into '준서를', should the sentence constituent be changed into an object from essential adverb? In conclusion, it would be reasonable to consider '-을/를' as an auxiliary particle, because it is grammatical to say that '?피자가 나에 의해 준서에게 주어졌다', but ungrammatical to say "*준서가 나에 의해 선물을 주어졌다'. In other words, the particle '-을/를' in '준서를' is an auxiliary particle that distinguishes Jun-Seo as 'nobody else but Jun-Seo'.

8.2.1.3 Complement particle

Complement particles(보격 조사), which include '-이/가', make the preceding word the complement of the sentence.

준서가 의사가 되었다. / Jun-Seo became a doctor.
존은 미국인이 아니다. / John is not an American.

Complement particle '-이/가' are the same as subject particles in form, but they have completely different functions. In other words, complement particles detail and complement incomplete verbs like '되다, 아니다'.

8.2.1.4 Adnominal particle

Adnominal particles(관형격 조사) are similar to 'apostrophe plus s[-'s]', or 'of, on, for, to, by, at, in' in function, and make the preceding word an adnominal phrase of the sentence. In other words, they make the preceding word modify the following word. They are often referred to as genitive particle. However, special attention is needed when using genitive particle '-의', since it has a various semantic functions, albeit in a single form.

① '-의' means 'owned by someone'. For example, Jun-Seo, which precedes '-의', is the owner of the book, and the following '책' is the object owned by him. It is the same as 'apostrophe plus s[-'s]' in English.

이것은 준서<u>의</u> 책입니다. / This is Jun-Seo's book.

② It means 'belonging to something'. In the sentence below, '한글학회'(Korean Language Research Society), which precedes '-의', is the name of the organization Min-Seo belongs to, and the following 회원 'member' refers to those belonging to the organization.

민서는 한글학회<u>의</u> 회원이다.
Min-Seo is a member of the Korean Language Society.

③ It means 'written by someone'. In the sentence below, '이광수', which precedes '-의', is the author, and the following '무정' is the name of the novel he wrote.

그것은 이광수<u>의</u> 무정이다. / It is Kwang-Soo Lee's Moojeong.

④ It means 'about something'. In the sentence below, '서울', which precedes '-의', is the subject, and the following '찬가' is a detail about the subject.

준서는 '서울<u>의</u> 찬가'라는 노래를 잘 부른다.
Jun-Seo can sing the 'Anthem of Seoul' very well.
그는 생물학<u>의</u> 권위자이다. / He is an authority in biology.

⑤ Fifth, it means 'than something/someone'. In the sentence below, '우리집' which precedes '-의' is the subject matter, the subject '그녀의

집' is the target of comparison, and '세 배' refers to the difference between the two.

그녀의 집은 우리집의 세 배는 된다.
Her house is three times bigger than our house.

⑥ It means 'for something/someone'. In the sentence below, '합격' immediately preceding '-의' is the goal, '길' the process of achieving the goal.

합격의 길은 멀고 험하다.
The path of passing the exam is long and winding.

⑦ It means 'produced in a certain place'. In the sentence below, '대구' immediately preceding '-의' is the place and '사과' following '-의' the product of '대구'.

대구의 사과 맛이 가장 좋다. / Apples produced in Daegu are the best.

⑧ It means 'becoming something/someone'. For example, in the sentence below, '문제' preceding '-의' is the detail and '인물' the subject matter.

문제의 인물이 드디어 나타났다. / The person at issue finally turned up.

Since '-의' has a wide range of semantic functions, it is sometimes difficult to capture the meaning of a sentence just by looking at the sentence alone.

형의 사진 / elder brother's photograph

It means 'photographs held by elder brother, photographs taken by elder brother, photographs of elder brother', etc. Readers must observe the context in order to have an accurate understanding of the phrase.

Also, '-의', when combined with '나, 저, 너, 누구', can be condensed into '나의 → 내, 저의 → 제, 너의 → 네, 누구의 → 뉘', which is usually the case in spoken language.

> 내 고향은 대구다. / My hometown is Daegu.
> 이 사람은 제 남동생입니다. / This is my younger brother.
> 이것은 네 책이다. / This is your book.
> 뉘 도움이 가장 컸니? / Who helped you most?

8.2.1.5 Adverbial particle

Adverbial particles(부사격 조사), which can be employed in a broad range of forms, make word with the particle into adverbial word or phrase.

① **Giving**(줌) and **receiving**(받음)

'To give' and 'to receive' here refer to not only giving and receiving material objects, but also abstract things such as 'influence' or 'impact'. To convey the meaning of 'giving' and 'receiving', verbs such as 주다 'to give', 드리다 'to give something to a respectable person', 받다 'to receive', 전하다 'to tell', 얻다 'to obtain', 말하다 'to speak', 듣다 'to hear', 시키다 'to have someone do something', 던지다 'to throw', 전수하다 'to pass down' can be used.

Use adverbial particle '-에게, -한테' when the subject gives something to an animate noun (e.g. person or animal), and use '-에게서, -한테서, -(으)로부터' when the subject receives something from an animate noun. As mentioned earlier, '-에게' is for indirect objects in English.

준서는 민서{**에게**/**한테**} 선물을 주었다.
Jun-Seo gave Min-Seo a present.
민서는 준서{**에게서**/**한테서**/**로부터**} 선물을 받았다.
Min-Seo received a present from Jun-Seo.

As for '–에게서, –한테서', it is easy to understand who is the giver
and the receiver through the context. Therefore, even if '–서' is deleted
from '–에게, –한테', there would be no problem understanding the sentence. Thus, Koreans usually prefer using '–에게, –한테' in conversations.
'–(으)로부터' is hardly ever used in spoken language, but mostly in written
language.

If the target of giving or receiving something is a respectable person
such as grandfather, teacher or pastor, attach '–께' to the respectable
person when the subject is giving something to the person, and attach '–께, –께로부
터' to the respectable person when the subject is receiving something
from the person.

그는 할아버지**께** 선물을 드렸다.
He gave his grandfather a present.
그는 할아버지{**께**/**께로부터**} 선물을 받았다.
He received a present from his grandfather.

When it comes to in-animate nouns (e.g. objects, places), use '–에,
–에다가' if the subject is giving something to the in-animate noun and
use '–에서, –(으)로부터' if the subject is receiving something from the
in-animate noun.

준서는 나무{**에**/**에다가**} 물을 주었다.
Jun-Seo gave water to the tree.
그 회사는 IT산업{**에**/**에다가**} 1조 원을 투자했다.

The company invested 1 trillion won in the IT sector.

그는 성경{에서/<u>으로부터</u>} 지혜를 얻었다.

He learned wisdom from the Bible.

게으른 자여, 꿀벌{<u>에게서</u>/로부터} 지혜를 얻으라.

The lazy, learn wisdom from bees.

② **Social status**(지위), **ranking**(신분) and **eligibility**(자격)

'-(으)로, -(으)로서' are adverbial particles that represent social status, ranking or eligibility. They are mainly referred to people and animals, or even trees and flowers from time to time. '-(으)로' and '-(으)로서' have a slightly different usage.

'-(으)로서' is attached to the back of a noun which functions as a predicate for the subject. In other words, '그는 선생으로서' is equal to '그는 선생이다' and '준서는 아들로서' is equal to '준서는 아들이다'.

그는 선생<u>으로서</u> 열심히 학생들을 가르치고 있다.

He, as a teacher, is keen on teaching students.

준서는 아들<u>로서</u> 부모님께 효도를 다했다.

Jun-Seo, as a son, did his best to be a good son to his parents.

'-(으)로' is attached to the back of a noun which functions as a predicate of the object for the sentence. In other words, '준서는 남편으로' is equal to '준서가 남편이다' and '민서를 수양딸로' is equal to '민서가 수양딸이다'.

민서는 준서를 남편<u>으로</u> 맞이했다.

Min-Seo accepted Jun-Seo as her husband.

그는 민서를 수양딸<u>로</u> 받아들였다.

He accepted Min-Seo as his foster daughter.

③ **Togetherness**(함께 함) and **dealing with each other**(상대가 됨)

Adverbial particles that represent 'togetherness' and 'dealing with each other' include '-와/과, -(이)랑, -하고'. Use '-와' when the preceding word ends in a vowel, and '-과' when the preceding word ends in a consonant. '-(이)랑, -하고' are mainly for spoken language. Readers need to pay attention to the verb to distinguish two different semantic functions of adverbial particles, 'togetherness' and 'dealing with each other'.

'-와/과, -(이)랑, -하고' in the sentences below refer to the target of 'togetherness'.

준서는 민서{**와**/**랑**/**하고**} 결혼했다. / Jun-Seo married Min-Seo.
그는 형{**과**/**이랑**/**하고**} 함께 생활하고 있다.
He is living with his elder brother.

'-와/과, -(이)랑, -하고' in the sentence below refer to the target of symmetrical relationship or comparison.

준서는 민서{**와**/**랑**/**하고**} 수영 시합을 했다.
Jun-Seo had a swimming competition with Min-Seo.
준서는 민서{**와**/**랑**/**하고**} 성격이 너무 다르다.
Jun-Seo is too different from Min-Seo.

④ **Approaching**(다가감) and **distancing**(떨어짐)
'-에게, -한테' are used to convey approaching to animate nouns (e.g. people, animals) and '-에게서, -한테서' are used to convey distancing from animate nouns.

아기가 엄마{**에게**/**한테**} 안겼다.
The baby is cuddled up in the mother's arms.
아기 곰이 엄마 곰{**에게서**/**한테서**} 떨어졌다.
The cub distanced itself from the mother bear.

'-에' is used to describe approaching to in-animate nouns (e.g. objects, places) and '-에서' to describe distancing from in-animate nouns.

존은 미국<u>에서</u> 왔다. / John came from America.
준서는 자리<u>에서</u> 일어났다. / Jun-Seo stood up from his seat.
존이 미국<u>에</u> 왔다. / John came to America.
민서는 자리<u>에</u> 앉았다. / Min-Seo sat on her seat.

⑤ **Time**(시간) and **order**(순서)
Use '-에' to refer to a certain time, era and order.

준서는 민서를 아침 9시<u>에</u> 만났다.
Jun-Seo met Min-Seo at 9 o'clock in the morning.
한글은 조선시대<u>에</u> 만들어졌다.
Hangul was made in the Chosun dynasty.
준서가 처음<u>에</u> 미국으로 유학을 갔고, 그 다음<u>에</u> 민서가 미국으로 유학을 갔다.
First, Jun-Seo went to America to study, and then Min-Seo followed.
어떤 일이든 처음<u>에</u>는 어렵지만, 나중<u>에</u>는 쉬워지는 법이다.
The beginning is the hardest part.

In particular, use '-에, -부터' to represent the beginning of something or the beginning of a certain change.

예배는 내일 11시{**에**/**부터**} 시작됩니다.
The service will begin at 11 am tomorrow.
오늘 오후{**에**/**부터**} 비가 많이 온다고 합니다.
It is going to rain a lot from this afternoon.

However, the semantic function of '-에' and '-부터' changes if the verb of the sentence does not convey the meaning of 'beginning', 'change' or 'process', as in the case of 공부하다 'to study', 일하다 'to work', 읽다

'to read', 놀다 'to play'. With those verbs, '-에' means 'at a certain time', while '-부터' means 'a certain period of time'.

> 민서는 오늘 아침{에/부터} 매우 아팠어요.
> Min-Seo was very sick this morning.
> Min-Seo has been very sick since this morning.
> 준서는 어젯밤{에/부터} 춤을 추었어요.
> Jun-Seo danced last night.
> Jun-Seo has been dancing since last night.

In particular, use '-부터' to refer to an actor or entity that engages in a certain behavior.

> 나부터 먼저 일을 시작하겠습니다.
> I will start the work first.
> 우리 부서부터 조사를 받기 원합니다.
> I hope that my department will be the first to be investigated.

Sometimes, '-(으)로' is attached to the back of a word that represents time, or a period of time during which a certain action is in progress, in order to convey the meaning of 'at such a time'.

> 오늘로 한국에 온 지 1년이 되었다.
> Today marks one year since I came to Korea.
> 남편이 죽은 후로 그녀의 모습은 제주도에서 영영 보이지 않았다.
> She could never be seen in Jeju Island after the death of her husband.

⑥ Location of existence(존재의 위치)

Use '-에' to denote the location or spot where people, animals or objects exist. '-에' is used in combination with existential verbs, such as 있다 'to exist', 계시다 '(a respectable being) to exist', 놓여 있다 'to be placed somewhere', 살아 있다 'to remain alive', 없다 'not to exist', 살다 'to live', 머무르다 'to stay', 남다 'to remain', 숨다 'to hide'.

민서는 지금 뉴욕에 가 있다. / Min-Seo is now in New York.
책상 위에 책이 많이 놓여 있다. / There are many books on the desk.

⑦ **Place of a certain action**(행동이 일어나고 있는 장소)

Use '-에서' to denote a place where a certain action is taking place. '-에서' is used in combination with motional verbs such as 먹다 'to eat', 놀다 'to play', 공부하다 'to study', 살다 'to live', 받다 'to receive', 주다 'to give', 부르다 'to call'.

존은 어제 한국 식당에서 저녁을 먹었다.
John had dinner at a Korean restaurant yesterday.
노래방에서 노래를 불러 본 적이 있어요?
Have you ever sung in a karaoke?

⑧ **Location or place in which a certain action has an impact**(행동의 결과가 미치는 위치)

'-에' is used to refer to a place or location on which a certain action has an impact. It is used in combination with words representing objects or a certain spot.

준서는 결혼 서약서에 사인을 했다. / Jun-Seo signed on the wedding vow.
민서는 소파에 앉아서 텔레비전을 보았다.
Min-Seo watched the TV on the sofa.
그는 지갑에 돈을 넣었다. / He put the money in his wallet.
벌써 동쪽 하늘에 해가 떴다. / The sun has already risen in the Eastern sky.

⑨ **Point of start**(출발점) and **point of arrival**(도달점)

'-에서, -에서부터' indicate the starting point of an action or status, meaning 'with something as the starting point'. They are used in combination with verbs of 'departure', such as 시작되다 'to start', 출발하다 'to depart' and 가다 'to go'. '-에서부터' can clarify the 'starting point' specifically than '-에서'.

> 경부고속도로는 서울{<u>에서/에서부터</u>} 시작된다.
> Gyeongbu Highway starts from Seoul.
> 뉴욕{<u>에서/에서부터</u>} 기다리던 소식이 왔다.
> We have some long-awaited news from New York.
> 이번 산사태는 무분별한 벌목{<u>에서/에서부터</u>} 시작되었다.
> The landslide was caused by reckless logging.

'-에' represents the point of arrival, and is used in combination with arrival-related verbs such as 도착하다 'to arrive', 도달하다 'to reach', 다다르다 'to come, reach', 이르다 'to get to, to arrive', 미치다 'to reach' and 오다 'to come'.

> 그는 드디어 에베레스트 산 정상<u>에</u> 도착했다.
> He finally arrived at the peak of Mountain Everest.
> 서울<u>에</u> 오는 데 얼마나 시간이 걸렸습니까?
> How long did it take you to come to Seoul?

⑩ **Directions**(방향) and **orientation**(지향점)

'-(으)로', which means 'with something as the destination and/or towards something', represents the direction and orientation of a certain action or status, usually in combination with directional verbs such as 가다 'to go', 오다 'to come', 떠나다 'to leave', 출발하다 'to depart', 향하다 'to head towards', 이사하다 'to move to a new location', 옮기다 'to move something', 돌아가다 'to return', 돌아서다 'to turn around' and 이끌다 'to lead'.

민서는 작년에 서울로 이사했다.
Min-Seo moved to Seoul last year.
요즘 경기가 상승 쪽으로 돌아섰다.
The economy started to pick up recently.
성공으로 이끄는 친구는 좋은 친구다.
Good friends guide you to success.

⑪ **Ingredients**(재료), **tools**(도구), **methods**(방법)
'-(으)로', which means 'by using something and/or with something', refers to ingredients, apparatuses, tools, methods, etc. '-(으)로써' is attached to nouns that end as '-(으)ㅁ'.

준서는 포도로 포도주를 만들었다. / Jun-Seo made wine with grapes.
하늘이 먹구름으로 온통 뒤덮여 있다.
The sky is covered with dark clouds.
그는 주식 투자로 돈을 많이 벌었다.
He earned a lot of money by investing in stocks.
군인은 모름지기 죽음으로써 고지를 사수해야 한다.
Soldiers must capture the enemy's fortress on a hill by death.

⑫ **Extent**(범위)
When it comes time and space, '-에서, -부터, -에서부터' refer to the starting point of a certain space or starting time, and '-까지' refers to the finishing point of a certain space or finishing time.

여기서부터 한국 땅입니다. / From here, you are on the Korean soil.
한국어 수업은 9시부터 시작됩니다. / The Korean class starts at 9.

여덟 시까지 학교에 도착해야 합니다. / I have to get to school by 8.
뉴욕까지 시간이 얼마나 걸리죠? / How long does it take to get to New York?

Use '-에서, -부터, -에서부터 … -까지' when talking about the extent of a certain period or space. '-까지' refers to the ending, finishing point or a point when changes come to an end.

어제 9시{에서/부터/에서부터} 12시까지 축구 경기가 있었다.
There was a football match yesterday from 9 to 12.
하숙집{에서/부터/에서부터} 학교까지 시간이 얼마나 걸립니까?
How long does it take to get to school from the boarding house?

Use '-부터' only if the time is not detailed enough, as in the case of 조금 전 'a while ago', 며칠 전 'a few days ago', 조금 뒤 'shortly', 언제 'some day', 오늘 'today', 어제 'yesterday', 내일 'tomorrow'.

지난 2002년 6월{*에서/부터} 9월까지 월드컵이 한국에서 열렸다.
The World Cup was held in Korea from June to September 2002.
며칠 전{*에서/부터} 지금까지 연락이 없습니다.
We have not heard from him/her since a few days ago.

⑬ **Reason**(이유) and **cause**(원인)
'-(으)로, -에' refer to the reason or cause behind a certain status or action. They are attached to a word representing the reason or cause, to imply 'because of something', or 'with something as the cause'.

인도네시아에서는 쓰나미로 많은 사람이 죽었다.
Many died from tsunami in Indonesia.
선생님의 도움으로 입학시험에 합격했습니다.
With the help of the teacher, I passed the entrance exam.
이번 폭설에 비닐하우스가 모두 무너졌다.

All greenhouses collapsed due to the heavy snow.

폭발 소리<u>에</u> 놀라 모두들 잠이 깼다.

Everyone awoke from sleep by the sound of explosion.

⑭ **Changes**(변화) **and regeneration**(변성)

'-(으)로' indicates the change of an object or change of a perception of a certain person or object. It is attached to the changed target to imply 'to become something'.

증오가 순식간에 애정<u>으로</u> 바뀌었다.

All of a sudden, hatred turned into affection.

물이 수증기<u>로</u> 변해 날아가 버렸다.

Water evaporated into steam.

그는 결국 사기꾼<u>으로</u> 드러났다.

In the end, he turned out to be a fraudster.

⑮ **Units**(단위)

'-에', which means 'by receiving something, by having something as the price for something, by giving something, in the order of something', represents prices, or units such as weight, number of times, order, etc.

이 수박은 한 개<u>에</u> 얼마입니까?

How much is one watermelon?

쇠고기는 만 오천 원<u>에</u> 한 근을 살 수 있습니다.

Beef costs 15,000 won per 600g.

이 약은 한 번<u>에</u> 두 개씩 먹어야 합니다.

Take two pills at one taking.

네가 첫 번째<u>에</u> 할 일은 무엇이냐?

What is the first thing you have to do?

⑯ **Comparison**(비교)

'-보다' expresses the difference between two things in a sentence, while '-와/과, -만큼' represent the sameness of two things in a sentence.

꿈<u>보다</u> 해몽이 좋다. / Interpretation may be better than the dream itself.
준서는 민서<u>보다</u> 키가 크다. / Jun-Seo is taller than Min-Seo.
준서는 민서<u>와</u> 키가 같다. / Jun-Seo is as tall as Min-Seo.
슈퍼 감자는 수박<u>만큼</u> 크기가 크다.
Super potatoes are as big as watermelons.

⑰ **Figure of speech**(비유)

'-처럼, -같이' can liken a certain object to something similar.

그녀는 천사{<u>처럼</u>/<u>같이</u>} 아름답다.
She is as beautiful as an angel.
준서는 사실을 알고 있는 것{<u>처럼</u>/<u>같이</u>} 이야기했다.
Jun-Seo was talking as if he knew the truth.
그가 그림{<u>처럼</u>/<u>같이</u>} 멋있는 슛을 날렸다.
He made a shot which was as fantastic as a picture.

■ **Ambivalent meanings of particles and sentences**

Ambivalence in the sentences below is caused by the varying semantic extent of particles.
First, adnominal particle '-의' can cause ambivalence:

그녀<u>의</u> 옷에 대한 관심이 대단했다.
She had huge interest in clothes.
→ She had huge interest in her own clothes.
→ Others had huge interest in the clothes she was wearing.

Second, adverbial particle '-보다', which represents comparison, may cause ambivalence:

준서는 민서**보다** 민서를 더 사랑한다.
Jun-Seo loves Min-Seo more than Min-Seo.
  → If the subject is Jun-Seo: Jun-Seo loves Min-Seo more than Min-Seo.
  → If the subject is Jun-Seo and Min-Seo: Jun-Seo loves Min-Seo more than Min-Seo loves Min-Seo.

Third, connective particle '-와/과' can cause ambivalence:

준서**와** 민서는 어제 서울에 갔다.
Jun-Seo and Min-Seo went to Seoul yesterday.
  → Connection of words: Jun-Seo and Min-Seo went to Seoul together at the same time.
  → Connection of clause: Jun-Seo went to Seoul yesterday, and Min-Seo went to Seoul yesterday but not with each other.

8.2.1.6 Vocative particle

Vocative particles(호격 조사), which include '-아/야, -(이)여, -(이)시여', serve to make the preceding word the 'summon' or 'address' of the sentence. '-아' should come at the end of a consonant, and '-야' at the end of a vowel.

민준**아**, 잘 있었니? / Min-Jun, how have you been?
준서**야**, 이리 와. / Jun-Seo, come this way.

Summons or addresses are used to summon friends or younger people, not someone older or higher in status. Instead, those older or higher in status should be addressed by their title, such as teacher, manager, CEO or mayor.

'-(이)여, -(이)시여' are usually spoken in prayers, funeral addresses or poems, but hardly ever in everyday speech.

사랑하는 친구**여**, 그동안 평안하였는가?
Dear friend, how have you been?
사랑하는 그대**여**, 내 곁을 떠나지 말아 주오.
My dearest, please do not leave me.
하나님**이시여**! 저의 기도를 들어 주소서.
O Lord! Listen to my prayer.

8.2.2 Auxiliary particle

Auxiliary particle(보조사) carries certain meanings as in the case of English prepositions or adverbs, and it incorporates its meaning to the preceding word. Readers should pay more attention to auxiliary particles to have a correct understanding of the sentence, since auxiliary particles always have sister members. Also, auxiliary particles can be affixed to not only subjects, but also objects, complements, adverbs, etc.

① **Topic**(주제)
In Korean, subject particle '-이/가' and topic particle '-은/는' are quite different in forms and functions.

Topics(화제), which are usually placed at the beginning of a sentence, come with auxiliary particle '-은/는'. Also, '-은/는' are attached to a person, object or circumstance which was mentioned at least once in the dialogue, or which are already known to the speakers of the dialogue. In other words, they come with old information, implying 'as for something'.

토끼<u>는</u> 앞발이 짧다.

Rabbits have short forelegs.

→ 토끼에 대해 말하자면, 앞발이 짧다.

　As for rabbits, they have short forelegs.

한국인들<u>은</u> 김치를 잘 먹는다.

Koreans are very fond of Kimchi.

→ 한국인으로 말할 것 같으면, 김치를 잘 먹는다.

　As for Koreans, they are very fond of Kimchi.

　While English is a subject-oriented language, Korean is a topic-oriented language. Therefore, a subject is a must in English sentences. Even if there is no certain subject, a placeholder 'it' has to be used in the place of the subject so as to make the sentence grammatically correct. However, Koreans usually skip the subject. Instead, Koreans mention the topic at the beginning of the sentence and then make descriptions or propose ideas about the topic. In other words, when Koreans make up a sentence, Koreans use subject particle '-이/가' first in the first sentence so as to introduce new information, and then use topic particle '-은/는' in the following sentences to introduce old information and put forward the topic, and then talk about new information in the following comments.

옛날 옛적에 한 할아버지와 할머니<u>가</u> 살았습니다. 그런데 그 할아버지와 할머니에게<u>는</u> 자식<u>이</u> 없었습니다. 그래서 할아버지와 할머니<u>는</u> 하나님께 자식을 낳게 해 달라고 빌었습니다. 하나님<u>은</u> 할아버지와 할머니를 불쌍히 여겨서 예쁜 딸을 낳게 해 주었습니다. 그 딸<u>은</u> 무럭무럭 자라서 할아버지와 할머니를 매우 기쁘게 해 드렸습니다.

Once upon a time, there was an old man and his wife. The couple did not have children, so they prayed to God for children. God had mercy on them and let them give birth to a pretty daughter. The daughter grew healthy and strong and was a great pleasure to the old couple.

In the first sentence, subject particle '-가' is attached to '할아버지와 할머니' to introduce new information. In the following sentence, '할아버지와 할머니', now an old piece of information, is attached with topic particle '-는'. Then, the new information '하나님께' appears, and in the following sentence, '하나님', old information, is attached to topic particle '-은', which is also the case for '딸은'.

In Korean, any sentence component can become the topic if put at the beginning of the sentence with '-은/는'. Therefore, words combined with '-은/는' may not necessarily be the subject of the sentence.

준서가　　민서를　학교에서　만났다.
Subject　　Object　　Adverb　　Predicate
Jun-Seo met Min-Seo at the school.

→ Subject = Topic:　준서는 민서를 학교에서 만났다.
　　　　　　　　　　　Jun-Seo met Min-Seo at school.
→ Object = Topic:　　민서는 준서가 학교에서 만났다.
　　　　　　　　　　　Min-Seo was met by Jun-Seo at school.
→ Adverb = Topic:　학교에서는 준서가 민서를 만났다.
　　　　　　　　　　　At school, Jun-Seo met Min-Seo.
→ Predicate = Topic:　준서가 민서를 만난 것은 학교에서였다.
　　　　　　　　　　　Where Jun-Seo met Min-Seo was school.

② **Contrast**(대조)
'-은/는' can convey 'contrast(대조)'. The contrastive objects may or may not be explicit in the sentence.

준서가 사과는 좋아하지만, 배는 싫어한다.
Jun-Seo likes apples but dislikes pears.
민서가 런던은 가 보았다.
Min-Seo has been to London (among other places).

'-은/는' can be used several times in a single sentence. In this case, the preceding '-은/는' modifies the topic, and the following '-은/는' modifies the target of contrast.

나는 뉴욕에는 가 보았지만, 런던에는 가 보지 못했다.
I have been to New York, not London.
민서는 얼굴은 예쁘다.
Min-Seo is pretty.

'-은/는' may also be placed at the beginning of a sentence to convey 'contrastive meanings'. In this case, the accent is on the '-은/는' combined sentence component, emphasizing the meaning of the word. The contrastive factor is hidden in the context, so readers should read between the lines.

나는 안 먹을래.
I won't eat.
피아노는 칠 줄 알아요.
I can play the piano (among other musical instruments).

'나는 안 먹는다' means 'I will neither eat nor care about whatever you're going to do'. The 'I' in the sentence, and 'You' hidden in the context, are in a contrastive relationship. Also, '피아노는 칠 줄 안다' means 'I can play the piano, but not violin, clarinet, etc.' thus, piano, and violin, clarinet, etc. are in a contrastive relationship. Therefore, it is important to keep in mind that auxiliary particles always have a sister member.

③ **Limitation**(제한) or **restriction**(한정)
Auxiliary particle '-만' and '-밖에' convey limitation(제한) the extent of something or restriction(한정) something, thereby excluding others that

are beyond such limitations. They are equivalents of 'only' or 'just'. '-만' can be combined with both positive and negative verbs, but '-밖에' can come with only negative verbs such as '없다, 아니하다'.

> 준서**만** 아직 안 왔구나. / Only Jun-Seo has yet to come.
> 민서가 눈물**만** 흘리고 있다. / Min-Seo is just shedding tears.
> 그 사실을 아는 사람은 준서**밖에** 없다. / Only Jun-Seo knows the fact.
> 준서**밖에** 아직 아무도 오지 않았구나. / Only Jun-Seo has turned up.

④ **Addition**(더함) or **equivalence**(같음)

Auxiliary particle '-도' means 'also, in addition to, too'. When combined with positive verbs, all sentence components become positive. When combined with negative verbs, all sentence components become negative. In other words, there is no partial negation when it comes to '-도'.

> 엄마, 나**도** 한국에서 살고 싶어요. / Mom, I also want to live in Korea.
> 준서**도** 책을 읽고 있어요. / Jun-Seo is also reading a book.

'-도' serves to list the same kind of status or actions, while conveying the sameness of all things listed.

> 그에게는 돈**도** 명예**도** 없다.
> He has neither money nor honor.
> 그것에 대해서는 듣지**도** 보지**도** 못했어요.
> I have neither seen nor heard of it.
> 민서는 공부**도** 잘하고, 운동**도** 잘한다.
> Min-Seo is good at studying as well as sports.

⑤ **Concession**(양보) or **indiscrimination**(가리지 않음)

Auxiliary particle '-(이)라도, -(이)나마' convey 'concession(양보)', in which the subject is not completely happy with something but is willing to accept it.

> 먹을 게 없다면, 빵{**이라도**/**이나마**} 먹고 가자.
> If there is nothing to eat, let's just eat some bread.
> 동전 한 개{**라도**/**나마**} 남아 있으면 좋겠다.
> I would be happy if I had just one coin left.

'-(이)라도, -(이)나마' are sometimes combined with quantitative words or '행여, 혹시', to stress the meaning of 'concession'.

> 한 살{**이라도**/**이나마**} 더 먹기 전에 정신을 차려야죠.
> I should come to my senses before I get one year older.
> 혹시{**라도**/**나마**} 네가 마음이 바뀌면 연락해 다오.
> If you ever change your mind, contact me.

'-(이)라도' can be combined with '아무, 언제, 어느' to imply 'indiscri-mination(가리지 않음)', in which the subject does not care whichever option he or she is given.

> 지금 같아서는 어떤 일**이라도** 할 수 있을 것 같다.
> I think I will be able to do just about anything now.
> 어느 곳**이라도** 가고 싶다.
> I want to go somewhere, wherever that be.

'-(이)나' means the subject accepts the option as it is, even though he or she is not completely happy with it. It also means 'indiscrimination'.

> 잠**이나** 자자. / Let's just sleep.
> 밥이 없으면 라면**이나** 먹자.
> If we don't have rice, let's just have some noodle.

⑥ **Extremity(극단)**

Auxiliary particle '-까지, -마저, -조차' convey a sense of 'extremity(극단)' by adding something to a certain fact, or going beyond such a fact. Among them, '-까지' means 'to come to a certain extent that is difficult to reach' or 'beyond the normal extent'.

> 그는 대학원**까지** 졸업했다.
> He even graduated from a graduate school.
> 김치는 맛이 좋을 뿐 아니라, 영양**까지** 만점이다.
> Kimchi is not only tasty but also nutritious.
> 네가 이렇게**까지** 나를 사랑하는 줄 몰랐다.
> I never knew that you loved me this much.

On the other hand, '-마저' and '-조차' have a negative sense, meaning 'to fall short of something that is easy to reach', 'subpar', or even 'unsatisfactory'. Thus, they are usually connected to negative verbs.

> 그는 초등학교{**마저**/**조차**} 졸업하지 못했다.
> He even failed to graduate from elementary school.
> 너{**마저**/**조차**} 나를 믿지 못하는구나.
> Even you are distrustful of me.

In addition, '-도, -까지도, -마저도, -조차도' can convey 'extremity'.

> 김치는 맛이 좋을 뿐 아니라, 영양{**도**/**까지도**} 만점이다.
> Kimchi is not only tasty but also nutritious.
> 그는 초등학교{**도**/**마저도**/**조차도**} 졸업하지 못했다.
> He even failed to graduate from elementary school.

⑦ **Rationale(당위)** or **inevitability(필연)**

Auxiliary particle '-(이)야' serves to stress something contrastive. It is affixed to the end of the contrastive object to imply 'even if others may not do something, the target will definitely do something'.

준서**야** 당연히 여기 오겠지요.
Jun-Seo will definitely come here.
남**이야** 어떻게 되든 상관이 없다.
I don't care about what others end up with.

'-(이)야' can be affixed to a word representing something trivial, to imply 'something will not matter much' or 'something is nothing special'.

그 사람의 속셈**이야** 어찌 알 수 있겠는가?
How can we know his hidden intentions?
사랑싸움**이야** 언제든지 할 수 있는 것 아닌가?
Lovers can engage in quarrels any time, can't they?

'-(이)야' can also be affixed to general adverbs or adverbs representing time, to imply 'finally'. In this case, '-(이)야' can be used interchangeably with '-(에)서야'.

이제{**야/서야**} 그 사람의 속셈을 알겠다.
Finally, I realized his hidden intentions.
그때{**야/서야**} 집으로 돌아가도 좋다고 허락했다.
Finally, he/she allowed me to go home.

⑧ **Each**(각자) and **every**(모두)
Auxiliary particle '-마다' conveys the sense of 'each and every', thus meaning 'fully', 'one by one', or 'every one of something'.

준서는 만나는 사람**마다** 인사를 했다.
Jun-Seo said hello to everyone he met.

집집**마다** 웃음소리가 끊이지 않았다.

There was laughter from house to house.

'-마다' may be affixed to words representing time, to imply 'per' or 'frequency'.

월드컵은 4년**마다** 열린다. / The World Cup is held every four years.
두 시간**마다** 물을 한 컵씩 마셔라. / Drink one cup of water every two hours.

8.2.3 Connective particle

Connective particles(접속조사), which link words, phrases and clauses, include serial, selective and contrastive particles.

① **Serial**(나열)

Particles that list at least two words, phrases or clauses in a parallel relationship, include '-와/과, -(이)랑, -하고, -(이)고, -(이)며, -에다(가)'.

First, '-와/과, -(이)랑' and '-하고' list the sentence components, putting such components in a parallel, collective relationship. '-와/과' are usually for written language whereas '-(이)랑' and '-하고' are for spoken language. '-(이)랑' is widely spoken in Seoul.

준서{**와**/**랑**/**하고**} 민서는 한동대학교 학생이다.
Jun-Seo and Min-Seo are students of Handong Global University.
그는 책{**과**/**이랑**/**하고**}, 노트{**와**/**랑**/**하고**} 연필을 사러 갔다.
He went out to buy books, notebooks and pencils.
음악을 듣는 것{**과**/**이랑**/**하고**} 운동을 하는 것이 나의 취미다.
My hobby is listening to music and playing sports.

'-(이)며' lists the sentence components connected therewith to imply 'and'.

여기는 사과**며**, 배**며**, 수박**이며** 없는 게 없다.

There is everything here, from apples, pears to watermelons.

준서는 음악**이며**, 수학**이며**, 운동**이며**, 모두 다 잘한다.

Jun-Seo is good at everything, from music, maths to sports.

'-(이)고' lists the sentence components connected therewith to imply 'indiscriminateness'.

소주**고** 맥주**고** 간에 닥치는 대로 마셔 버렸다.

I drank everything available from soju to beer.

사랑**이고** 나발**이고** 난 졸려 죽겠다.

I am so sleepy, I don't give a damn about love or whatever.

'-에' and '-에다(가)' list the sentence components connected therewith to imply 'in addition to something'. They can be used in the form of '-에 -에' or '-에다(가) -에다(가)'.

과일{**에/에다(가)**} 음료수{**에/에다(가)**} 실컷 먹었다.

I ate a lot, I had apples and drinks and everything.

그는 권력{**에/에다(가)**} 부{**에/에다(가)**} 부러울 게 없는 사람이다.

He has everything from power to wealth, so he has nothing to envy.

Using '-에, -에다(가)' just once conveys a sense of 'addition(첨가)' rather than 'series'.

3{**에/에다(가)**} 4를 더하면 7이 된다. / Three plus four is seven.

국수{**에/에다(가)**} 야채를 얹어 먹어라.

Put some vegetables on the noodle.

② **Selection(선택)**

Connective particle '-(이)거나, -(이)건, -(이)든지, -(이)든, -(이)든가, -

(이)나' convey 'selection of something out of several things', 'not being selective at all about something', or 'not to care about something'.

First, '-(이)나' means selecting one thing out of several things.

> 나는 이 돈으로 책이나 노트를 사야겠다.
> I should buy books or notebooks with this money.
> 서울이나 부산 가운데 어느 곳이 더 살기가 좋을까?
> Where would be better to live, Seoul or Busan?

'-(이)거나, -(이)든지, -(이)든가' mean 'not being selective about something' or 'not to care about something'. In particular, they are affixed to '누구, 무엇, 어느, 아무, 어떤', or used in the form of '-(이)거나 -(이)거나 간에, -(이)든지 -(이)든지 (간에), -(이)든가 -(이)든가 (간에)'.

> 무슨 말{이거나/이든지/이든가} 해 보세요.
> Please say anything, whatever that may be.
> 누구{건/든} 만날 뜻이 있습니다.
> I am willing to meet anyone.
> 나는 1년{이건/이든} 2년{이건/이든} 당신을 기다리겠어요.
> I will wait for you, even if it means one or two years.

In spoken Korean, '-(이)거나' is usually condensed to '-(이)건, -(이)든지' to '-(이)든' and '-(이)든가' to '-(이)든'.

③ Contrast(대립) or contradiction(반대)

Connective particle '-마는' is used when the subject, while admitting or acknowledging the preceding fact, puts forth something contrastive or contradictory to the aforementioned fact. It acts as a direct bridge between the preceding sentence and the following sentence. Also, it is affixed to sentential endings such as '-(ㄴ/는)다, -(으/느)냐, -자, -지, -(으)

라' and used in the form of '-(ㄴ/는)다마는, -(으/느)냐마는, -자마는, -지마는, -(으)라마는'.

서울에 갑니**다마는** 준서를 만나지는 않을 예정입니다.
I am going to Seoul, but I am not going to see Jun-Seo.
빨리 고향에 가 보**지마는** 옛 친구들은 만날 수 없을 것이다.
I will go to Seoul as soon as possible, but I won't be able to see my old friends.

In spoken language, '-마는' is usually condensed to '-만'.

■ Meaning and grammatical function of '-요'

What is the grammatical function of '-요' and how should we address this?
'-요', which is placed at the end of a sentence, can be addressed as a listener-honorific suffix, because it elevates the listener if attached to sentential endings of ordinary non-honorific speech such as '-거든, -네, -(ㄴ/는)다고, -(ㄴ/는)다니까, -(으)ㄴ/는데, -아/어, -지, -아/어야지, -(으)ㄹ게, -(으)ㄹ래' [declarative] ; '-게? -고? -(ㄴ/는)다면서? -아/어? -(으)ㄹ까? -(으)래? -지?' [interrogative] ; '-아/어, -지' [imperative] ; '-아/어, -지' [propositive] ; '-(는)군' [exclamatory]. When these sentential endings are combined with '-요', the sentential ending of ordinary non-honorific speech changes into hearer-honorific style.

Declarative:　준서는 축구를 잘해**요**.
　　　　　　　Jun-Seo is good at football.
Interrogative:　요즘 잘 지내고 있지**요**?
　　　　　　　How have you been?
Imperative:　책 좀 읽어**요**.
　　　　　　　Read some books.
Propositive:　우리 함께 가**요**.
　　　　　　　Let us go together.
Exclamatory:　민서가 노래를 굉장히 잘하더군**요**.
　　　　　　　Min-Seo was very good at singing.

Also, '-요' can be put in the middle of a sentence to humble the speaker, or to convey friendliness or hesitation, since '-요' can be spoken several times in the identical form in a single sentence unlike auxiliary particles.

선생님요, 저는요 어제요 서울에요 갔어요.
Sir, I went to Seoul yesterday.
며칠 전부터요 날씨가요 매우 안 좋아요.
The weather has been quite nasty since a few days ago.

*누구나 첫사랑이나 항상이나 특별한 법이다.
For anyone, first love is special and others too.
*그마저 오늘마저 한 모금의 물마저 마셔 버렸다.
Even he drank the last drop of water even today.

It is also possible to omit '-요' while it is impossible for auxiliary particles.

날씨가 좋으면(요) 언제든지(요) 소풍을 가셔야 해(요).
If the weather is nice, at any time, you should go on a picnic.
졸업하기 전에(요) 많은 경험을(요) 쌓으면(요) 좋은 일이죠.
It is good to accumulate good experiences before you graduate from school.

한 마디의 말{이라도/*∅} 진심으로 하고 있는가?
Have you ever spoken a word of truth?
한 방울의 눈물{이나마/*∅} 뜨겁게 흘린 적이 있는가?
Have you ever shed scalding tears?

8.3 Multiple use of particles in a sentence

Many times, Korean particles are used in conjunction with each other. Having several particles in a single sentence can clarify the meaning of the sentence. There are four types of particle additions, which include: 'case particle + case particle', 'auxiliary particles + case particle', 'case particle + auxiliary particle' and '(case particle) + auxiliary particle + auxiliary particle'.

First, 'case particle + case particle' is usually 'adverbial particle + other case particle'.

지난 2년간 서울<u>에서의</u> 생활은 정말 행복했습니다.
My life in Seoul for the last two years was great.
잔소리를 한 것은 준서<u>에게가</u> 아닙니다.
I did not nag Jun-Seo (but someone else).
런던<u>에를</u> 가 보긴 했으나 별 기억이 없어요.
I have been to London, but I do not remember much about it.

Adverbial particles can be added to another adverbial particle.

이제 그만 부모님<u>에게로</u> 돌아가거라.
Please return to your parents now.
서울에서는 런던<u>에서보다</u> 훨씬 행복했다.
I was much happier in Seoul than London.
부모님<u>으로부터</u> 편지가 왔다.
A letter from my parents arrived.

'Case particle + auxiliary particle' is usually 'adverbial particle + auxiliary particle'.

민서는 워싱턴<u>에도</u> 가 보았단다.
Min-Seo has been to Washington as well.
준서<u>에게도</u> 안부를 전해 다오.
Please give my regard to Jun-Seo.
그 일<u>로는</u> 성을 낼 것이 없단다.
There is nothing to be angry with that matter.

'Auxiliary particle + case particle' is usually 'auxiliary particle -만, -까지 + case particle -을/를, -이/가'.

> 나는 너**만을** 사랑해. / I love you only.
> 너**만이** 우리의 희망이다. / Only you are our hope.
> 너**까지를** 합격자로 처리할 것이다. / Up to you are successful candidates.

In addition, '(case particle) + auxiliary particle + auxiliary particle' is usually in the form of '(adverbial particle) + auxiliary particle + auxiliary particle'.

> 준서**에게만이라도** 진실을 말하고 싶다.
> I just want to tell the truth to Jun-Seo [if not anyone else].
> 애야, 밖**으로만이나마** 돌지 말아 다오.
> Please do not stay out of home for too long.
> 민서**조차도** 그 의견에 동의하지 않았어요.
> Even Min-Seo did not agree with the idea.

8.4 Korean cultural aspects as reflected in particles

Korean particles are often omitted in everyday speech, but not every particle can be omitted, there is certain particle which can be omitted in certain situation.

Case particles can be omitted, while auxiliary particles, which add a certain meaning to the preceding word, cannot be omitted. Also, among case particles, only subject particle, object particle, adnominal particle and some adverbial particles can be omitted.

First, particles can be omitted if they are recoverable with the help of the context. In general, they are highly likely to be recovered if the sentence order is consistent with the general Korean word order.

Adnominal particle, which is affixed to a noun, make the noun modify the following noun. Therefore, the adnominal particle '-의' in '누구의 책(whose book)' can be easily omitted, as: 1) it is clear that '누구' is modifying '책' with the help of particle '-의'; 2) the particle is easily recoverable with the help of the context; and 3) the sentence has a conventional word order.

A: 그것은 누구의 책이니? → 그것∅ 누구∅ 책이니?
   Whose book is it?
B: 준서의 책이에요. → 준서∅ 책이에요.
   It is Jun-Seo's.

Since '가다' is an intransitive verb, the sentence with '가다' can be grammatical without the use of a particle if there is a noun acting as a subject. In other words, subject particle '-이/가' can be easily omitted, since: 1) '배' before '가다' can be easily predicted as the subject of the sentence; and 2) the particle is easily recoverable. The same goes for the answer statements.

A: 배가 잘 가네. → 배∅ 잘 가네.
   The ship is smooth sailing.
B: 예, 배가 잘 가요. → 예, 배∅ 잘 가요.
   Yes, the ship is smooth sailing.

'사랑하다' is a transitive verb, which requires a subject and an object noun. Since Jun-Seo is already stated as the subject, Min-Seo can be easily assumed as the object. Therefore, object particle '-을/를' can be omitted.

A: 준서가 민서를 사랑하니? → 준서가 민서∅ 사랑하니?

Does Jun-Seo love Min-Seo?

B: 예, 민서를 사랑해요. → 예, 민서∅ 사랑해요.

Yes, he loves Min-Seo.

However, omission of both the subject particle and object particle can lead to three different interpretations, making it difficult to grasp the meaning of the sentence. Therefore, the two particles should not be omitted altogether.

준서가 민서를 사랑하니?

Does Jun-Seo love Min-Seo?

준서를 민서가 사랑하니?

Is Jun-Seo loved by Min-Seo?

준서와 민서가 사랑하니?

Are Jun-Seo and Min-Seo in love?

As such, if any one particle of essential sentence components is omitted, the particle of another sentence component cannot be omitted. '받다(to receive)' requires three essential sentence components, such as 'someone receives something from someone'. If subject '나는' and adverbial particle '-한테' are omitted, it is difficult to see whether '준서∅' means 'of Jun-Seo', 'to Jun-Seo', or just 'Jun-Seo'. Therefore it is impossible to omit the particle, as it would be impossible to see what kind of grammatical relationship Jun-Seo and '받다' have.

나는 준서한테 책을 받았다. → *준서∅ 책을 받았다.

I received a book from Jun-Seo.

The same goes for 꼬집다 'to pinch'. '꼬집다' also requires two essential sentence components, as in 'someone pinches someone'. Therefore, object particle '-을/를' should not be omitted as omission of both the subject '아내가' and object particle '-을/를' will result in ambivalence.

아내가 남편을 꼬집었다. → *남편Ø 꼬집었다.
The wife gave her husband a pinch.

'아니다' and '되다' are complement-requiring verbs. In following sentences, Jun-Seo and water at the beginning act as subjects, thus, the following sentence component is bound to be the complement. Therefore, readers can easily predict that complement particle '-이/가' was omitted.

준서가 범인이 아니야. → 준서가 범인Ø 아니야.
Jun-Seo is not the culprit.
물이 벌써 얼음이 됐어. → 물이 벌써 얼음Ø 됐어.
Water has already frozen.

'있다' requires a subject and a locational adverb. As '어디' and '워싱턴' indicate locations, it is easy to predict that the adverbial particle is '-에', thus, it can be omitted.

A: 민서가 지금 어디에 있니? → 민서가 지금 어디Ø 있니?
   Where is Min-Seo now?
B: 워싱턴에 있어요. → 워싱턴Ø 있어요.
   In Washington.

However, most of the adverbial particles have certain lexical meanings, which means omission of adverbial particles may change the meaning of the sentence. Therefore, it is difficult to omit adverbial particles.

준서가 민서**보다** 몸무게가 무거워요.

→ *준서가 민서**Ø** 몸무게가 무거워요.

Jun-Seo is heavier than Min-Seo.

나는 어제 한국 식당**에서** 저녁을 먹었어요.

→ *나는 어제 한국 식당**Ø** 저녁을 먹었어요.

I had dinner at a Korean restaurant yesterday.

어디**에서부터** 여행을 시작할까요?

→ *어디**Ø** 여행을 시작할까요?

From where shall we start the journey?

그녀는 학부모**로서** 학교에 왔다.

→ *그녀는 학부모**Ø** 학교에 왔다.

She came to the school as a parent.

Auxiliary particles also have lexical meanings, so omitting them can change the meaning of the sentence or make the sentence ungrammatical. Therefore, auxiliary particles cannot be omitted.

여기는 준서**밖에** 아무도 없어요.

There is nobody but Jun-Seo here.

→ *여기는 준서밖에 아무**Ø** 없어요.

　*여기는 준서**Ø** 아무도 없어요.

　?*여기**Ø** 준서밖에 아무도 없어요.

　*여기**Ø** 준서**Ø** 아무**Ø** 없어요.

If the subject or object comes with a long modifier, it is impossible to omit the subject and object particle even if it is obvious which word is the subject and object.

뉴욕에서 온 존**이** 오늘은 집 안에 있다.

→ *뉴욕에서 온 존**Ø** 오늘은 집 안에 있다.

John, who is from New York, is at home today.

마이클이 학교에서 공부를 하고 있는 존**을** 만났다.

→ ^{?*}마이클이 학교에서 공부를 하고 있는 존**Ø** 만났다.

Michael met John who was studying at school.

The subject particle in implied sentences cannot be left out even if it is easy to predict which word is the subject, because it is not clear what kind of relationship the word with the omitted particle has with which predicate.

준서**가** 거짓말을 했다는 사실이 분명히 드러났다.

→ [*]준서**Ø** 거짓말을 했다는 사실이 분명히 드러났다.

It has become clear that Jun-Seo lied.

Particles affixed to the answers to interrogative '누가(who)', '어디가 (where)', '언제가(when)', '무엇이(what)', '어떤 것이(which)', '어느 것이 (which)', '어떻게(how)' cannot be omitted, because the meaning of the answer has to be clear, and the core sentence component that clarifies the answer is particles.

A: **누가** 이 그림을 그렸니? / Who drew this picture?

B: [*]**민서Ø** 이 그림을 그렸어요. / Min-Seo drew this picture.

A: 한국에서 **어디가** 제일 아름답습니까?

Where is the most beautiful place in Korea?

B: ^{?*}**금강산Ø** 제일 아름답습니다.

Mountain Geumgang is most beautiful.

A: 하루 중 **언제가** 가장 바쁩니까?

What time of the day are you busiest?

B: ^{?*}**오후 2시경Ø** 가장 바쁩니다.

I am busiest at around 2pm.

A: 지금 네게 **무엇이** 문제니? / What is your most urgent issue now?

B: ?*대학 입시**Ø** 문제야. / Entering the college.

A: 여름에 나는 과일로는 **어떤 것이** 있니?

What kind of fruits are produced in summer?

B: ?*수박**Ø** 있어요. / Watermelons.

A: **어느 것이** 네 책이야? / Which one is your book?

B: ?*이 책**Ø** 제 거예요. / This one is mine.

A: **어떻게** 런던까지 갔습니까? / How did you travel to London?

B: ?*비행기**Ø** 갔었습니다. / By airplane.

In following sentences, object '매' is placed at the very beginning of the sentence to be given emphasis. '산이' is placed at the beginning of the sentence because the object '산' in '사람들이 산을 좋아한다(people love mountains)' was combined with subject particle '-이' to be given emphasis. As such, subject and object particles that are intended for emphasis cannot be omitted.

매**를** 형이 나에게 댔다.

→ *매**Ø** 형이 나에게 댔다.

My elder brother put the rod towards me.

산**이** 좋은 사람들이 모였다.

→ *산**Ø** 좋은 사람들이 모였다.

This is the gathering of people who love mountains.

09 Verb

9.1 What is a verb?

Verb(동사) represents the movement, actions or process of the subject, and acts a predicate in a sentence. Verbs are classified into intransitive verbs and transitive verbs depending on the subject that influences its movement and action. Verbs classified into main verbs and auxiliary verbs depending on the function which does in the sentence, or classified into regular verbs and irregular verbs according to the types of verbal conjugation.

The most distinctive characteristic of the Korean verbs is that they have various verbal conjugation. Conjugation means the changing form of the verb as various endings are added on the verb stems, and verbs will have new features accordingly.

먹다 'to eat'
먹-(stem) + -다(basic form, dictionary ending)
　　　　　-는다([declarative] final ending)
　　　　　-으면([condition] relation connective ending)
　　　　　-었-다([past] tense prefinal ending)

-으시-다([subject honorific] prefinal ending)

-게 하다([causative] ending)

-게 되다([passive] ending)

-지 아니하다([negation] ending)

-는(adnominal ending)

-음(noun ending)

Verbs can represent sentence ending, conjunction, time, aspect, politeness, causative, passive and negation through the verbal conjugation thus, and a way of representing such is very different from English.

Also, verbs can be modified by adverbial phrases, and the main verb always comes at the end of a sentence.

9.2 Types and characteristics of verbs

9.2.1 Intransitive verb and transitive verb

- Intransitive verb

Intransitive verbs(자동사) are verb which movement or action of a verb only affects the subject. Therefore, as an intransitive verb being a one valency predicate one-place predicate, it becomes a grammatical sentence when one subject is given as a subject that takes the movement or action of the verb.

준서가 학교에 **간다**.(◁가-ㄴ다) / Jun-Seo goes to school.
시냇물이 졸졸 **흐른다**.(◁흐르-ㄴ다) / A brook murmurs along.
눈이 많이 **내린다**.(◁내리-ㄴ다) / It snows a lot.

- Transitive verb

Transitive verbs(타동사) are verb which movement or action of a verb affects object or essential adverbial phrases not subject. As a transitive verb being a more than two valencies predicate two-places predicate, it becomes grammatical sentence when there are other essential components other than subject, in other words, objects or essential adverbial phrases.

아버지는 우표를 **모으신다**.(◁모으-시-ㄴ다) / My father collects stamps.
준서가 민서에게 동화책을 **선물하였다**.(◁선물하-였-다)
Jun-Seo presented a storybook to Min-Seo.
그는 자기 아들을 의사로 **만들었다**.(◁만들-었-다)
He made his son a doctor.

- Intransitive and transitive verb

There are some Korean verbs that can act as intransitive verb and transitive verb without any changes in the form, and they are called **intransitive and transitive verbs**(양용동사). Therefore, The structure is completely different depending on whether the verb is used as intransitive or transitive, it should be determined by distinguishing the meaning of a sentence and grammatical relations.

Intransitive verb: 오늘은 **바람이** 많이 **분다**.(◁불-ㄴ다)
It is very windy today.
Transitive verb: 군악대가 **나팔을** 잘 **분다**.(◁불-ㄴ다)
A military band blow horns very well.

Verbs like 돌다 'to turn around', 놀다 'to play', 트다 'to sprout, to go break something open', 넘다 'to exceed, to cross over', 끼다 'to become cloudy, to join' have a similar attribute to 불다 'to blow, to breathe out'.

9.2.2 Main verb and auxiliary verb

Auxiliary verbs(보조동사) refer to verbs that come after the main verb to add aspectual or grammatical meanings to the main verb.

준서는 워싱턴에 **가 보았다**. Jun-Seo has been to Washington.

'가' is the main verb and '보았다' the auxiliary verb. In this case, '보다' means 'attempt, experience', not 'to see'. Therefore, '가 보았다' means 'have been there/have experienced', not 'something that someone went and saw'.

Auxiliary verbs are accompanied with connective endings such as '-아/어, -게, -지, -고, -아/어야, -기는, -는가, -(이)ㄴ가, -(으)ㄹ까' since they always come after the main verb. And just like regular verbs, auxiliary verbs can be freely combined with the present-tense prefinal ending '-는-', imperative ending '-아/어라' or propositive ending '-자'.

① **Progress**(진행): -아/어 가다/오다, -고 있다/계시다

그는 지금 저녁을 다 **먹어 간다**. / He has almost eaten dinner now.
이제 날이 **밝아 온다**. / Now, the whole sky is bright.
민서는 점심을 **먹고 있어요**. / Min-Seo is eating lunch.
아버지께서는 회사에서 일을 **하고 계셔요**.
My father is working at the company.

② **Completion**(완료) + **Regret**(아쉬움)/**Good riddance**(속 시원함): -아/어 버리다, -고(야) 말다

이제야 빚을 다 **갚아 버렸다**. / I finally paid off my debts.
주식 투자에 실패에서 재산을 다 **날려 버렸다**.
He lost all his fortune in the stock market.
사랑하는 강아지가 **죽고(야) 말았다**. / My beloved dog died.

③ **Completion**(완료) + **Fulfillment**(수행): -아/어 내다, -고 나다

드디어 '토지'라는 소설을 다 읽**어 냈다**.
I eventually read off the novel Toji(The land).
저녁을 먹**고 나서** 우리는 TV를 보았다.
We ate our dinner, then we watched television.

④ **Possession**(보유) + **Completion**(완료): -아/어 놓다/두다

준서는 자기가 맡은 일을 잘**해 놓았다**. / Jun-Seo has done his job well.
내 말을 잘 들**어 두어라**. / You mark what I say.

⑤ **Experience**(경험) + **Try**(시도): -아/어 보다

너 한국 김치 먹**어 보았니**?
Have you ever tried Korean food Kimchi?
'사랑한다'는 말을 들**어 보았습니까**?
Have you ever heard the expression 'I love you'?

⑥ **Help**(도움) + **Service**(봉사): -아/어 주다/드리다

민서는 나를 위해 문을 열**어 주었다**.
Min-Seo opened the door for me.
나는 어머니가 저녁 준비를 하는 것을 도**와 드렸습니다**.
I helped my mother to get dinner.

⑦ **Negation**(부정) + **Intention of speaker**(화자의 의도): -지 않다

준서는 피자를 먹**지 않았다**. / Jun-Seo did not eat pizza.
그는 일부러 서울에 가**지 않았다**. / He intentionally did not go to Seoul.

⑧ **Impossibility**(불능) + **Restriction on situation**(상황에 의한 제약): -지
못하다

　준서는 피자를 먹**지 못했다**. / Jun-Seo has not eaten pizza.
　어제는 홍수가 나서 학교에 오**지 못했다**.
　I could not come to school because of the flood.

⑨ **Prohibition**(금지): -지 말다

　애야, 마약은 절대 하**지 마라**. / Honey, never take drugs.
　술을 너무 많이 먹**지 마세요**. / Don't drink so much.

⑩ **Inevitability**(필연) + **Emphasis**(강조): -아/어야 하다

　이번에는 꼭 승리**해야 한다**. / (We) must win this time.
　어떻게 하든, 대학 시험에 합격**해야 한다**.
　It requires passing a university entrance exam, one way or another.

⑪ **Ordering**(시킴): -게 하다

　어머니는 항상 나에게 일기를 쓰**게 했다**.
　My mother always made me write a diary.
　우유를 많이 마시**게 하자**. / Let's make (him) drink a lot of milk.

⑫ **Admission**(시인) + **Partial or Additional Acknowledge**(부분/추가 인정):
　-기는/기도 하다

　그가 잘못했다고 말하**기는 했다**. / He did say he was wrong.
　민서가 다시 오겠다고 하**기는 했다**.
　Min-Seo did say she would come again.
　그녀는 돈이 많다고 하**기도 했다**. / She did say she has much money.

⑬ **Sequence**(계기) + **Supplement**(보유): -아/어 가지다

눈이 너무 많이 **와 가지고** 결석을 했다.
I was absent, because it was so snowy.
민서는 항상 지각을 **해 가지고** 문제다.
The problem with Min-Seo is, she is always late.
서울에 직접 **가 가지고** 준서를 만났다.
I went to Seoul in person, and met Jun-Seo.

⑭ **Schedule**(예정) + **Result**(결과): -게 되다

내일 우리 가족은 경주로 여행을 가**게 되었다**.
My family are going to travel to Gyeongju tomorrow.
사랑을 하**게 되면** 모두들 시인이 된다.
At the touch of love, everyone becomes a poet.

⑮ **Repetition**(반복) + **Emphasis**(강조): -아/어 쌓다/대다

학생들이 교실에서 너무 떠들**어 쌓는다**.
The students are being too noisy in the classroom.
갓난애가 끝없이 울**어 댔다**. / The veriest baby was crying endlessly.

⑯ **Guess**(추측): -(으)ㄴ/는/(으)ㄹ 듯하다, -(으)ㄹ 성싶다, -(으)ㄹ 법하다

오늘은 비가 **올 듯하다**. / It seems likely to rain.
걔는 공부를 잘**할 성싶지** 않다.
He doesn't seem to be doing well in school.
그가 이제 항복**할 법한데도** 전혀 그런 기색이 안 보인다.
I thought he'd have surrendered now, he has shown no signs.

⑰ **Pretense**(시늉) + **Non-fact**(비사실): ﹣(으)ㄴ/는 척하다/체하다/양하다

준서는 나를 보고 아**는 척했다**.
Jun-Seo acknowledged me before I greeted him.
앞으로 나를 만나거든 아**는 체하지** 마라.
If we meet in the future, don't pretend that you know me.
민서는 그 사건의 진실을 다 아**는 양했다**.
Min-Seo pretended to know about the facts of the case.

⑱ **Value**(가치) + **Degree**(정도): ﹣(으)ㄹ 만하다

한국 김치는 좀 맵기는 하지만 먹**을 만하다**.
Korean Kimchi is a little spicy, but edible.
한국에 있는 경주는 한번 가 **볼 만하다**.
Gyeongju in Korea is worth a visit.

9.2.3 Regular verb and irregular verb

Korean verbs can be divided into regular and irregular verbs with the basis of **verbal conjugation**(어미활용). Regular verb is a verb of unchanging verb stems even when the verb stems are followed by any endings, and irregular verb is a verb with changing verb stems that can not be explained by certain rules. Because regular verbs and irregular verbs has same dictionary forms, they have to be determined whether it is a regular or irregular verb by looking at the changing form when endings are added at the end of stems.

The following are 12 kinds of irregular forms in Korea, and there are 11 types of irregular verbs except ㅎ irregularity.

① ㄷ, ㄹ, ㅂ, ㅅ, 르, 우, 으

② 거라, 너라, 러, 여

③ ㅎ

① are verbs with changes in the stem, ② with changes in the ending, and ③ with changes in both stem and ending. Such irregularities generally occur before prefinal endings like '-았/었-, -아/어서', and endings where '으' can be added, such as '-(으)러, -(으)려고, -(으)며, -(으)면, -(으)면서, -(으)니까'.

① **Irregular verb ㄷ**: the stem 'ㄷ' is changed into 'ㄹ'.

> 듣다 'to hear': 듣고, 듣니? 듣자 ; 들었다/*듣었다, 들어서/*듣어서, 들으러 /*듣으러, 들으려고/*듣으려고, 들으면/*듣으면, 들으면서/* 듣으면서, 들으니까/*듣으니까

Verbs that are subject to the stem change above include: 묻다 'to ask', 걷다 'to walk', 싣다 'to load', 붇다 'to swell', 깨닫다 'to realize', 일컫다 'to call', 눋다 'to scorch'.
묻다 'to stick, to bury', 닫다 'to close', 믿다 'to believe', 얻다 'to get' are regular verbs.

② **Irregular verb ㄹ**: the stem 'ㄹ' is eliminated before prefinal ending '-시-', adnominal ending '-는, -(으)ㄴ, -(으)ㄹ', sentence ending '-습니다' and connective ending starting with 'ㄴ' such as '-니(까), -느라(고)'.

> 살다 'to live': 살고, 살며, 살자 ; 사시고/*살시고, 사는/*살는, 산/*살은, 살/*살을 ; 삽니다/*살습니다, 사니까/*살니까, 사느라고/*살 느라고

Verbs that are subject to 'ㄹ' elimination above include: 살다 'to live',

알다 'to know', 돌다 'to go around', 울다 'to cry', 밀다 'to push', 빌다 'to beg', 틀다 'to turn on', 털다 'to shake off', 들다 'to lift up, to eat', 끌다 'to draw'.

③ **Irregular verb** ㅂ: the stem 'ㅂ' changes into '오/우' or is outright eliminated.

> 돕다 'to help': 돕고, 돕니? 돕자 ; 도왔다/*돕았다, 도와서/*돕아서, 도우러
> /*돕으러, 도우려고/*돕으려고, 도우면/*돕으면, 도우면서/*
> 돕으면서, 도우니까/*돕으니까
> 뵙다 'to see': 뵙고, 뵙니? 뵙자 ; 뵈었다/*뵙었다/*뵈웠다, 봬서/*뵙어서/*뵈
> 워서, 뵈러/*뵙으러/*뵈우러, 뵈려고/*뵙으려고/*뵈우려고,
> 뵈면/*뵙으면/*뵈우면, 뵈면서/*뵙으면서/*뵈우면서, 뵈니까
> /*뵙으니까/*뵈우니까

Verbs that are subject to the stem change above include: 굽다 'to roast', 눕다 'to lie', 줍다 'to pick up', 깁다 'to sew', 여쭙다 'to ask'.

잡다 'to catch', 뽑다 'to pull out', 접다 'to fold', 씹다 'to chew' are regular verbs.

④ **Irregular verb** ㅅ: the stem 'ㅅ' is eliminated.

> 잇다 'to link': 잇고, 잇니? 잇자 ; 이었다/*잇었다, 이어서/*잇어서, 이으러/*
> 잇으러, 이으려고/*잇으려고, 이으면/*잇으면, 이으면서/*잇
> 으면서, 이으니까/*잇으니까

Verbs that are subject to 'ㅅ' elimination above include: 긋다 'to draw', 낫다 'to recover', 짓다 'to make', 젓다 'to row', 붓다 'to swell'.

웃다 'to laugh', 벗다 'to undress', 빼앗다 'to take something by force', 씻다 'to wash', 솟다 'to rise' are regular verbs.

⑤ **Irregular verb** 르: '__' from the last syllable of the stem '르' is eliminated and then combined with '르'.

부르다 'to call': 부르고, 부르니? 부르자 ; 불렀다/*부르었다/*부렀다, 불러
서/*부르어서/*부러서, 불러도/*부르어도/*부러도, 부르러,
부르려고, 부르면, 부르면서, 부르니까

고르다 'to choose': 고르고, 고르니? 고르자 ; 골랐다/*고르았다/*고랐다,
골라서/*고르아서/*고라서, 골라도/*고르아도/*고라
도, 고르러, 고르려고, 고르면, 고르면서, 고르니까

Verbs subject to the application above include 가르다 'to divide', 고르다 'to choose', 기르다 'to grow', 나르다 'to carry', 모르다 'to do not know', 오르다 'to climb', 이르다 'to reach', 흐르다 'to flow'.

⑥ **Irregular verb** 우: the stem '우' is eliminated.

푸다 'to scoop out' : 푸고, 푸니? 푸자 ; 펐다/*푸었다, 퍼서/*푸어서, 퍼도/*
푸어도, 푸러, 푸려고, 푸면

푸다 is the only irregular verb '우', and 주다 'to give', 두다 'to put', 낮추다 'to make low', 멈추다 'to stop', 지우다 'to erase', 피우다 'to make a fire', 비우다 'to empty out', 세우다 'to found', 데우다 'to make warm', 배우다 'to learn', 싸우다 'to fight', 부수다 'to break', 이루다 'to accomplish', 그만두다 'to cease', 바꾸다 'to change' are regular verbs.

⑦ **Irregular verb** 으: the stem '으' is eliminated before prefinal ending '-았/었-' and connective ending '-아/어서, -아/어도'.

쓰다 'to write': 쓰고, 쓰니? 쓰자 ; 썼다/*쓰었다, 써서/*쓰어서, 써도/*쓰어
도, 쓰러, 쓰려고, 쓰면, 쓰면서, 쓰니까

모으다 'to collect': 모으고, 모으니? 모으자 ; 모았다/*모으았다, 모아서/*모
으아서, 모아도/*모으아도, 모으러, 모으려고, 모으면,
모으면서, 모으니까

Verbs subject to the application above include 따르다 'to follow, to pour', 치르다 'to pay', 끄다 'to extinguish', 모으다 'to collect', 트다 'to sprout', 들르다 'to drop in', 뜨다 'to float'.

⑧ **Irregular verb** 거라: imperative sentence ending '-아라' changes into '-거라'.

가다 'to go': 가고, 가니? 가자 ; 갔다, 가서, 가려고, 가면, 가면서, 가니까, 가거라/*가라

Verbs subject to the application above include 자다 'to sleep', 자라다 'to grow', 일어나다 'to get up', 서다 'to stop, to stand up' and '가다' compound verbs such as 나아가다 'to advance', 들어가다 'to enter', 살아가다 'to lead a life', 올라가다 'to climb up'.
차다 'to kick', 싸다 'to wrap up', 사다 'to buy', 만나다 'to meet' are regular verbs.

⑨ **Irregular verb** 너라: imperative sentence ending '-아라' changes into '-너라'.

오다 'to come': 오고, 오니? 오자 ; 왔다, 와서, 오려고, 오면, 오면서, 오니까, 오너라/*오거라/*와라

Verbs subject to the application above include '오다' compound verbs such as 나오다 'to come', 들어오다 'to come in', 내려오다 'to come down', 넘어오다 'to come over', 돌아오다 'to come back'.

보다 'to see', 쏘다 'to shoot', 쪼다 'to pick', 꼬다 'to twist' are regular verbs.

⑩ **Irregular verb 러**: the first syllable of the ending '-어' changes into '-러'.

> 이르다 'to reach': 이르고, 이르니? 이르자 ; 이르렀다/*이르었다/*일렀다,
> 이르러서/*이르어서/*일러서, 이르려고, 이르면, 이르니까

이르다 is the only irregular verb 러.

⑪ **Irregular verb 여**: the first syllable of the ending '-어' changes into '-여'.

> 하다 'to do': 하고, 하니? 하자 ; 하였다/*하었다/*핬다, 하여서/*하어서/*하
> 서, 하러, 하려고, 하면, 하면서, 하니까

Verbs subject to the application above include compound verbs such as 공부하다 'to study', 사랑하다 'to love', 생각하다 'to think', 일하다 'to work', 말하다 'to say'. Since verbs and adjectives that end with '-하다' look the same, readers should tell whether the word is a verb or adjective by looking at its meaning and function in the sentence.

9.3 Switch-over of verb

By putting a suffix on the verb stem, an intransitive verb can be changed into a transitive verb or transitive verb into a intransitive verb, and this is called the switch-over of verb.

- Switch-over of intransitive verb to transitive verb

An intransitive verb can be turned into a transitive verb by using causative suffixes such as '-이-, -히-, -리-, -기-, -우-, -구-, -추-', and these converted transitive verbs have the meaning of 'causative'.

아기가 웃는다. / A baby is laughing.
→ 어머니가 아기를 웃긴다.(◁웃-기-ㄴ-다)
 A mother makes a baby to laugh.

If causative suffix '-기-' is added to the intransitive verb 웃다 'to laugh', it becomes '웃기다', and because this '웃기다' means 'to make laugh', it needs a subject of laughing, in other word a object. Therefore, it can be considered as being derived into transitive verb.

Few examples with these grammatical characteristics as these are as follows.

먹다 'to eat' → 먹이다 'to let eat'
입다 'to wear' → 입히다 'to let wear'
울다 'to cry' → 울리다 'to let cry'
깨다 'to wake up' → 깨우다 'to let wake up'
솟다 'to rise high' → 솟구다 'to let rise high'

- Switch-over of transitive verb to intransitive verb

An transitive verb can be turned into a intransitive verb by using passive suffixes such as '-이-, -히-, -리-, -기-', and these converted intransitive verbs have the meaning of 'passive'.

경찰이 도둑을 잡았다. / The police caught the robber.
→ 도둑이 경찰에게 잡혔다.(◁잡-히-었-다)

The robber was caught by the police.

If passive suffix '-히-' is added to the transitive verb 잡다 'to catch', it becomes '잡히다', and because this '잡히다' means 'be caught', it needs not a object but an adverbial phrases such as '경찰에게'. Therefore, it can be considered as being derived into intransitive verb.

Few examples with these grammatical characteristics as these are as follows.

놓다 'to put' → 놓이다 'to be put'
듣다 'to hear' → 들리다 'to be heard'
안다 'to embrace' → 안기다 'to be embraced'

9.4 Derivation into a verb

The following three ways are of deriving adjective into a verb.

① **Adjective stem** + -아/어지다
If '-아/어지다' is attached at the end of adjective stem, it becomes a verb, and it will have a meaning of 'gradually becoming certain state'.

민서는 무척 예쁘다. / Min-Seo is very pretty.
→ 민서가 무척 예뻐졌다.(◁ 예쁘-어지-었-다)
　　Min-Seo has become prettier.

Few examples with these grammatical characteristics as these are as follows.

크다 'to be large' → **커지다** 'to grow larger'
작다 'to be small' → 작**아지다** 'to become smaller'
길다 'to be long' → 길**어지다** 'to become longer'
짧다 'to be short' → 짧**아지다** 'to shorten'
좋다 'to be good' → 좋**아지다** 'to become better'
싫다 'to be hate' → 싫**어지다** 'to become disgusted'
같다 'to be same' → 같**아지다** 'to become equal'
다르다 'to be different' → 달**라지다** 'to change'

② Adjective stem + -아/어하다

If '-아/어하다' is attached at the end of adjective stem, it also becomes a verb, and it has a meaning of 'do certain action'. However, '-아/어하다' cannot be attached at the end of every adjectives, and mostly, psychological adjectives such as '좋다, 슬프다, 기쁘다, 무섭다, 싫다' are attached and changes them into verbs.

나는 바다가 싫다. / I dislike sea.
→ 나는 바다를 싫**어한다**.(◁싫-어하-ㄴ다) / I dislike sea.

민서는 예쁘다. / Min-Seo is pretty.
→ 어머니는 민서를 예**뻐한다**.(◁예쁘-어하-ㄴ다)
(My) mother likes Min-Seo so much.

When '-하다' is combined with verbal nouns such as 강조 'emphasis', 공부 'study', 공연 'performance', 명상 'meditation', 운동 'exercise', 보호 'protection', it changes them into verbs.

민서는 한국어를 열심히 공부**한다**. / Min-Seo studies Korean hard.
건강을 지키기 위해 준서는 매일 운동**한다**.
Jun-Seo exercises every day for keeping his health.

③ **Adjective stem + causative suffix**

If causative suffix such as '-이-, -히-, -우-, -추-' is attached at the end of adjective stem, it becomes a verb.

서울은 도로가 넓다. / The roads in Seoul are wide.
→ 서울시가 서울의 도로를 더 넓혔다.(◁ 넓-히-었-다)
  Seoul city widened the roads in Seoul.

The words as follows have grammatical characteristics above.

높다 'to be high' → 높<u>이</u>다 'to make something higher'
괴롭다 'to be painful' → 괴롭<u>히</u>다 'to harass'
크다 'to be large' → 키<u>우</u>다 'to enlarge'
낮다 'to be low' → 낮<u>추</u>다 'to lower'

One step forward ▶▶

■ Agreement of subject and verb

English verbs change their forms according to the person and number of subjects, and this is called as an **agreement** of subject and verb. In other words, the form of a verb changes depending on whether the subject is the first person or the third person, and whether it is singular or plural.

I go ↔ He/she/it goes ↔ They go

However, this does not affect much in Korean. In other word, the form of a verb does not change according to the person, number or gender of a subject. To be more precise, it is the verb stem which is not changing, not the entire verb, and a wide variety of verb endings are attached at the end according to the tense and mood.

Person			Tense		Mood	
Singular	1st person (나)	먹다	Present	먹는다	Declarative	먹는다
	2nd person (너)	먹다	Past	먹었다	Interrogative	먹니?
	3rd person (그/그녀)	먹다	Future	먹겠다	Imperative	먹어라
Plural	1st person (우리)	먹다	Present progressive	먹고 있다	Propositive	먹자
	2nd person (너희들)	먹다	Past progressive	먹고 있었다	Exclamatory	먹는구나
	3rd person (그들/그녀들/그것들)	먹다	Future progressive	먹고 있겠다	Promise	먹으마

9.5 Korean cultural aspects as reflected in verbs

First, Koreans often omit subject and object and use only verb in everyday conversation. In other words, they omit information that the listener and speaker already are aware of, and communicate by only using new information.

A: (비가 오는데도 지금 서울에) 갈래?

Do you want to go (to Seoul despite the rain)?

B: 갈 거야. / I'm gong to Seoul.

A: 비가 오는데도 (네가 간다고)?

In spite of the rain (are you gong to Seoul)?

B: 시간이 없는데 어떡해. (가야지.)

I don't have time what can I do? (I have to go.)

A: (비가 많이 오니까 너는 서울에) 나중에 가.

(It is raining a lot,) go (to Seoul) later.

B: 아니야, 그래도 (나는 서울에 지금) 가야 돼.

No. Nevertheless I have to go (to Seoul now).

Second, there are many cases that irregular verbs ㄹ are used as regular verbs. Of course, they are used as regular verbs in poems or lyrics to meet the rhythm, but this is an exception.

어제 하늘을 {*날으는/나는} 꿈을 꾸었다.

Yesterday I dreamed of flying.

→ regular: *날으는, irregular: 나는

며칠 되지도 않았는데, 그사이에 준서의 영어회화 실력이 많이 {*늘은/는} 것 같다.

It's been only a few days since Jun-Seo studied English conversation, but he seems to make a remarkable improvement in it.

→ regular: *늘은, irregular: 는

Verbs which phenomenalize as these are as follows.

놀다 'to play': *놀은/논

물다 'to bite': *물은/문

벌다 'to earn': *벌은/번

살다 'to live': *살은/산

울다 'to cry': *울은/운

이끌다 'to lead': *이끌은/이끈

풀다 'to untie': *풀은/푼

헐다 'to form a boil': *헐은/헌

Third, there is a tendency to pronounce the 'intention' connective ending '-(으)려고' by attaching 'ㄹ' at front of '-려'.

우리 아이는 밥을 잘 안 {먹**을려고**/먹**으려고**} 해서 걱정이에요.
I worry that my child don't eat much rice.
→ 먹을려고: 먹-을-려고, 먹으려고: 먹-으려고

나는 내년에 뉴욕에 {**갈려고**/**가려고**} 해요.
I try to go to New York nest year.
→ 갈려고: 가-ㄹ-려고, 가려고: 가-려고

Verbs which phenomenalize as these are as follows.

잡다 'to catch': 잡을려고/잡으려고
배우다 'to learn': 배울려고/배우려고
가르치다 'to teach': 가르칠려고/가르치려고
듣다 'to listen': 들을려고/들으려고
쓰다 'to write': 쓸려고/쓰려고
양보하다 'to concede': 양보할려고/양보하려고
가다 'to go': 갈려고/가려고
오다 'to come': 올려고/오려고
서다 'to stand (up)': 설려고/서려고

In contrast, irregular verbs ㄹ and adjectives can not eliminate 'ㄹ' when verb conjugated, there are some cases that they pronounce the word by eliminating 'ㄹ'.

나는 가능한 한 한국에서 {살려고/*사려고/*살을려고} 해.
I try to live in Korea as passible.
→ 살려고: 살-려고, *사려고: 사-려고, *살을려고: 살-을-려고

자꾸 {울려고/*우려고/*울을려고} 하지 마세요.
Try not to cry again and again.
→ 울려고: 울-려고, *우려고: 우-려고, *울을려고: 울-을-려고

Fourth, there are cases that irregular use of '-거라' and '-너라' tends to become regular.

가려거든 빨리 {가거라/가라} / Go fast if you had intended to go.
→ regular: 가라, irregular: 가거라

늦어도 내일까지는 서울로 {돌아오너라/돌아와라}
Come back to Seoul tomorrow at the latest.
→ regular: 돌아와라, irregular: 돌아오너라

10 Adjective

10.1 What is an adjective?

Adjective(형용사) represents the state, characteristics and attributes of the subject, and acts as a predicate in a sentence.

English adjectives modify or explain nouns. However, Korean adjectives, though somewhat similar to English, can be very different from English adjectives. Thus, they require special attention.

The biggest difference from English is that Korean adjectives act similarly to verbs. In other words, Korean adjectives can become the predicate of a sentence without the help of other words.

이 연필은 **길다**. / This pencil **is long**.

In the sentence above, '연필' is the subject and '길다' the predicate. However, in English, 'is' is just a predicate and 'long' a complement which stands to explain the characteristics of the subject. 'Long' itself does not act as a predicate. In other words, '길다' is equal to 'be long', thus, it has a very similar function to 'verbs'.

Korean adjectives are similar to English in that they can modify nouns if put before a noun.

예쁜 꽃 / beautiful flower
└─↑   └────↑

Yet, the English adjective 'beautiful' is used in its dictionary form, whereas the Korean adjective is slightly changed into [예쁘-(stem) + -(으) ㄴ(adnominal ending) = 예쁜].

For example, Korean adjectives, which signify the characteristics, state, properties and situation of the subject, act as a predicate in a sentence. They are classified into attributive adjectives, psychological adjectives and demonstrative adjectives according to their state and attributes.

10.2 Types and characteristics of adjectives

10.2.1 Types of adjective

There are three types of adjective:

- Attributive adjective

Attributive adjectives(성상형용사) refer to the state, attributes and circumstance of the subject. A majority of adjectives are in fact attributive adjectives. They represent how the subject feels, how the subject is compared to others, or how the subject is assessed by others.

한국 김치는 매우 **맵다**. / Korean Kimchi is very spicy.
이 산은 매우 **높다**. / This mountain is very lofty.
한국어는 영어와 **다르다**. / Korean is different from English.
민서는 성격이 참 **밝다**. / Min-Seo is very cheerful.

- Psychological adjective

Psychological adjectives(심리형용사) denote the psychological state of the subject. They are subjective assessment of something or someone by the subject based in its own experience, so the assessment may vary between individuals. Psychological adjectives fall under the category of attributive adjectives in a broader context.

The subject of psychological adjectives in an declarative sentence should always be the speaker. In other words, the subject must be the first person, not second or third person, because the speaker does not know for sure the psychological state of others.

> {나/*너/*그}는 거짓말하는 사람이 **싫다**. / {I/*You/*He} dislike(s) liars.
> {나/*너/*그}는 지금 매우 **슬프다**. / {I/*You/*He} am/*are/*is very sad.

However, if predictive prefinal ending '-겠-' is added to the stem of a verb, the subject can be the second or third person, but not the first person.

> {*나/너/그}는 참 좋**겠**다. / {*I/You/He} must be very happy.
> {*나/너/그}는 참 슬프**겠**다. / {*I/You/He} must be very sad.

The subject of a psychological adjective in an interrogative sentence must be the second person, as interrogative sentences are used to ask how the other is feeling.

> {*나/너/*그}는 지금 기쁘**니**? / {*Am/Are/*Is} *I/you/*he happy now?
> {*나/너/*그}는 정말 민서가 싫**니**?
> {*Do/Do/*Does} *I/you/*he really dislike Min-Seo?

Nonetheless, psychological adjectives denote 'prediction' if combined with '-(으)ㄴ 것 같니?'. In this case, the subject can be the first and third person, but not the second person, because 'prediction' is estimation of something that we do not know very well.

{나/*너/그}가 지금 기**쁜 것 같니**?
Do you think {I/*you/he} am/*are/is happy now?
{나/*너/그}가 정말 민서가 **싫은 것 같니**?
Do you think {I/*you/he} really dislike Min-Seo?

- Demonstrative adjective

Demonstrative adjectives(지시형용사) represent 'indication' as in the case of demonstrative pronouns. They include '이러하다, 그러하다, 저러하다 ; 어떠하다, 아무러하다. 이렇다, 그렇다, 저렇다 ; 어떻다, 아무렇다' are short for '이러하다, 그러하다, 저러하다 ; 어떠하다, 아무러하다'.

상황이 **그러하다**면, 빨리 집에 가 보아라.
If the situation is such, go home quickly.
저렇게 아름다운 꽃은 처음 보았다.
I have never seen such a beautiful flower in my life.

'그러하다면' is short for '그러하다고 하면', and '저렇게' is for '저러하게'.

10.2.2 Main adjective and auxiliary adjective

Auxiliary adjectives(보조형용사) refer to adjectives that come after the main verb or adjective to add aspectual or grammatical meanings to the main adjective.

준서는 책을 읽고 있다. / Jun-Seo is reading a book.

'읽고' is the main verb and '있다' the auxiliary adjective. In this case, '있다' means 'to be in progress', not 'to be'. Therefore, '읽고 있다' means 'Jun-Seo is in the midst of reading'.

Auxiliary adjectives are accompanied with connective endings such as '-아/어, -게, -지, -고, -기는/기도, -(으)ㄴ/는가, -(이)ㄴ가, -(으)ㄹ까, -나' since they always come after the main adjective. In general, auxiliary adjectives cannot be combined with the present-tense prefinal ending '-는-', imperative ending '-아/어라' or propositive ending '-자'.

① **Progress**(진행): -고 있다, -는 중이다, -고 있는 중이다

그는 요즈음 한국어 공부를 하고 **있다**.
He is studying Korean these days.
준서는 책을 읽**는 중이다**. / Jun-Seo is reading a book.
민서는 수영을 하**고 있는 중이다**. / Min-Seo is swimming.

② **State**(상태) + **Continuum**(지속): -아/어 있다/계시다, -아/어 있는/계시는 중이다

할아버지께서 침대 위에 한 시간 동안이나 누**워 있다/계신다**.
My grandfather has been lying on the bed for one hour.
아버지는 고향에 **가 계시는 중이다**. / My father has gone to his hometown.

③ **Guess**(추측): -지 싶다, -(으)ㄴ/는가 싶다/나 싶다, -(으)ㄴ/는가 보다/나 보다

축구 경기가 다 끝났**지 싶다**. / I guess the football match is nearly over.
그녀가 곧 오**는가 싶다**. / I guess she will be here soon.
이렇게 우리가 잘 사는 것은 바로 우리 부모님의 은혜가 아**닌가 싶다**.
I guess we are well off thanks to the grace of our parents.

비가 많이 {**왔는가**/**왔나**} 보다. / I guess it rained a lot.
저 사람이 바로 민서의 엄마**인가 보다**. / I guess she is Min-Seo's mom.

④ **Intention**(의도) + **Indefiniteness**(미확정): -(으)ㄹ까 싶다

다음 달에 고향으로 돌아**갈까 싶다**.
I guess I shall come back to my hometown next month.
오늘 저녁은 가족과 함께 저녁을 먹**을까 싶다**.
I guess I shall have dinner with my family this evening.

⑤ **Hope**(희망): -고 싶다

나도 한국어 공부를 잘하**고 싶다**. / I hope I can study Korean well.
된장찌개를 먹**고 싶어요**. / I want to eat Doenjang stew.

⑥ **Expectation**(예정) + **Fact**(사실): -게 되어 있다

캘시 양은 내년에 한국으로 유학을 오**게 되어 있다**.
Kelsie is to come to Korea to study next year.
한국인이라면 김치는 잘 먹**게 되어 있다**.
It is natural for Koreans to enjoy Kimchi.

⑦ **Admission**(시인) + **Partial or Additional Acknowledgement**(부분/추가 인정): -기는/기도 하다

민서가 참 예쁘**기는 하다**. / I approve that Min-Seo is pretty.
그 사람은 키가 참으로 크**기도 하다**. / I think he is indeed very tall.

⑧ **Negation**(부정): -지 않다

민서는 몸무게가 그다지 무겁**지 않다**. / Min-Seo does not weigh that much.

이 과자는 달**지 않아서** 좋다. / I like this snack as it is not sweet.

⑨ **Shortage(불급): -**지 못하다

준서는 성격이 좋**지 못해서** 모두들 싫어한다.
Jun-Seo is disliked by everyone as he has a bad personality.
민서는 잘생기**지는 못해도** 성격은 매우 좋다.
Min-Seo has a good personality even though she is not good-looking.

⑩ **Emphasis(강조) + Exaggeration(과장): -**아/어 죽다

나는 그 애가 예**뻐 죽겠더라**. / The child was so damn lovely.
요즘 같은 날은 아이스크림이 먹고 싶**어 죽겠어**.
On days like this, I'm dying for some ice cream.

10.2.3 Regular adjective and irregular adjective

There are eight irregular adjectives in Korean as follows:

① 르, ㅂ, ㅅ, 르, 으
② 러, 여
③ ㅎ

① are adjectives with changes in the stem, ② with changes in the ending, and ③ with changes in both stem and ending. Such irregularities generally occur before prefinal endings like '-았/었-, -아/어서', and endings where '으' can be added, such as '-(으)며, -(으)면, -(으)면서, -(으)니까'.

① **Irregular adjective** 르: the stem '르' is eliminated before prefinal ending '-시-', adnominal ending '-(으)ㄴ, -(으)ㄹ', sentence ending '-습니

다' and connective ending starting with 'ㄴ' such as '-니, -니까'.

멀다 'to be far': 멀고, 멀며, *멀자 ; 머시고/*멀시고, 먼/*멀은, 멀/*멀을
 ; 멉니다/*멀습니다, 머니(까)/*멀니(까)

Adjectives that are subject to 'ㄹ' elimination above include: 멀다 'to
be far', 달다 'to be sweet', 길다 'to be long', 가늘다 'to be thin', 잘다
'to be even', 솔다 'to be narrow'.

② **Irregular adjective** ㅂ: the stem 'ㅂ' changes into '오/우' or is outright
eliminated.

춥다 'to be cold': 춥고, 춥니? *춥자 ; 추웠다/*춥었다/*추었다, 추워서/*춥
    어서/*추어서, 추우려고/*춥으려고/*추으려고, 추우면/*
    춥으면/*추으면, 추우면서/*춥으면서/*추으면서, 추우
    니까/*춥으니까/*추으니까
무겁다 'to be heavy': 무겁고, 무겁니? *무겁자 ; 무거웠다/*무겁었다/*무거
    었다, 무거워서/*무겁어서/*무거서, 무거우려고/*무
    겁으려고/*무거려고, 무거우면/*무겁으면/*무거면,
    무거우면서/*무겁으면서/*무거면서, 무거우니까/*
    무겁으니까/*무거니까

Adjectives that are subject to the stem change above include: 춥다
'to be cold', 덥다 'to be hot', 사랑스럽다 'to be lovely', 밉다 'to be ugly',
괴롭다 'to be distressed', 무겁다 'to be heavy', 가볍다 'to be light', 쉽다
'to be easy', 어둡다 'to be dark', 새롭다 'to be new'.
굽다 'to be bent', 좁다 'to be narrow' are regular adjectives.

③ **Irregular adjective** ㅅ: the stem 'ㅅ' is eliminated.

낫다 'to be better': 낫고, 낫니? *낫자 ; 나았다/*낫았다, 나아서/*낫아서,

나으려고/*낫으려고, 나으면/*낫으면, 나으면서/*낫으면서, 나으니까/*낫으니까

Only 낫다 'to be better' is subject to the application above.

④ **Irregular adjective 르:** '_' from the last syllable of the stem '르' is eliminated and then combined with '르'.

> 다르다 'to be different': 다르고, 다르니? *다르자 ; 달랐다/*다르았다/*다랐
> 다, 달라서/*다르아서/*다라서, 달라도/*다르아도
> /*다라도, 다르면, 다르면서, 다르니까
> 게으르다 'to be idle': 게으르고, 게으르니? *게으르자 ; 게을렀다/*게으르
> 었다/*게으랐다, 게을러서/*게으르아서/*게으라서,
> 게을러도/*게으르어도/*게으러도, 게으르면, 게으
> 르면서, 게으르다니까

Adjectives subject to the application above include 이르다 'to be early', 고르다 'to be even', 다르다 'to be different', 게으르다 'to be lazy', 배부르다 'to be full', 무르다 'to be soft'.

⑤ **Irregular adjective 으:** the stem '으' is eliminated before prefinal ending '-았/었-' and connective ending '-아/어서, -아/어도'.

> 슬프다 'to be sad': 슬프고, 슬프니?, *슬프자 ; 슬펐다/*슬프었다, 슬퍼서/*슬
> 프어서, 슬퍼도/*슬프어도, 슬프면, 슬프면서, 슬프니까
> 바쁘다 'to be busy': 바쁘고, 바쁘니?, *바쁘자 ; 바빴다/*바쁘았다, 바빠서/*바
> 쁘아서, 바빠도/*바쁘아도, 바쁘면, 바쁘면서, 바쁘니까

Adjectives subject to the application above include 슬프다 'to be sad', 고프다 'to be hungry', 크다 'to be big', 바쁘다 'to be busy', 나쁘다 'to be bad', 뜨다 'to be slow'.

⑥ **Irregular adjective 러**: the first syllable of the ending '-어' changes into '-러'.

푸르다 'to be blue': 푸르고, 푸르니?, *푸르자 ; 푸르렀다/*푸르었다/*푸렀
다, 푸르러서/*푸르어서/*푸러서, 푸르려고, 푸르면,
푸르니까

Adjectives subject to the application above include 푸르다 'to be blue', 누르다 'to be yellow'.

⑦ **Irregular adjective 여**: the first syllable of the ending '-어' changes into '-여'.

깨끗하다 'to be clean': 깨끗하고, 깨끗하니?, *깨끗하자 ; 깨끗하였다/*깨
끗하었다/*깨끗했다, 깨끗하여서/*깨끗하어서/*깨
끗하서, 깨끗하면, 깨끗하면서, 깨끗하니까

Adjectives subject to the application above include compound adjectives such as 깨끗하다 'to be clean', 튼튼하다 'to be strong', 부지런하다 'to be hardworking', 축축하다 'to be wet' and 익숙하다 'to be familiar with something'. Since verbs and adjectives that end with '-하다' look the same, readers should tell whether the word is a verb or adjective by looking at its meaning and function in the sentence.

⑧ **Irregular adjective ㅎ**: the final sound of the stem 'ㅎ' is eliminated, but a new form is made with a partial combination of the stem and the ending.

파랗다 'to be blue': 파랗고, 파랗니?, *파랗자 ; 파랬다/*파랗았다/*파랐다,
파래서/*파랗아서/*파라서, 파라면/*파랗으면/*파래

면, 파라니까/*파랗으니까/*파래니까, 파란데도/*파랗
은데도/*파랜데도, 파란들/*파랗은들/*파랜들, 파랄뿐
더러/*파랗을뿐더러/*파랠뿐더러, 파랗다면, 파랗거
든, 파랗거나, 파랗든지

Adjectives subject to the application above include: 누렇다 'to be yellow', 벌겋다 'to be reddish', 빨갛다 'to be red', 까맣다 'to be black', 하얗다 'to be white' ; 둥그렇다 'to be round', 널따랗다 'to be broad' ; 이렇다, 그렇다, 저렇다, 어떻다, 아무렇다 'to be like this or that'.

좋다 'to be good' is a regular adjective.

10.3 Derivation into an adjective

A noun or a pronoun becomes an adjective with a simple addition of '-답다, -스럽다, -롭다, -하다' at the end.

- ● Noun/pronoun + -답다

'-답다' usually is attached to nouns representing people, to mean that 'something/someone deserves to' or 'something/someone is well suited to someone's standing or characteristics'.

준서는 늘 학생**답다**. / Jun-Seo always behaves like a student.
그분은 어른**답다**. / He acts like an adult.

- ● Noun/pronoun + -스럽다

'-스럽다' is usually attached to nouns representing people, or abstract nouns such as love, happiness, mercy, hardship and glory, to mean that 'someone/something feels like'.

그 사람은 바보스럽다. / He is foolish.

민서는 매우 사랑스럽다. / Min-Seo is very lovely.

- ● Noun/pronoun + -롭다

'-롭다' is attached to abstract nouns that end with a vowel (e.g. 슬기 'wisdom', 향기 'scent', 흥미 'interest', 수고 'hard work'), or adnominal 새 'new', irregular stems '괴-, 번거-, 애처-, 와-, etc.', to mean that it is natural for the subject to be like something.

진달래는 향기롭다. / Azaleas are fragrant.

미국에 오니 모든 게 새롭다. / Everything seems strange is the US.

친구가 없어서 너무 외롭다. / Without any friends, I feel so lovely.

- ● Noun/pronoun + -하다

'-하다' comes after abstract nouns (e.g. 가난 'poverty', 건강 'health', 겸손 'modesty', 단순 'simpleness', 순수 'innocence', 정직 'honesty', 진실 'truth'), or mimetic words (e.g. 깨끗 'clean', 둘쭉날쭉 'uneven or volatile', 또랑또랑 'clear or clearly', 미끈미끈 'slimy') to transform them into an adjective.

시냇물이 깨끗하다. / The stream is clean.

목소리가 또랑또랑하다. / The voice is very clear.

10.4 Dual-use adjective

There are some Korean verbs that can act as adjective without any changes in the form. Therefore, the word appears the same whether it is acting as a verb or adjective, but the ending or the whole sentence structure would be different, so readers should check whether the word is a verb or an adjective in the given sentence. For example, '밝다' is an adjective and also a verb. If it is a verb, the present-tense prefinal ending '-는-' can be accompanied to make '밝는다'.

Adjective: 오늘은 달이 **밝다**. / The moon is bright today.
Verb: 날이 이제 **밝는다**. / The day is dawning.

Adjectives like 크다 'to be big', 늙다 'to be old', 늦다 'to be late', 낫다 'to be better', 맞다 'to be correct', 틀리다 'to be wrong' have a similar attribute to 밝다. If they are acting as a verb, they should be used in the form of '큰다, 늙는다, 낫는다, 맞는다 and 틀린다'.

One step forward

■ **About 있다 and 계시다**

'있다' means 'existence of human, animals and objects'. In other words, '있다' means '(someone/something) exists/is located (somewhere)'. '계시다' is the honorific form of '있다'.

• 있다
Since '있다' is an adjective, particle '-에' comes at the end of the word representing locations. The negative form of '있다' is '있지 아니하다/않다'. However, Koreans use '없다', the antonym of '있다', more frequently in spoken language.

A: 책이 책상 위에 있습니까? / Is a book on the desk?
B: 예, 책이 있습니다. / Yes, the book is.
  아니요, 책이 있지 않습니다. / No, the book isn't.
  아니요, 없습니다. / No, (it) isn't.

Moreover, '있다' means to have '가지다'. In other words, '있다' means '(someone) has (something)'. In this case, the subject particle '-이/가' comes after the subject (owner) of the sentence. The antonym is '있지 아니하다/않다', but Koreans typically prefer '가지고 있지 않다' to '안 가지고 있다'. In spoken language, 없다 is used most of the time.

A: 돈이 <u>있습니까</u>? / Do you have money?
B: 예, (가지고) 있습니다. / Yes, I do.
아니요, 가지고 있지 않습니다. / No, I don't.
아니요, 안 가지고 있습니다. / No, I don't.
없습니다. / No, I don't.

The negative form, tense and honorifics of '있다' are as follows.

있다		Positive	Negative
Present	Basic	있다	있지 아니하다/않다
	Honorific	있습니다	있지 아니합니다/않습니다
Past	Basic	있었다	있지 아니하였다/않았다
	Honorific	있었습니다	있지 아니하였습니다/않았습니다
Future	Basic	있겠다, 있을 것이다/거다	있지 아니하겠다/않겠다, 있지 아니할 것입니다/않을 거다
	Honorific	있겠습니다, 있을 것입니다/겁니다	있지 아니하겠습니다/않겠습니다, 있지 아니할 것입니다/않을 겁니다

* 계시다

'계시다' is the honorific form of '있다', which means 'someone exists'. '계시다' acts as a predicate in a sentence in which the subject is older than the speaker or someone to be respected (e.g. grandfather, teacher, CEO, pastor). In other words, '계시다' cannot be used for ordinary people, animals, materials or plants.

Simply, '계시다' means '(respectable person) exists/is located (somewhere)'. The negative form of '계시다' is '계시지 아니하다/않다' or '안 계시다', but Koreans tend to use '없다' in spoken language.

The respectable subject must come with subject particle '-께서' instead of '-이/가'. Adverbial particle '-에' should come after the place in which the subject is located.

A: 선생님께서 댁에 계십니까? / Is the teacher at home?

B: 예, (선생님께서 댁에) 계십니다. / Yes, (he/she) is at home.

아니요, (선생님께서 댁에) 계시지 않습니다. / No, (he/she) isn't at home.

아니요, (선생님께서 댁에) 안 계십니다. / No, (he/she) isn't at home.

아니요, 없습니다. / No, (he/she) isn't.

The negative form, tense and honorifics of '계시다' are as follows.

계시다		Positive	Negative
Present	Basic	계시다	계시지 아니하다/않다
	Honorific	계십니다	계시지 아니합니다/않습니다
Past	Basic	계셨다	계시지 아니하였다/않았다
	Honorific	계셨습니다	계시지 아니하였습니다/않았습니다
Future	Basic	계시겠다, 계실 것이다/거다	계시지 아니하겠다/않겠다, 계시지 아니할 것입니다/않을 거다
	Honorific	계시겠습니다, 계실 것입니다/겁니다	계시지 아니하겠습니다/않겠습니다, 계시지 아니할 것입니다/않을 겁니다

10.5 Korean cultural aspects as reflected in adjectives

First, Koreans consider 청(靑) 'blue', 홍(紅) 'red', 흑(黑) 'black', 백(白) 'white', 황(黃) 'yellow' as the five basic colors and use them frequently in their idioms.

For example, in sports games, players are divided into 청군(靑軍) 'Blue Team' and 백군(白軍) 'White Team', who use blue and red symbols respectively. Players can also be divided into Black Team and White Team to compete against each other. Also, distinguishing right and wrong is also referred to as '흑백(黑白)을 가리자' 'distinguish black and white'.

Generally, Koreans put money gift for happy occasions and contribution for funeral expenses in white envelopes in belief that white symbolizes innocence and abstinence. Therefore, red or blue envelops should do a great disservice to the recipients. However, it is proper to be dressed in black suits and ties for funerals.

Second, colors can be used metaphorically.

새빨간 거짓말(a red lie) 'big lie'
빨갱이(the Red) 'dismiss communists'
싹이 노랗다(yellow sprouts) 'young people who seem to be absolutely
        hopeless'
속이 시커멓게 타다(the heart is burning black) 'to be very worried'
검은 속셈(black intentions) 'self-serving, wicked and heinous intentions'
까맣게 잊다(to forget in black) 'to forget completely'
시꺼멓게 멍들다(to get a black bruise) 'to get seriously bruised'
하얗게 몰려들다(to be crowded as white) 'to be crowded'
밤을 하얗게 지새우다(to spend white nights) 'to spend sleepless nights'

Third, Koreans express the five basic colors in a wide range of derivations, which all give a different feelings and tones. For instance, '붉다' have 31 derivatives as follows:

-갛다: 발갛다, 빨갛다, 벌겋다, 뻘겋다
-긋하다: 발긋하다, 빨긋하다, 벌긋하다, 뻘긋하다, 볼긋하다, 뽈긋하다,
        불긋하다, 뿔긋하다
-대대하다: 발그대대하다, 빨그대대하다
-댕댕하다: 발그댕댕하다, 빨그댕댕하다, 볼그댕댕하다
-그레하다: 발그레하다, 벌그레하다, 볼그레하다, 불그레하다
-그름하다: 발그름하다, 빨그름하다, 벌그름하다, 뻘그름하다, 볼그름하다,
        뽈그름하다, 불그름하다, 뿔그름하다
-그속속하다: 발그속속하다, 볼그속속하다

Fourth, taste terms can also be expressed metaphorically.

달게 먹었다(to eat sweetly) 'to enjoy one's meal'
단잠(a sweet sleep) 'a good night's sleep'
쓴맛을 보았다(to taste bitterness) 'to undergo serious hardships'
매운 성미(hot/spicy character) 'a notorious and irritable character'
매운 맛을 보여 주다(to give (someone) a hot taste) 'to give a serious
                      shock'
싱거운 말(bland words) 'joke'
싱거운 행동(bland behavior) 'clumsy behavior'
학점이 짜다(to give salty scores) 'to be onerous in giving scores'
월급이 짜다(salty salary) 'small salary'
수입이 짭짤하다(the wage is savory) 'to be well-paid'
눈꼴 시린 행동(eye-souring behavior) 'disturbing behavior'
떫은 표정(sour face) 'disgruntled face'

11 Copula

11.1 What is a copula?

The form of 'to be' in English changes very differently according to the person and tense such as 'am, are, is ; was, were'. However, an interesting fact is that there are two different verbs that has a meaning of 'to be' in Korean, such as 이다 'to be' and 있다(계시다) 'there is'. Unlike English, there is no change in the form according to the person, but they represent tense and honorific through morphological changes of ending.

The biggest feature of a **copula**(지정사) 이다 is that it does a wide variety of ending conjugation as a verb.

(책)이다 'to be'
(책)이-(stem) + -다(basic form, dictionary ending)
　　　　　　　-니?([interrogative] final ending)
　　　　　　　-면([condition] relation connective ending)
　　　　　　　-었-다([past] tense prefinal ending)
　　　　　　　-시-다([subject honorific] prefinal ending)
　　　　　　　-ㄴ(adnominal ending)
　　　　　　　-ㅁ(noun ending)

A copula can represent the sentence ending, connection, tense and aspect, and honorific through the use of ending words as above, and this is a proof that a copula 이다 falls under the categories of verbs.

Also 이다 is often called as copula or predicative particle, and it has the ability to make an substantive as the predicate by attaching it at the end of most of the substantives without any constraints. '학생이다' in the sentence below is a combined form of a noun '학생' with a copula 이다, and it works as a predicate in this sentence.

준서는 학생<u>이다</u>. / Jun-Seo **is** a student.

11.2 Types and characteristics of copula

There is only 이다 for copula, and it is being as an obstacle of setting up parts of speech, called a copula. In other words, is it necessary to set parts of speech, called copula for one word '이다'? However, because 이다 has a very different aspect from verbs or adjectives in grammatical and semantic aspects, setting up parts of speech, called 이다 is considered very convenient to explain it to the foreigner.

이다 has the following characteristics.

First, 이다 is used to indicate the characteristics, a state, identity, classes or a number of the target which subject instructs, and it has the ability to make an substantive into a predicate by attaching it at the end of an substantive with this meaning.

이것은 책<u>이다</u>. / It **is** a book.
이 사람이 바로 나의 친구<u>이다</u>. / This **is** just my friend.

독도는 누가 뭐래도 한국 땅<u>이다</u>.

Anyway, Dokdo island <u>is</u> Korean territory.

웅변은 은<u>이고</u>, 침묵은 금<u>이다</u>. / Speech <u>is</u> silver, silence <u>is</u> gold.

강의실 안이 엉망<u>이다</u>. / The whole classroom <u>is</u> in utter disorder.

그 사람은 매우 양심적<u>이다</u>.

He <u>is</u> a sort of conscientious person very much.

이번에 한국에 서울에 온 사람은 셋<u>이다</u>.

The person who came to seoul **are** three.

Second, it also indicates the aspect of behavior or state by being attached at the end of adverbs. And it indicates situation of the behavior or state by being attached at the end of connective endings such as '-어서, -고, -고서, -다가, -자마자, etc.'

그 사람의 골프 실력이 **제법**이다.(◁ 제법-이-다)

He is pretty useful at golf.

준서가 사고 현장에 도착한 것은 사고가 모두 수습되고 **나서**였다.
(◁ 나-아서-이-었-다)

Jun-Seo arrived on the accident scene after cleaning up accident.

민서를 처음 만난 것은 사회 봉사활동을 하**다가**였다.(◁ 하-다가-이-었-다)

I met Min-Seo first while doing social-minded activities.

Third, the negation of 이다 is '-이/가 아니다', and the types of tense and the types of honorific are as follows.

이다		Positive type	Negative type
Present	Plain form	이다	-이/가 아니다
	Honorific form	입니다	-이/가 아닙니다
Past	Plain form	이었다	-이/가 아니었다
	Honorific form	이었습니다	-이/가 아니었습니다

Future	Plain form	이겠다, 일 것이다/거다	-이/가 아니겠다, -이/가 아닐 것이다/거다
	Honorific form	이겠습니다, 일 것입니다/겁니다	-이/가 아니겠습니다, -이/가 아닐 것입니다/겁니다

Fourth, the '-다' is used as a declarative final ending.

준서는 한국 {사람이**다**/*사람인다} / Jun-Seo is a Korean.
이것은 {수박이**다**/*수박인다} / This is a watermelon.

Fifth, it cannot be used with an imperative sentence ending and a propositive sentence ending together.

*우리는 좋은 선생님이**자**. / Let's be a good teacher.
*너는 정직한 사람이**어라**. / Be an honest man.

Sixth, for the exclamatory endings '-도다, -로다' is used and for '-구나, -로구나' is used.

과연 진정한 한국인이**로다**. / Indeed, (he) is a true Korean.
아, 드디어 봄이**로구나**! / Ah, spring at last!

Seventh, for the connective endings '-어', '-라' is used, for '-어서', '-라서', for '-어도', '-라도' and for '-어야', '-라야' is used.

한국은 지금 8월이**라서** 매우 덥다.
It is very hot in Korea because it is August.
그가 아무리 똑똑한 학생이**라도** 이 문제는 풀 수 없을 것이다.
Even thought he is a smart student he cannot solve this problem.
그 사람이 내가 사랑하는 사람이**라야** 결혼을 하지.
I don't want to get married to him, because he is not a person I love.

Eighth, the '-ㄴ'[present], '-ㄹ'[future/prediction] are used as an adnominal ending.

현재 대학생<u>인</u> 사람은 누구예요? / Who is a university student now?
어제 생일이었<u>던</u> 분 없어요?
Isn't there anyone whose birthday was yesterday?
그 일을 할 사람이 꼭 한국 사람<u>일</u> 필요는 없다.
Someone who does that work doesn't need to be a Korean.
아마 그것이 정답<u>일</u> 거예요. / That's probably the answer.

Ninth, for the sentence ending '-어', '-야' is used at the end of vowels and '-이야' is used at the end of consonants.

여기가 청와대<u>야</u>. / This is the Blue House.
여자는 흔들리는 갈대<u>야</u>. / Woman is as fickle as a reed.
그 사람이 바로 범인<u>이야</u>. / He is the criminal.
나도 네 말에 찬성<u>이야</u>. / I agree with what you say.

Tenth, for the sentence ending '-어요', '-여요, -예요' is used at the end of vowels and '-이어요, -이에요' is used at the end of consonants.

이제 {가을<u>이어요</u>/가을<u>이에요</u>/*가을<u>이여요</u>/*가을<u>이예요</u>}
Finally it's fall.
제 아버지는 {군인<u>이어요</u>/군인<u>이에요</u>/*군인<u>이여요</u>/*군인<u>이예요</u>}
My father is a soldier.
준서는 제 {*친구<u>이어요</u>/*친구<u>이에요</u>/친구<u>여요</u>/친구<u>예요</u>}
Jun-Seo is my friend.
그 사람은 {*의사<u>이어요</u>/*의사<u>이에요</u>/의사<u>여요</u>/의사<u>예요</u>}
He is a doctor.

Multiple views on 이다

First, view as a predicate particle

This attached great importance to the conjugation and the use of using 이다 mainly at the end of substantives. However, a case is a concept that generally indicates grammatical relationship between the predicate and the preceding noun phrases, and since the term, the predicate particle, becomes a predicate particle by adding 이다 to the noun itself. It does not match the above concept. Also, in terms of form, a particle is a word that does not change forms, and because the form changes by using 이다, there is difficulty of admitting only 이다 as an exception. However, 이다 is regarded as a predicate particle in the current school grammar.

Second, view as a suffix

이다 is viewed as a suffix such as '-답다' 'to be like, be worthy of, be becoming to' or '-스럽다' 'to be like, look like, seem'. However, the preceding components of suffix are generally used very limitedly, but 이다 can be attached to almost every substantive without any constraints. And this is a proof that 이다 is not just a simple derivational affix. Besides, how 이다 cannot take any modification of degree adverbs represents that 이다 is not a derivational suffix.

그는 {매우/무척/아주} 한국인답다.
He is (very) worthy of a Korean.
*그는 {매우/무척/아주} 한국인이다.
He is a (very) Korean.

Third, view as a copula

This put stress on how 이다 works as a predicate and how it is different from verbs or adjectives syntactically and semantically. However, since a particle cannot be used in front of 이다, how it is always used by being attached to the previous word, and how palatalization is made as in 끝-이다→[끄치다] 'to stop, cease, end', 밑-이다→[미치다] 'to reach' it is actually difficult to call it as a copula.

11.3 Differences of grammatical characteristics among verb, adjective and copula

A verb, adjective and copula work as a predicate in a sentence, and they are very similar in terms of conjugation. However, the ending forms at the end are different in few aspects.

① Verbs can be combined with present tense prefinal ending '-ㄴ/는-', but adjectives cannot be combined.

먹다 'to eat' → 먹는다
웃다 'to laugh' → 웃는다
가다 'to go' → 간다
오다 'to come' → 온다
공부하다 'to study' → 공부한다

작다 'to be small' → *작는다
높다 'to be high' → *높는다
좋다 'to be good' → *좋는다
예쁘다 'to be pretty' → *예쁜다
부지런하다 'to be diligent' → *부지런한다

Also, '-ㄴ/는-' cannot be combined with 이다 and 있다, but they can be combined with 계시다. In this sense, 이다 and 있다 are similar to the adjectives, and 계시다 is similar to the verbs.

(책)이다 → *(책)이는다/*인다
있다 → *있는다
계시다 → 계신다

② Verbs can be combined with imperative ending '-아/어라' and propositive ending '-자', but adjectives cannot be combined.

먹다 'to eat' → 먹**어라**/먹**자**
웃다 'to laugh' → 웃**어라**/웃**자**
나누다 'to divide' → 나누**어라**/나누**자**
공부하다 'to study' → 공부**해라**/공부하**자**

작다 'to be small' → *작**아라**/*작**자**
좋다 'to be good' → *좋**아라**/*좋**자**
예쁘다 'to be pretty' → *예**뻐라**/*예쁘**자**

Also, '-아/어라' and '-자' cannot be combined with 이다 and 계시다, but they can be combined with 있다. In this sense, 이다 and 계시다 are similar to the adjectives, and 있다 is similar to the verbs.

(책)이다 → *(책)이**어라**/*이**자**
있다 → 있**어라**/있**자**
계시다 → *계**셔라**/*계시**자**

However, the reason imperative ending '-아/어라' and propositive ending '-자' cannot be combined with 계시다 is because of semantic constraint not morphological constraints. It is because, since the subject of 계시다 has to be a person of older age or respectable person than the speaker, a speaker cannot make a low non-honorific style command to such person. Therefore, forms such as '계십시오' and '계십시다' are made by adding a high honorific style imperative ending '-(으)십시오' and a propositive ending '-(으)십시다'.

③ Verbs can be combined with connective ending '-(으)려고' which means intention, but adjectives cannot be combined.

먹다 'to eat' → 먹<u>으려고</u>
웃다 'to laugh' → 웃<u>으려고</u>
가다 'to go' → 가<u>려고</u>
오다 'to come' → 오<u>려고</u>
공부하다 'to study' → 공부하<u>려고</u>

작다 'to be small' → *작<u>으려고</u>
높다 'to be high' → *높<u>으려고</u>
좋다 'to be good' → *좋<u>으려고</u>
예쁘다 'to be pretty' → *예쁘<u>려고</u>

Also, '-(으)려고' cannot be combined with 이다, but they can be combined with 있다 and 계시다. In this sense, 이다 is similar to the adjectives, and 있다 and 계시다 are similar to the verbs.

(사람)이다 → *(사람)이<u>려고</u>
있다 → 있<u>으려고</u>
계시다 → 계시<u>려고</u>

④ Verbs can be combined with '-고 있다' or '-는 중이다' which means 'progress', but adjectives cannot be combined.

먹다 'to eat' → 먹<u>고 있다</u>/먹<u>는 중이다</u>
웃다 'to laugh' → 웃<u>고 있다</u>/웃<u>는 중이다</u>
오다 'to come' → 오<u>고 있다</u>/오<u>는 중이다</u>
공부하다 'to study' → 공부하<u>고 있다</u>/공부하<u>는 중이다</u>

작다 'to be small' → *작<u>고 있다</u>/*작<u>는 중이다</u>
좋다 'to be good' → *좋<u>고 있다</u>/*좋<u>는 중이다</u>
예쁘다 'to be pretty' → *예쁘<u>고 있다</u>/*예쁘<u>는 중이다</u>

Also, '-고 있다' cannot be combined with '이다, 있다, 계시다'. However, '-는 중이다' can be combined with 계시다.

(사람)이다 → *(사람)이고 있다/*(사람)이는 중이다
있다 → *있고 있다/*있는 중이다
계시다 → *계시고 있다/계시는 중이다

⑤ Verbs can be combined with exclamatory ending '-는구나', adjective can be combined with '-구나', not vice versa.

먹다 'to eat' → 먹는구나/*먹구나
웃다 'to laugh' → 웃는구나/*웃구나
가다 'to go' → 가는구나/*가구나
나누다 'to divide' → 나누는구나/*나누구나
공부하다 'to study' → 공부하는구나/*하구나

작다 'to be small' → *작는구나/작구나
좋다 'to be good' → *좋는구나/좋구나
예쁘다 'to be pretty' → *예쁘는구나/예쁘구나

Also, '-는구나' cannot be combined with '이다, 있다', but they can be combined with 계시다. In this sense, '이다, 있다' are similar to the adjectives, and 계시다 is similar to the verbs.

(사람)이다 → *(사람)이는구나/이구나
있다 → *있는구나/있구나
계시다 → 계시는구나/*계시구나

⑥ Present tense adnominal ending '-는' can be combined with verbs, '-(으)ㄴ' can be combined with adjectives, not vice versa.

서울에 가는 사람 'people going to Seoul'
한국말을 잘하는 사람 'people speaking Korean fluently'
한국 김치를 잘 먹는 존 'John who eats Korean Kimchi well'
기쁜/*기쁘는 날 'a happy day'
깨끗한/*깨끗하는 옷 'a clean cloth'
키가 작은/*작는 민서 'short Min-Seo'

Also, '-ㄴ' cannot be combined with 이다, but '-는' can be combined with 있다 and 계시다. In this sense, 이다 is similar to the adjectives, and 있다 and 계시다 are similar to the verbs.

미국 국민인 마이클 'American Michael'
흥미가 있는 일 'a fascinating work'
고향에 계시는 부모님 'my parents in my hometown'

However, because adjectives change into verbs when '-아/어지다' is combined, '-ㄴ/-는, -아/어라, -자, -(으)려고, -고 있다, -는 중이다, -는구나' can be attached at the end.

작아지다 'to become smaller': 작아진다, 작아져라, 작아지자, 작아지려고, 작아지고 있다, 작아지는 중이다, 작아지는 구나

11.4 Korean cultural aspects as reflected in copula

First, no matter how 이다 is named, 이다 in Korean has very different characteristics from English or Japanese. In other words, 'be' verbs in English have meanings of 이다 'to be', 되다 'to become', 있다/존재하다 'to exist' as below.

He **is** such a bright boy. / 그는 머리가 참 좋은 **아이예요**.

She **will be** great writer. / 그녀는 위대한 작가가 **될 거예요**.

Tyrants **have been**, and **are**. / 폭군은 지금까지 **있었고**, 현재에도 **있다**.

Unlike it, 이다 is used in Korean when specifying something, and when expressing presence, 있다 is used to express these two concepts differently. This shows that it is clearly distinguishing the concept of 이다 ↔ 아니다 that represents facts from a concept of 있다 ↔ 없다 which represents the existence of people or things.

In Japanese, です(desu) is used to specify things, and ある(aru) and いる(iru) to represent existence. Specially, as いる(iru) is used when the subject is a living thing, such as a person or animal, and ある(aru) is used for lifeless things, it shows that it is subdividing the existents more. Of course, their negative words, いません(imasen) and ありません (arimasen), are different from each other.

ここは 私の 學校**です**.

여기는 저의 학교**입니다**.

This is my school.

教員室に 韓國語の 先生が **います**.

교무실에 한국어 선생님이 **있습니다**.

The Korean teacher is in the teacher's room.

わたいの うちの にわには うさぎが **います**.

우리집 정원에 토끼가 **있습니다**.

There is a rabbit in my garden.

ここに 新聞が **あります**.

여기에 신문이 **있습니다**.

Here is a newspaper.

Second, Koreans use verbs or adjectives as the predicate of a sentence more frequently than 'substantive + 이다'. It is because, if 'substantive + 이다' is used as the predicate, a sentence not only becomes a written language, but it is also because it is difficult for the speaker to express his own thoughts or feelings.

[?]오늘 날씨는 대단히 **맑음이다**.
→ 오늘 날씨는 대단히 **맑다**.
It's very sunny today.

며칠 동안 불법 폭력 시위가 계속 되었음은 **물론이다**.
→ 물론 며칠 동안 불법적인 폭력 시위가 **계속되었다**.
Of course, illegal violent protest continued for several days.

대단히 실망스러운 것은 준서가 보여준 비상식적인 언행 **때문이다**.
→ 준서가 보여준 비상식적인 언행 때문에 대단히 **실망스러웠다**.
I was so disappointed about Jun-Seo's preposterous speech and behavior.

12 Adnominal

12.1 What is an adnominal?

Adnominal(관형사) qualifies nouns, pronouns and numerals to clarify their meaning. Adnominals always come before the word they qualify.

나는 어제 **새 옷**을 샀다. / I bought **new clothes** yesterday.

Adnominals do not change their form and no particles can be affixed to adnominals. Adnominals are not an essential component of a sentence, since sentences can be formed without adnominals. There are three types of adnominals: characteristic, indicative and numeric adnominals.

12.2 Types and characteristics of adnominals

12.2.1 Characteristic adnominals

Characteristic adnominals(성상관형사) represent properties or state of the following noun or pronoun. They are divided into native Korean adnominals and Sino-Korean adnominals.

- Native adnominals:

새 책 'new book'   갖은 양념 'various condiments'
헌 양말 'old socks'   외딴 섬 'isolated island'
옛 이야기 'old stories'   웬 떡 'unexpected rice cake'
온갖 정성 'all one's hearts'   맨 꼴찌 'the very last'
온 세상 'the whole world'   헛 걸음 'vain step: a trip for nothing'

- Sino-Korean adnominals:

순(純) 거짓말 'a complete lie'
구(舊) 시청 건물 'the old City Hall premise'
고(故) 박정희 대통령 'deceased former president Jeong-Hee Park'
성(聖) 베드로 'St. Peter'

12.2.2 Indicative adnominals

Indicative adnominals(지시관형사) indicate an object or situation outside the sentence. They are divided into native Korean adnominals and Sino-Korean adnominals.

- **Native adnominals**: 이, 그, 저 ; 이런, 그런, 저런 ; 어떤, 어느 ; 아무
이 'this' and 이런 'this, this kind of' indicate something close to the speaker.

이/이런 사람 'this/this kind of person'
이/이런 고양이 'this/this kind of cat'

이/이런 책 'this/this kind of book'
이/이런 옷 'these/these kinds of clothes'
이/이런 시계 'this/this kind of clock'

그 'that' and 그런 'like that/that sort of' indicate something close to the listener.

그/그런 학생 'that/that kind of student'
그/그런 호랑이 'that/that kind of tiger'
그/그런 책상 'that/that kind of desk'
그/그런 양말 'that/that kind of socks'
그/그런 구두 'that/that kind of shoes'

저 'over there' and 저런 'like that over there' indicate something far from both the speaker and listener.

저/저런 남자 'the man over there/like that over there'
저/저런 사자 'the tiger over there/like that over there'
저/저런 연필 'the pencil over there/like that over there'
저/저런 넥타이 'the necktie over there/like that over there'
저/저런 안경 'the glasses over there/like those over there'

Also, 어떤 'a certain/some', 어느 'one/unnamed' are used if the speaker indicates something, but the speaker does not want to specify one out of something.

어떤 선생님 'some teacher'   어떤 바지 'some trousers'
어떤 동물 'some animal'   어떤 목걸이 'some necklace'
어떤 연필 'some pencil'

어느 것 'something'   어느 고래 'some whale'

어느 걸상 'some chair'   어느 장갑 'some gloves'
어느 반지 'some ring'

'아무' is used when the speaker is not indicating anything.

아무 것 'anything'   아무 개 'any dog'
아무 지우개 'any rubbers'   아무 모자 'any hat'
아무 팔찌 'any bracelets'

● **Sino-Korean adnominals**: 귀(貴) 'your', 모(某) 'some/any', 본(本) 'this', 전(前) 'former', 현(現) 'current/incumbent'

<u>귀</u>(貴) 회사 'your company'
<u>모</u>(某) 월 'some month'
<u>본</u>(本) 건물 'this building'
<u>전</u>(前) 서울 시장 'former mayor of Seoul'
<u>현</u>(現) 세대 'current generation'

12.2.3 Numeric adnominals

Numeric adnominals(수관형사) indicate the quantity of an object. They are always accompanied with a unit of measurement.

● **Native adnominals**: Adnominals for whole numbers are as follows.

한 'one'   두 'two'
세/석/서 'three'   네/넉/너 'four'
다섯/닷 'five'   여섯/엿 'six'
일곱 'seven'   여덟 'eight'
아홉 'nine'   열 'ten'

열한 'eleven'   열두 'twelve'
열세/열석/열서 'thirteen'   열네/열넉/열너 'fourteen'
스무 'twenty'

Adnominals for rough numbers are as follows.

한두 'one or two'   두세 'two or three'
두서너 'two to four'   서너 'three to four'
서너너덧 'three to five'   너덧 'four to five'
댓 'around five'   대여섯 'five to six'
예닐곱 'six to seven'   일여덟 'seven to eight'
여남은 'around ten or over ten' 여러 'several'
모든 'all'   온 'all'
온갖 'all, all kinds of'   갖은 'all sorts of'

In particular, '세, 네' is changed into '석, 넉' to qualify 장(張) 'a sheet' and into '서, 너' to qualify 말(斗) 'Korean unit of measurement for volume'.

- **Sino-Korean adnominals**: 전(全) 선수 'all contestants', 제(諸) 명령 'all orders'

12.3 Order and omission of adnominals

In Korean, several adnominals can be used in a single sentence, and they all serve to qualify the following noun. In other words, the characteristic adnominal 새 'new' qualifies 책 'book', and indicative adnominal 저 'that' qualifies 새 책 'new book'.

- Indicative adnominals generally come before characteristic adnominals.

저 새 책이 나의 책이다. / That new book is my book.

이 <u>외딴</u> 마을이 나의 고향이다. / This remote village is my hometown.

- Indicative adnominals come before numeric adnominals.

이 <u>온</u> 세상에 사랑이 가득하길 기원하자.
Let's hope that this whole world will be filled with love.
저 <u>모든</u> 것이 소떼들이다. / Those all things are a herd of cows.

- Indicative adnominals come before numeric adnominals, and numeric adnominals before characteristic adnominals.

저 <u>온갖 새</u> 건물을 지난해에 지었다.
Those all buildings were built last year.
이 <u>모든 헌</u> 책은 준서의 것이다. / These all old books are Jun-Seo's.

Adnominals are not an essential component of a sentence. However, adnominals must not be omitted if they come with certain dependent nouns as follows:

- If adnominals are used in conjunction with formal dependent noun '것' and '때문'

태풍이 지나가고 나자 {<u>아무</u>/<u>*Ø</u>} <u>것</u>도 남은 게 없었다.
There was nothing left after the hurricane.
{<u>그</u>/<u>*Ø</u>} <u>때문</u>에 많은 사람들이 행복을 느꼈다.
Many felt happy because of him.

- If adnominals are used in conjunction with unit dependent nouns

나는 강아지 {<u>한</u>/<u>*Ø</u>} <u>마리</u>를 샀다. / I bought a puppy.

차 {한/*Ø} 잔 할까요? / Shall we have a cup of tea?

{여러/*Ø} 송이의 장미꽃이 피었다. / Several roses have bloomed.

준서는 대구에서 서울로 가는데 {두/*Ø} 시간밖에 안 걸렸다.

It took only two hours for Jun-Seo to get to Seoul from Daegu.

■ Position of modifiers and meaning of sentences

Adnominals, which act as a modifier, delineate the meaning of the following noun. However, it will be difficult to do so if adnominals are placed too far from the noun.

최근 뜻있는 이 정부의 보수적 분위기는 사람들을 실망시키고 있다.
Recently, the conservative posture of the government under a meaningful cause is disappointing many people.
→ 이 정부의 보수적 최근 분위기는 뜻있는 사람들을 실망시키고 있다.
Recently, the conservative posture of the current administration is disappointing those with a meaningful cause.

아름다웠던 우리 고향 사람들이 살았던 마을이 수몰되어 버렸다.
The village in which our beautiful home folks had lived was submerged.
→ 우리 고향 사람들이 살았던 아름다웠던 마을이 수몰되어 버렸다.
The beautiful village in which my home folks lived was submerged.

그 연속극은 대부분의 주부와 남편들에게 불쾌감을 안겨 주었다.
The soap opera displeased a majority of housewives and husbands.
→ 그 연속극은 대부분의 주부와, 남편들에게 불쾌감을 안겨 주었다.
The soap opera displeased a majority of housewives, as well as husbands.
→ 그 연속극은 대부분의 주부와 대부분의 남편들에게 불쾌감을 안겨 주었다.
The soap opera displeased a majority of housewives and a majority of husbands.

어서 완전 서비스 공짜폰 받아 가세요.
Come and get this free cellphone with complete service.
→ 서비스로 주는 완전 공짜폰 어서 받아 가세요.
Come and get this completely free cellphone.

12.4 Making an adnominal phrase

A word class can be changed into a word that has the same function as an adnominal, which is called adnominal phrase. Therefore, these adnominal phrases maintain the characteristics of their original word class, and they simply function as an adnominal.

- **Adnominal particle '-의'** is for nouns, pronouns and numerals

저 책이 바로 **민서의** 책이다. / That book is Min-Seo's book.
그의 얼굴은 늘 밝았다. / His face was always bright.
요즈음 **둘의** 관계가 어떤지 모르겠다.
I don't know how the two are getting on these days.

Koreans tend to skip '-의' from 'noun + -의', particularly in spoken language.

{제주**의**/제주**Ø**} 귤이 가장 맛이 좋다. / Jeju tangerines are the best.
이것은 {준서**의**/준서**Ø**} 옷이다. / These are Jun-Seo's clothes.

Sometimes, the use of adnominal particle '-의' can make a very awkward or ambiguous sentence. It is better to leave out '-의' in such sentences.

{[?]외국**의**/외국**Ø**} 사람을 만나면, 항상 한국말로 얘기를 하세요.
Always talk in Korean if you meet foreigners.
{[?]대문**의**/대문**Ø**} 앞에 {[?]고향**의**/고향**Ø**} 친구가 와 있다.
Your friend from hometown is in front of the door.

- **Adnominal ending '-(으)ㄴ, -는, -(으)ㄹ'** come after verbs, adjectives, 있다, 이다, etc.

'Verb + adnominal ending ‑(으)ㄴ' refers to things of the past, 'verb + adnominal ending ‑는' to the present and 'verb + ‑(으)ㄹ' to the future.

> 먹다 'to eat' → 먹은 'ate', 먹는 'eating', 먹을 'to eat'
> 잡다 'to catch' → 잡은 'caught', 잡는 'catching', 잡을 'to catch'
> 가다 'to go' → 간 'gone', 가는 'going', 갈 'to go'

Since **adjectives** do not represent the tense, use '‑은' if the stem of the adjective ends in a consonant and '‑ㄴ' if the stem ends in a vowel.

> 작다 'to be small' → 작은
> 싫다 'to dislike' → 싫은
> 희다 'to be white' → 흰
> 크다 'to be big' → 큰

있다 'to be' represents the present tense with '‑는', the future tense with '‑을' and the past tense with '‑었던'. '‑었던' is the combination of '‑었' (prefinal ending in the past tense), '‑더‑' (prefinal ending used to convey reminiscence), '‑ㄴ' (adnominal ending).

이다 'to be' represents the present tense with '‑ㄴ', the future tense with '‑ㄹ' and the past tense with '‑었던'.

> (한국 사람)이다 / 'Someone is Korean'
> → (한국 사람)인 준서 / 'Jun-Seo who is Korean'
>
> (주인)이다 / 'Someone is the owner'
> → (주인)일 (것 같다) / 'I think someone will be the owner'
>
> (곰)이었던 여자 / 'a girl who used to be a bear'

12.5 Korean cultural aspects as reflected in adnominals

First, Koreans use '이, 그, 저' to indicate something, but 요 'this', 고 'that', 조 'over there' ; '요런, 고런, 조런' to signify cute, little children or people they look down on.

요 놈 봐라, 제법이네.
Look at him/her, she/he is better than expected.
고 애 참 똑똑해. 아직 두 살도 안 된 애가 벌써 한글을 읽을 줄 알아.
That kid is so smart. He is not even two years old but he can read Hangul.
조 녀석 대단하네, 어린 애가 피아노를 저렇게 잘 쳐?
That kid is so great. How can a little child play the piano so well?

Second, if adnominal phrases are used in conjunction with dependent nouns that are units of measurements, the 'adnominal + dependent noun' should come after the noun at issue.

나는 어제 **한 마리의** 강아지를 샀다. / I bought a puppy yesterday.
→ 나는 어제 **강아지 한 마리**를 샀다. / I bought a puppy yesterday.

한 잔의 커피를 마시자. / Let's drink a cup of coffee.
→ **커피 한 잔**을 마시자. / Let's drink a cup of coffee.

Third, adnominals can be used in sequence in a sentence, but it is very unnatural for Koreans to do use two or more adnominals in sequence: in such a case, adnominals should be changed into an adnominal clause or adverb.

저 온갖 새 건물을 지난해에 지었다.
All those new buildings were built last year.
→ 저기 있는 새 건물은 **모두** 지난해에 지었다.

Those new buildings were all built last year.

이 모든 헌 책은 준서의 것이다. / These all old books are Jun-Seo's.
→ 이 헌 책은 모두 준서의 것이다. / All these old books are Jun-Seo's.

Fourth, adnominal particle '-의' is spoken as [에] to facilitate the pronunciation.

저 책이 바로 민서의[민서에] 책이다. / That book is Min-Seo's book.
그의[그에] 얼굴은 늘 밝았다. / His face was always bright.
요즈음 둘의[둘에] 관계가 어떤지 모르겠다.
I don't know how the two are getting on these days.

13 Adverb

13.1 What is an adverb?

Adverb(부사) modifies verbs, adjectives and other adverb to clarify their meaning. Adverbs always come before the word they qualify.

준서는 민서를 **매우 사랑한다**. / Jun-Seo loves Min-Seo very much.

Adverbs do not change their form. Auxiliary particles can be affixed to adverbs but case particles cannot be affixed to them. Adverbs are not an essential component of a sentence, since sentences can be formed without adverbs. Adverbs can be classified into component adverbs and sentential adverbs depending on modifying range.

13.2 Types and characteristics of adverbs

13.2.1 Component adverbs

Component adverbs(성분부사) modify components in a sentence such as adjectives, verbs, other adverbs, adnominals and particular substantives.

They are divided into characteristic adverbs, time adverbs, indicative adverbs, negative adverbs and onomatopoeia · mimetic adverbs according to meaning.

● Characteristic adverbs

Characteristic adverbs(성상부사) represent properties or state of the predicate. They indicate generally degree, frequency, modality.

For degree: 가장 'most', 매우 'very', 정말 'really', 대단히 'very', 아주 'very', 실컷 'to one's heart's contest', 상당히 'fairly', 한참 'for a time', 한결 'conspicuously', 퍽 'very much', 꽤 'quite', 잘 'well', 많이 'aplenty', 적당히 'properly', 제법 'fairly', 좀 'kindly', 조금 'a little', 약간 'a few', 겨우 'barely', 전혀 'entirely', 훨씬 'by far', etc.

modifying predicates

잘 간다 'go well'   가장 높다 'be the highest'
매우 잘한다 'do very well'   실컷 먹었다 'ate to excess'
한결 가볍다 'be much lighter'   좀 잡으세요 'kindly hold the door'
전혀 없다 'there is nothing'

modifying adverbs

가장 천천히 'most slowly'   아주 빨리 'very fast'
훨씬 더 높이 난다 'fly much higher'

modifying nouns

바로 위 'just above'   겨우 이틀 'only two days'
아주 겁쟁이 'altogether a coward'

modifying adnominals

<u>매우</u> 새 차 'very new car'   <u>아주</u> 헌 옷 'very old clothes'

For **frequency**: 자주 'often', 가끔 'sometimes', 때때로 'sometimes', 종종 'occasionally', 매일 'every day', 매년 'every year', etc.

<u>자주</u> 온다 'often come'
<u>가끔</u> 간다 'sometimes go'
<u>때때로</u> 음악을 듣는다 'sometimes listen to music'
<u>매일</u> 기도한다 'pray every day'

For **comparison**: 더 'more', 덜 'less', etc.

민서가 준서보다 키가 <u>더</u> 크다. Min-Seo is taller than Jun-Seo.
토끼가 사슴보다 <u>덜</u> 무겁다. A rabbit is less scary than a deer.

For **modality**: 천천히 'slowly', 밝히 'brightly', 분명히 'clearly', 따뜻이 'warmly', 슬피 'sadly', 즐거이 'pleasantly', 쓸쓸히 'lonely', 바로 'exactly, straight, at once', 모두 'all', 멀리 'far', 홀로 'alone', 함께 'together', etc.

<u>천천히</u> 걸었다 'walked slowly'
<u>따뜻이</u> 안아 준다 'hug someone warmly'
<u>모두</u> 모였다 'everyone was assembled'
<u>멀리</u> 떠났다 'left far away'
<u>홀로</u> 살아간다 'live alone'
<u>함께</u> 노래한다 'sing together'
<u>바로</u> 그 장소 'the exact spot'

- Indicative adverbs

Indicative adverbs(지시부사) indicate specific time, place or some word which was in the sentence.

For **time**: 일찍 'early', 일찍이 'early', 늦게 'late', 접때 'not long time ago', 장차 'in the future', 아까 'a while ago', 곧 'at once', 줄곧 'continuously', 이미 'already', 아직 'still', 문득 'suddenly', 앞서 'before', 난데없이 'suddenly', 갑자기 'suddenly', 늘 'always', 만날 'always', 잠깐 'short time', 오늘 'today', 내일 'tomorrow', 모레 'the day after tomorrow', etc.

일찍 일어난다 'get up early'
아까 뭐랬니? 'What did you say a while ago?'
아직 서울에 있다 'be still in Seoul'
접때 만났던 사람 'the person who met a few days ago'
늘 상냥하다 'be always friendly'
잠깐 들러 주겠니? 'Would you like to drop in for a while?'

Sometimes time adverbs 오늘 'today', 내일 'tomorrow', 모레 'the day after tomorrow' are used both adverb and noun.

'내일' in '민서야, 우리 **내일** 만나자'. 'Min-Seo, Let's meet tomorrow'. is an adverb, and it does not have a particular effect on grammaticality of sentence when it is omitted. '내일' in '**내일**은 바로 우리의 결혼기념일이다'. 'It is our wedding anniversary tomorrow'. is a noun, and plays a role of the subject, therefore if it is omitted, the sentence becomes ungrammatical and very awkward.

For **place**: 이리 'this way', 그리 'that way', 저리 'that way', 요리 'this way', 고리 'that way', 조리 'that way', 여기 'here', 거기 'there', 저기 'over there', 어디 'where', etc.

For manner of action: 이렇게 'like this' → 이리 'in this way', 그렇게 'like that' → 그리 'in that way', 저렇게 'like that' → 저리 'in that way', etc.

<u>이리</u> 오세요. 'Come here'.
<u>저리</u> 가거라. 'Get away'.
어떻게 {<u>이렇게/이리</u>} 좋을까? 'How good it is?'
{<u>저렇게/저리</u>} 하면 곤란하다. 'It is difficult to do so'.

Sometimes place adverbs '여기, 거기, 저기' are used both adverb and pronoun.

'여기' in '<u>여기</u>에다 놓아라'. 'Put it here'. is an indicative pronoun, and particle '-에다' is attached to it. However, '여기' in '민서가 또 <u>여기</u> 올 수 있을까?' 'Can Min-Seo come here again?' is an indicative adverb, and there is no difference on grammaticality particularly.

● Negative adverbs

Negative adverbs(부정부사) are used for negating the meaning of verb, adjective and copula. In the case of verb, '아니' is used when denies with subject's assertive intention. Abbreviation of '아니' is '안', and '안' is mainly used in spoken language. And when denied regardless of speaker's intention because situation is not good, '못' is used for negation.

{안/못} 먹겠다. 'I {will not/can not} eat'.
너는 {안/못} 뛰겠니? '{Don't/Can't} you run?'
{안/*못} 가려고 한다. 'I {am not/can not} going'.
{안/못} 오도록 해라. '{Don't try to/Don't} come'.

Connective endings such as '-(으)려고, -고자, -(으)러' cannot be used with '못' which expresses situation negation, because they express assertive intention of subject. And '안' and '못' are used as the forms of auxiliary inflectional word '-지 않다, -지 못하다'.

In the case of adjective, only '안' can be used. Because circumstantial judgement that adjective is has nothing to become subjective judgement according to will of subject ultimately.

{안/*못} 예쁘다 'be not pretty'
{안/*못} 높다 'be not high'
{안/*못} 싫다 'do not hate'
{안/*못} 달다 'be not sweet'

● Symbolic adverbs(상징부사)

Mimetics are words that imitate movement of person, animal and things, and onomatopoeia are words that imitate sound of them.

Typical **mimetic words**(의태어) are as follows:

깡충깡충 'hippity-hoppity'	살금살금 'secretly'
성큼성큼 'stride'	사뿐사뿐 'lightly'
데굴데굴 'rolling continuously'	올통볼통 'uneven'
구불텅구불텅 'meanderingly'	흥청망청 'in profusion'
아장아장 'toddlingly'	올망졸망 'in lots of small units'
살랑살랑 'gently'	알쏭달쏭 'motley'
느릿느릿 'slowly'	파릇파릇 'freshly green'
생긋생긋 'sweetly'	울긋불긋 'colorfully'
티격태격 'wranglingly'	들썩들썩 'restlessly'
푸석푸석 'crumbly'	빤질빤질 'sleekly'
오싹오싹 'shiveringly'	

Typical **onomatopoeic words**(의성어) are as follows:

졸졸 'murmuring'	철썩철썩 'splashing'
덜컹덜컹 'brattle'	땡땡 'ding-dong'
둥둥 'boom-boom'	빵빵 'honk'
붕붕 'buzzing'	퐁당퐁당 'plop, plop'
따르릉따르릉 'ting-a-ling'	뽀글뽀글 'boiling'
껄껄 'haha'	빠지직빠지직 'sputteringly'
꼬르륵꼬르륵 'gurgle'	후루룩후루룩 'flap-flap'
쾅쾅 'rat a tat'	뽀도독뽀도독 'with a grating sound'
찌직찌직 'crackle'	짹짹 'twee'
호호호 'ho-ho'	

13.2.2 Sentential adverbs

Sentential adverbs(문장부사) modify not a particular component in a sentence, but whole sentence. They are classified into modal adverbs and conjunctive adverbs.

- Modal adverbs

Modal adverbs(화식부사) are used for expressing attitude of the speaker about sentence.

제발 'please'	설마 'surely'
아마 'probably'	과연 'indeed'
결코 'never'	모름지기 'by all means'
바야흐로 'about to'	부디 'by all means'
하물며 'much more'	도리어 'on the contrary'
정녕(코) 'surely'	응당 'for sure'
다행히 'fortunately'	확실히 'certainly'

분명히 'clearly'   특히 'specially'
만약 'if'   말하자면 'so to speak'
왜냐하면 'because'   아무쪼록 'as much as one can'
별안간 'in the twinkling of an eye'

- Conjunctive adverbs

Conjunctive adverbs(접속부사) are used for connecting word and word, sentence and sentence or paragraph and paragraph.

Adverbs for connecting word and word are 혹은 'or', 또는 'or', and 그리고 'and', etc. And adverbs for connecting sentence and sentence are, classifying depending on semantic function in detail are as follows:

supplement · addition(보충 · 첨가)
  더구나 'in addition'   또 'and'
  게다가 'what is more'   더욱이 'moreover'

contrast · conflict(대조 · 대립)
  그러나 'but'   하지만 'but'
  그렇지만 'but'   아니면 'either...or'

switch topic(화제전환)
  그런데 'by the way'   한편 'one side'

example · figure of speech(예시 · 비유)
  예컨대 'for instance'   말하자면 'so to speak'
  이를테면 'as it were'   즉 'namely'
  곧 'that is to say'

cause · result(원인 · 결과)

그러므로 'so'   따라서 'accordingly'

그러니(까) 'so'   그러자 'and then'

그제야 'only then'

Adverbs for connecting sentence and sentence are 따라서 'therefore', 요컨대 'in short', 요약하면 'to sum up', 결론적으로 'in its final analysis', etc.

13.3 Order and omission of adverbs

In Korean, several component adverbs can be used in a single sentence, indicative adverbs generally come before characteristic adverbs, and characteristic adverbs come before negative adverbs.

일찍 잘 왔다. / You did well to come early.

독수리가 그리도 높이 나니? / Does an eagle fly so high?

차가 잘 안 간다. / The car does not go well.

지난번보다 훨씬 못 뛰었다. / I ran much worse than the last.

In the case of sentential adverbs, conjunctive adverbs come before modal adverbs. Of course, sentential adverbs come before component adverbs.

그러나 제발 좀 도와주세요. / However, could you help me?

이를테면 바야흐로 봄이 제대로 왔다고 할 수 있다.

Spring is really here, so to speak.

그리고 부디 건강하게 잘 생활하기 바란다.

And I wish you a healthy life.

If a component adverb used in the middle of sentence move in front of the sentence, and put comma in the back, the meaning of adverb is emphasized.

오늘은 온 가족이 **모처럼** 모여서 함께 외식을 했다.
→ **모처럼**, 오늘은 온 가족이 모여서 함께 외식을 했다.
Today my whole family got together and ate out for a long time.

그녀는 그렇게 큰 교통사고에서도 **다행히** 다치지 않았다.
→ **다행히**, 그녀는 그렇게 큰 교통사고에서도 다치지 않았다.
Fortunately she wasn't hurt in such a big accident.

▪ Co-occurrence of adverbial phrase

Co-occurrence refers to the limited usage that a particular word comes after another particular word in a sentence. In Korean there are many adverbs like it.

● Adverbs co-occurred with predicates which mean negation
나는 오늘은 **별로** 할일이 {**없다**/*있다} / Today I have very little to do.
그 사람은 **결코** 그녀를 {미워하**지 않겠다**/*미워하겠다} / He will never hate her.
준서는 **전혀** 거짓말을 한 적이 {**없다**/*있다} / Jun-Seo never told a lie.
나는 **차마** 그 아이의 얼굴을 쳐다볼 수 {**없었다**/*있었다}
I could not bear the sight of the child.
그 사람을 **일절** 이곳에 {들어오**지 못하게**/*들어오게} 했다.
I never let him come in here.
그가 **기껏** 가 봐야 멀리는 {**못** 갔을/*갔을} 거야. / He couldn't go far, at best.
오늘은 **여간** 더운 {날씨가 **아니다**/*날씨이다} / It is very hot today.
비단 그 사람뿐만 **아니라**, 많은 사람들이 부정을 저지르며 살고 있다. Not only he, but many other people have been misbehaving.

- Adverbs co-occurred with predicates which mean affirmation

너는 이번에는 **반드시** 서울에 {가야 한다/*가지 말아야 한다}
You must go to Seoul this time.

아무쪼록 네가 합격하기를 {바란다/*바라지 않는다} / I hope that you will pass the exam.
{**가까스로/간신히**} 그 일을 {끝냈다/*끝내지 못했다} / I've managed to finish the work.
삼가 고인(故人)의 명복을 {빕니다/*빌지 않습니다}
I respectfully pray for the bliss of dead.

- Adverbs co-occurred with predicates which mean supposition

아마 지금쯤 서울에 {도착했을 거야/*도착했다} / He must have arrived in Seoul by now.
그는 **마치** 고향 친구를 {만난 듯이/*만나고} 반가워했다.
He was glad as if he met a homie.

- Adverbs co-occurred with interrogative endings or exclamatory endings

도대체 왜 이렇게 늦게 {*온다/오니?/*오너라/*오자/*오는구나!}
Why in the world did you come in so late?
설마 그가 거짓말을 {*했다/했겠니?/*해라/*하자/*하는구나!}
Don't tell me that he told a lie.
오죽 화가 났으면 그런 소리를 {*했다/했겠니?/*해라/*하자/*했으랴!}
Would he/she have said something like that unless he/she was really angry?
나도 내 마음을 잘 이해하지 못하는데 **하물며** 남을 다 이해할 수 {*있다/있겠는가?/*있어라/*있자/있으랴!} / I can't understand my mind, even less others.
이 **얼마나** 행복한 {*일이다/일인가?/*일이어라/*일이자/*일이구나!} / What a happy event!

- Adverbs co-occurred with particular ending forms

어제는 학교에 가지 않았다. **왜냐하면** 어제는 공휴일이었기 **때문이다.**
I didn't go to school. Because yesterday was a holiday.
{**응당/당연히/마땅히/모름지기**} 너는 내 말에 순종해**야 한다.**
You should by all means be obedient to my words.

- Adverbs co-occurred with particular connective endings

{**만약/만일**} 내일 비가 {오거든/오면} 내게 꼭 전화해 다오.
If it should rain tomorrow, be sure to call me.
{**비록/설령**} 시험에 합격하지 못 {하여도/하더라도/할지라도} 결코 실망하지 마라.
Even if you don't pass the exam, you should never be disappointed.
아무리 사람이 {악해도/악하더라도/악할지라도} 사람을 사형시킬 수는 없다.
Were a man ever so bad, he can not be executed.

13.4 Making an adverbial phrase

A word class can be changed into a word that has the same function as an adverb, which is called adverbial phrase. Some adverbial phrases are transformed into adverb by adding the suffix. And other adverbial phrases maintain the characteristics of their original word class, and they simply function as an adverb.

13.4.1 Derived adverbs

• **Adverbializing suffix '-이'** is for adjectives, reduplications and adverbs

깨끗이 'clean'	따뜻이 'warmly'
많이 'aplenty'	반듯이 'straight'
같이 'like'	굳이 'firmly'
깊이 'deeply'	높이 'highly'
길이 'for a long time'	가까이(◁가깝-이) 'close at hand'
고이(◁곱-이) 'beautifully'	새로이(◁새롭-이) 'newly'
쉬이(◁쉽-이) 'easily'	일일이 'one by one'
낱낱이 'one by one'	집집이 'from house to house'
틈틈이 'in one's spare time'	줄줄이 'one after the other'
앞앞이 'before each person'	번번이 'each time'
짬짬이 'in one's spare time'	샅샅이 'thoroughly'
다달이(◁달+달-이) 'every month'	더욱이(◁더욱-이) 'besides'
일찍이 'early'	생긋이 'smiling'
곰곰이 'deliberately'	

- **Adverbializing suffix '-히' is for adjectives**

솔직히 'frankly'	가만히 'motionlessly'
각별히 'particularly'	분명히 'clearly'
쓸쓸히 'lonely'	심히 'very'
조용히 'quietly'	상당히 'fairly'
섭섭히 'regretfully'	간편히 'conveniently'
엄격히 'strictly'	급히 'in a hurry'
딱히 'not exactly'	족히 'enough'
속히 'quickly'	능히 'easily'
익히 'fully'	작히 'how much'
특히 'specially'	

- **Adverbializing suffix '-오' and '-우' are for some verbs and adjectives**

자주(◁잦-우) 'frequently'	모두(◁몯-우) 'all'
마구(◁막-우) 'recklessly'	고루(◁고르-우) 'evenly'
겨우(◁겹-우) 'barely'	너무(◁넘-우) 'too'
이루(◁이루-우) 'by any means'	두루(◁두르-우) 'without exception'
바로(◁바르-오) 'straight'	따로(◁따르-오) 'separately'
도로(◁돌-오) 'again'	

- **Adverbializing suffix '-(으)로' is for some nouns and 'Sino-Korean word-적(的)'**

날로 'day by day'	홀로 'alone'
참으로 'really'	진실로 'truly'
정말로 'truly'	겉으로 'outwardly'
속으로 'inly'	여러모로 'in various ways'
대대로 'for generations'	갖가지로 'variously'
일반적으로 'commonly'	대체적으로 'typically'

실제적으로 'practically'   전적으로 'completely'
광적으로 'madly'   총체적으로 'generally'
전통적으로 'traditionally'   단적으로 'directly'

13.4.2 Adverbial phrases which has function of adverb

- **Adverbial ending '-게'** is for adjectives

꽃이 아름답게 피어 있다. / Flowers are in beautiful bloom.
그는 전쟁에서 용감하게 싸웠다. / He fought bravely in the war.
민서는 존에게 한국 문화에 대해 친절하게 설명해 주었다.
Min-Seo kindly explained Korean culture to John.

- **Adverbial particle** is for adjectives nouns, pronouns and numerals

준서와 스미스는 광화문 앞에서 만났다.
Jun-Seo and Smith met in front of Gwanghwamun Gate.
엘리스는 3년 전에 한국으로 유학을 왔다.
Ellis came to Korea to study three years ago.
이 버스는 서울역으로 갑니다.
This bus goes to Seoul Station.
나도 너만큼 농구를 잘 할 수 있다.
I can play basketball as much as you.
눈이 꽃송이처럼 아름답다.
The snow is as beautiful as flowers.
그는 국회의원으로서 최선을 다해 일했다.
He worked as best he could as a member of the Nation Assembly.

13.5 Korean cultural aspects as reflected in adverbs

First, in Korean symbolic adverbs are very developed, these make various nuance by vowel harmony phenomenon according to mix of yang vowel [ㅏ, ㅗ], yin vowel [ㅓ, ㅜ, ㅡ] and neutral vowel [ㅣ]. And Koreans use apposite onomatopoeic words and mimetic words to affectivity when they are speaking.

Type		Yang vowel(ㅏ, ㅗ)	Yin vowel(ㅓ, ㅜ, ㅡ)	Neutral vowel(ㅣ)
Mimetic word		살금살금(stealthily)	슬금슬금	실금실금
		반질반질(sleekly)	번질번질	빈질빈질
Onomatopoeic word		따르릉따르릉(ting-a-ling)	떠르렁떠르렁	띠리링띠리링
		퐁당퐁당(plop-plop)	풍덩풍덩	
		졸졸(murmuring)	줄줄	질질
		호호호(ho-ho)	후후후	히히히

Second, in addition to vowel harmony, as change consonants, in other words, as change relaxed sounds [ㄱ, ㄷ, ㅂ, ㅈ] into tensed sounds [ㄲ, ㄸ, ㅃ, ㅉ] or aspirated sounds [ㅋ, ㅌ, ㅍ, ㅊ] Koreans can make symbolic adverbs which have various nuance and they express their feeling delicately.

시냇물이 {졸졸/쫄쫄/촐촐 ; 줄줄/쭐쭐/출출 ; 질질/찔찔/칠칠} 흐른다.
There is a brook murmuring.
그녀는 화가 나서 빨래를 {박박/빡빡/팍팍 ; 벅벅/뻑뻑/퍽퍽} 문질러 댔다.
She was so angry and rubbed laundry.

14 Exclamation

14.1 What is an exclamation?

Exclamation(감탄사) represents emotions or commitment, such as surprise, joy, sorrow, summon and answer, revealing the emotions of the speaker.

아! 경치가 정말 아름답**구나**. / Ah! The scenary is so beautiful.

Exclamations do not change their form, and do not come with any particles. Also, they are not an essential component of a sentence, since sentences can be formed without exclamations. They are always used independently, thus, they do not have direct relationship with other sentence components, but they usually come at the end of a sentence. Exclamations include emotional, volitional, respondent and tonal exclamations.

14.2 Types and characteristics of exclamations

14.2.1 Emotional exclamations

Emotional exclamations(감정감탄사) are when the speaker wants to convey his/her feelings (e.g. joy, sorrow, surprise, sigh, reprimand, realization) without being conscious of others.

Joy: 하하, 호호, 허허, 껄껄
Sorrow: 아이고, 응~응~
Surprise: 아이쿠! 아뿔싸! 이크, 이런! 아! 와! 어머나! 엄마야! 아이고!
　　　　야~! 에구머니!
Sigh: 휴우! 아이고 맙소사
Reprimand: 에끼! (이놈), 어라! (이 녀석)
Realization: 아하?, 아! 아~아!

14.2.2 Volitional exclamations

Volitional exclamations(의지감탄사) are when the speaker wants to express his/her thoughts while being conscious of others.

Affirmative: 옳지, 옳소! 그렇지! 'good, right, yes!'
Negative: 천만에, 아서라, 그만! 'no way, stop!'
Cheer: 만세! 야호! 'hooray!'
Suggestion/presentation: 자, 옜다 'here you go'

14.2.3 Respondent exclamations

Respondent exclamations(호응감탄사) are used to call or answer someone.

Summon: 여보세요! 보세요, 이봐! 헤이! 저기요! 'hello!'
Affirmative answer: 예, 그래(요), 오냐, 응, 좋아요 'yes, good'
Negative answer: 아니, 아냐! 아니오, 아녜요, 싫어요, 으으으 'no'
Hesitation: 글쎄, 글쎄올시다, 잠시만 'well'

14.2.4 Tonal exclamations

Tonal exclamations(음조감탄사) do not convey a particular meaning, but let the speaker choose the tone or put a pause in his speech.

있지요, 있잖아요, 말이야, 말입니다 'you know what'
어~, 음~, 에~, 에~또!, 뭐, 머, 저, 거시기, 에헴 'hmm, ah...'

14.3 Korean cultural aspects as reflected in exclamations

First, Koreans hardly use exclamations in front of those older than themselves. In other words, Koreans tend to restrain their feelings to a certain extent and try to fit in with the situation they are in. This can be hugely attributed to Confucian belief that refining one's words, rather than letting it all out, is a virtue in all circumstances.

Therefore, Koreans tend to be a very cautious speaker, and even restrain from talking a lot in meetings. In other words, in official occasions like meetings, the elderly tends to be the main speaker, while younger people listen and go with the flow. This is why Koreans try to be rather reserved and polite when it comes to expressing their emotions.

Second, exclamations are used more by women, as women vent their feelings more easily than men. Men are educated to be reticent from their early age, so they do not frankly express their feelings. It is especially true for men from Gyeongsang Province.

Third, men and women use different emotional exclamations when they laugh.

하하하: the most general form of laughter used by both men and women

허허허: laughter used by male adults

호호호: laughter generally used by women

히히히: laughter intended to sneer or laugh at others

헤헤헤: a slightly sycophantic or flattering laughter

후후후: laughter with a slightly wicked intentions

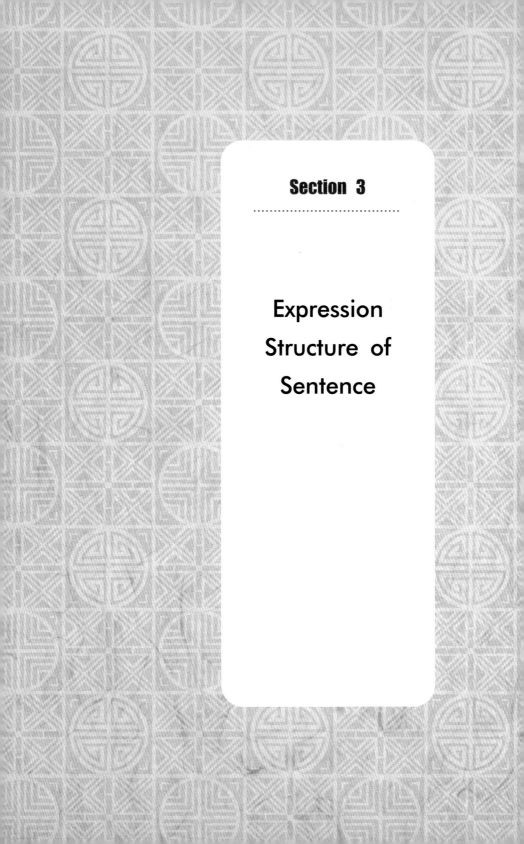

Section 3

Expression Structure of Sentence

Standard Korean Grammar for Foreigners

15 Sentence ending

15.1 What is a sentence ending?

Sentence endings are the way of ending the sentence, Korean sentences are ended by using a final ending. Korean has five types of final endings; declarative, interrogative, imperative, propositive and exclamatory endings.

15.2 Types and characteristics of sentence endings

15.2.1 Declarative sentence

Declarative sentence(평서문) is the sentence which ends in declarative final endings. Declarative sentences are used when the speaker intends to express his/her thoughts, feelings, convey related information, or to answer a question.

준서가 노래를 부르고 있**습니다**.(◁있-습니다) / Jun-Seo is singing a song.
날씨가 참 덥**다**.(◁덥-다) / The weather is hot.

A: 이것은 뭐죠? / What is this?

B: 이것은 내가 새로 산 컴퓨터**예요**.(◁ 컴퓨터-예요)

This is my new computer.

There are about 60 different declarative endings including '-(스)ㅂ니다, -아/어요, -(는)군요, -이에요/예요, -(ㄴ/는)다, -아/어, -지, -(으)마, -(ㄴ/는)단다, -는데, etc'. and if these endings are used, declarative sentence is made. If declarative ending '-(ㄴ/는)다' is used with prefinal ending such as '-더, -(으)라, -(으)나', it is changed into '-라' like such as '-더라, -(으)리라, -(으)니라'. And because '-(으)마' is used when speaker promises listener to do so it sometimes called promise type ending.

And as sentence below, when constructing an indirect quotative sentence, all declarative endings are changed into '-(ㄴ/는)다고'. As seen this, it can be known that '-(ㄴ/는)다' is the most representative and litmusless declarative ending.

준서는 "토마스는 김치를 잘 먹습니다." 하고 말했다.

Jun-Seo said, "Thomas eats Kimchi well."

→ 준서는 토마스는 김치를 잘 먹**는다고** 말했다.(◁ 먹-는다고)

Jun-Seo said that Thomas eats Kimchi well.

15.2.2 Interrogative sentence

Interrogative sentences(의문문) are used when questioning a person for an answer. However, the form of Korean interrogative sentence is very different from English. In English, interrogative sentence is made by changing word order or using auxiliary verbs.

He **bought** a book yesterday. → **Did** he **buy** a book yesterday?

Korean neither change word order nor use auxiliary verbs. Declarative final endings can be changed into interrogative final endings.

그가 어제 책을 샀다.(◁사-았-다) / He bought a book yesterday.
→ 그가 어제 책을 샀니?(◁사-았-니?) / Did he buy a book yesterday?

Korean interrogative sentences can be classified into four types according to forms of asking answer and contents.

- Explanation interrogative sentence

Explanation interrogative sentence(설명의문문) is an interrogative sentence which has the form that requires explanation of the other party as using interrogatives such as 누가 'who', 언제 'when', 어디서 'where', 무엇을 'what', 어떻게 'how', 왜 'why'. It is equivalent to *Wh-question* in English.

Jun-Seo: 지난 주말에 **무엇**을 했습니까? / What did you do last weekend?
Min-Seo: 경주로 여행을 갔습니다. / I went on a trip to Gyeongju.

- Judgment interrogative sentence

Judgment interrogative sentence(판정의문문) is an interrogative sentence which is asked using only interrogative ending, and has the form that requires judgment whether speaker's content of asking of the other party is correct or wrong. It is equivalent to *Yes-No question* in English.

Jun-Seo: 어제는 날씨가 추웠**습니까**? / Was it cold yesterday?
Min-Seo: **예**, 날씨가 매우 추웠습니다. / Yes, it was very cold.
아니오, 별로 춥지 않았습니다. / No, it wasn't so cold.

- Rhetorical interrogative sentence

Rhetorical interrogative sentence(수사의문문) takes the form of explanation interrogative sentence or judgment interrogative sentence, however it is used for expressing speaker's positive or negative intention very strongly not for asking something au fond. Negative rhetorical interrogative sentence is used when emphasizes affirmations, positive rhetorical interrogative sentence is used when emphasizes negation. It is equivalent to *Rhetorical question* in English.

> Min-Seo: 이번 축구 시합에서 상대편을 이길 수 있겠어요?
> In this soccer match, can you win the opponent?
> Jun-Seo: 제가 **못** 이길 것 같**습니까**? / Do you think I will not win?

As Jun-Seo expresses his intention using the form of negative rhetorical interrogative sentence, he emphasizes positive fact which is 'Jun-Seo himself can win'.

> Jun-Seo: 민서가 피아노도 잘 치지요?
> Min-Seo is good at playing the piano, isn't she?
> Min-Jun: 민서가 **무엇** 하나 제대로 하는 게 있**나요**?
> Min-Seo does not do anything right.

As Min-Jun expresses his intention using the form of positive rhetorical interrogative sentence, he emphasizes negative fact which is 'Min-Seo can't do anything right'.

- Affixation interrogative sentence

Affixation interrogative sentence(부가의문문) is an interrogative sentence which is used for reconfirming listener in contents of preceding phrase as adding affixation elements such as '그렇지? ; 안 그렇지? 안 그렇니? 안 그래?' in the back of declarative and interrogative ending. Here, speaker has the opinion that the contents of preceding phrase is certainly 'right', and this sentence has the meaning that speaker expect to confirm once again of fact which his/her opinion is right. It is equivalent to *Tag question* in English.

However, in tag question in English, if preceding phrase is positive, negative word is added, while if preceding phrase is negative, positive word is added as below.

> John loves Judy, **doesn't he**?
> John doesn't love Judy, **does he**?

However, in the case of Korean, there is no such grammatical restriction.

> 오늘 날씨가 참 좋다, {그렇지?/안 그래?/안 그렇니?}
> The weather is nice today, isn't it?
> 오늘 날씨가 참 안 좋다, {그렇지?/안 그래?/안 그렇니?}
> The weather is terrible today, isn't it?
> 와! 꽃이 멋있게 피었구나, {그렇지?/안 그래?/안 그렇니?}
> Wow! Beautiful flowers are blooming, aren't they?
> 야! 참 비가 안 와도 너무 안 오는구나, {그렇지?/안 그래?/안 그렇니?}
> Oh, it hasn't rained, has it?

There are more than 60 interrogative endings including '-(스)ㅂ니까? -아/어요? -이에요/예요? -(으)ㄴ/는가? -(으/느)냐? -(으)ㄹ까? -니? -아/어? -지? -(ㄴ/는)대? -(ㄴ/는)다면서?'. And as sentence below, when these endings are used in an indirect quotative sentence, all endings alter into '-(으/느)냐고'. As seen this, it can be known that '-(으/느)냐?' is the most representative and litmusless interrogative ending.

Jun-Seo: 어제 숙제를 다 했습니까?

Did you do your homework yesterday?

Min-Seo: 어제 숙제를 다 했<u>느냐고</u> 준서가 내게 물었다.(◁했-느냐고)

Jun-Seo asked me if I had done all my homework.

15.2.3 Imperative sentence

Imperative sentence(명령문) is the sentence which ends in imperative final endings. Imperative sentences is the sentence of form that speaker demands listener for acting something or not. However the form of Korean imperative sentence is very different from English. As sentence below, imperative sentence in English is made by omitting subject and placing infinitive at the front of sentence.

He goes to his hometown.

→ Go to your hometown.

However, in the case of Korean, word order is not changed and auxiliary verbs are not used. Just declarative final endings change into imperative final endings.

[Declarative] 그는 의자에 앉았**다**.(◁앉-았-다)

He sat on a chair.

[Imperative] 너는 의자에 앉**아라**.(◁앉-아라)

Sit on a chair.

Because the object of fulfillment is always listener, subject has to be second person pronoun such as '너, 너희, 당신'. And because the time of listening the command is present, imperative sentence can not be used with not only prefinal ending such as '-았/었-, -겠-, -더-, -(으)리-, etc'.

but also present tense prefinal ending '-ㄴ/는-'. Because present is premised in the imperative ending itself, adding '-ㄴ/는-' again is meaningless.

{*나/*그/너}는 책 좀 읽어라. / (You) read the book.
너는 이것을 잡{*-았-/*-겠-/*-더-/*으라-/*-는-}아라. / Hold this.

For negative imperative sentence, the form of '-지 말다' is taken, '-지 아니-' or '-지 못-' is not used.

더 이상 거짓말을 하<u>지 마라</u>.(◁하-지 말-아라) / Don't tell lies any more.
서울에 가<u>지 마세요</u>.(◁가-지 말-으세요) / Don't go to Seoul.

Also, for verbs compounded '-가다' including 가다 such as 돌아가다 'to return', 읽어가다 'to read', 뛰어가다 'to run', 물러가다 'to move backward', 건너가다 'to go across', 쫓아가다 'to follow', 찾아가다 'to go on a visit to', 올라가다 'to climb up', '-거라' is used instead of '-아라' for imperative ending. However, it does not become ungrammatical sentence because '-아라' is used in the back of these verbs, the new generation mostly use rather '-아라' instead of '-거라'.

어머니를 {쫓아가거라/[?]쫓아가라} / Follow your mother.
이제 집으로 {돌아가거라/[?]돌아가라} / Return home now.

For verbs compounded '-오다' including 오다 such as 다가오다 'to approach', 올라오다 'to come up', 건너오다 'to come across', 뛰어오다 'to come running', 내려오다 'to come down', 넘어오다 'to come over', 데려오다 'to bring with one', 달려오다 'to come running', 들어오다 'to come in', '-너라' is used instead of '-아라' for imperative ending. However, of course, it does not become ungrammatical sentence because '-아라' is used in the back of these verbs, the new generation mostly use rather

'-아라' instead of '-너라'.

> 이리로 {올라오너라/$^?$올라와라} / Come here.
> 민서를 서울로 {데려오너라/$^?$데려와라} / Bring Min-Seo to Seoul.

There are more than 20 imperative endings including '-(으)십시오, -아/어요, -(으)세요, -게, -아/어, -지, -(으)라니까, -아/어라', and when these endings are used in an indirect quotative sentence, they are changed into '-(으)라고'.

> Jun-Seo: 제 손을 꼭 잡으십시오. / Please hold my hand tightly.
> Customer: 준서가 자기의 손을 꼭 잡으라고 말했다.(◁잡-으라고)
> Jun-Seo told me to hold his hand tightly.

15.2.4 Propositive sentence

Propositive sentence(청유문) is the sentence which ends in propositive final endings. Propositive sentence is the sentence of form that speaker suggest to listener that they do some action together. Therefore the subject of propositive sentence is 'we' which indicates that speaker and listener do something together, and generally this 'we' is dropped. For predicate, verb can be used.

> 도서관에 공부하러 (우리) 함께 **갑시다**.(◁가-ㅂ시다)
> Let's go to the library and study together.
> 이제 (우리) 좀 **쉽시다**.(◁쉬-ㅂ시다) / Let's rest now.
> {*나/*너/*그/우리}는 책 좀 읽자. / Let's read the book.

Because the time of listening the suggestion is present, propositive sentence can not be used with not only prefinal ending such as '-았/었-,

-겠-, -더-, -(으)리-, etc.' but also present tense prefinal ending '-ㄴ/는-'. Because present is premised in the propositive ending itself. When requests to do something in the future, add the words which express particular time and date such as 당장 'at once', 곧 'immediately', 조금 이따가 'a little later', 조금 뒤 'after a little', 한 시간 뒤에 'in one hour', 내일 'tomorrow', 1년 후 'a year later', etc.

이 옷은 한 달 뒤에 사{*-았-/*-겠-/*-더-/*-리-/*-는-}ㅂ시다.
Let's buy this cloth one month later.
우리 곧 결혼하{*-였-/*-겠-/*-더-/*-리-/*-는-}ㅂ시다.
Let's get married soon.

For negative propositive sentence, the form of '-지 말다' is taken, '-지 아니-' or '-지 못-' is not used.

더 이상 거짓말을 하<u>지 말자</u>.(◁하지 말자) / Let's not tell lies any more.
서울에 가<u>지 맙시다</u>.(◁가지 마ㄴㅂ시다) / Let's not go to Seoul.

There are more than 20 propositive endings including '-(으)ㅂ시다, -아/어요, -(으)세, -자, -자구나, -아/어, -지, -자니까'. All of them are changed into '-자고' in an indirect quotative sentence.

Teacher: 이제 수업을 마칩시다. / Let's finish the class now.
Jun-Seo: 선생님께서 이제 수업을 마치<u>자고</u> 말씀하셨다.(◁마치-자고)
　　　　　The teacher told students to finish the class now.

15.2.5 Exclamatory sentence

Exclamatory sentence(감탄문) is the sentence which ends in exclamatory final endings. Exclamatory sentence is the sentence of form that the speaker expresses his/her feeling such as joy, sorrow and surprises naturally, freely, as if to oneself. Therefore the subject has to be first person, and for the predicate, adjective is mostly used because there are many descriptions about speech situation or state.

And in most cases, exclamations such as 야 'oh', 와 'wow', 어머나 'oh', etc. or adverbs such as 아주 'very', 정말 'really', 대단히 'very', 무척 'very', etc. are used in exclamatory sentence. Also punctuation marks ! is attached in the end of sentence.

> 와, 날씨가 너무 좋**구나**!(◁좋-구나!) / Wow, what a beautiful day!
> 이 오렌지 정말 맛있**네**!(◁맛있-네!) / This orange is very delicious!

There are about 20 exclamatory endings, including '-(는)구나! -(는)군! -(는)군요! -(는)구려!' And when these endings are used in an indirect quotative sentence, all endings are changed into '-(ㄴ/는)다고'. This '-(ㄴ/는)다고' is the same as declarative ending of indirect speech, there is not particular form for exclamatory ending of indirect speech.

> Teacher: 장미꽃이 정말 예쁘구나! / The Rose is really beautiful.
> Jun-Seo: 선생님께서 장미꽃이 정말 예쁘**다고** 말씀하셨다.(◁예쁘-다고)
> The teacher said to me that the rose is really beautiful.

▪ Final ending which indicates promise

Promise is something that speaker arranges to do some action to listener, there are '-(으)마, -(으)ㄹ게, -(으)리다, -(으)ㅁ세, -(으)오리다, -(으)ㄹ게요', etc. for expressing the meaning of this promise. Final endings which indicate promise generally belongs to declarative final endings, but there are instances where promise type set up to one independent ending type.

Final endings which indicate promise has the following characteristics.

● It can be combined with verbs and 있다 only.

내가 내일 서울에 {가마/갈게/가리다/감세} / I will go to Seoul tomorrow.
나는 집에 {있으마/있을게/있으리다/있음세} / I will be at home.
*우리가 배가 {고프마/고플게/고프리다/고픔세} / *We will be hungry.
*제가 대학생{이마/일게/이리다/임세} / *I am a university student.

● For subject, first person pronouns such as '나/내, 저/제, 소자, 본인, 우리, 저희' can be used.

{내/우리/*너/*그/*그녀}가 먼저 서울에 가마. / I/we will go to Seoul first.
{나/우리/저희/*너/그/*그녀/*그들/*너희들}도 먼저 춤을 출게요.
I/we will dance first, too.
{저/저희들/*그들/*너희들}은/는 나중에 점심을 먹을게요.
I/we will eat lunch later.

● It can be used with prefinal endings which express present tense only.

내가 이번에는 양보하{ø/*-였-/*-더-/*-겠-/*-라-}ㄹ게.
I will make a concession this time.
우리는 나중에 책을 읽{ø/*-였-/*-더-/*-겠-/*-라-}으마.
We will read the book later.

● For negative promise, '안, -지 않-' can be used, while '말다' cannot.

나는 미국으로 유학 {안 갈게/가지 않을게/*가지 말게} / I will not go to USA to study.
저희들은 거짓말을 {안 할게요/하지 않을게요/*하지 말게요} / We will not tell lies.

15.3 Korean cultural aspects as reflected in sentence endings

Korean male have tendencies to be Confucian and authoritative, therefore they tend to use imperative form for final ending, however, because female regard obedience to male as a virtue, they tend to use interrogative form for final ending.

For example, when they want their children to open the window at home, they use the expressions as follows.

> man: 문을 열어라. / Open the door.
> 문 좀 열지. / Why don't you open the door?
> 문 좀 열어.
> woman: 문 좀 열어 주겠니? / Could you open the door?
> 문 좀 열어 줄래?

However, because this is changeable depending on individual personalities and regional differences, how sentence ending of male or female should be is not at all. Because sentence endings tend to express speaker's personality and mental state comparatively well, the speaker's character can be known by looking around what kind of final ending the speaker choose mostly.

Second, same meaning can be expressed by using various ending such as declarative, interrogative, imperative, propositive, exclamatory form, so Koreans express variously according to their individual personality. For example, when parents want their children to go to school after eating breakfast, they use the expressions as follows. Therefore, the speaker's mental state and the meaning of a sentence can be grasped when look what kinds of final ending is used.

[Imperative] 아침 먹어라. 아침 먹어. 아침 먹지.
[Interrogative] 아침 안 먹니? 아침 안 먹어? 아침 안 먹을래?
[Propositive] 아침 먹자.
[Declarative] 아들! 아침을 먹는다.

Third, final endings can be used variously interchangeably. For example, even though '-(ㄴ/는)다' is a declarative final ending, sometimes it can be used as exclamatory form as following example.

야, 그거 정말 멋있다! / Oh, it looks really cool!
와, 정말 노래 잘한다! / Wow, what a good singer (you are)!

Also for more euphemism, propositive ending is used a lot instead or imperative ending. In other word, even thought it is the situation that imperative ending should be used, propositive interrogative endings are used roundabout way not for giving nuance of command to listener.

[Imperative] 공부 좀 해라. / Hit the books.
　→ [Propositive] 공부 좀 하자.
　→ [Interrogative] 공부 좀 안 할래?

16 Elevation of speech level

16.1 What is an elevation of speech level?

Elevation of speech level(높임법) is when the speaker raises or lowers the level of speech he/she makes to the listener. The Korean language has a highly sophisticated level of speech elevation, so it is very important to use the appropriate elevation in everyday speech.

The level of elevation depends on the age, social position and relationship with the hearer. It is expressed by sentence endings, prefinal endings, particles and words. There are three types of elevation: subject-honorific speech, hearer-honorific speech and object-honorific speech.

16.2 Types and characteristics of speech elevation

16.2.1 Subject-honorific speech

Subject-honorific speech(주체높임) elevates the subject of a sentence by adding a prefinal ending '-(으)시-' to the predicate, when the subject is older or ranks higher than the speaker. Substituting the subject particle

'-이/가' with '-께서' can represent an even higher level of elevation. Prefinal ending '-(으)시-' and subject particle '-께서' are generally used in conjunction with each other. Also, the use of suffix '-님' before '-께서' can help make a more natural honorific speech.

It would be impolite for the speaker to elevate himself, so the subject is usually the second person or third person in a subject-honorific speech.

할아버지{가/께서} 우리를 부르신다.(◁-께서, 부르-시-ㄴ다)
Grandfather is calling us.
선생님{이/께서} 우리 집에 오셨다.(◁-께서, 오-시-었-다)
My teacher came to my house.
당신{이/께서} 가시는 길에 꽃을 뿌려 드리겠어요.(◁-께서, 가-시-는)
I will scatter flowers on the path you tread.
{*내가/*나께서} 서울에 가시겠습니다.(◁가-시-겠-습니다)
I will go to Seoul.

However, the first person subject can be used in exceptional cases. The first person subject can be elevated in film or theater play scripts, or in a particular situation where the speaker wants to crack a joke.

잘 봐라! 이번엔 내가 나가신다.(◁나가-시-ㄴ다)
Hey look! Here I come now.
여기가 바로 본인이 태어난 곳이시다, 알겠냐?(◁곳-이-시-다)
This is where I the great was born, got it?

Moreover, even though the subject is older or ranks higher than the speaker, prefinal ending '-(으)시-' is usually skipped if the listener is older or ranks higher than the subject.

할아버지, 아버지 어디 갔습니까?(◁가-Ø-았-습니까?)
Grandfather, where is dad?

부장님, **계장님**은 벌써 출장지로 **떠났습니다**.(◁떠나-∅-았-습니다)
Mr(team head), the chief has already gone on the business trip.

Yet, young people tend to ignore the above and use honorific forms to the hearer, such as 가셨습니다(◁가시-었-습니다), 떠나셨습니다(◁떠나-시-었-습니다) in above situations, so it is also considered correct by the standard speech of Korean for the time being. Even in this case however, the subject is not elevated as much as to use the elevated subject particle '-께서'. (e.g. 아버지께서/아버(님)께서, 계장님께서)

Furthermore, prefinal ending '-(으)시-' can indirectly elevate the subject of a sentence. Indirect elevation refers to elevation of certain business, things or even part of the body that is related to the subject. Since the expressions below can be paraphrased into 큰아버지의 재산 'uncle's wealth', 부장님의 양복 'team head's suit', 사장님의 사업 'CEO's business', 할머니의 얼굴 'grandmother's face', the use of prefinal ending '-(으)시-' can have an elevation effect.

> 큰아버지는 **재산**이 **많으십니다**.(◁많-으시-ㅂ니다)
> My uncle is very wealthy.
> 부장님, 검은 **양복**이 참 잘 어울리십니다.(◁어울리-시-ㅂ니다)
> Mr, the black suit goes very well with you.
> 사장님의 **사업**이 잘되셔야, 저도 안심이 되겠지요.(◁잘되-시-어야)
> I guess I will find relief if your business goes well.
> 할머니는 **얼굴**이 늘 밝으셨습니다.(◁밝-으시-었-습니다)
> My grandmother was always cheerful.

Some verbs have two forms of elevation. The two forms can be used either interchangeably or not, depending on whether the subject is being directly or indirectly elevated. For example, the elevated form of 있다, which means 'to own or exist', is 있으시다 and 계시다. The two of them can directly elevate the subject.

대통령께서는 현재 롯데호텔에 머물고 {있으십니다/계십니다}
The president is currently staying at Lotte Hotel.
어머니는 소파에 앉아 {있으십니다/계십니다}
Mother is sitting on the sofa.
김 교수님은 경제학에 대한 지식을 많이 가지고 {있으십니다/계십니다}
Professor Kim has profound knowledge in economics.

However, when it comes to indirect elevation, it is possible to use only 있으시다, not 계시다.

그 사장님은 **재산**이 많이 {있으십니다/*계십니다}
The CEO is very wealthy.
우리 선생님은 여러 **취미**가 {있으십니다/*계십니다}
My teacher has several hobbies.
장모님은 서울에 **일**이 {있으셔서/*계셔서} 가셨습니다.
My mother-in-law left for Seoul because she had something to do.

Aside from 계시다, the subject can be elevated with verbs such as 편찮다(◁아프다) 'to be sick', 잡수다/들다(◁먹다) 'to eat', 주무시다(◁자다) 'to sleep', 돌아가시다(◁죽다) 'to pass away', 말씀하시다(◁말하다) 'to speak'.

16.2.2 Hearer-honorific speech

Hearer-honorific speech(상대높임) is used when the speaker wants to elevate the hearer. Hearer-honorific speech is the most sophisticated form of elevation. There are four types of hearer-honorific speech according to the hearer's age and social position (high honorific, ordinary honorific, ordinary non-honorific and low non-honorific style), which can be represented in following sentence endings.

High honorific style: 책을 읽으시오.(◁ 읽-으시오)
　　　　　　　　High honorific style: Please read the book.
Ordinary honorific style: 책을 읽어요.(◁ 읽-어요)
　　　　　　　　Ordinary honorific style: Read the book.
Ordinary non-honorific style: 책을 읽어.(◁ 읽-어)
　　　　　　　　Ordinary non-honorific style: Read the book.
Low non-honorific style: 책을 읽어라.(◁ 읽-어라)
　　　　　　　　Low non-honorific style: Read the book.

However, the line is blurring between these four types of elevation. For instance, the high honorific and ordinary honorific style, ordinary honorific and ordinary non-honorific style and ordinary honorific and low non-honorific style are generally used in conjunction with each other, because the level of elevation may slightly vary between the mood at the time of speaking.

16.2.2.1 High honorific style

High honorific(아주높임) style can be classified by following sentence endings.

[Declarative] 책을 읽습니다.(◁ 읽-습니다)
[Interrogative] 책을 읽습니까?(◁ 읽-습니까?)
[Imperative] 책을 읽으시오.(◁ 읽-으시오)
[Propositive] 책을 읽읍시다.(◁ 읽-읍시다)
[Exclamatory] 와! 책 잘 읽으시는구나!(◁ 읽-으시는구나)

High honorific style is employed when the speaker wants to honor the hearer as much as possible, if the hearer is older or ranks higher than the speaker. It is also known as '-(스)ㅂ니다' style.

The high honorific style can also be referred to as official style, due to its widespread use in official occasions, such as lectures, presentations, discussions, reports, radio and TV programs and interviews, regardless of the hearers' age or social position. It is also used in unofficial occasions or everyday speech, for example, to talk to clients, strangers, or hearers who are much older or rank higher than the speaker. In general, the high honorific style is more preferred by men than women, especially by elderly men.

High honorific style can be represented by following sentence endings.

[Declarative] -(스)ㅂ니다
[Interrogative] -(스)ㅂ니까?
[Imperative] -(으)시오, (으)십시오
[Propositive] -(으)ㅂ시다, (으)십시다
[Exclamatory] -(으)시(는)구나!

The combination of exclamatory phrase and degree verbs with the sentence ending '-(스)ㅂ니다' (e.g. "야! 정말 잘 읽었습니다.") can also make an exclamatory expression.

16.2.2.2 Ordinary honorific style

Ordinary honorific(예사높임) style can be classified by following sentence endings.

[Declarative] 책을 읽어요./읽으오.(◁ 읽-어요/읽-으오)
[Interrogative] 책을 읽어요?/읽으오?(◁ 읽-어요?/읽-으오?)
[Imperative] 책을 읽어요./읽으오.(◁ 읽-어요/읽-으오)

[Propositive] 책을 읽<u>어요</u>./읽<u>으오</u>.(◁ 읽-어요/읽-으오)
[Exclamatory] 와! 책 잘 읽<u>는군요</u>!/읽<u>는구려</u>!(◁ 읽-는군요/읽-는구려)

Ordinary honorific style is when the speaker wants to moderately elevate the hearer if the hearer is at the same age or slightly older than the speaker, or if the hearer is ranks similar or slightly higher than the speaker. Ordinary honorific style can be represented by '-아/어요' and '-(으)오' endings.

- '-아/어요' form

'-아/어요' form is very frequently used by men and women alike in everyday speech, and is the most common form of elevation which enables the speaker and hearer to be polite but comfortable with each other at the same time. '-아/어요' is when the speaker is very friendly with the hearer, or when the speaker wants to convey his/her intention in a very amiable way.

Among men and women, women prefer using '-아/어요' form, and among men, younger generations prefer using the '-아/어요' form. In the current Korean society, '-아/어요' is the most prevalent style, and is likely to have more followings in the foreseeable future.

- '-(으)오' form

'-(으)오' form can be referred to as an authoritative male style, yet, this style is hardly ever used even by elderly men except only a few: the style is sometimes spoken in period dramas or soap operas, so it seems to have become almost archaic.

The ordinary honorific style can be classified by following sentence endings.

- '-아/어요' form endings

[Declarative] ┑(ㄴ/는)다고요, ┑(ㄴ/는)다나요, ┑(ㄴ/는)다니까요, ┑(ㄴ/는)
대요, ┑(는)군요, ┑(으)ㄴ/는걸요, ┑(으)ㄴ/는데요, ┑(으)ㄹ걸
요, ┑(으)ㄹ게요, ┑(으)ㄹ래요, ┑(으)ㄹ테지요, ┑(으)라고요,
┑(으)라니까요, ┑(으)세요, ┑거든요, ┑네요, ┑아/어야지요, ┑아/
어요, ┑지요
[Interrogative] ┑(ㄴ/는)다니요? ┑(ㄴ/는)다며요? ┑(ㄴ/는)대요? ┑(느)냐고
요? ┑(는)지요? ┑(으)ㄴ/는가요? ┑(으)ㄴ/는데요? ┑(으)ㄹ까
요? ┑(으)ㄹ래요? ┑(으)라고요? ┑(으)라면서요? ┑(으)려고
요? ┑(으)세요? ┑거요? ┑고서요? ┑고요? ┑아/어야지요? ┑아/
어요? ┑자면서요? ┑지요?
[Imperative] ┑(으)라고요, ┑(으)라니까요, ┑(으)세요, ┑아/어요, ┑자고요, ┑자
니까요, ┑지요
[Propositive] ┑아/어요, ┑지요, ┑(으)세요
[Exclamatory] ┑(는)군요! ┑(으)세요!

- '┑(으)오' form endings

[Declarative] ┑(ㄴ/는)다오, ┑(으)오, ┑(으)오이다, ┑소, ┑소이다
[Interrogative] ┑(으)오? ┑(으)오이까? ┑소? ┑소이까?
[Imperative] ┑(으)소, ┑(으)오
[Propositive] ┑(으)오
[Exclamatory] ┑(는)구려!

16.2.2.3 Ordinary non-honorific style

Ordinary non-honorific(예사낮춤) style can be classified by following sentence endings.

[Declarative] 책을 읽어./읽네.(◁ 읽-어/읽-네)

[Interrogative] 책을 읽<u>어</u>?/읽<u>는가</u>?(◁ 읽-어?/읽-는가?)
[Imperative] 책을 읽<u>어</u>./읽<u>게</u>.(◁ 읽-어/읽-게)
[Propositive] 책을 읽<u>어</u>./읽<u>으세</u>.(◁ 읽-어/읽-으세)
[Exclamatory] 와! 책 잘 읽<u>는다</u>!/읽<u>는구려</u>!(◁ 읽-는다/읽-는구려)

Ordinary non-honorific style is when the speaker wants to slightly lower the level of speech if the hearer is at the same age or younger than the speaker, or if the hearer is at the similar or lower position than the speaker. There are two forms of ordinary non-honorific style: '-아/어' and '-네' form.

- '-아/어' form

'-아/어' form is often referred to as half speech, which is spoken mostly by close friends about the same age, or by the senior to the younger in a friendly way. In particular, '-아/어' form is spoken by teenagers at elementary, middle and high school, even if they are not close friends. However, those aged 20 or higher, including college students, do not use this style to those about the same age if they are strangers. If they do, they may sound very insulting and arrogant. The younger can use this style to the senior if they have a very special relationship. For example, a son or daughter can use this style to his/her mother and the younger sibling to the senior sibling. A son or daughter can use this style to his/her mother as a token of intimacy, but not usually to his/her father however close they are. In general, husbands use this style to wives, and wives use the '-아/어' form to husbands. However, husbands and wives alike are increasingly using '-아/어' form these days.

- '-네' form

'-네' form is a friendly adult style, but it is more of a literary language since it has become almost extinct, just like '-(으)오' form. This is spoken by the senior to the younger who has a certain social position, or between older adults who try to elevate each other in a polite way.

However, this can never be used by the younger to the senior. It is still frequently used in period dramas or historical novels.

Ordinary non-honorific style can be classified by following sentence endings.

● '-아/어' form endings

[Declarative] -(ㄴ/는)다고, -(ㄴ/는)다나, -(ㄴ/는)다니까, -(ㄴ/는)대, -(으)ㄴ/
  는걸, -(으)ㄴ/는데, -(으)ㄹ걸, -(으)ㄹ게, -(으)ㄹ래, -(으)ㄹ테
  지, -(으)라고, -(으)라니까, -거든, -아/어야지, -아/어, -지
[Interrogative] -(ㄴ/는)다니? -(ㄴ/는)다며? -(ㄴ/는)대? -(느)냐고? -(는)
  지? -(으)ㄴ/는가? -(으)ㄴ/는데? -(으)ㄹ까? -(으)ㄹ래? -
  (으)라고? -(으)라면서? -(으)려고? -게? -고서? -고? -나?
  -니? -아/어야지? -아/어? -자면서? -지?
[Imperative] -(으)라고, -(으)라니까, -아/어, -자고, -자니까
[Propositive] -아/어, -지
[Exclamatory] -아/어! -지! -(으)리!

● '-네' form endings

[Declarative] -(ㄴ/는)다네, -(ㄴ/는)단다, -(으)마, -네
[Interrogative] -(느)뇨? -(으)ㄴ/는가?
[Imperative] -게, -게나
[Propositive] -(으)세, -(으)세나
[Exclamatory] -네! -(는)군! -(는)구먼!

16.2.2.4 Low non-honorific style

Low non-honorific(아주낮춤) style can be classified by following sentence endings.

> [Declarative] 책을 읽**는다**.(◁ 읽-는다)
> [Interrogative] 책을 읽**느냐**?(◁ 읽-느냐?)
> [Imperative] 책을 읽**어라**.(◁ 읽-어라)
> [Propositive] 책을 읽**자**.(◁ 읽-자)
> [Exclamatory] 책을 잘 읽**는다**!(◁ 읽-는다)

Low non-honorific style is spoken between intimate friends who are about the same age, by parents to offsprings, by the older sibling to the younger sibling, by teachers to students, by father-in-law or mother-in-law to son-in-law or daughter-in-law. The younger the speaker and the hearer are, the more this style is used.

However, using the low non-honorific style in everyday speech does not mean that the speaker is looking down on the hearer or the hearer is at a lower stature than the speaker. Rather, the use of low non-honorific style implies that the speaker is very intimate with the hearer.

Low non-honorific style can be classified by following sentence endings.

> [Declarative] -(ㄴ/는)다
> [Interrogative] -(느)냐?
> [Imperative] -아/어라
> [Propositive] -자
> [Exclamatory] -(는)구나! -(는)다! -(는)도다!

● **Print style**

Other than the styles mentioned above, there is a peculiar honorific form used in prints, such as newspapers, magazines and novels. This is called 'print style'(인쇄체). It employs sentence endings of low non-honorific style, but does not convey anything honorific or non-honorific. In other words, it is when Koreans want to express their ideas regardless of sex, age, or social positions of the reader. '-(으)라' acts as the imperative ending in print style instead of '-아/어라'.

알맞은 답을 고르라.(◁고르-라) / Choose the correct answer.
손잡이를 꼭 잡으라.(◁잡-으라) / Grab the handle tight.

Since the print style uses the ending of low non-honorific style, it is tentatively classified as a type of low non-honorific style in this book.

One thing to take note is that Korean's hearer-honorific speech can vary between age, position, sex, friendship, situation, mood and the intention of the speaker. In other words, Koreans tend to mix several levels of honorific speech in everyday speech, rather than sticking to a single form of honorific speech.

16.2.3 Object-honorific speech

Object-honorific speech(객체높임) honors the object of a predicate, i.e., people who are represented as the object or adverbial phrase of a sentence. In order to honor objects, speakers can use honorific words 드리다(◁주다), suffix '-님' or adverb particle '-께'.

● Honorific words

The object can be honored by using following honorific words, such as 모시다(◁데리다) 'to come to pick up someone', 여쭈다(◁묻다) 'to ask', 뵙다(◁만나다) 'to meet', 진지(◁밥) 'meal', 성함(◁이름) 'name', 연세(◁나이) 'age', 치아(◁이) 'teeth', 댁(◁집), 'house', 부인(◁아내) 'wife', 생신(◁생일) 'birthday', 말씀(◁말) 'words'.

선생님, 조금 있다가 **뵙겠습니다.**(◁만나다) / Sir, I will see you soon.
자네 아버님의 **연세**는 올해 얼마이신가?(◁나이)
How old is your father?

● Suffix '-님'

A person's title or position can be combined with honorific suffix '-님', for example, 아드님(◁아들) 'son', 따님(◁딸) 'daughter', 선생님(◁선생) 'teacher', 과장님(◁과장) 'manager', 부장님(◁부장) 'general manager', 사장님(◁사장) 'CEO', 어머님(◁어머니) 'mother', 아버님(◁아버지) 'father', 할아버님(◁할아버지) 'grandfather'.

이 사건에 대해서는 댁의 **아드님**에게 물어 보십시오.(◁아들)
Ask your son about this incident.
사장님께 말씀드립시다.(◁사장) / Let's tell this to the CEO.

● Particle '-께'

A honorific adverb particle '-께' can be used in the place of adverb particle '-에게' to honor the object. It should be noted that '-님' can be added only to respectable objects or deities, such as teachers, reverends, team heads, presidents, grandfather, mother, God, etc.

이 책을 아버님**께** 갖다 드려라.(◁-에게)
Take this book to your father.
이 문제의 해법을 선생님**께** 여쭈어 보았다.(◁-에게)
I asked the teacher the answer to this question.

네가 명문 대학에 꼭 합격할 수 있도록 하나님**께** 기도하마.(◁-에게)
I will pray for you so that you will enter a prestigious university.

■ Various views on the hearer-honorific speech

Hearer-honorific speech is the most sophisticated form of elevation in Korean. While there are varying views on how to categorize this speech, the school grammar classifies the hearer-honorific speech as follows:

	Formal	Informal
Honorific	High honorific style (하십시오)	Universal honorific style (해요)
	Ordinary honorific style (하오)	
Non-honorific	Ordinary non-honorific style (하게)	Universal non-honorific style (해: half speech)
	Low non-honorific style (해라)	

The above is founded by Seong(1970) and Suh(1984). Honorific speech is initially divided into formal and informal style, and then the formal style is categorized into high honorific, ordinary honorific, ordinary non-honorific, low non-honorific style, and the informal style into universal honorific and universal non-honorific style.

The formal style indicates a psychological distance between the speaker and the hearer, whereas the informal style is a rather amiable, friendly and kind expression. Universal honorific style can be readily interchangeable with high honorific or ordinary honorific speech, and universal non-honorific style with ordinary non-honorific and low non-honorific speech.

However, sometimes, 하십시오 form cannot be replaced by 해요 form, and 해라 form cannot be replaced by 해 form. Furthermore, 하오 form and 해라 form can sound informal in certain circumstances. Therefore, the classification system above does not seem to fully reflect the reality of the Korean language.

Moreover, it is quite problematic to establish a honorific speech system which is based on ordinary honorific endings like '-(으)오, -소, -(는)구려' and ordinary non-honorific endings like '-게, -네, -세, -(으)렴, -(는)구먼', which all fell out of use in the contemporary Korean language.

Therefore, it would be more reasonable to build a honorific system centering on more familiar honorific endings, such as '-(스)ㅂ니다, -(스)ㅂ니까? -아/어요, -지요, -(으)세요, -아/어요? -지요? -(으/느)냐? -아/어라, -자'.

Aside from the above classification, Choi(1937=1980) divided the speech into five levels (high honorific, ordinary honorific, ordinary non-honorific, low non-honorific and half speech), and Lee(1973) classified the speech into six levels ('-(스)ㅂ니다, -아/어요, -(으)오, -네, -아/어, -(ㄴ/는)다') and Kim(1981) classified the speech into honorific and plain speech, with the former divided into speech for the senior and speech for the younger.

16.3 Korean cultural aspects as reflected in honorific expressions

First, honorific speech is a long-standing tradition and one of the highly significant characteristics of the Korean language. The right honorific expressions should be used in the right situation, because people who fail to use adequate honorific expressions are considered poorly cultured. If the speaker does not use honorific expressions when he or she is supposed to, or uses honorific expressions when he or she is not supposed to, the conversation becomes very awkward.

Adults generally use ordinary non-honorific and low non-honorific speech to children, but they still have to use high honorific or ordinary honorific speech to children if they are not familiar with each other. However, adults can naturally switch to ordinary non-honorific or low non-honorific style when they have become close enough to the children.

Second, children tend to use ordinary non-honorific speech to their mother, since ordinary non-honorific speech sounds more friendly than other levels of honorific speech. However, children tend to use ordinary honorific speech to their father to respect and uphold his authority. However, children hardly ever use the high honorific speech to their father.

Third, there is a special way for the speaker to honor the hearer by humbling himself, which is called the 'polite strategy(공손법)'. Polite strategy is primarily used by adults aged 50 or higher working in the religious and business community, and especially in period dramas as it gives an archaic impression. Prefinal ending '-사오-, -사옵-, -(으)옵-' and pronoun 저 or 제 (in place of 나) can be used to exercise the polite strategy.

> 아주 싼 가격으로 모시고 있<u>사오</u>니 한번 왕림해 주시기 바랍니다.
> Please come visit us as we are offering a deep discount.
> 제가 그렇게 하지는 않았<u>사오</u>나 사과 말씀 드립니다.
> Even though I didn't do that, I would like to make apologies.
> <u>제</u>가 그 일을 하겠<u>사옵</u>니다.
> I will do it.
> 결혼식이 무사히 잘 끝나기를 바라<u>옵</u>니다.
> I hope the wedding goes smoothly.

Fourth, the honorific level of sentence endings in hearer-honorific speeches should be compatible with the rank of the hearer.

> <u>선생님</u>, 그동안 {평안하셨습니까?/평안하셨어요?/*평안하셨어?/*평안하 셨니?}
> Sir, how have you been?
> <u>누나</u>, 한국어사전 좀 빌려 {*주십시오/주세요/줘요/줘?/*줘라}
> Sister, please lend me the Korean dictionary.
> <u>준서야</u>, 숙제 다 {*했습니까?/*했어요?/했어?/했니?}
> Jun-Seo, have you done your homework?

Fifth, '말씀' has an ambiguity in its use. When the speaker wants to honor older people, or those at a higher position, or when the hearer is older or ranks higher than the speaker, the speaker condescends him/herself by using '말씀'.

선생님의 **말씀**을 귀담아 듣겠습니다. / I'll heed to your words.
제가 한 **말씀** 드리겠습니다. / I would like to make a comment.

Sixth, the honorific level of a speech may depend on the nuance or tone of the speaker, even if the speech sounds the same in pronunciation.

애, 빨리 집에 {가[→] / 가[→↑] / 가[↓]} / Hey, go home immediately.
어서 {오세요[→] / 오세요~[→↑] / 오세요[↓]} / Welcome.

Seventh, in an official lecture or interview, the high honorific style '-(스)ㅂ니다' form is commonly spoken. However, once the speakers get to know the audience better, they tend to mix '-(스)ㅂ니다' form and '-아/어요' form. This is because continued use of the high honorific style can make the conversation too stiff, and the hearer may even be misled to believe that the speaker intentionally wants to distance him/herself from the him/her. Thus, the speaker should refrain from using '-아/어요' form throughout the speech. However, not using '-아/어요' form at all during the conversation can also be considered impolite, as the speaker may appear not to consider the hearer as the subject of highest elevation.

17 Tense and aspect

17.1 What is tense and aspect?

Tense(시제) and aspect(상) express when and how a certain event action takes place. They can be divided into: present, past and f̶u̶t̶u̶re according to the time of the discourse and the relationship bet̶w̶e̶e̶n the preceding and following clause; or completion, progress, surm̶i̶s̶e̶, volition and experience according to the aspect of the matt̶e̶r̶.

In Korea, tense and aspect are represent̶e̶d̶ ̶b̶y̶ ̶t̶e̶rminal endings that are attached to the verbal stem (̶i̶.̶e̶.̶ ̶-̶는̶-̶,̶ -았/었-, -더-, -겠-, -(으)라-'); or verbal ph̶r̶a̶s̶e̶s̶ ̶l̶i̶k̶e̶ ̶-̶고 있다, -는 중이다, -아/어 있다'. Korean tense a̶s̶pect, however, neither change in form according to gender, number person as in German, nor are broken down into 12 different tenses in English. Tense and aspect can be indicated by adverbs like 지금 'now', 방금 'a moment ago', 아까 'a while ago', 나중 'later' and 이따가 'after a while' or nouns like 어제 'yesterday', 오늘 'today' and 내일 'tomorrow'.

What is also noteworthy is that Korean's tense and aspect are a broader concept which signifies not only the tense or aspect showing how a certain event or action takes place, but also modality, which displays the speaker's psychological attitude towards a certain event or action.

17.2 Types and characteristics of tense and aspect

17.2.1 Present tense and aspect

- Present tense

Present tense(현재시제) refers to a tense and aspect which locates the speaker's discourse in present time, denoting the present action, situation or facts. If the predicate is a verb, '-는-' (for verbs ending in a consonant) and '-ㄴ-' (ending in a vowel) are attached to the verbal stem. '-∅-' is used if the predicate is an adjective. However, the form of the tense does not change according to the gender, number or person of the subject.

> [Verb] 잡는다(◁잡-는-다) 'to catch'
> 먹는다(◁먹-는-다) 'to eat'
> 간다(◁가-ㄴ-다) 'to go'
> [Adjective] 작다(◁작-∅-다) 'to be small (in size)'
> 적다(◁적-∅-다) 'to be small (in number)'
> 높다(◁높-∅-다) 'to be high'

Prefinal ending of present tense '-ㄴ/는-' implies the **tense of the** sentence and refers to the present fact, and at the same time, signifies the aspect of the sentence, meaning that the action of the sentence is currently in progress. In other words, the sentence '나는 간다'. means both 'I go' and 'I am going'. The present tense can be expressed differently according to the level of elevation as follows:

가다 'to go': 갑니다/가십니다 ; 가오/가요 ; 가네/가 ; 간다
읽다 'to read': 읽습니다/읽으십니다 ; 읽으오/읽어요 ; 읽네/읽어 ; 읽는다

Furthermore, the marker for the present tense of adjectives 이다 and 있다 is [-Ø-]. In other words, prefinal endings should not be inserted.

오늘은 날씨가 **차다.**(◁차-Ø-다) / Today, the weather is cold.
독도는 한국 **땅이다.**(◁이-Ø-다) / Dokdo island is Korea's territory.
한국에는 네 계절이 **있다.**(◁있-Ø-다) / Korea has four seasons.

If present tense time adverbs, such as 지금 'now', 현재 'at present', 바로 이제 'right now', 이 시간에 'at this time' are used in combination with '-ㄴ/는-, -Ø-, -고 있다, -는 중이다', the presentness of the sentence becomes even more clear.

독도는 **현재** 한국 **땅이다.**(◁이-Ø-다)
Dokdo island is currently Korea's territory.
준서가 **지금** 책을 **읽고 있다.**(◁읽-고 있다)
Jun-Seo is now reading a book.
민서는 **지금** 서울에 **가는 중이다.**(◁가는 중이다)
Min-Seo is going Seoul now.

The present tense refers to the current action or status as shown above, but it can also refer to the following:

① **Current habitual action or status**

나는 늘 저녁 늦게까지 **공부한다.**(◁공부하-ㄴ-다)
I always study till late in the evening.
한국인들은 추석에 송편을 **먹는다.**(◁먹-는-다)
Koreans eat song-pyeon in Chuseok.

준서는 회사일 때문에 늘 **바쁘**다.(◁바쁘-∅-다)

Jun-Seo is always busy due to his business.

우유 속에는 유익한 영양 성분이 많이 들어 **있**다.(◁있-∅-다)

There are lots of useful nutrients in milk.

② Unchanging truth

지구는 태양의 주위를 **돈**다.(◁돌-ㄴ-다)

The Earth rotates around the Sun.

삼(3) 더하기 사(4)는 칠(7)**이**다.(◁이-∅-다)

Three plus four is seven.

물은 산소와 수소로 이루어져 **있**다.(◁있-∅-다)

Water consists of oxygen and hydrogen.

③ Actions that the speaker believes will happen in the future

그는 다음 주에 미국에 **간**다.(◁가-ㄴ-다)

He will go to America next week.

내일은 토요일**이**다.(◁이-∅-다)

Tomorrow is Saturday.

오는 11월 5일에 수능시험이 **있**다.(◁있-∅-다)

On November 5th, the college entrance exam is scheduled.

④ Actions or situations that the speaker wants to describe in detail

이순신 장군이 거북선을 이용해 왜적을 물리**친**다.(◁물리치-ㄴ-다)

General Sun-Sin Lee defeats the Japanese invaders with Turtle Ship.

시저가 루비콘 강을 건너 이탈리아로 진격**한**다.(◁진격하-ㄴ-다)

Caesar crosses Rubicon River to advance to Italy.

닐 암스트롱이 바로 달에 첫발을 내디딘 사람**이**다.(◁이-∅-다)

Neil Armstrong is the very person who landed on the moon for the first time.

예수에게는 유다라는 몹쓸 제자가 **있다**.(◁있-∅-다)
Jesus has a wicked disciple called Judas.

● Present progressive tense

Present progressive tense(현재시제진행) can be indicated by prefinal endings '-ㄴ/는-' as well as '-고 있다, -는 중이다, -는 가운데 있다, -아/어 가다, -아/어 오다'. It is possible to make present progressive tense with verbs alone.

민서는 춤추는 것을 좋아**한다**.(◁좋아하-ㄴ-다) / Min-Seo likes dancing.
준서가 책을 읽**고 있다**.(◁읽-고 있다) / Jun-Seo is reading a book.
민서는 서울에 가**는 중이다**.(◁가는 중이다)
Min-Seo is on her way to (going to) Seoul.
현재 새 건물을 짓**는 가운데 있다**.(◁짓-는 가운데 있다)
Currently, the new building is under construction (being constructed).
그녀는 숙제를 다 **해 간다**.(◁하-여 가-ㄴ-다)
She is about to complete her homework.
먹구름이 자꾸 몰**려 온다**.(◁몰리-어 오-ㄴ-다)
Dark clouds are crowding the sky.

● Present perfect tense

Present perfect tense(현재완료시제) is described by '-아/어 있다, -아/어 오다, -부터 (지금까지) … -고 있다, -부터 (지금까지) -아/어 오고/가고 있다, -아/어 있는 중이다', and can be made with verbs only.

준서는 현재 하버드 대학교에 유학을 **가 있다**.(◁가-아 있다)
Jun-Seo is currently studying in Harvard University.
나는 10년 전**부터** 여기서 살**아 왔다**.(◁살-아 오-았-다)
I have lived here for 10 years.
5천 년 전**부터 지금까지** 한국인들은 한반도에서 살**아 오고 있다**.(◁살-아

오고 있다.)

From 5,000 years ago, Koreans have lived on the Korean peninsula.
민서는 지난해**부터** **지금까지** 영국에 유학을 **가 있는 중이다.**(◁가-아 있는
중이다) / Min-Seo has studied in the UK since last year.

17.2.2 Past tense and aspect

● Past tense

Past tense(과거시제) refers to the tense where the event described in
the discourse takes place before the time of the discourse, and conveys
past actions, status, habits or experience. If the predicate is a verb or
an adjective, '-았-' is attached to verbal stems ending in yang vowels
[ㅏ, ㅗ], and '-었-' is attached to verbal stems ending in other types of
vowels. If the verb is a '하-' verb, '-였-' is used in written language,
and 했다 (condensed form of '하-' and '-였-') is used in spoken language.
However, the verb does not change in form according to the gender,
number or person of the subject.

> [Verb] 잡았다(◁잡-았-다) 'caught'
> 　　　 먹었다(◁먹-었-다) 'ate'
> 　　　 기뻐하였다/기뻐했다(◁기뻐하-였-다) 'was/were glad'
> 　　　 갔다(◁가-았-다) 'went'
> [Adjective] 작았다(◁작-았-다) 'was/were small (in size)'
> 　　　　　 적었다(◁적-었-다) 'was/were small (in number)'
> 　　　　　 불쌍하였다/불쌍했다(◁불쌍하-였-다) 'was/were pitiful'
> 　　　　　 예뻤다(◁예쁘-었-다) 'was/were pretty'

If the stem of the verb ends in a vowel, '-았-' or '-였-' is either deleted
or condensed. Refer to below for more details.

① If the verbal stem ends in such vowels as ' ㅏ, ㅓ, ㅕ ': the vowel must be deleted.

가다 'to go': 갔다/[?]가았다(◁ 가-았-다)

서다 'to stop': 섰다/[?]서었다(◁ 서-었-다)

켜다 'to light': 켰다/[?]켜었다(◁ 켜-었-다)

② If the verbal stem ends in such vowels as 'ㅗ, ㅜ': depends on the word.

오다 'to come': 왔다/[*]오았다(◁ 오-았-다)

보다 'to see': 봤다/보았다(◁ 보-았-다)

외우다 'to memorize': 외웠다/[*]외우었다(◁ 외우-었-다)

주다 'to give': 줬다/주었다(◁ 주-었-다)

③ If the verbal stem ends in vowel ' ㅣ ': if the vowel ' ㅣ ' comes after consonants like 'ㅅ, ㅈ, ㅊ, ㅉ, ㄹ', the verb must be used in a condensed form. If not, both the full and condensed forms can be used interchangeably.

지다 'to be defeated': 졌다/[*]지었다(◁ 지-었-다)

치다 'to hit': 쳤다/[*]치었다(◁ 치-었-다)

찌다 'to steam': 쪘다/[*]찌었다(◁ 찌-었-다)

마시다 'to drink': 마셨다/[?]마시었다(◁ 마시-었-다)

④ If the verbal stem ends in vowel 'ㅟ': it is impossible to use condensed forms.

뛰다 'to jump': [*]뛨다/뛰었다(◁ 뛰-었-다)

쉬다 'to rest': [*]쉤다/쉬었다(◁ 쉬-었-다)

⑤ If the verb is a irregular verb 'ㅅ': it is possible to use both the condensed and original forms in spoken language, but only original form should be used in written language.

붓다 'to pour': ^{?*}붰다/부었다(◁붓-었-다)
긋다 'to draw': ^{?*}겄다/그었다(◁긋-었-다)
잇다 'to link': ^{?*}였다/이었다(◁잇-었-다)

Past tense prefinal endings '-았/었/였-' convey facts of the past as a **tense** and also completion of an action or event as an **aspect**(상, 相). In other words, the sentence '그는 갔다' can be understood as not only 'he went' but also 'he has gone'.

Past tense can be expressed differently depending on the level of elevation as shown in the following:

가다 'to go': 갔다/가셨습니다 ; 갔소/갔어요 ; 갔네/갔어 ; 갔다
읽다 'to read': 읽었습니다/읽으셨습니다 ; 읽었소/읽었어요 ; 읽었네/읽었
        어 ; 읽었다

Also, the marker for past tenses 이다 and 있다 is always '-었-'.

마이클은 1년 전에는 미국인이**었**다.(◁이-었-다)
Michael was an American one year ago.
예전에 한국에는 야간 통행 금지법이 있**었**다.(◁있-었-다)
In the past, there was a curfew system in Korea.

If past tense time adverbs such as 아까 'a while ago', 방금 'a moment ago', 지난달/지난해 'last month/year' are combined with '-었-, -고 있었다, -는 중이었다, -는 가운데 있었다', more emphasis can be placed on the pastness of the sentence.

독도는 **옛날에도** 한국 땅이**었다**.(◁이-었-다)

Dokdo island has been Korean territory.

준서가 **어제** 책을 읽고 **있었다**.(◁읽-고 있었다)

Jun-Seo was reading a book yesterday.

민서는 **아까** 도서관에 가**는 중이었다**.(◁가는 중이었다)

Min-Seo was going to the library a while ago.

수년 전에 새 건물을 짓**는 가운데 있었다**.(◁짓-는 가운데 있었다)

The building was under construction several years ago.

Past tense conveys not only past actions or status, but also the following:

① **An action or status of the future that the speaker believes will definitely happen**: the sentences below respectively mean 'you will definitely be scolded', 'you will never be able to get married', and 'you will never be able to come to Korea'.

너 자꾸 까불면 죽**었어**.(◁죽-었-어)

If you keep behaving badly, you will be dead.

(= I won't put up with it any longer.)

너 이제 시집은 다 **갔다**.(◁가았다)

You have gotten married at all.

(= You will never be able to get married.)

그래 가지고는 한국에 다 **왔다**.(◁오-았다)

You have come to Korea in such a way.

(= You will never be able to come to Korea in such a way.)

② **The present status or fact (used in combination with adjectives)**: Not all adjectives are used in the past tense to describe the present status or facts, except 생기다 'to appear like', 닮다 'to resemble', 늙다 'to get old', (몸이) 마르다 'to get thin', (살이) 찌다 'to get fat', 낡다 'to get worn out', 멀다 'to be far'.

그 아이 참 잘생겼어.(◁잘생기-었-어)

The kid is very good-looking.

준서는 자기 아버지를 많이 닮았다.(◁닮-았-다)

Jun-Seo looks very much like his father.

갈 길이 아직 멀었니?(◁멀-었-니?)

Do you still have a long way to go?

● Past progressive tense

Past progressive tense(과거진행시제) can be expressed by verbs only with prefinal endings like '-고 있었다, -는 중이었다', and '-는 가운데 있었다'.

준서가 책을 읽고 있었다.(◁읽-고 있었다)

Jun-Seo was reading a book.

민서는 서울에 가는 중이었다.(◁가는 중이었다)

Min-Seo was going to Seoul.

10년 전 그때 새 건물을 짓는 가운데 있었다.(◁짓는 가운데 있었다)

Ten years ago, the new building was under construction.

● Past perfect tense

Past perfect tense(과거완료시제) can be expressed by verbs only with such phrases as '-아/어 있었다, -아/어 왔었다, -부터 … -까지 … -고 있었다, -부터 … (-까지) -아 오고/가고 있었다'.

준서는 작년에 하버드 대학에 유학을 가 있었다.(◁가아 있었다)

Jun-Seo had studied in Harvard University last year.

그는 이 책을 재미있게 읽어 왔었다.(◁읽-어 왔었다)

He had read this book with great interest.

민서는 1년 전부터 지난달까지 서울에서 살고 있었다.(◁살-고 있었다)

Min-Seo had lived in Seoul from one year ago until last month.

그 팀은 10년 전부터 작년까지 우승을 기다려 오고 있었다.(◁기다리-어
오고 있었다)
The team had waited for success from ten years ago till last year.

- **'-았/었었-'** and experience

Prefinal ending '-았/었었-' denotes a past experience, and the subject
is usually human. '-았/었었-' can be used interchangeably with '-(으)ㄴ
적이 있다', and '-(으)ㄴ 경험이 있다'.

나는 작년에 뉴욕에 **갔었다**.(◁가-았었-다)
I went to New York last year.
→ 나는 작년에 뉴욕에 **간 적이/경험이 있다**.
I had been to New York last year.

준서는 몇 년 전에 경주에 **왔었다**.(◁오-았었-다)
Jun-Seo came to Gyeongju a few years ago.
→ 준서는 몇 년 전에 경주에 **온 적이/경험이 있다**.
Jun-Seo had been to Gyeongju a few years ago.

If the subject is an object, a matter or a status; or the subject is a
human and predicate an adjective, both cases represent 'isolation from
the past'. In other words, they mean 'the matter or status existed in the
past, but no longer so in the present'.

선생님, 어제 댁에서 **전화가 왔었**어요.(◁오-았었-어요)
Sir, you had a phone call from your home yesterday.
→ Implication: There were no more phone calls from then on.

민서는 예전에 **얼굴이 예뻤었**다.(◁예쁘-었었-다)
Min-Seo used to be pretty.
→ Implication: She is no longer pretty now.

어제는 **바람이** 많이 **불었었**다.(◁불-었었-다)

Yesterday, it was very windy.

→ Implication: It is no longer windy now.

준서는 어렸을 때 매우 **약했었**다.(◁약하-였었-다)

Jun-Seo was very weak when he was young.

→ Implication: He is no longer weak.

- '**-더-**' and retrospection

'**-더-**' is used when the speaker wants to talk about his or her past experience in reminiscence or wants to convey his or her past experience. In other words, '**-더-**' is used when the speaker wants to recollect his own experience or something that he heard of at a time in the past, or when he wants to ask the hearer to recollect what the hearer experienced. Therefore, neither first person subject is used in an declarative sentence nor second person subject in an interrogative sentence. Imperative or propositive endings cannot end the retrospective sentence.

지난해에 금강산에 갔었는데, 경치가 대단하**더**라.(◁대단하-더-라)

(I) went to Mountain Geumgang last year, and the scenary was great.

민서는 피아노를 잘 치**더**냐?(◁치-더-냐?)

Did Min-Seo play the piano well?

{?*나/너/그}는 컴퓨터 게임을 잘하**더**라.(◁잘하-더-라)

{I/you/he} played the computer game very well.

{나/?*너/그}는 한국 사람이 맞**더**냐?(◁맞-더-냐?)

Was it right that {I/*you/he} was Korean?

준서가 축구를 {하**더**라/하**더**냐?/*하**더**라/*하**더**자/하**더**구나}

Jun-Seo played soccer./Did Jun-Seo play soccer?/Jun-Seo is playing soccer.

Also, '**-더-**' is used when the speaker realizes something that he did not know in the past, or the speaker wants to tell others what happened to himself in an objective manner.

알고 보니 **그 사람** 참 멋있는 사람이**더**라.(◁이-더-라)
As it turned out, he/she was a very nice person.
준서의 이야기를 듣고 보니, **내가** 잘못했**더**라.(◁잘못하-였-더-라)
As I was listening to Jun-Seo's story, I realized that it was my fault.

In a very exceptional case, '-더-' is employed when the speaker wants to tell others something that will happen in the future. In other words, the sentences below show how the speaker, with knowledge about the waiting list of surgery or the schedule for the mid-term exam, tells others about such facts.

그 사람 다음 달에 수술 받**더**라.(◁받-더-라)
He/she will undergo an operation next month.
준서 다음 주에 중간고사 보**더**라.(◁보-더-라)
Jun-Seo will have his mid-term exam next week.

● Overlap of prefinal endings

Past-representing prefinal ending '-았/었-' can be combined with '-더-, -았/었-, -(으)리-, -겠-, etc'. The preceding prefinal ending '-았/었-' represents the past tense and the following prefinal ending signifies the aspect.

For example, '-았겠/었겠-' represents past-surmise, '-았더/었더-' past-retrospective/delivery, '-았으리/었으리-' past-surmise, '-았겠더/었겠더-' past surmise-retrospective/delivery and '-았었겠/었었겠-' and '-았었으리/었었으리-' past-experience/isolation-surmise.

지금쯤 편지가 뉴욕에 도착**했겠**지?(◁도착하-였-겠-지?)
I guess the letter has arrived in New York by now.
저 아이에게 어떤 일이 일어**났던**가?(◁일어나-았-더-ㄴ가?)

Did anything happen to that kid?

이미 위험한 상황이 종결되**었겠더**라.(◁종결되-었-겠-더-라)

I guess the dangerous situation has ended.

민서가 사랑한다고 먼저 고백을 **했었겠**지?(◁하-였었-겠-지?)

I guess Min-Seo confessed her love first?

나는 준서가 그 일을 **했었으리**라 생각한다.(◁하-였었-으리-라)

I believe that Jun-Seo had done the work.

17.2.3 Future tense and aspect

• Future tense

Future tense(미래시제), which represents actions or status of the future, is when the event mentioned in the dialogue happens ex-post. Prefinal endings signifying the future tense include '-겠-' and '-(으)리-'. '-(으)리-' is hardly ever spoken, except for old-fashioned expressions such as '-(으)리다, -(으)리라, and -(으)리까'. Moreover, the future tense is very often represented by '-(으)ㄹ 것', which is a combination of modifier ending '-(으)ㄹ' and dependent noun '것'. In spoken language, '-(으)ㄹ 것' is condensed into '-(으)ㄹ 거'.

> [Verb] 잡겠다(◁잡-겠-다) 'to catch'
> 먹겠다(◁먹-겠-다) 'to eat'
> 기뻐하겠다(◁기뻐하-겠-다) 'to be joyful'
> 잡으리라(◁잡-으리-라) 'to catch'
> 먹으리라(◁먹-으리-라) 'to eat'
> 기뻐하리라(◁기뻐하-리-라) 'to be joyful'
> 잡을 것이다(◁잡-을 것-이-다) 'to catch'
> 먹을 것이다(◁먹-을 것-이-다) 'to eat'
> 기뻐할 것이다(◁기뻐하-ㄹ 것-이-다) 'to be joyful'
> [Adjective] 작겠다(◁작-겠-다) 'to be small'

적겠다(◁적-겠-다) 'to be few'
불쌍하겠다(◁불쌍하-겠-다) 'to be pitiful'
작으리라(◁작-으리-라) 'to be small'
적으리라(◁적-으리-라) 'to be few'
불쌍하리라(◁불쌍하-리-라) 'to be pitiful'
작을 것이다(◁작-을 것-이-다) 'to be small'
적을 것이다(◁적-을 것-이-다) 'to be few'
불쌍할 것이다(◁불쌍하-ㄹ 것-이-다) 'to be pitiful'

Future-tense prefinal ending '-겠-, -(으)리-' and '-(으)ㄹ 것' represent future in terms of **tense**, and intention, surmise, plan, and possibility of the speaker in terms of **aspect**.

① If the speaker is the first person subject and the predicate is a verb, the prefinal endings symbolize intentions of the speaker.

제가 그 일을 {하**겠**습니다/ʔ하**리**다/**할 거**예요} / I will do the job.
나는 내일 도서관에 공부하러 {가**겠**습니다/ʔ가**리**다/**갈 거**예요}
I will go to the library tomorrow to study.

If the subject is second person or somebody, and the predicate is a verb, the prefinal endings stand to ask the intentions of the hearer.

네가 나를 좀 {도와주**겠**니?/도와**줄 거**야?} / Will you help me?
누가 그 일을 {하**겠**어요?/**할 거**예요?} / Who will do the job?

② If the subject is third person or an object, the prefinal endings represent surmise, plan, or possibility.

[Surmise]: 지금쯤 서울에는 비가 많이 {오**겠**다/ʔ오**리**라/**올 것** 같다}
I guess it is raining heavily in Seoul now.

[Plan]: 잠시 후 경기가 {열리겠습니다/?*열리리라/열릴 것이다}
The game shall start in a while.
[Possibility]: 어린애라도 그것쯤은 {하겠다/?*하리라/할 것이다}
Even a child can do the job.

Furthermore, combination of future-representing time adverbs (i.e. 곧 'soon', 조금 뒤 'a little later', 다음 달/해 'next month/year' and '-겠-, -(으)라, -(으)ㄹ 것' can emphasize the meaning of future tense even more.

독도는 **영원히** 한국 땅으로 남**을 것**이다.(◁남-을 것-이다)
Dokdo island shall forever remain Korea's territory.
공연이 **곧** 시작되**겠**다.(◁되-겠-다) / I guess the show will start soon.
수년 뒤에 새 건물을 짓고 있**을 것**이다.(◁짓고 있-을 것-이다)
I guess (I) will be building a new building in the coming years.

● Future progressive tense

Future progressive tense(미래진행시제) can be represented by prefinal endings '-고 있겠다, -고 있으리라', and '-고 있을 것이다'. This future progressive tense always conveys not only future but also surmise of the speaker.

준서가 책을 읽**고 있겠**다.(◁읽-고 있겠다)
I guess Jun-Seo would be reading a book.
민서는 서울에 가**고 있으리**다.(◁가-고 있으리라)
I guess Min-Seo will be on her way to Seoul.
현재 새 건물을 짓**고 있을 것**이다.(◁짓-고 있을 것이다)
I guess (they) will be building a new building now.

● Future perfect tense

Future perfect tense is expressed by '-아/어 있겠다, -아/어 있으리라,

-아/어 있을 것이다, -아 오고/가고 있겠다/있으리라/있을 것이다', and can be made by verbs only. They also signify the speaker's surmise.

준서는 내년쯤에 하버드 대학에 유학을 **가 있겠다**.(◁가-아 있겠다)
I guess Jun-Seo will have gone to Harvard University next year.
나는 10년 후에 부자가 **되어 있으리라**.(◁되-어 있으리라)
I guess I will have become rich in ten years.
나는 수년 후에 어르신들을 돕는 자원봉사를 **해 오고 있을 것이다**.(◁하-여 오고 있을 것이다)
I will have been volunteering to help old people several years later.

- ● Overlap of prefinal endings

Future-representing '-겠-' is used in combination with '-더-' to convey future-surmise-retrospective/delivery.

준서는 축구를 잘하**겠더**라.(◁잘하-겠-더-라)
I guess Jun-Seo is good at football.
민서는 입이 짧아서 밥을 잘 안 먹**겠더**라.(◁먹-겠-더-라)
I guess Min-Seo, who is picky about food, does not eat much.

17.3 Tense and aspect in an adnominal clause

- ● Present tense

Attach '-는' to a verb. If the stem of an adjective ends in a consonant, use '-은', and if ending in a vowel, use '-ㄴ'. Use '-ㄴ' for '이다' and '-는' for '있다'.

한국에는 눈이 오**는** 날이 많다.(◁오-는)
There are many snowy days in Korea.

우리 반에는 키가 작**은** 학생이 별로 없다.(◁작-은)
There are not many short students in my class.
화단에 예**쁜** 꽃이 많이 피어 있다.(◁예쁘-ㄴ)
There are many beautiful flowers in flower beds.
한국 민요**인** 아리랑은 부르기가 매우 쉽다.(◁이-ㄴ)
Korean folk song, Arirang, is easy to sing.
저기에 서 있**는** 분이 바로 김 교수님이다.(◁있-는)
The man standing over there is Professor Kim.

● Past tense

Attach '-(으)ㄴ' or '-던' to a verb. '-던' is a combination of recollective prefinal ending '-더-' and modifier ending '-ㄴ'. If the sentence is a 있다 sentence, attach '-은' or '-던' to the verb. Moreover, past-tense prefinal ending '-았/었-' can be added in front of '-(으)ㄴ' and '-던' to stress the pastness of the sentence.

나는 불고기를 {먹**은**/먹**던**/먹**었던**} 적이 있다.(◁먹-은/먹-더-ㄴ/먹-었-더-ㄴ) / I have eaten Bulgogi before.
키가 {작**던**/작**았던**} 어린이가 요즘 무척 많이 자랐다.(◁작-더-ㄴ/작-았-더-ㄴ) / The kid who was short got much taller recently.
{철부지이**던**/철부지이**었던**} 준서가 이제 의젓해졌다.(◁이-더-ㄴ/이-었-더-ㄴ) / Jun-Seo, who was just a kid, became quite mature.
여기 {있**던**/있**었던**} 책이 어디 갔지?(◁있-더-ㄴ/있-었-더-ㄴ)
Where have the books that were here gone?

● Future tense

Attach '-(으)ㄹ' to a verb and use '-을' for 있다 sentences.

나는 오늘 저녁에 불고기를 먹**을** 예정이다.(◁먹-을)
I am going to have Bulgogi for dinner tonight.

준서는 내일 워싱턴으로 떠날 계획이 있다.(◁떠나ㄹ)

Jun-Seo plans to leave for Washington tomorrow.

전쟁터에 그냥 남아 있을 사람은 없다.(◁있-을)

No one will remain on the battlefield.

■ Absolute tense and relative tense

It is very useful to explain the tense of adnominal clause and connective clause with absolute and relative tense. As mentioned earlier, the **absolute tense**(절대시제) refers to the tense based on the time of the dialogue, while the **relative tense**(상대시제) is based on the time the event takes place.

In the sentence below, the predicate of the encompassing sentence is in the past tense '만났다', and the predicate of the encompassed sentence is in the present tense '가는', so the sentence seems to be in conflict. However, it is easy to understand the conflicting tenses from the perspective of relative tense. In other words, based on the past of the tense of predicate '만나았다' in the encompassing sentence, 'the bus going to Seoul' in the encompassed sentence is interpreted as present, thus, present-tense adnominal ending '-는' can be used in the sentence.

나는 서울로 가는 버스에서 준서를 만났다.(◁만나았다)
I met Jun-Seo in the bus to Seoul.

The same applies to following sentences. Based on the tense of the encompassing sentence's predicate '않았다', 'my meeting friends' is an event of the future, so future-tense adnominal ending '-(으)ㄹ' can be used in the sentence. Moreover, based on the presentness of '그리워하다', 'meeting Jun-Seo in London' is already an event of the past, so it is possible to use past-tense adnominal ending '-(으)ㄴ'.

서울역에서 만날 친구들이 아직 도착하지 않았다.(◁않았다)
My friends, who I will meet at Seoul Station, have not yet arrived.
그녀는 지난해에 런던에서 만난 준서를 그리워한다.(◁그리워하-ㄴ-다)
She misses Jun-Seo, whom she met last year in London.

In connective clauses, it is necessary to introduce the relative tense. In each of the following sentences, the predicate of the following clause is in the past tense '만났다', and the encompassed sentence has no tense indicator '가-ø-아서', so it seems as if the tense of the sentence is in error. However, based on the predicate of the following clause '만나-았-다', it is clear that 'my going to Seoul' is an event of the past, thus it is easy to see that the tense of the preceding clause is past even though past-tense prefinal ending '-았/었-' is not used.

나는 서울에 가서, 민서를 만났다.(◁가-ø-아서, 만나-았-다)
I went to Seoul and met Min-Seo.
준서는 공부하러, 도서관에 갔다.(◁공부하-ø-러, 가-았-다)
Jun-Seo, to study, went to the library.

17.4 Korean cultural aspects as reflected in tense and aspect

In the Korean language, the use of aspect is more sophisticated than tense. In other words, Koreans put significance on the aspect of an action over the time of the action.

In fact, '-ㄴ/는-' in the sentences below is known as a prefinal ending representing the present tense, but it is used to convey not only present but also past and even future tenses, therefore it is difficult to say that '-ㄴ/는-' represents the present tense only. Therefore, '-ㄴ/는-' can be a prefinal ending that indicates a certain action is in progress.

[Present+progressive]: 준서는 지금 간다.(◁가-ㄴ-다)
　　　　　　　　　　　Jun-Seo is now going.
[Future+progressive]: 나는 내일 그 사과 먹는다.(◁먹-는-다)
　　　　　　　　　　　I will eat the apple tomorrow.

The same applies to '-았/었-' which represents the past tense. In the following sentences, '-았/었-' conveys not only the present but also the future. Therefore, '-았/었-' can be used when the speaker is convinced that the situation at issue is happening or will definitely happen in the future, rather than simply conveying the pastness of the sentence.

[Present+conviction]: 야, 정말 큰일 **났**다.(◁나-았-다)
       Hey, by heavens!
[Past+conviction]: 너 정말 그렇게 자꾸 말하면 끝**났**어.(◁끝나-았-어)
       If you keep talking like that, I will no longer be a
       friend of yours.

'-겠-' and '-(으)리-', which represent the future tense, can also be used for the past, present and future circumstances. Therefore, they do not simply indicate future tense but future-volition or future-surmise.

[Past+surmise]: 이미 축구 경기가 끝났**겠**지?(◁끝나-았-겠-지)
      I guess the football match is already over?
[Past+surmise]: 일이 잘 마무리가 되었**으리**라 믿는다.(◁되-었-으리-라)
      I guess things have been well done.
[Present+surmise]: 서울에는 지금쯤 눈이 많이 오**겠**다.(◁오-겠-다)
      I guess it is snowing heavily in Seoul.
[Present+surmise]: 현재 런던에 도착하**리**라 생각되지만, 네가 준서의 도착
      여부를 확인해 보렴.(◁도착하-리-라)
      I guess Jun-Seo has arrived in London now, but please
      confirm Jun-Seo's arrival.
[Present+volition]: 내가 그 일을 지금 하**겠**다.(◁하-겠-다)
      I will do the work now.
[Future+surmise]: 내일쯤 일을 마무리할 수 있**겠**다.(◁있-겠-다)
      I guess I can wrap up the work probably tomorrow.
[Future+volition]: 나의 꿈을 언젠가는 꼭 이루**리**라.(◁이루-리-라)

I will certainly achieve my dream some day.

Therefore, it can be witnessed that Koreans place more importance on the process or the perspective of a certain action than the time of the action.

18 Negation

18.1 What is negation?

Negation(부정법) negates what is written in a positive sentence. Koreans use negative adverbs such as 아니, 못 or negative auxiliary verb 말다 to negate the sentence.

18.2 Types and characteristics of negation

18.2.1 Negation by 아니

● Subject-intended negation

In order to represent negation which is intended by the subject, 아니(or 안) and 아니하다(or 않다) can be used. 아니, which is always put before verbs, is called short negation whereas 아니하다, which is always put after verbs in the form of '-지 아니하다' is called long negation. To represent intended negation, the subject must be human and the predicate must be a verb.

The following sentence means that 'I can keep the promise, but did not keep the promise because I did not want to'.

> [Affirmative] 나는 약속을 지켰다. / I kept the promise.
> [Negative] 나는 약속을 **안** 지켰다.
>> I did not keep the promise (on purpose).
>> 나는 약속을 지키**지 않**았다.
>> I did not keep the promise (on purpose).

Intended negation by 아니 has an emphasis if combined with prefinal ending '-겠-' or connective ending '-(으)려 하다', which represent the intention of the subject.

> 나는 약속을 **안** 지키**겠**다. / I will not keep the promise.
> 나는 약속을 **안** 지키**려 한다**. / I try not to keep the promise.

Intended negation by 아니 is used in declarative and interrogative sentences, but not in imperative or propositive sentences. In imperative or propositive sentences, 말다 is used instead in the form of '-지 말다'.

> [Declarative]   나는 약속을 **안** 지켰다. / I did not keep the promise.
> [Interrogative] 너는 약속을 **안** 지키겠니?
>> Are you not going to keep the promise?
> [Imperative]   너는 약속을 {***안** 지켜라/*지키**지 않**아라/지키**지 마라**}
>> You should not keep the promise.
> [Propositive] 우리 함께 약속을 {***안** 지키자/*지키**지 않**자/지키**지 말자**}
>> Let us not keep the promise.

- Simple negation

'아니, 아니하다' and 아니다 can be used to represent not only intended negation but also negation of given facts and phenomena.

In this case, the subject tends to be an object or an animal, and the predicate an adjective or an intransitive verb. The following sentences are an objective description of the current weather condition.

[Affirmative] 오늘은 비가 온다. / It is raining today.
[Negative] 오늘은 비가 **안** 온다. / It does not rain today.
오늘은 비가 오<u>지 않</u>는다. / It does not rain today.

아니다 is a combination of negative adverb 아니 and predicate '-이다'. 아니다 negates sentences that end in '-이다'. It is always written in the form of '-이/가 아니다'.

[Affirmative] 준서는 의사<u>이다</u>. / Jun-Seo is a doctor.
[Negative] 준서는 의사<u>가 아니다</u>. / Jun-Seo is not a doctor.

● Characteristics of a 아니 sentence

① There are no semantic differences between the short and long negative sentence, but the short negation is usually for colloquial use and the long negation for written language. Of course, the short negation may be used in the written language and the long negation vice versa, but this will only make the phrase very awkward.

A: 이 사과 먹을래요? / Will you eat this apple?
B: 아니, **안** 먹을래요. / No, I will not.
    ?아니, 먹<u>지 않</u>을래요. / No, I will not.

However, the long negation can be used in colloquial speeches to emphasize a specific sentence component, for example, by adding an auxiliary particle '-는' to '먹지 않을 거야' in order to make '먹지는 않을 거야'.

② 아니 or 아니하다 may not be compatible with certain verbs. In other words, sentences with such verbs as 견디다 'to endure', 알다 'to know', 모르다 'to be ignorant of something', 깨닫다 'to realize' cannot be negated because affirmation or negation of these verbs depend on external factors, not the intention of the subject. Instead, 못 can negate these verbs.

준서는 지구가 둥글다는 사실을 깨달았다.
Jun-Seo realized that the earth is round.
*준서는 지구가 둥글다는 사실을 {**안** 깨달았다/깨닫**지 않았다**}
Jun-Seo did not realize that the earth is round.
준서는 지구가 둥글다는 사실을 {**못** 깨달았다/깨닫**지 못했다**}
Jun-Seo could not realize that the earth is round.

③ The meaning of 아니 sentences is subject to change according to which sentence components 아니 negates. The following sentences can be understood in four ways.

ⓐ<u>준서가</u> ⓑ<u>어제</u> ⓒ<u>학교에</u> ⓓ<u>가지</u> <u>않았다</u>.

Jun-Seo   yesterday   school   go   didn't.

ⓐ It was not Jun-Seo who went to school. Negation of [Jun-Seo]
ⓑ It was not yesterday that Jun-Seo went to school. Negation of [YESTERDAY]
ⓒ It was not school that Jun-Seo went yesterday. Negation of [SCHOOL]
ⓓ Jun-Seo did not go to school yesterday. (= Jun-Seo was absent yesterday.): negation of [GO]

④ If adverbs like 모두 'all', 다 'all, every', 많이 'many', 적당히 'moderately', 조금 'a little', 약간 'slightly' are in a negative sentence, the meaning of the sentence is subject to change according to whether the adverb falls under the scope of negation.

숙제를 ⓐ<u>다</u> ⓑ<u>안 했다</u>.

(I) Homework all not did

ⓐ I did some homework. Negation of [ALL]: In this case, '-는' should
be combined with the adverb 다.
ⓑ I did not do any homework. Negation of [DID]

To eliminate ambiguity caused by the scope of negation, the speaker
can stress the sentence component that is being negated, or add a differen-
tiating auxiliary particle '-은/는' to the adverb. The following sentences,
in which the sentence component combined with '-은/는' is negated, mean
that 'the subject went to a place other than school, and did some of
his homework'.

준서가 <u>학교에</u> 가지 않았다.
Jun-Seo did not go to school.: 'school' is stressed
준서가 숙제를 다<u>는</u> 안 했다.
Jun-Seo did not do all of his homework.: '-는' is added to the adverb

⑤ Short negation of '-하다' verbs, such as 공부하다 'to study', 명상하다
'to meditate', 운동하다 'to play sports', 반대하다 'to oppose' should be
'공부 안 하다, 명상 안 하다, 운동 안 하다, 반대 안 하다', instead of '*안
공부하다, *안 명상하다, *안 운동하다, *안 반대하다'. However, not all verbs
(including other 하- verbs) are subject to the short negation above. As
for verbs like 두려워하다 'to fear something', 부지런하다 'to be hardworking', 부족하다 'to lack something', they can be negated in both ways:
'안 두려워하다/두려워 안 하다, 안 부지런하다/부지런 안 하다, 안 부족하다/부

족 안 하다'.

> [Affirmative] 준서는 요즘 한국어 공부한다.
>> Jun-Seo is studying Korean these days.
> [Negative] 준서는 요즘 한국어 공부 **안** 한다.
>> Jun-Seo is not studying Korean these days.
> *준서는 요즘 한국어 **안** 공부한다.
>> Jun-Seo is not studying Korean these days.

⑥ The use of negative auxiliary verb 아니하다 may not sometimes denote negation. Rather, the verbs may imply confirmation or surmise of facts, in which case, '-지 않-' can be contracted to '-잖-'.

> 네가 예전에 민서를 {사랑했**지 않**니?/사랑했**잖**니?}
> Didn't you love Min-Seo in the past?
> 올 여름도 큰 홍수가 {나**지 않**을까/나**잖**을까} 걱정이야.
> I am worried that there might be a severe flood this summer again.

18.2.2 Negation by 못

- Negation caused by the subject's incapability or unfavorable circumstances

못 and 못하다 represent negations caused by the subject's incapability. 못 is always inserted before a verb, and is referred to as short negation, whereas 못하다 is always put after a verb in the form of '-지 못하다', and is referred to as long negation. In both cases, the predicate must be a verb to denote negation that is caused by the subject's incapability or unfavorable circumstances. In other words, 못 and 못하다 cannot be used with adjectives or 이다.

The following sentences show that 'the subject wants to keep the promise, but cannot do so due to lack of capability or some external difficulties'.

[Affirmative] 나는 약속을 지켰다. / I kept the promise.
[Negative] 나는 약속을 **못** 지켰다. / I could not keep the promise.
나는 약속을 지키<u>지 **못했다**</u>. / I could not keep the promise.

In the following sentences, the speaker believes that 'the inanimate subject airplane can fly since it is in good condition, but the airplane cannot fly well due to unfavorable environment'.

[Affirmative] 이 비행기는 잘 난다. / This plane flies well.
[Negative] 이 비행기는 잘 날<u>지 **못한다**</u>. / This fly does not fly well.
이 비행기는 잘 **못** 난다. / This fly does not fly well.

Negation by incapability, which is expressed in 못, becomes even clearer if used with causal expressions such as '-아/어서, -(으)니까, -(으)므로, -느라(고), -때문에, -는 바람에, -는 통에' or '더 이상, 도저히'. Also, these expressions can be converted into '-(으)ㄹ 수 없(었)다'.

[Negation by incapability]
힘이 없기 **때문에** **더 이상**은 걷<u>지 **못**</u>하겠다. (= 걸을 수가 없다)
With no strength left, no more can I walk.
[Negation by circumstance]
전쟁이 나<u>서</u> 나는 약속을 **못** 지켰다. (= 지킬 수 없었다)
Due to the outbreak of the war, I could not keep the promise.

못 is used in declarative and interrogative sentences, not in imperative or propositive sentences. Imperative and propositive sentences always use 말다 in the form of '-지 말다'.

> [Declarative] 나는 약속을 **못** 지킨다. / I cannot keep the promise.
> [Interrogative] 너는 약속을 **못** 지키겠니?
> > Can't you keep the promise? (= Do you not have the ability to keep the promise?
> [Imperative] 너는 약속을 {[*]**못** 지켜라/[*]지키<u>지 못해</u>라/지키<u>지 마라</u>}
> > You should not keep the promise.
> [Propositive] 우리 함께 약속을 {[*]**못** 지키자/[*]지키<u>지 못하</u>자/지키<u>지 말자</u>}
> > Let's not keep the promise.

- ● Characteristics of **못** sentence

① Short negation is typically for colloquial use and long negation for written language, as in the case of 아니 sentences.

> A: 너 이 사과 먹을래? / Will you eat this apple?
> B: 아니요, **못** 먹겠어요. / No, I cannot.
> > [?]아니요, 먹<u>지 못</u>하겠어요. / No, I cannot.

② **못** denotes a condition in which the subject cannot do certain actions due to a specific situation rather than his/her own will. Therefore, **못** cannot be used with non-action adjectives or 이다.

> [*]민서는 {**못** 아름답다/아름답<u>지 못하</u>다}
> Min-Seo cannot be/is unable to be beautiful.
> [*]준서는 {**못** 대학생이다/대학생이<u>지 못하</u>다}
> Jun-Seo cannot be/is unable to be a college student.

However, it is possible for **못** to negate positive adjectives combined with '-하다', such as 깨끗하다 'to be clean', 검소하다 'to be frugal', 다양하

다 'to be various', 독실하다 'to be devout', 똑똑하다 'to be smart', 만족하다 'to be satisfied with something', 민감하다 'to be sensitive', 부유하다 'to be wealthy', 공평하다 'to be fair', 상냥하다 'to be nice and friendly', 자신만만하다 'to be self-confident', 자상하다 'to be thoughtful', 청렴하다 'to be upright', 결백하다 'to be innocent'. If 못 is used in conjunction with these adjectives, the sentence will imply that the subject falls short of the positive expectations. The adjectives can be negated only in the form of long negation.

그는 생활이 {검소하지 못하다/*못 검소하다} / He is not frugal.
준서는 성격이 {자상하지 못하다/*못 자상하다} / Jun-Seo is not considerate.

③ Prefinal ending which signifies the tense and aspects should be inserted after '-지 못하-'.

[Affirmative] 준서는 민서를 만났다. / Jun-Seo met Min-Seo.
[Negative] 준서를 민서를 만나지 못했다.(◁만나-지 못하-였-다)
        Jun-Seo could not meet Min-Seo.
        *준서는 민서를 만났지 못하다.(◁만나-았-지 못하-다)
        Jun-Seo could not meet Min-Seo.

Honorific prefinal ending '-시-' can be affixed before '-지 못하-', but is generally put after 못하다.

[Affirmative] 선생님께서는 준서에게 선물을 주셨다.
        The teacher gave Jun-Seo a present.
[Negative] 선생님께서는 준서에게 선물을 주지 못하셨다.(◁주-지 못하-시-었-다) / The teacher could not give Jun-Seo a present.
        선생님께서는 준서에게 선물을 주시지 못했다.(◁주-시-지 못하-였-다) / The teacher could not give Jun-Seo a present.

18.2.3 Negation by 말다

말다 implies prohibition or negative recommendation. 말다 is a long negation since it is always inserted after a verb in the form of '-지 말다'. 말다 is always attached to verbs or 있다, and cannot be used in conjunction with adjectives or 이다.

> 너는 서울에 가<u>지 마</u>라. / You should not go to Seoul.
> 당신은 여기 있<u>지 마</u>십시오. / (You) Do not stay here.
> *너는 예쁘<u>지 마</u>라. / You should not be pretty.
> *너는 죄인이<u>지 마</u>라. / You should not be a sinner.

'말다, 아니, 못' complement each other, since 말다 is for commands and proposals whereas '아니, 못' are for statements and questions.

> [Declarative] 너는 약속을 지키지 {***만다**/**않는다**/**못한다**}
>   You do not keep your promise.
> [Interrogative] 너는 약속을 지키지 {**말겠니?**/**않겠니?**/**못하겠니?**}
>   Are you not going to keep your promise?
> [Imperative] 너는 약속을 지키지 {마라/***않아라**/***못해라**}
>   You should not keep your promise.
> [Propositive] 우리 함께 약속을 지키지 {말자/***않자**/***못하자**}
>   Let's not keep the promise.

- ● Characteristics of 말다 negation

① Even declarative sentences can use '-지 말다' with verbs representing wishes and hopes (e.g. 바라다 'to wish', 원하다 'to want', 희망하다 'to hope', 기대하다 'to look forward to'), or phrases denoting hope or assumption (e.g. '-았/었으면 하다, -았/었더라면 좋겠다').

나는 네가 거짓말을 하지 {말기/않기/못하기}를 **바란다**.
I wish that you do not lie.
나는 네가 거짓말을 하지 {말**았으면**/않**았으면**/못**했으면**} **한다**.
I wish that you do not lie.
네가 서울에 가지 {말**았더라면**/않**았더라면**/못**했더라면**} **좋을** 뻔했다.
It would have been better if you did not/were not able to go to Seoul.

② 말다 can be used in conjunction with adjectives to denote prayer or wishes, typically in the form of '-지만 마라'.

이제 제발 날씨가 덥**지만 마라**. / I hope it won't be hot any more.
거리가 너무 멀**지만 마라**. / I hope it will not be too distant.
지금부터는 아프**지만 마라**. / Please don't be sick from now on.

③ 말다 is often used in set phrases, such as '-다가 말다가, -자마자, -(으)ㄹ 듯 말 듯, -는 듯 마는 듯, 마지못해, -고(야) 말다, 감사해 마지않다'.

준서는 **마지못해** 춤을 추었다. / Jun-Seo reluctantly danced.
드디어 전쟁이 터지고**(야) 말았다**. / At last, the war broke out.

④ '-하다' verbs (e.g. 간섭하다 'to interfere', 감동하다 'to be impressed by something', 강요하다 'to force someone/something', 거래하다 'to trade with someone', 걱정하다 'to be worried', 구경하다 'to watch', 근심하다 'to be concerned', 당황하다 'to be embarrassed', 도망하다 'to run away', 명령하다 'to order', 배웅하다 'to see someone out', 상납하다 'to offer a bribe', 수교하다 'to establish diplomatic ties with', 탄식하다 'to lament' may skip '하지' in its negation, for example, '간섭 말다, 강요 말다, 도망 말다'.

이제 제발 **간섭** 좀 **마세요**. / Please do not interfere any more.

그만하면 됐으니까, **강요** 좀 **말아** 주시겠습니까?
That's enough. Will you stop forcing me?

⑤ Prefinal ending which denotes tenses and aspects should come after
'-지 말-'.

이제 그만 말**겠**니?(◁말-겠-니?) / Will you not stop it?
드디어 사업을 그만두고 말**았**다.(◁말-았-다) / Finally, I quit the business.
어제 날짜로 대통령직을 말**았을 것**이다.(◁말-았-을 것-이-다)
I think (he) quit the presidency as of yesterday.
아버지는 쉰여섯 살을 살고 마**셨**다.(◁말-시-었-다)
Father ended up living only 56 years.

18.3 Double negation

Double negation(이중부정) occurs when two forms of negation out of
'아니(하다), 못(하다), 말다' are used in the same sentence to produce
a positive meaning. However, this is not the same as general affirmative
sentences.

The difference of double negation from affirmative sentences is made
clear with the use of auxiliary particle '-는' after '-지'. The following
double negatives imply that 'I ate lunch, which was not sufficient', or
'I ate lunch, which was not very good'.

[Affirmative] 나는 점심을 먹었다. / I had lunch.
[Negative] 나는 점심을 **못** 먹었다. / I could not have lunch.
　　　　　 나는 점심을 먹**지 못했**다. / I could not have lunch.
[Double negative] 나는 점심을 **못** 먹**지(는) 않**았다.
　　　　　 It isn't that I didn't have lunch.

나는 점심을 먹<u>지 못하지(는)</u> <u>않</u>았다.
It isn't that I didn't have lunch.

Negative elements may be used more than twice, but they are hardly ever spoken in everyday speech because the meaning is not very clear. The following sentences have used negative elements three times, meaning that 'the subject could not have lunch'.

나는 점심을 <u>못</u> 먹<u>지 않지는</u> <u>않</u>았다.
나는 점심을 먹<u>지 못하지 않지는</u> <u>않</u>았다.

● **Characteristics of double negation**

① Double negatives in the form of '-지 않으면 안 된다' or '-지 않을 수 없다' stand for strong affirmation, i.e. 'somebody has to be/do something'.

네가 그 일을 하<u>지 않으면 안 된다</u>.
You have to do it. (= The work must be done by you.)
이번에는 엄마의 뜻을 따르<u>지 않을 수 없다</u>.
I cannot help but follow mother's will this time. (= Mother's will must be followed.)

② Double negatives in the form of '-지 않은 것은 아니다' or '안 -(으)ㄴ/는 것은 아니다' indicate a weak affirmation, i.e. 'someone/something does/is something, but not to a significant degree'.

눈이 <u>안 온 것은 아니다</u>.
It is not that it was not snowy. (= It was snowy, but only a little.)
그녀를 사랑하<u>지 않은 것은 아니다</u>.
It is not that I did not love her. (= I loved her, but not much.)

준서가 범인<u>이 아닌 것은 아니다</u>.

It is not that Jun-Seo isn't the culprit. (= Jun-Seo did commit the crime, but a light one.)

③ '-(으)ㄹ 수 없다' may be used with negative elements to constitute a double negative.

[Affirmative] 준서는 서울에 간다. / Jun-Seo is going to Seoul.
[Negative] 준서는 서울에 <u>안</u> 간다./가<u>지 않</u>는다.
            Jun-Seo is not going to Seoul.
[Double negative] 준서는 서울에 <u>안 갈 수 없다</u>./가<u>지 않을 수 없다</u>.
            Jun-Seo has to go to Seoul.

④ There are five types of double negatives: '아니-아니, 아니-못, 못-아니, 아니-없다, 못-없다'. '못-못' cannot make a double negative.

민서는 책을 <u>안</u> 읽지 <u>않</u>았다.
민서는 책을 <u>안</u> 읽지 <u>못</u>했다.
민서는 책을 <u>못</u> 읽지 <u>않</u>았다.
민서는 책을 <u>안</u> 읽을 수 <u>없</u>다.
민서는 책을 <u>못</u> 읽을 수 <u>없</u>다.
민서가 책을 <u>못</u> 읽는 경우는 <u>없</u>다.
[*]민서는 책을 <u>못</u> 읽지 <u>못</u>했다.

Using negative elements twice does not always make a double negative. The following sentences have used double negatives in the form of '아니-아니, 못-못', but they still convey negativity.

너는 서울에 <u>안</u> 가면 <u>안</u> 간다고 처음부터 말을 했어야지.
You should have said that you are not going to Seoul at the first place.
준서는 그 일을 <u>못</u> 하면 <u>못</u> 한다고 솔직히 얘기를 하는 사람이다.

Jun-Seo is frank enough to say that he cannot do something beyond his ability.

말다 has a negative meaning, but cannot make a double negative. 말다 in the following sentences act as an auxiliary verb, having a nuance of being sorry.

준서는 그 일을 **안** 하고 **말**았다.
Jun-Seo did not do the job in the end.
민서는 결국 대학에 **못** 가고 **말**았다.
Min-Seo was not able to enter college in the end.

18.4 Negative phrases as an answer to questions

To give an affirmative answer to an affirmative question, the speaker can say '예, 네, 응, 그래'. To give a negative answer, the speaker can say '아니(요)'.

[Question] 너 어제 서울에 갔니?/ Did you go to Seoul yesterday?
[Affirmative answer] {<u>예</u>/<u>네</u>} 갔습니다. / Yes, I did.
　　　　　　　　　 {<u>응</u>/<u>그래</u>} 갔어. / Yes, I did.
[Negative answer] <u>아니요</u>, 안 갔습니다. / No, I didn't.
　　　　　　　　 <u>아니</u>, 안 갔어. / No, I didn't.

However, the answer to a negative question is completely different from above. In other words, the speaker should say '아니(요)' to give an affirmative answer, and '예, 네, 응' to give a negative answer. This is opposite to English.

[Question] 너 어제 서울에 안 갔니? / Didn't you go to Seoul yesterday?

[Affirmative answer] 아니요, 갔습니다. / No, I did.

아니, 갔어. / No, I did.

[Negative answer] {예/네}, 안 갔습니다. / Yes, I didn't go.

{응/그래}, 안 갔어. / Yes, I didn't go.

■ Negative expressions that are not negative

There are some affirmative expressions which use 아니. They are used to check the hearer's opinion, or to clarify one's own opinion based on a surmise. The hearer can say '예, 네, 응' to give an affirmative answer and 아니(요) to give a negative answer. In this case, '-지 않-' is usually condensed to '-잖-'.

In the following sentences, the speaker believes that 'there is too little money'. The speaker can express his thoughts in an ordinary way, for example, 'the money is too little, isn't it?', but may want to stress what he's saying and sound the hearer out about his thoughts, wishing that the hearer sympathizes with him.

[Question] 돈이 너무 {적지 않니?/적잖니?} / Don't you think the money is too little?
[Affirmative answer] 예, 너무 적어요. / Yes, it is too little.
[Negative answer] 아니요, 적지 않아요. / No, it is not little.

If the hearer wants to answer that 'the snow is highly likely', but is not completely sure, thus wants to make a guess, he can use expressions such as '-지 않-/-잖-' as below.

[Question] 내일쯤 눈이 내릴까? / Will it snow tomorrow?
[Affirmative answer] 예, 눈이 {내리지 않을까/내리잖을까} 싶어요.
예, 눈이 내릴 것 같아요.
예, 눈이 내리지 싶어요. / Yes, I guess it will snow.
[Negative answer] 아니요, 내리지 않지 싶어요. / No, I guess not.

Sometimes, rhetorical questions, which serve to emphasize the speaker's intention or coerce the hearer to accept the speaker's intention, may employ negation. The speaker in the following sentences is trying to say 'hurry up' by using a negative question.

[Question] 너 빨리 학교에 안 갈래? / Won't you hurry up to school?
[Affirmative answer] 예, 빨리 갈게요. / Yes, I will.
[Negative answer] 아니요, 빨리 안 갈 거예요. / No, I won't.

When it comes to general questions asking the hearer's thoughts, the hearer should answer as follows.

[Question] 너 빨리 학교에 안 갈래? / Won't you hurry up to school?
[Affirmative answer] 예, 빨리 안 갈 거예요. / Yes, I won't hurry to school.
[Negative answer] 아니요, 빨리 갈 거예요. / No, I will hurry up to school.

18.5 Korean cultural aspects as reflected in negation

First, Koreans tend to make negation using the antonym, rather than with negative elements such as '아니, 못, 말다'. For example, 있다 is typically negated as 없다, rather than '있지 않다' or '안 있다'. In some cases, negating the statement using negative elements may produce a rather awkward or ungrammatical sentence as below.

[Question] 너 돈 가진 것 있니? / Do you have any money?
[Answer] [?]나는 돈 가진 것 <u>있지 않</u>아요. / I don't have any money.
[*]나는 돈 가진 것 <u>안 있</u>어요. / I don't have any money.
나는 돈 가진 것 <u>없</u>어요. / I don't have any money.

This holds particularly true for adjectives. Adjectives are generally negated by their antonyms instead of 아니.

있다 'to be' 'to have' ↔ 없다 'not to be' 'not to have'
맞다 'to be correct' ↔ 틀리다 'to be incorrect'
옳다 'to be right' ↔ 그르다 'to be wrong'
곧다 'to be straight' ↔ 굽다 'to be bent'
넓다 'to be wide' ↔ 좁다 'to be narrow'
길다 'to be long' ↔ 짧다 'to be short'
굵다 'to be thick' ↔ 가늘다 'to be lean'
깊다 'to be deep' ↔ 얕다 'to be shallow'
무겁다 'to be heavy' ↔ 가볍다 'to be light'
두껍다 'to be thick' ↔ 얇다 'to be thin'
뚱뚱하다 'to be fat' ↔ 홀쭉하다 'to be thin'
깨끗하다 'to be clean' ↔ 더럽다 'to be dirty'
크다 'to be big' ↔ 작다 'to be small'
많다 'to be many' ↔ 적다 'to be small in quantity'
밝다 'to be bright' ↔ 어둡다 'to be dark'
빠르다 'to be fast' ↔ 느리다 'to be slow'
쉽다 'to be easy' ↔ 어렵다 'to be difficult'
강하다 'to be strong' ↔ 약하다 'to be weak'
귀하다 'to be rare' ↔ 흔하다 'to be common'

Some verbs are also negated by their antonym.

알다 'to know' ↔ 모르다 'to be ignorant'
죽다 'to die' ↔ 살다 'to be alive'
가다 'to go' ↔ 멈추다/멎다 'to stop'
묵다 'to stay' ↔ 떠나다 'to leave'
울다 'to cry' ↔ 그치다 'to stop crying'
이기다 'to win' ↔ 지다 'to lose'
잠들다 'to fall asleep' ↔ 깨다 'to wake up'
저축하다 'to save' ↔ 쓰다/낭비하다 'to spend/waste'

The dialogue below clearly reflects Korean's language culture.

[Question] 너 이 문제의 답이 무엇인지 아니?
　　　　　Do you know the answer to this question?
[Answer] ?아니요, 나는 알고 있지 않아요. / No, I don't.
　　　　*아니요, 나는 안 알고 있어요. / No, I don't.
　　　　아니요, 나는 몰라요. / No, I don't.

[Question] 지난번 게임에서 너희 팀이 이겼니?
　　　　　Did your team win the last game?
[Answer] ?아니요, 우리 팀이 이기지 않았어요. / No, we didn't.
　　　　*아니요, 우리 팀이 안 이겼어요. / No, we didn't.
　　　　아니요, 우리 팀이 졌어요. / No, we didn't.

Second, even if the older person is wrong, Koreans tend to refrain from explicitly pointing out the person's misjudgment, or from expressing their denial or rejection immediately. This is due to the fact that the Korean traditional culture is rooted in Confucius ideas, which consider that it is seriously impolite to deny, or explicitly indicate any flaw in the senior's assertion.

If the speaker wants to point out the misjudgment of the senior in a polite way, the speaker should slightly beat around the bush, while making necessary additions to the senior's idea or stressing a different point of view.

19 Causative

19.1 What is causative?

Causative(사동법), which lies in contrast with active, is when the subject influences a person, an animal or an object to make them do something, or make them come to a certain status.

Korean causative can be categorized into: lexical causative, derivative causative and syntactic causative.

19.2 Types and characteristics of causative

19.2.1 Lexical causative

Lexical causative(어휘적 사동) makes a causative sentence by using lexicons such as 시키다 'to make somebody do'. If motional nouns like 'marriage(결혼), seeing(구경), discussing(토론), etc.' are used as object followed by predicate 하다, 하다 is changed into 시키다 and a new subject is introduced in order to make a lexical causative. Here, the syntactic form of 'object + 시키다' as witnessed in '결혼을 시키다' is interchangeable with the lexical form, 'object + 시키다' as in 결혼시키다.

[Active] 준서가 민서와 **결혼**을 **했다**.(◁ 하-였-다)
　　　　Jun-Seo and Min-Seo got married.
[Causative] 김 선생은 준서와 민서를 **결혼**을 **시켰다**.(◁ 시키-었-다)
　　　　Mr. Kim made Jun-Seo and Min-Seo got married.
　　　　김 선생은 준서와 민서를 **결혼시켰다**.
　　　　Mr. Kim made Jun-Seo and Min-Seo got married.

This applies to following verbs:

감동하다 'to be impressed'	개발하다 'to develop'
거절하다 'to decline'	결심하다 'to make up one's mind'
결합하다 'to combine'	경쟁하다 'to compete'
경험하다 'to experience'	공부하다 'to study'
구원하다 'to save'	기도하다 'to pray'
긴장하다 'to be nervous'	단련하다 'to discipline'
당황하다 'to be embarrassed'	대립하다 'to be in confrontation with'
동거하다 'to cohabit'	되풀이하다 'to repeat'
마감하다 'to finish'	멸망하다 'to be destroyed'
민박하다 'to lodge'	발언하다 'to make a remark'
발전하다 'to develop'	발표하다 'to announce'
복습하다 'to revise'	보존하다 'to preserve'
복원하다 'to restore'	분리하다 'to separate'
사죄하다 'to beg pardon'	설득하다 'to persuade'
설치하다 'to install'	수행하다 'to perform'
시행하다 'to enforce'	연기하다 'to postpone'
이식하다 'to transplant'	이야기하다 'to tell'
이해하다 'to understand'	이혼하다 'to divorce'
인사하다 'to greet'	자랑하다 'to boast'
주문하다 'to order'	참석하다 'to participate'
출발하다 'to depart'	침투하다 'to infiltrate'

타협하다 'to compromise'   통과하다 'to pass through'
포기하다 'to give up'   합격하다 'to pass (an exam or test)'
함락하다 'to fall down'   합의하다 'to agree'
혼인하다 'to get married'   흥분하다 'to get excited'

However, if the object of the sentence is adverbs such as 고분고분 'obediently', 기웃기웃 'peeping', 들쭉날쭉 'jaggedly', 몰랑몰랑 'soft', 삐죽삐죽 'jagged' and conditional nouns such as 가득 'fullness', 간절 'earnestness', 건강 'health', 겸손 'humility', 어색 'awkwardness' as well as concrete nouns such as 밥 'rice', 떡 'rice cake', 머리 'head', 아침 'morning' 자리 'seat', it is impossible to make a causative sentence with 시키다.

민서는 아버지의 말에 **고분고분하다**.
Min-Seo became obedient at her father's words.
→ *아버지는 민서에게 **고분고분시켰다**.

준서는 비교적 **건강하다**. / Jun-Seo is relatively healthy.
→ *어머니는 준서에게 비교적 **건강시켰다**.

언니가 오늘 **머리**를 **했다**. / My elder sister had her hair done today.
→ *어머니가 언니에게 **머리**를 **시켰다**.

Moreover, lexicons that are inseparable from 하다, such as 급(急)하다 'to be in hurry', 망(亡)하다 'to go under', 면(面)하다 'to be exempted from', 반(反)하다 'to be opposed to', 변(變)하다 'to change', 전(傳)하다 'to deliver', 청(請)하다 'to ask a favor', 취(取)하다 'to take', 칭(稱)하다 'to name', 피(避)하다 'to avoid', and 향(向)하다 'to head to', cannot make a causative sentence by simply attaching 시키다.

준서는 성질이 {**급하다**/*급을 하다} / Jun-Seo is quick in temper.
→ *아버지는 준서의 성질을 **급을 시켰다**.

19.2.2 Derivative causative

In **derivative causative**(파생적 사동), derivative suffixes such as '-이-, -히-, -리-, -기-, -우-, -구-, -추-, -애-', are attached to the verb, and a new subject is introduced to the sentence. The suffix can be attached to both the adjective and the verb.

- Derivative causative of adjectives

Attach '-이-, -히-, -리-, -기-, -우-, -구-, -추-, -애-' to the adjective, make the subject the object of the sentence and introduce a new subject.

<u>안방이</u>   <u>넓다.</u>
[Subject]   [Predicate]
The bedroom is big.

→ <u>아버지가</u>   <u>안방을</u>   <u>넓혔다.</u>(◁ 넓-히-었-다)
   [New subject]   [Object]   [Predicate]
   Father enlarged the bedroom.

This applies to following adjectives:

높다 'to be high' → 높이다 'to heighten'
(죽이) 눅다 '(a porridge) to become soft' → 눅이다 'to soften'
줄다 'to be reduced' → 줄이다 'to reduce'

넓다 'to be large' → 넓히다 'to enlarge'
좁다 'to be narrow' → 좁히다 'to narrow'
밝다 'to be bright' → 밝히다 'to brighten'
괴롭다 'to be in agony' → 괴롭히다 'to agonize'
굳다 'to be hard' → 굳히다 'to harden'
더럽다 'to be dirty' → 더럽히다 'to make something dirty'
붉다 'to be red' → 붉히다 'to redden'

덥다 'to be hot' → 덥히다 'to make hot'
간지럽다 'to feel ticklish' → 간지럽히다 'to tickle'

(배가) 부르다 'to feel stuffed' → 불리다 'to stuff'
(방이) 너르다 '(the room)to be broad' → 널리다 'to broaden'

(땅이) 걸다 '(the soil)to be fertile' → 걸우다 'to fertilize'
크다 'to grow' → 키우다 'to make something grow'
비다 'to be empty' → 비우다 'to empty'
길다 'to be long' → 길우다 'to lengthen'

곧다 'to be straight' → 곧추다 'to straighten'
낮다 'to be low' → 낮추다 'to lower'
늦다 'to be late' → 늦추다 'to make something late'

없다 'to be out of existence' → 없애다 'to remove or eliminate'

Derivative causative verbs above shall have the same grammatical characteristics as verbs.

넓힌다(◁넓히-ㄴ-다) 'to broaden'
넓히고 있다(◁넓히-고 있-다) 'to be broadening'
넓히자(◁넓히-자) 'let's broaden'
넓혀라(◁넓히-어라) 'broaden'

- Derivative causative of intransitive verbs

Attach '-이-, -히-, -리-, -기-, -우-, -구-, -추-, -시-, -(으)키-' to the intransitive verb, make the subject the object of the sentence and introduce a new subject.

<u>아기가</u>   <u>웃는다.</u>

[Subject]   [Predicate]

The baby is smiling.

→ <u>어머니가</u>   <u>아기를</u>   <u>웃겼다.</u>(◁ 웃-기-었-다)

    [New subject]   [Object]   [Predicate]

    Mother made the baby smile.

This applies to following intransitive verbs:

녹다 'to melt' → 녹이다 'to make something melt'

죽다 'to die' → 죽이다 'to kill'

속다 'to deceive' → 속이다 'to be deceived'

(싸움이) 붙다 'to fight' → 붙이다 'to be entangled in fight'

(속이) 썩다 'to be worried' → 썩이다 'to make somebody worry'

기울다 'to tilt' → 기울이다 'to be tilted'

(배추가 소금에) 절다 'to salt the cabbage' → 절이다 'to be salted'

(국이) 졸다 'to be boiled down' → 졸이다 'to boil down'

앉다 'to seat' → 앉히다 'to be seated'

눕다 'to lie down' → 눕히다 'to be layed'

익다 'to cook' → 익히다 'to be cooked'

날다 'to fly' → 날리다 'to make something fly'

살다 'to be alive' → 살리다 'to make someone alive, to save'

얼다 'to freeze' → 얼리다 'to be frozen'

흐르다 'to trickle' → 흘리다 'to make something trickle'

(몸무게가) 늘다 'to gain weight' → 늘리다 'to make somebody gain weight'

울다 'to cry' → 울리다 'to make somebody cry'

웃다 'to laugh' → 웃기다 'to make somebody laugh'

숨다 'to hide from somebody' → 숨기다 'to hide something'

남다 'to be left' → 남기다 'to leave'

굶다 'to be starved' → 굶기다 'to starve'
넘다 'to exceed' → 넘기다 'to make something exceed'

피다 'to blossom' → 피우다 'to make something blossom'
(살이) 찌다 'to gain weight' → 찌우다 'to make somebody gain weight, to fatten somebody'
비다 'to be empty' → 비우다 'to empty'
깨다 'to be awake' → 깨우다 'to wake up somebody'
지다 'to carry' → 지우다 'to make somebody carry'
(배가) 뜨다 'to be afloat' → 띄우다 'to set a ship afloat'

솟다 'to rise' → 솟구다 'to raise'

(햇빛이) 비치다 '(the sun) to shine' → 비추다 'to shine'

(옷이 물에) 젖다 'to be wet' → 적시다 'to make wet'

(물결이) 일다 '(the wave) to rise' → 일으키다 'to make waves'

Such derivative causative verbs above shall have the same grammatical characteristics as transitive verbs, as they can now have an objective as in 국을 졸이다 'to boil down the soup', 종이비행기를 날리다 'to fly a paper airplane', 살을 찌우다 'to gain weight'.

- ● Derivative causative of transitive verbs
Attach '-아, -하, -라, -가, -우-' to the transitive verb, and add '-에게/-한테/-께' to the subject to change the subject into an essential adverb, and introduce a new subject.

준서가	책을	읽는다.
[Subject]	[Object]	[Predicate]

Jun-Seo is reading a book.

→ <u>선생님이</u>   <u>준서에게</u>   <u>책을</u>   <u>읽혔다.</u>(◁읽-히-었-다)
[New subject] [Adverb]   [Object]   [Predicate]
The teacher made Jun-Seo read a book.

This applies to following transitive verbs:

보다 'to see' → 보이다 'to be made capable of seeing, to be able to see'
먹다 'to eat' → 먹이다 'to feed'
닦다 'to wipe' → 닦이다 'to be wiped'

입다 'to put on' → 입히다 'to make somebody put on'
잡다 'to catch' → 잡히다 'to be caught'

듣다 'to hear' → 들리다 'to be made capable of hearing, to be able to hear'
알다 'to know' → 알리다 'to tell'
말다 'to stop' → 말리다 'to make somebody stop'
싣다 'to load' → 실리다 'to be loaded'
물다 'to bite' → 물리다 'to be bitten'
털다 'to steal' → 털리다 'to be stolen'

(머리를) 감다 'to wash one's own hair' → 감기다 'to make somebody wash hair'
넘다 'to exceed' → 넘기다 'to make somebody exceed'
벗다 'to strip' → 벗기다 'to be stripped'
신다 'to put on shoes' → 신기다 'to make somebody put on shoes'
씻다 'to wash' → 씻기다 'to make somebody wash'
맡다 'to be assigned' → 맡기다 'to assign'

차다 'to be filled' → 채우다 'to fill'
깨다 'to wake oneself up' → 깨우다 'to make somebody wake up'
(날이) 새다 '(the day) to break' → 새우다 'to stay up all night'
타다 'to be in flames' → 태우다 'to burn something'

(짐을) 지다 'to load (some baggage)' → 지우다 'to be loaded'

Such derivative causative verbs shall have the same grammatical characteristics as transitive verbs as they make the sentence into a form of '-에게 ⋯ -을/를 읽히다'. They shall also have to have an adverb that corresponds to '-에게'.

● Characteristics of derivative causative

① There can be two to three causative suffixes in a sentence in some exceptional cases. However, using plural causative suffixes does not necessarily stress the causative.

세우다(◁ 서-이-우-다) 'to found or to make somebody stand up'
재우다(◁ 자-이-우-다) 'to make somebody sleep'
태우다(◁ 타-이-우-다) 'to give a ride to somebody'
키우다(◁ 크-이-우-다) 'to rear up somebody'

② Not all adjectives or verbs can be made into a causative verb with a causative suffix. Only a few of them can be made into a causative verb, and there are no known rules about attachment of causative suffixes.

준서가 서울로 떠났다. / Jun-Seo left for Seoul.
*아버지는 준서를 서울로 떠나<u>이</u>었다.

Verbs that cannot become derivative causative include:

['-하다' adjective] 강하다 'to be strong', 건강하다 'to be healthy', 다양하
다 'to be diverse', 미개하다 'to be uncivilized', 부족하
다 'to lack', 엄격하다 'to be strict', 죄송하다 'to be
sorry', 행복하다 'to be happy'

[Dative verbs] 드리다 'to present', 바치다 'to offer', 받다 'to receive',
  주다 'to give'
[Symmetrical verbs] 결혼하다 'to marry', 닮다 'to resemble', 만나다 'to
  meet', 싸우다 'to fight'
[Moving verbs] 가다 'to go', 도착하다 'to arrive', 오다 'to come', 출발하
  다 'to depart'

19.2.3 Syntactic causative

In **syntactic causative**(통사적 사동), syntactic forms such as '-게 하다/만
들다, -도록 하다/만들다' are attached to the end of a verb, and a new
subject is introduced. Since syntactic causatives have less syntactic or
semantic constraints, they can be attached to almost all adjectives and
verbs.

- Syntactic causative of adjectives
  Attach '-게 하다/만들다, -도록 하다/만들다' to an adjective, make the
subject the object of the sentence and introduce a new subject.

<u>안방이</u>　　　<u>넓다.</u>
[Subject]　　[Predicate]
The bedroom is large.
→ <u>아버지가</u>　　　<u>안방을</u>　　<u>넓게 했다/만들었다.</u>
　　[New subject]　　[Object]　　[Predicate]
　　Father enlarged the bedroom.

Sometimes, 안방이 remains unchanged. In this case, 안방이, the subject
of the embedded sentence, corresponds with '넓-', and the subject of the
matrix sentence, 아버지가, corresponds with '-게 하다/만들다'. However,
it sounds more natural to attach '-을' to 안방 than leaving the subject

as it is. Therefore, '-을/를' is affixed to the subject of the embedded sentence in most cases to make syntactic causative.

→ 아버지가　　　안방이　　　　　　　　　넓게 했다/만들었다.
[New subject] [Subject of embedded sentence] [Predicate]
Father made the bedroom large.

- Syntactic causative of intransitive verbs

Affix '-게 하다/만들다, -도록 하다/만들다' to the verb, make the subject to object of the sentence and introduce a new subject.

아기가　　　　　　웃는다.
[Subject]　　　　[Predicate]
The baby is smiling.

→ 어머니가　　　　아기가/아기를　　　웃게 했다/만들었다.
[New subject]　　[Subject/Object]　[Predicate]
Mother made the baby smile.

As in the case of the adjective mentioned above, 아기가 can be left unchanged at times. However, it is more natural to make 아기 the object of the sentence by affixing '-을/를' than leaving it as it is.

- Syntactic causative of transitive verbs

Affix '-게 하다/만들다, -도록 하다/만들다' to the transitive verb, and either leave the subject as it is or change it into the object/adverbial phrase of the sentence, and introduce a new subject.

준서가　　　　책을　　　　읽는다.
[Subject]　　　[Object]　　[Predicate]
Jun-Seo is reading a book.

→ 선생님이　　준서가/준서를/준서에게　책을　읽게 했다/만들었다.
[New subject] [Subject/Object/Adverbial phrase][Object] [Predicate]
Teacher made Jun-Seo read a book.

● Characteristics of syntactic causative

① Syntactic causatives are used more commonly than derivative causatives due to less semantic or syntactic constraints. Syntactic causatives can be fixed to almost all verbs except 이다 verbs. For instance, it is impossible to make 열다 into a causative phrase with derivative causative, but it is possible with syntactic causative.

[Active] 준서가 문을 열었다. / Jun-Seo opened the door.
[Derivative causative] *김 선생님은 준서에게 문을 열이었다.
[Syntactic causative] 김 선생님은 준서에게 문을 열게 하였다.
　　　　　　　Mr Kim made Jun-Seo open the door.

Verbs and adjectives that cannot be made causative with derivative causative are as follows:

가르치다 'to teach'	곱다 'to be lovely'
놀라다 'to be surprised'	늙다 'to get old'
돌보다 'to take care of'	둥글다 'to be round'
마시다 'to drink'	많다 'to be abound with'
바라다 'to wish'	부럽다 'to envy'
쉬다 'to rest'	새롭다 'to be new'
어기다 'to violate'	어렵다 'to be difficult'
주다 'to give'	즐겁다 'to be joyful'
참다 'to withstand'	춥다 'to feel cold'
캐다 'to dig'	파다 'to burrow'
훔치다 'to steal'	

② Lexicons that are inseparable from 하다, such as 급(急)하다 'to be in hurry', 망(亡)하다 'to go under', 면(面)하다 'to be exempted from', 반(反)하다 'to be opposed to', 변(變)하다 'to change', 전(傳)하다 'to deliver', 청(請)하다 'to ask a favor', 취(取)하다 'to take', 칭(稱)하다 'to name', 피(避)하다 'to avoid', and 향(向)하다 'to head to', cannot be made into a causative sentence by simply attaching 시키다 and derivative causative. However, it is possible to make it into a syntactic causative with '-게 하다'.

> [Active] 준서는 성질이 급하다. / Jun-Seo is impetuous.
> [Lexical causative] *아버지는 준서의 성질을 급을 <u>시켰</u>다.
> [Derivative causative] *아버지는 준서의 성질을 급<u>이</u>다.
> [Syntactic causative] 아버지는 준서의 성질을 급하<u>게 했</u>다.

③ Derivative causatives are direct causative, while syntactic causatives are indirect causative in general. Direct causative refers to when the subject does something himself, whereas indirect causative is when the subject does something only indirectly.

In the derivative causative sentence below, the subject policeman kills the criminal with a knife or a gun, thus the subject himself is engaging in the act of killing. On the other hand, in a syntactic causative sentence, the policeman does not directly kill the criminal, but instructs others to do so or set conditions to bring about the criminal's death, thus, syntactic causatives are indirect causatives. In other words, the biggest reason behind the criminal's death is the car accident caused by the criminal, and the actor is the criminal himself.

However, even though syntactic causative sentences have indirect causative, they can sometimes convey direct causative, while derivative causative can, from time to time, imply not only direct causative but also indirect causative. Therefore, special attention is needed to identify the meaning of the sentence. In other words, derivative causative can be used as follows even if the policeman did kill the criminal.

[Active] 범인이 죽었다. / The criminal died.
[Derivative causative] 경찰이 범인을 죽**였**다.
　　　　　　　　　　The policeman killed the criminal.
[Syntactic causative] 경찰이 범인을 죽**게 했**다.
　　　　　　　　　　The policeman made the criminal die.

④ Derivative and syntactic causative have a difference in the applicable range of negative elements (i.e. 아니, 못). In the following derivative causative sentence, 아니 negates the action of the policeman, implying that someone else killed the criminal. However, in the syntactic causative sentence ⓐ, 아니 negates the action of the subject (the policeman), while in the syntactic causative sentence ⓑ, 아니 negates the action of the object (the criminal).

[Derivative causative] **경찰이** 범인을 죽이지 않았다.
　　　　　　　　↑＿＿＿＿＿＿＿｜
　　　　　　　　The policeman did not kill the criminal.
[Syntactic causative ⓐ] **경찰이** 범인을 죽게 하지 않았다.
　　　　　　　　　↑＿＿＿＿＿＿＿＿｜
　　　　　　　　The policeman did not make the criminal die.
[Syntactic causative ⓑ] 경찰이 **범인을** 죽지 않게 하였다.
　　　　　　　　　　　↑＿＿＿＿＿｜
　　　　　　　　The police did something so that the criminal won't die.

Moreover, 시키다-oriented lexical causatives usually mean direct causative, or indirect causative in exceptional cases.

김 선생은 준서와 민서를 결혼 시키지 않았다.

Mr. Kim did not make arrangements to make Jun-Seo and Min-Seo get married.

김 선생은 준서와 민서를 결혼을 안 시켰다.

Mr. Kim did not make Jun-Seo and Min-Seo get married.

⑤ There is a difference in the use of time adverbial phrases. In derivative causative, causative events have to take place concurrently, but in syntactic causative, there are no such constraints. In the following derivative causative, the subject policeman killed the criminal (past or past perfect), thus it is possible to use time adverbs such as 어제 'yesterday' or 오늘 'today', but impossible to use future adverbs such as 한 시간 뒤에 'one hour later' or 내일 'tomorrow'. Yet, syntactic causative sentences impose no such constraints, so any time adverbial phrases, whether past or future, can be used.

[Derivative causative] 경찰이 범인을 {어제/지금/*한 시간 뒤에/*내일} 죽였다.
　　　　　　　　　　　　　The policeman killed the criminal {yesterday/just now/*one hour later/*tomorrow}

[Syntactic causative] 경찰이 범인을 {어제/지금/한 시간 뒤에/내일} 죽게 했다.
　　　　　　　　　　　The policeman made the criminal die {yesterday/ just now/one hour later/the day after}

■ Syntactic causative and the use of prefinal endings

First, in syntactic causative, the meaning of the sentence depends on where the subject-elevating prefinal ending '-(으)사-', is located. This is because the location of '-(으)사-' can either expand or narrow its applicable range.

어머니께서 자기 아들을 미국으로 유학을 가게 하셨다.(◁하-사-었-다)
Mother made her son go to the US to study.
형이 어머니를 고향으로 돌아가시게 했다.(◁돌아가-사-게)
Elder brother made mother return to her hometown.

Second, in syntactic causative, such prefinal endings as '-았/었-, -겠-, -다-, -(으)라-' come with the predicate of the matrix sentence, 하다.

준서는 민서에게 노래를 부르게 하였다.(◁하-였-다)
Jun-Seo made Min-Seo sing.
*준서는 민서에게 노래를 불렀게 한다.(◁부르-었-게)

나는 준서를 뉴욕에 가게 {하겠다/하리다}(◁하-겠-다/하-라-다)
I made Jun-Seo go to New York.
*나는 준서를 뉴욕에 {가겠게/가리게} 한다.(◁가-겠-게/가-라-게)

엄마가 아기를 자게 하더라.(◁하-더-라)
Mother made the baby sleep.
*엄마가 아기를 자더게 한다.(◁자-더-게)

19.3 Korean cultural aspects as reflected in causative

Koreans usually express what is supposed to be causative in non-causative phrases.

> 내가 이번에 새 집을 **짓느라고** 고생이 많았다.
> I made lots of efforts to build a new house.
> 나는 이번 추석에 자가용을 **몰고** 고향에 다녀왔다.
> I drove to my hometown this Chuseok.

나 above is neither a building engineer nor a professional chauffeur, thus, 짓느라고 should be corrected to '짓게 하고' and 몰고 to '몰게 하고'. However, no Koreans use causatives correctly. In the sentences above, causative is not used since 나 is the supervisor of the situation. The same applies to a broad range of situations.

20 Passive

20.1 What is passive?

Passive(피동법), which lies in contrast with active, is when the subject does something by the power or action of others.

Korean passive can be categorized into: lexical passive, derivative passive and syntactic passive.

20.2 Types and characteristics of passive

20.2.1 Lexical passive

Lexical passive(어휘적 피동) makes a passive sentence with phrases like 되다 and 당하다. When motional nouns (i.e. 개발 'development', 긴장 'tension', 대립 'confrontation', 체포 'arrest', 감금 'detention') act as the object of the sentence, and when they are combined with predicate 하다, a passive sentence can be constructed by changing 하다 into '-이/가 되다, -을/를 당하다', the objective into the subject and the subject into an essential adverbial phrase with '-에게'. Here, the typical passive form

체포가 되다, 체포를 당하다 'to be arrested' can be changed into a single phrase, 체포되다, 체포 당하다 'to be arrested'.

> [Active] 경찰이 범인을 체포를 했다.(◁ 하-였-다)
>> The police arrested the criminal.
> [Passive①] 범인이 경찰에게 체포가 되었다.(◁ 되-었-다)
>> 범인이 경찰에게 체포되었다.
> [Passive②] 범인이 경찰에게 체포를 당했다.(◁ 당하-였-다)
>> 범인이 경찰에게 체포당했다.
>> The criminal was arrested by the police.

Nouns representing the passive modification above are usually motional nouns attached to 하다, and they have a lot of semantic constraints. The 'Noun + 하다' form, which can become passive by 되다, include:

감동하다 'to be impressed'	개발하다 'to develop'
거절하다 'to refuse'	결심하다 'to make up one's mind'
결합하다 'to combine'	경쟁하다 'to compete'
경험하다 'to experience'	구원하다 'to save/rescue'
긴장하다 'to become nervous'	단련하다 'to train'
당황하다 'to be embarrassed'	
대립하다 'to conflict with something/someone'	
되풀이하다 'to repeat'	마감하다 'to finish/close'
멸망하다 'to perish'	발언하다 'to comment'
발전하다 'to develop'	발표하다 'to announce'
보존하다 'to preserve'	복원하다 'to restore'
분리하다 'to separate'	설득하다 'to persuade'
설치하다 'to install'	소탕하다 'to wipe someone out'
수행하다 'to perform'	시행하다 'to enforce'
연기하다 'to delay'	이식하다 'to transplant'
이해하다 'to understand'	이혼하다 'to divorce'
주문하다 'to order'	참석하다 'to attend'

출발하다 'to depart'   침투하다 'to penetrate'
타협하다 'to compromise'   통과하다 'to pass through'
합격하다 'to pass (an exam)'
함락하다 'to take (the enemy's fortress)'
합의하다 'to agree'   흥분하다 'to be excited'

Some of them have either positive or negative implications.
The 'Noun + 하다' form, which can become passive by 당하다 include:

간섭당하다 'to be interfered'   강요당하다 'to be forced'
거절당하다 'to be rejected'   겁탈당하다 'to be raped'
격퇴당하다 'to be repelled'   곤란당하다 'to go through difficulty'
공격당하다 'to be attacked/assaulted'
금지당하다 'to be prohibited'   멸망당하다 'to be perished'
배신당하다 'to be betrayed'   부상당하다 'to be injured'
분리당하다 'to be separated'   살생당하다 'to be killed'
설득당하다 'to be persuaded'   섬멸당하다 'to be annihilated'
소탕당하다 'to be wiped out'   순교당하다 'to be martyred'
습격당하다 'to be attacked'   실패당하다 'to be failed'
암살당하다 'to be assassinated'   연기당하다 'to be delayed'
유혹당하다 'to be lured'   이식당하다 'to be transplanted'
이용당하다 'to be sucked in/to be played on'
이혼당하다 'to be divorced'   창피당하다 'to be humiliated'
처형당하다 'to be executed'
침몰당하다 'to be shipwrecked/sunken'
침입당하다 'to be invaded'   침투당하다 'to be penetrated'
탄압당하다 'to be suppressed'
포기당하다 'to be forced to abandon/give up'
폭행당하다 'to be assaulted'
함락당하다 'to fall/ to be defeated by the enemy'

Most of them have a negative implication.

Provided however, if adjective nouns (i.e. 사랑하다 'to love', 칭찬하다 'to commend', 격려하다 'to encourage', 공경하다 'to respect') are used as an object of the sentence, the nouns cannot become passive by 되다 or 당하다.

[Active] 준서는 민서를 사랑한다. / Jun-Seo loves Min-Seo.
[Passive] *민서는 준서에게 {**사랑된다**/**사랑당한다**}
        Min-Seo is loved by Jun-Seo.

Lexicons that are inseparable from 하다, such as 구(救)하다 'to ask', 금(禁)하다 'to prohibit', 당(當)하다 'to suffer', 원(願)하다 'to want', 전(傳)하다 'to deliver', 청(請)하다 'to ask a favor', 취(取)하다 'to take', 표(表)하다 'to express', cannot become passive by 되다 or 당하다.

[Active] 준서는 민서에게 사랑을 구했다.
        Jun-Seo asked love from Min-Seo.
[Passive] *사랑이 준서에 의해 민서에게 {**구되었다**/**구당했다**}
        Love is asked by Jun-Seo to Min-Seo.

20.2.2 Derivative passive

Derivative passive can be constructed by affixing derivative suffix '-이-, -히-, -리-, -기-' to the verb, changing the object into subject and the subject into an essential adverbial phrase with '-에게'.

[Active] 엄마가 아기를 안았다.(◁안았-다)
        The mother cuddled her baby.
[Passive] 아기가 엄마에게 안**겼**다.(◁안-기-었-다)
        The baby was cuddled by his/her mother.

Only transitive verbs can be used in derivative passive sentences. It is impossible to construct a passive sentence with adjectives or intransitive verbs with derivative passive.

놓다 → 놓이다 'to put'   묶다 → 묶이다 'to tie'
보다 → 보이다 'to see'   쌓다 → 쌓이다 'to pile up'
섞다 → 섞이다 'to mix'   쓰다 → 쓰이다 'to use'
파다 → 파이다 'to dig'

닫다 → 닫히다 'to close'   먹다 → 먹히다 'to eat'
묻다 → 묻히다 'to bury'   박다 → 박히다 'to hammer'
밟다 → 밟히다 'to step on'
엎다 → 엎히다 'to put something onto something'
잡다 → 잡히다 'to catch'

누르다 → 눌리다 'to press'   듣다 → 들리다 'to hear'
물다 → 물리다 'to bite'   밀다 → 밀리다 'to push'
풀다 → 풀리다 'to come loose'

감다 → 감기다 'to wind up'   안다 → 안기다 'to hug'
끊다 → 끊기다 'to cut off'   찢다 → 찢기다 'to tear'

However, not all transitive verbs can become derivative passive.

[Active] 준서가 어머니께 용돈을 드렸다.(◁ 드리-었-다)
     Jun-Seo gave his mother some spending money.
[Passive] *어머니가 준서에게 용돈을 드리<u>히</u>었다.(◁ 드리-히-었-다)
     Mother was given some spending money by Jun-Seo.

Transitive verbs that cannot become derivative passive include:

[Dative verbs] 건네다 'to hand over', 드리다 'to give something to a

respectable person', 바치다 'to dedicate', 주다 'to give',
(대금을) 치르다 'to pay the price for something'

[Benefactive verbs] 돕다 'to help', 바라다 'to hope', 받다 'to receive',
얻다 'to gain', (은혜를) 입다 'be indebted to some-
one', 찾다 'to find', (월급을) 타다 'to receive a salary'

[Symmetrical verbs] 겨루다 'to compete for', 견주다 'to compare with',
닮다 'to resemble', 만나다 'to meet', 맞먹다 'to
equivalent to', 비기다 'to tie with'

[Empirical verbs] 깨닫다 'to realize', 느끼다 'to feel', 모르다 'to be
ignorant of', 배우다 'to learn', 알다 'to know', 익히다
'to master'

[Verbs whose stem ends with ㅣ] 가르치다 'to teach', 때리다 'to hit',
마시다 'to drink', 만지다 'to touch',
모시다 'to live with [parents, parents-
in-law], to take someone respectable
to somewhere', 사귀다 'to go out with',
이기다 'to win', 지키다 'to keep'

[하- verbs] 감시하다 'to monitor', 개혁하다 'to reform', 사랑하다 'to
love', 슬퍼하다 'to grieve over something', 예습하다 'to
prepare for tomorrow's lessons', 좋아하다 'to like'

20.2.3 Syntactic passive

In **syntactic passive**(통사적 피동), syntactic forms such as '-아/어지다,
-게 되다' are attached to the end of a verb. This has less syntactic or
semantic constraints, so almost all verbs which cannot become derivative
passive can become syntactic passive.

- ### Syntactic passive by -아/어지다

'-아/어지다' is the combination of connective ending '-아/어' and

auxiliary verb 지다. Its passive form can be constructed by attaching '-아/어지다' to certain transitive verbs, changing the object into the subject and making the subject into an adverbial phrase by attaching '-에게' or '-에 의해서' to the subject.

[Active] 준서는 그 일을 성공적으로 이루었다.(◁이루-었-다)
    Jun-Seo did the work successfully.
[Passive] 그 일은 준서에 의해 성공적으로 이루**어졌**다.(◁이루-어자-었-다)
    The work was done successfully by Jun-Seo.

Sometimes, passive forms with '-아/어지다' can sound awkward. In such a case, use derivative suffix '-이-, -히-, -리-, -기-' to make a natural sentence.

[Active] 한국 사람들은 아리랑을 많이 불렀다.(◁부르-었-다)
    Koreans sang Arirang a lot.
[Passive①] ?아리랑이 한국 사람들에게 많이 불**러졌**다.(◁부르-어자-었-다)
    Arirang was sung a lot by Koreans.
[Passive②] 아리랑이라는 민요는 한국 사람들에게 많이 불**리어졌**다.
    (◁부르-이-어자-었-다)
    A folk song called Arirang was sang a lot by Koreans.

However, if '-아/어지다' is put after an adjective, it refers to a change of state of the adjective, as well as passivity. Thus, 'adjective + -아/어지다' shall have the same syntactic characteristics as verbs. Therefore, imperative expressions and sentence endings like *길어라/길어져라 'grow longer!', *길자/길어지자 'let's become longer', which are impossible with adjectives alone, can be made possible.

기린의 목이 길다. / Giraffe's neck is long.

기린의 목이 길**어졌**다.(◁ 길-어지-었-다)
Giraffe's long has become long.

민서는 키가 크다. / Min-Seo is tall.
민서는 키가 커**졌**다.(◁ 크-어지-었-다)
Min-Seo has become tall.

● Syntactic passive by '-게 되다'

'-게 되다' is the combination of connective ending '-게' with auxiliary verb 되다. If '-게 되다' is affixed to a verb, the verb becomes passive. This way of making passive forms has little syntactic or semantic constraints, so '-게 되다' can be usually put after verbs to make a passive expression.

준서는 서울에서 한국어를 배운다. / Jun-Seo is learning Korean in Seoul.
준서는 서울에서 한국어를 배우**게 되**었다.(◁ 배우-게 되-었-다)
Jun-Seo got to learn Korean in Seoul.

준서는 민서를 그리워한다. / Jun-Seo is nostalgic for Min-Seo.
준서는 민서를 그리워하**게 되**었다.(◁ 그리워하-게 되-었-다)
Jun-Seo grew nostalgic for Min-Seo.

Also, combination of '-게 되다' with passive derivative suffix '-이-, -하-, -라-, -기-' or syntactic passive '-아/어지다', can clarify the meaning of the passive.

[Active] 준서는 민서를 껴안았다. / Jun-Seo hugged Min-Seo.
[Passive①] 민서는 준서에게 껴안**졌**다.(◁ 껴안-기-었-다)
　　　　　Min-Seo was hugged by Jun-Seo.
[Passive②] 민서는 준서에게 껴안**기게 되**었다.(◁ 껴안-기-게 되-었-다)
　　　　　Min-Seo was hugged by Jun-Seo.

[Active] 준서는 자기의 꿈을 이루었다. / Jun-Seo realized his dream.
[Passive①] 준서의 꿈이 이루**어졌**다.(◁이루-어지-었-다)
　　　　　Jun-Seo's dream came true.
[Passive②] 준서의 꿈이 이루**어지게 되**었다.(◁이루-어지-게 되-었-다)
　　　　　Jun-Seo's dream came true.

Moreover, if '-게 되다' is put after an intransitive verb, the combination refers to not only passivity but also refer to the result of a change in the action.

준서가 워싱턴으로 왔다. / Jun-Seo came to Washington.
준서가 워싱턴으로 오**게 되**었다.(◁오-게 되-었-다)
Jun-Seo was made to come to Washington.

Combination of '-게 되다' with adjectives refers to not only passivity but also a change in the status of the adjective.

민서의 방이 깨끗하다. / Min-Seo's room is clean.
민서의 방이 깨끗하**게 되**었다.(◁깨끗하-게 되-었-다)
Min-Seo's room was made clean.

준서는 매우 슬기롭다. / Jun-Seo is very wise.
준서는 매우 슬기롭**게 되**었다.(◁슬기롭-게 되-었-다)
Jun-Seo was made very wise.

■ Actor of passive sentences

　If the actor of a passive sentence is a person or animal, attach '-에게, -에 의해' to the actor. However, if the actor is an inanimate object, use adverbial particles such as '-에, -에서, -(으)로, -(으)로부터', since the subject of an active sentence is in fact an instrumental case semantically.

스텔스기가 적을 초토화했다. / The stealth aircraft annihilated the enemy.
→ 적이 스텔스기에 초토화됐다. / The enemy was annihilated by the stealth aircraft.

국회가 올해 추경 예산을 많이 깎았다.
The National Assembly curbed this year's revised supplementary budget sharply.
→ 올해 추경 예산이 국회에서 많이 깎였다.
    This year's revised supplementary budget was sharply curbed at (by) the
    National Assembly.

이라크 전쟁이 수많은 인명을 빼앗았다. / The Iraq war claimed the lives of many.
→ 수많은 인명이 이라크 전쟁으로 빼앗겼다.
    The lives of many were claimed by the Iraq war.

교육부가 많은 학생들을 입시 지옥으로 내몰았다.
The Ministry of Education drove many students into an examination hell.
→ 많은 학생들이 교육부로부터 입시 지옥으로 내몰렸다.
    Many students were driven by the Ministry of Education into an examination
    hell.

20.2.4 Characteristics of Korean passive

① Korean active and passive are semantically similar. However, active sentences usually emphasize the actor, whereas passive sentences highlight the object.

[Active] 경찰이[Actor] 범인을[Object] 체포했다.
        The police arrested the criminal.
[Passive] 범인이[Object] 경찰에게[Actor] 잡혔다.(◁ 잡-히-었-다)
        The criminal was arrested by the police.

② Expressions that signify figures or quantity can make the meaning of active and passive sentences very different. The active sentence below means that the criminals arrested by two policemen are three or six in number, whereas the passive sentence means that three criminals are caught by two policemen.

> [Active] 두 명의 경찰이 세 명(씩)의 범인을 체포했다.
>> Two policemen arrested three criminals (each).
> [Passive] 세 명의 범인이 두 명의 경찰에게 체포**되**었다.(◁체포-되-었-다)
>> Three criminals were arrested by two policemen.

③ Some passive sentences cannot be turned into active sentences. This is mostly when the subject is an inanimate object while the verb has a minor meaning. In the passive sentence below, inanimate beings such as the weather and appearance serve as the subject, while the verb has a minor meaning of 'getting better' (풀리다) and 'being remembered' (씹히다).

> [Passive] 요즈음 날씨가 많이 풀**렸**다.(◁풀-리-었-다)
>> The weather became warmer.
> [Active] [?](누군가) 날씨를 풀었다.
>> (Somebody) warmed the weather.

> [Passive] 그녀의 모습이 눈에 씹**혔**다.(◁씹-히-었-다)
>> I was constantly reminded of her.
> [Active] [?](누군가) 그녀의 모습을 눈에 씹었다.
>> (Somebody) reminded me of her.

④ Passive verbs or expressions in imperatives sometimes have an active meaning, in which the subject is the actor.

> 빨리 경찰에게 붙잡**혀**라.(◁붙잡-히-어라)
> Be caught by the police quickly.
> 아가야, 엄마 품에 안**겨**라.(◁안-기-어라)
> Babe, be held in mommy's arms.

너의 진실을 보여라.(◁보-이-어라)

Let your truth be shown.

어서 포승줄에 묶여라.(◁묶-이-어라)

Be bound in ropes quickly.

20.3 Korean cultural aspects as reflected in passive

First, Koreans sometimes express what should be passive in active sentences. In particular, if the object is an inanimate object, passive sentences hardly ever use inanimate objects as subjects. That is why birthday present below makes a very awkward sentence. Koreans hardly ever use such expressions, except for extremely peculiar cases.

[Active] 준서가 민서에게 생일 선물을 주었다.
         Jun-Seo gave Min-Seo a birthday present.
[Passive] ??생일 선물이 준서에 의해 민서에게 주어졌다.(◁주-어지-었-다)
         A birthday present was given by Jun-Seo to Min-Seo.
         → Min-Seo received a birthday present from Jun-Seo.

Second, it is impossible to change some Korean verbs to passive forms, which demonstrates Koreans' linguistic habit that tends not to use passive expressions in everyday speech.

[Active] 준서는 매일 영어를 배운다. / Jun-Seo learns English every day.
[Passive] *영어가 매일 준서에게 배워진다.(◁배우-어지-ㄴ-다)
         English is being learned every day by Jun-Seo.

[Active] 준서는 집에서 강아지를 기른다. / Jun-Seo raises a pet at home.
[Passive] *강아지가 준서에 의해 집에서 길린다/길러진다/기르게 된다.
         A pet is being raised by Jun-Seo at home.

[Active] 민서는 어머니를 공경한다. / Min-Seo respects her mother.

[Passive] *어머니는 민서에게 공경하<u>이</u>다/공경<u>해지</u>다/공경하<u>게 된</u>다.

Mother is being respected by Min-Seo.

Verbs that are impossible to change into passive forms include: 가르치다 'to teach', (꾸중을) 듣다 'to be scolded', 꾸짖다 'to scold', 되돌아보다 'to look back', 모르다 'to be ignorant of something', 무릅쓰다 'to risk', 바라다 'to wish', 비웃다 'to laugh at', 알아듣다 'to understand', 앞서다 'to precede', 야단맞다 'to get a sharp scolding', 여쭈다 'to ask (to a respectable person)', 잃다 'to lose', 쫓다 'to chase', 찾다 'to find', (말을) 타다 'to ride (on a horse)', and 혼내다 'to tell off'.

Third, when translating a foreign language into Korean, the passive expression in the foreign language is often literally translated into Korean, which makes a very awkward sentence.

[Passive] 베를린 지역에서 유대인들이 독일군들에 의해 몰아내<u>어진</u>대.

Jews are to be driven out of Berlin by German soldiers.

→ 독일군들이 유대인들을 베를린 지역에서 몰아낸대.

German soldiers are to drive out Jews from Berlin.

Fourth, Koreans sometimes turn even 받다 'to receive' into passive. However, it is difficult to call it a grammatically correct passive sentence.

그는 자기 아내를 매우 사랑한다. / He loves his wife very much.

→ 그의 아내는 그에게 매우 <u>**사랑**</u>을 <u>**받는다**</u>.

His wife is very much loved by him.

학생들이 그 선생님을 존경한다. / Students respect the teacher.

→ 그 선생님이 학생들에게 <u>**존경**</u>을 <u>**받는다**</u>.

The teacher is respected by students.

21 Subjunctive

21.1 What is subjunctive?

Subjunctive(가정법) refers to a way of expressing irreality. The subjunctive in Korean language is not as sophisticated as Indo-European languages, but this chapter is dedicated to subjunctive in the Korean language since it is certain that Korean has its own subjunctive and foreigners may want to express Korean in various subjunctive.

In Korean, the subjunctive is divided into present subjunctive, past subjunctive and future subjunctive according to the relationship between the time of the dialogue and the time of the event. Subjunctive can be used with combination of; time adverbial phrases (i.e. 어제 'yesterday', 오늘 'today', 내일 'tomorrow', 당장 'right now', 미래에 'in the future'); '-았/었-, -더-, -ㄴ/는-, -겠-' which come after the verb stem; ending of declarative sentences '-다'; and connective ending '-(으)면'.

21.2 Types and characteristics of subjunctive

21.2.1 Present subjunctive

Present subjunctive(가정법 현재) expresses irreality of the present, and is expressed in '만약 ··· -(ㄴ/는)다면, ··· -(으)ㄹ 텐데' in general. '-(ㄴ/는)다면' is a combination of present-tense prefinal ending '-ㄴ/는-' or '-∅-', declarative sentence ending '-다', and conditional connective ending '-면'. If adverbs such as '만약, 만일' are used in conjunction with speculative expressions like '-(으)ㄹ 텐데, -(이)ㄹ 것이다, etc.', the meaning of subjunctive can become even more clear.

> **만일** 내가 새**라면**, 네게 날아**갈 텐데**. / If I were a bird, I could fly to you.
> **만약** 네가 내 아들이**라면**, 네게 모든 것을 **줄 텐데**.
> If you were my son, I would have given everything to you.
> **만일** 해가 서쪽에서 뜬**다면**, 세상의 모든 것이 바**뀔 것이다**.
> If the Sun rises from the West, everything in the whole world would change.
> **만약** 민서가 날씬하**다면**, 훨씬 예**뻤으리라**.
> If Min-Seo were slim, she would have been much prettier.

The sentences above mean: 'Because I am not a bird now, I cannot fly to you; Because you are not my son now, I cannot give you everything; Because the Sun does not rise from the West at the moment, everything in the whole world will not change; and Because Min-Seo is not slim now, she is not pretty'.

Interrogative, propositive, imperative and exclamatory sentence endings can also be used.

> **만일** 그가 사람이**라면**, 과연 인류를 저버릴 수 있**을까**?
> If he were a human being, could he transgress moral laws?
> **만약** 오늘 하늘이 무너**진다면**, 아무것도 하지 말고 가만히 있**어라**.
> If the sky is to fall down today, don't do anything but stay still.
> **만일** 지금 로또 복권에 당첨**된다면**, 우리 당장 결혼하자.
> If I win the lottery now, let's get married right now.

만약 그 운전사가 현명하**다면**, 훨씬 사고를 줄일 수 있겠<u>군요</u>!
If the driver is wise, he can prevent many more accidents!

Sentences above mean: 'As he is too immoral to be a human being, he transgressed moral laws; The sky will never fall down, so we have to work hard; It is almost impossible to win the lottery in reality, so we cannot get married'.

21.2.2 Past subjunctive

Past subjunctive(가정법 과거) expresses irreality of the past, and is expressed in '만약 … -았/었다면/-(았/었)더라면, … -았/었을 텐데' in general. '-았/었더라면' is a combination of; past-tense prefinal ending '-았/었-'; recollective prefinal ending '-더-', declarative sentence ending '-다'; and conditional connective ending '-면'. If adverbs such as '만약, 만일' are used in conjunction with speculative expressions like '-았/었을 텐데, -았/었을 것이다', the meaning of past subjunctive becomes even more clear.

만일 내가 새**였다면**, 네게 날아<u>갔을 텐데</u>.
If I had been a bird, I would have flown to you.
만약 네가 내 아들이**었더라면**, 네게 모든 것을 주<u>었을 텐데</u>.
If you had been my son, I would have given you everything.
만일 해가 서쪽에서 **떴다면**, 세상의 모든 것이 바뀌<u>었을 것이다</u>. / If the Sun had risen from the West, everything in the whole would have changed.
만약 민서가 날씬**했더라면**, 훨씬 예<u>뻤으리라</u>.
If Min-Seo had been slim, she would have been much prettier.

Sentences above mean: 'Because I was not a bird in the past, I could not fly to you; Because you were not my son in the past, I could not give you everything; Because the Sun did not rise from the West, everything in the whole world did not change; and Because Min-Seo was not slim, she was not pretty'.

Moreover, '-았/었더라면' can signify subjunctive without '-라'.

만약 한국 전쟁이 나지 않**았더면**, 한국은 지금보다 훨씬 더 잘 살 수 있었을 텐데. / If the Korean War had not break out, Korea would be much wealthier than it is now.
네가 좀 더 현명한 판단을 내**렸더면**, 우리가 이 고생을 하지 않았을 것이다.
If you had made a wiser decision, we would not go through all these difficulties.
눈이 조금만 더 내**렸더면**, 눈싸움을 할 수 있었을 텐데.
If it had snowed a little more, we could have a snowball fight.

Also, interrogative and exclamatory sentence endings can be used as follows:

만일 그가 공자 같은 사람이**었더라면**, 과연 인류을 저버렸**을까**?
If he had been like Confucius, would he have transgressed moral laws?
만약 그 운전사가 현명**했었다면**, 훨씬 사고를 줄일 수 있었겠**군요**!
If the driver was wise, he could have prevented many more accidents!

21.2.3 Future subjunctive

Future subjunctive(가정법 미래) expresses irreality of the future, and is represented in '혹시(라도) ⋯ -이/가 된다면, ⋯ -(으)ㄹ 텐데' in general. '된다면' is a combination of verb '-되(다)', declarative sentence ending '-ㄴ다' and conditional connective ending '-면'. If adverbs such as 만약, 만일 are used in conjunction with speculative expressions like '-(으)ㄹ 텐데, -(이)ㄹ 것이다', the meaning of future subjunctive becomes even more clear.

혹시(라도) 내일 내가 새가 된다면, 네게 날아갈 텐데.
If I should become a bird tomorrow by any chance, I shall fly to you.
혹시(라도) 미래에 네가 내 아들이 된다면, 네게 모든 것을 줄 것이다.
If you could be my son in the future by any chance, I shall give you
everything.
혹시(라도) 내일 해가 서쪽에서 {뜬다면/뜨게 된다면}, 세상의 모든 것이
바뀔 것이다.
If the Sun should rise from the West tomorrow by any chance, everything
in the whole world shall change.

Sentences above mean: 'Because I will hardly become a bird tomorrow,
I will not be able to fly to you; Because you will highly unlikely become
my son in the future, I will not be able to give you everything; and
Because the Sun is highly unlikely to rise from the West, everything
in the whole world will not change'.

Also, '-게 된다면' and '-아/어진다면' can signify future subjunctive.

네가 산삼이라도 몇 뿌리 캐게 된다면, 우리 형편도 나아질 텐데.
If you can dig some wild ginseng, we shall be better off.
내가 너를 사랑하게 된다면, 너를 만나러 오겠다.
If I get to love you, I shall come to see you.
이 고목에 움이 돋게 된다면, 모를까 절대 그녀가 사랑을 고백하지 않을
거야.
Unless a sprout starts to burgeon from this old tree, she shall never
confess her love.
나중에 민서가 날씬해진다면, 지금보다 훨씬 예쁠 거야.
If Min-Seo can become slim in the future, she shall be much prettier
than now.

Moreover, interrogative, imperative, propositive and exclamatory sentence endings can be used as follows:

만일 그가 사람이 **된다면**, 과연 인류을 저버**릴까**?

If he should become a human being, will he transgress moral laws?

만약 내일 하늘이 무너지**게 된다면**, 아무것도 하지 말고 가만히 있**어라**.

If the sky should fall down tomorrow, don't do anything but stay still.

만일 내일 로또 복권에 당첨**이 된다면**, 우리 당장 결혼하**자**.

If I should win the lottery tomorrow, let's get married right away.

만약 그 운전사가 현명하**게 된다면**, 훨씬 사고를 줄일 수 있겠**군요**!

If the driver should become wise, he will be able to prevent accidents much more!

One step forward >>

■ Concessional subjunctive

Concessional connective endings '-던들, -더라도' can convey subjunctive. These mean concessional subjunctive. In their apodosis, either negative expressions like '없다, 아니다', etc. are used or interrogative endings like '-(으)ㄹ까? -(으)ㄴ/는가? -았/었겠는가?' are used.

비가 그만 {왔**던들**/왔**더라도**} 이런 홍수 피해는 **없었**을 것이다.
→ 비가 그만 왔**었다면**, 이런 홍수 피해는 없었을 것이다.
  If the rain had stopped, we would not have seen such flood damage.

자네가 {판사였**던들**/판사였**더라도**} 내가 유죄를 선고 당하지 **않았**을 텐데.
→ 자네가 판사였**더라면**, 내가 유죄를 선고 당하지 않았을 텐데.
  If you were a judge, I would not have been sentenced guilty.

내가 조국을 {떠**난들**/떠나**더라도**} 아주 떠**날까**?
→ 내가 조국을 떠**난다면**, 아주 떠날까?
  If I get to leave my home country, shall I leave for good?

그 사람이 부자가 {**된들**/되**더라도**} 남을 도울 수 **있을까**?
→ 그 사람이 부자가 **된다면**, 남을 도울 수 있을까?
  If he becomes rich, will he be able to help others?

21.2.4 Characteristics of Korean subjunctive

First, Korean's conditional expressions and subjunctive expressions are closely linked together, since they are all represented by connective ending '-(으)면'. It is possible to make conditional expressions with '-(ㄴ/는)다면' alone, and also to make subjunctive expressions with '-(으)면'. This is because the expressions can be interpreted as either subjunctive or conditional expressions according to what situation the speaker was in with what kind of intentions.

좋다면 and 좋으면 below can be subjunctive expressions if understood as 'supposing that the weather is going to be nice, even though the weather is hardly likely to be nice', or conditional expressions if 'the state of the weather' is understood as a condition for going on a picnic. However, '-(으)면' generally puts forward something of the real world as a direct condition, while '-(ㄴ/는)다면' puts forward something of irreality. Therefore, '-(ㄴ/는)다면' is more adequate for subjunctive expressions.

> 날씨가 좋**다면** 함께 놀러 가겠니?
> If the weather is nice, will you go on a picnic with me?
> 날씨가 좋**으면** 함께 놀러 가겠니?
> If the weather is nice, will you go on a picnic with me?

Moreover, if the role of '-(으)면' is to put forward conditions based upon the speaker's subjective judgment, the role of '-(ㄴ/는)다면' is to put forward something that is based on others' objective judgment as the speaker's subjective assumption. Therefore, '-(ㄴ/는)다면' is more appropriate for subjunctive expressions. It is easier to see the difference between '-(으)면' and '-(ㄴ/는)다면' if using 뉴스에서 (news, thus objective media outlet) in following sentences.

뉴스에서 날씨가 좋**다면** 함께 놀러 가겠니?
If the news reports that the weather is going to be nice, will you go on a picnic with me?
*뉴스에서 날씨가 좋**으면** 함께 놀러 가겠니?

Second, present subjunctive and future subjunctive usually overlap with each other in terms of phrases they use. In other words, '-(ㄴ/는)다면', which usually stands for present subjunctive, can also convey future subjunctive. '-이/가 된다면', which generally signify future subjunctive, can also convey present subjunctive. This is because, the present-tense prefinal ending '-ㄴ/는-' in '-(ㄴ/는)다면' refers to events that are currently underway, as well as something of the past; and '-이/가 된다면' also can be used for present and future expressions. In such cases, the meaning of '-(ㄴ/는)다면' and '-이/가 된다면' can become clearer if used in conjunction with time adverbs such as 내일 'tomorrow', 나중에 'later', 미래에 'in the future', 오늘 'today', 지금 'now', and 당장 'right now'.

In the following sentences, '-(ㄴ/는)다면' indicates future subjunctive, '-게 된다면' present subjunctive.

만일 내일 해가 서쪽에서 **뜬다면**, 세상의 모든 것이 바뀔 것이다.
If the Sun rises from the West tomorrow, everything in the whole world will change.
혹시(라도) 지금 해가 서쪽에서 뜨**게 된다면**, 세상의 모든 것이 바뀔 것이다.
If the Sun should rise from the West now by any chance, everything in the whole world will change.

Third, conditional connective ending '-거든' can indicate subjunctive. However, '-거든', which helps construct an objective and realistic conditional clause, needs to be used in conjunction with performative verbs (i.e. commands, questions, promises, volition, proposition). Thus, it is not generally used to express subjunctive.

내가 {천사라면/*천사이거든} 참 행복할 텐데.
If I were an angel, I would be so happy.
해가 서쪽에서 {뜨거든/뜨면/뜬다면} 우리 결혼하자.
If the Sun rises from the West, let's get married.

21.3 Korean cultural aspects as reflected in subjunctive

First, when supposed to use subjunctive expressions, Koreans tend to use conditional expressions. In particular, present subjunctive is usually confused with conditional clauses. '-(으)면' and '-ㄴ/는다면', as shown below, stand for conditions and subjunctive respectively, but they are usually confused in general discourse.

사람을 죽이고 돈을 빼앗아 {가면/간다면} 강도나 다름없다.
If somebody kills others and steals money from them, he is practically a robber.
내일 종말이 {오면/온다면} 누가 일을 하겠나?
If the world should end tomorrow, who shall work?

Second, if the speaker wants to make slight concessions and assumptions without revealing his own intentions or feelings, '-ㄴ/는다면 … -ㄴ/는다면' is generally used.

멀다면 멀고, 가깝다면 가까운 것이 법이다.
The law can be far if you think far, or near if you think near.
동지라면 동지고, 적이라면 적이랄 수 있는 사람이 바로 그 사람이다.
He is a kind of person who can be a comrade or an enemy.

Section 4

Sentence
Extension

Standard Korean Grammar for Foreigners

22 Connective

22.1 What is a connective?

Connective(연결) is one way of expanding a sentence by using connective endings. Connectives can be divided into equivalent connective and subordinate connective according to grammatical features and semantic relationship.

The Korean language has a very sophisticated level of connective endings. Therefore, a good knowledge of Korean connectives should help make a wide range of expressions. Koreans are currently using roughly 100 connective endings in various ways.

Connective sentences are subject to many grammatical constraints. Therefore, speakers should pay careful attention to the use of subject, predicate, tense, aspect, sentence endings and negation.

22.2 Types and characteristics of connectives

22.2.1 Equivalent connective

Equivalent connective(대등적 연결) connects the preceding and following clause so that the clauses will have an equivalent relationship. Equivalent relationship can be divided into serial, selection and contrast. Also, the meaning of the sentence connected by equivalent connectives does not change even if the order of the preceding and following clause is switched. It is important to note however, that the preceding and following clause form a semantic symmetry.

	Semantic relationship	Connective endings
1	Serial	-고, -(으)며
2	Selection	-거나/건, -든지/든, -든가, -(으)나
3	Contrast	-아/어도, -(으)나, -(으)되, -지만

22.2.1.1 Serial

Connective endings '-고, -(으)며' can form serial(나열) relationship. They simply link the preceding clause with the following clause symmetrically. '-고, -(으)며' can connect at least two sentences, and they are more or less the same as 'and' in English.

● **Meaning**: '-고' and '-(으)며' can list two or more situations or facts, and are able to connect several clauses with equivalent meanings.

준서는 학교에 {가고/가며} 민서는 집에 간다.
Jun-Seo goes to school and Min-Seo goes home.
민서는 지식이 {많고/많으며} 준서는 지혜가 많다.
Min-Seo has deep knowledge and Jun-Seo has deep wisdom.
5월 5일은 {어린이날이고/어린이날이며}, 5월 15일은 스승의 날이다.
May 5th is Children's day, and May 15th is teachers' day.

They sometimes connect clauses that have opposite meanings.

준서는 미국에서 한국에 {오고/오며} 민서는 한국에서 미국으로 간다.
Jun-Seo is coming to Korea from America and Min-Seo is going to America from Korea.
그는 키가 {크고/크며} 그녀는 키가 작다. / He is tall and she is short.
민서는 {모범생이고/모범생이며} 준서는 망나니이다.
Min-Seo is a model student and Jun-Seo is a roughneck.

'-고' and '-(으)며' have the same function in that they connect different clauses in a serial relationship, but only '-고' can be used to connect individual words.

사회에는 {크고/*크며} 작은 문제들이 많이 있을 수 있다.
The society may have problems, both big and small.
{달고/*달며} {쓰고/*쓰며}를 따질 상황이 아니다.
(We are) not in a situation to choose what is sweet or bitter.
{하얗고/*하야며} 곱게 쌓인 눈 위를 걸어갑니다.
(We are) walking on the white and lovely snow.
나는 서울에 {가고/*가며} 싶다.
I want to go to Seoul.
민서는 공부를 {하고/*하며} 나서 공원으로 놀러 나갔다.
Min-Seo, after studying, went out to the park to play.

Moreover, if '-고' and '-(으)며' are used in the same sentence, '-고' is usually to connect words and phrases, whereas '-(으)며' is for phrases and clauses.

어머니는 녹차를 마시고 있고 아버지는 커피를 마시고 있으며, 누나는 책을 읽고 있고 형은 컴퓨터 게임을 하고 있다.
Mother is drinking green tea, father is drinking coffee, elder sister is reading a book and elder brother is playing computer games.
→ *어머니는 녹차를 마시고 있으며 아버지는 커피를 마시고 있고, 누나는 책을 읽고 있으며 형은 컴퓨터 게임을 하고 있다.

이 물건은 크고 저 물건은 작으며, 이 사람은 착하고 저 사람은 악하다.
This object is large, that one small, this person good and that person vicious.
→ ^{?*}이 물건은 크며 저 물건은 작고, 이 사람은 착하며 저 사람은 악하다.

- **Order of the preceding and following clause**: The meaning of connective sentences in a serial relationship does not change even if the order of the preceding and following clause is switched.

민서는 집에 가고 준서는 학교에 간다.
Min-Seo goes home and Jun-Seo goes to school.
민서는 무용을 잘하는 학생이며 준서는 공부를 잘하는 학생이다.
Min-Seo is a student who is good at dancing, and Jun-Seo is a student who is good at studying.

- **Use of subject**: There are no special constraints for subjects. The same subject can be applied to both the preceding and following clause, or a different subject may also be applied. However, several clauses are usually listed in series under just one single topic.

<u>준서는</u> 한국 {사람이고/사람이며}, <u>**토마스는**</u> 미국 사람이다.
Jun-Seo is Korean and Thomas is American.
<u>민서는</u> 공부도 {잘하고/잘하며} 운동도 잘한다.
Min-Seo is good at studying and sports also.
<u>한국 사람은</u> 성격이 좀 {급하고/급하며} 솔직한 편이다.
Koreans tend to be impulsive and outspoken.

- **Use of prefinal endings**: Prefinal endings such as '-았/었-, -겠-, -았/었었-' usually come in the following clause, but it does not matter which clause they are in.

준서는 농구를 {잘**했**고/잘**했**으며} 민서는 배구를 잘**했**다.

Jun-Seo was good at basketball and Min-Seo was good at volleyball.

오늘은 비도 오지 {않겠고/않겠으며} 바람도 불지 않겠다.

Today, it is going to be neither rainy nor windy.

준서는 노래를 {불렀었고/불렀었으며} 민서는 춤을 추었었다.

Jun-Seo sang and Min-Seo danced.

However, '-더-' can be located only in the following clause. If put in the preceding clause, or in both clauses, the sentence would become ungrammatical.

준서는 서울에 {가고/가며} 민서는 부산에 가더라.

Jun-Seo went to Seoul and Min-Seo went to Busan.

*준서는 한국 음악을 {듣더고/듣더며} 민서는 중국 음악을 듣더라.

Jun-Seo listened to Korean music and Min-Seo listened to Chinese music.

*준서는 사과를 {먹더고/먹더며} 민서는 파인애플을 먹는다.

Jun-Seo is eating apples and Min-Seo is eating pineapples.

When using connective ending '-(으)며' in a past-tense sentence, '-았/었-' should be put in both the preceding and following clause to be grammatically correct. However, '-고' has no such constraints.

어제는 비도 많이 {왔으며/*오며} 눈도 많이 왔다.

Yesterday, it rained heavily and snowed heavily.

어제는 비도 많이 {왔고/오고} 눈도 많이 왔다.

Yesterday, it rained heavily and snowed heavily.

● **Use of predicates**: Since there are no constraints for predicates, verbs, adjectives, 이다 and 있다 may be used freely.

준서는 노래를 {부르고/부르며} 민서는 춤을 춘다.

Jun-Seo sings and Min-Seo dances.

그 사람은 {**용감하고**/**용감하며**} 정직하다. / The person is brave and honest.

준서는 {여행가**이고**/여행가**이며**} 민서는 무용가이다.

Jun-Seo is a traveler and Min-Seo is a dancer.

민서는 학식도 많이 {**있고**/**있으며**} 재산도 많이 있다.

Min-Seo has a lot of knowledge and a lot of property.

● **Use of sentence endings**: There are no special constraints for sentence endings, so it is possible to use all sorts of sentence endings, from declarative, interrogative, imperative, propositive to exclamatory endings. However, combination of '-(으)며' with propositive or imperative endings makes a very awkward sentence.

공부도 열심히 {하고/[?]하며} 운동도 열심히 {**해라**/하자}

Study hard and work out hard.

Let's study hard and work out hard.

음악도 {듣고/[?]들으며} 그림도 {그려라/그리자}

Listen to the music and draw pictures.

Let's listen to the music and draw pictures.

● **Use of negation**: There are no constraints for negation either. Yet, either negative elements or expressions appear in both preceding and following clauses, or not used at all in both clauses. Using negative expressions in only one of the clauses will make a very awkward, or even ungrammatical sentence.

오늘은 비도 **안** {오고/오며} 바람도 **안** 분다.

Today, it is neither rainy nor windy.

^{?*}오늘은 비도 **안** {오고/오며} 바람도 분다.

^{?*}오늘은 비도 {오고/오며} 바람도 **안** 분다.

● **Common use**: If serial relationship should be stated repeatedly, use

'-고' and '-(으)며' in turns, in the order of '⋯ -고 ⋯ -(으)며, ⋯ -고 ⋯ -(으)며', not '⋯ -(으)며 ⋯ -고, ⋯ -(으)며 ⋯ -고'.

그 백화점은 물건 값이 싸고 품질이 좋으며, 직원들이 친절하고 상냥하다.
In the department store, the price is cheap, the quality is good, and the staff are kind and friendly.
?그 백화점은 물건 값이 싸며 품질이 좋고, 직원들이 친절하며 상냥하다.

준서는 성실하고 친절하며, 게다가 일까지 잘한다.
Jun-Seo is hardworking, kind and very competent.
?준서는 성실하며 친절하고, 게다가 일까지 잘한다.

22.2.1.2 Selection

Connective endings for **selection**(선택) are '-거나, -든지, -(으)나'. '-거나, -든지' can be abbreviated to '-건, -든'. The endings connect the preceding and following clause so that the hearer may choose what to do between the preceding and following clause. They cannot choose more than two, or they may not choose anything at all. The endings are more or less the same as 'or' in English.

● **Meaning**: A single use of '-거나' and '-든지' in a sentence can give the hearer only one choice. Two or more '-거나' or '-든지' can give the hearer multiple choices.

[Singular choice] 오늘은 비가 {오거나/오든지} 눈이 올 것 같다.
It seems it's going to either rain or snow today.
준서는 밥을 {먹거나/먹든지} 빵을 먹을 것이다.
Jun-Seo will have some rice or bread.
[Multiple choice] 오늘은 비가 {오거나/오든지}, 눈이 {오거나/오든지}
할 것 같다. / It seems it's going to rain or snow today.

준서가 밥을 {먹**거나**/먹**든지**}, 빵을 {먹**거나**/먹**든지**}
나는 상관없다.
Whether Jun-Seo has rice or bread, I don't care.

'-거나' and '-든지' are identical in that they are connective endings for selection, but there is a slight difference in the scope of choice they offer. In other words, '-거나' limits the choice of the hearer to what is suggested in the sentence. Therefore, the sentences below with '-거나' allows the hearer to choose only apples or pears, folk songs or children's songs, Min-Seo or Yun-Seo, and nothing else whatsoever. The hearer must choose any one of them.

애야, 너는 사과를 먹**거나** 배를 먹어라. / Hey, eat apples or pears.
?애야, 너는 사과를 먹**거나** 배를 먹**거나** 마음대로 해라.
Hey, eat apples or pears, just do whatever you want.

너는 유치원생이니까 민요를 부르**거나** 동요를 불러라.
You are a preschooler, so sing a folk song or children's song.
너는 틀림없이 배우자로 민서를 선택하**거나** 윤서를 선택해야 한다.
You will have to choose Min-Seo or Yun-Seo as your spouse.

However, '-든지' gives an open-ended choice by expanding the choice of hearers to what lies outside the sentence. In other words, sentences below with '-든지' lets the hearer choose apples or pears, folk songs or children's songs, Min-Seo or Yun-Seo, and anything else they wish.

?애야, 너는 사과를 먹**든지** 배를 먹어라.
애야, 너는 사과를 먹**든지** 배를 먹**든지** 네 마음대로 해라.
Hey, eat apples or pears, or whatever you want.

애야, 너는 유치원생이니까 민요를 부르**든지** 동요를 부르**든지** 하면 될 것이야. / You are a preschooler, so sing a folk song, children's song or whatever you want.

너는 배우자로 민서를 선택하<u>든지</u> 윤서를 선택하면 좋을 거야.
You should choose Min-Seo, Yun-Seo or whoever as your spouse.

The difference between '-거나' and '-든지' becomes clearer if combined with indefinite pronouns such as 누구 'who', 언제 'when', 어디 'where', 무엇 'what'. '-든지', which indicates open-ended choice, can bond well with indefinite pronouns, whereas '-거나' (limited choice) cannot.

정답을 아는 사람은 {*누구<u>거나</u>/누구<u>든지</u>} 손을 들어 보세요.
Whoever knows the answer, put your hands up.

이곳에 오고 싶으면 {*언제<u>거나</u>/언제<u>든지</u>} 오세요. 환영합니다.
Please feel free to come whenever you want. You are welcome.

{*어디<u>거나</u>/어디<u>든지</u>} 네가 가고 싶은 곳에 가거라.
Go to the place wherever you want.

질문이 있으면 {*무엇이<u>거나</u>/무엇이<u>든지</u>} 물어 보세요.
You may ask whatever questions you may want to ask.

'-(으)나' also signifies open-ended choice, just like '-든지'. This becomes clearer with addition of '어떻게 해도, 어떠해도' to '-(으)나'.

그녀는 오<u>나</u> 가<u>나</u> (어떻게 해도) 말썽이다.
She is a menace everywhere you turn.

민서가 오<u>나</u> 준서가 오<u>나</u> (어떻게 해도) 결과는 마찬가지다.
Whether Min-Seo comes or Jun-Seo comes, things will be the same.

그 사람은 눈이 오<u>나</u> 비가 오<u>나</u> (상황이 어떠해도) 성실하게 일했다.
The person worked hard, come rain or come snow.

'-거나' and '-든지', connective endings of selection, mean that it does not matter whether the hearer chooses any one of the given situations, or that the hearer can choose all of the given situations.

네가 서울에 {오**거나**/오**든지**} {말**거나**/말**든지**} 나는 상관하지 않겠다.
Whether you come to Seoul or not, I will not care.
한국에 오고자 하는 외국인은 {남자(이)**건**/남자(이)**든**} {여자(이)**건**/여자
(이)**든**} 모두 올 수 있습니다.
All foreigners who wish to come to Korea can come to Korea whether
male or female.
그 친구와는 어디에서 {만나**건**/만나**든**} 반가웠습니다.
Wherever the place was, it was good to see the friend.

If used with interrogative pronouns, such as 누구 'who', 언제 'when',
어디 'where', 무엇 'what', 어떻게 'how', 왜 'why', 어떤 'which', 어느
'which', it becomes clearer that the hearer can choose everything.

누구와 만나**든** 나는 상관하지 않겠다. / I will not care whoever you meet.
언제 오**든** 문제 될 것은 없다. / It does not matter when you come.
어떤 것이**든** 고르십시오. / Choose whatever (you like).

● **Order of the preceding and following clause**: The meaning of the
whole sentence does not change even if the preceding and following
clauses change the order, in a sentence that conveys selection.

내일은 눈이 오**거나** 비가 올 것 같다.
Tomorrow, it looks like it will either snow or rain.
귤을 먹**든지** 사과를 먹**든지** 하자.
Let's eat something, whether tangerines or apples.
그 사람은 비가 오**나** 눈이 오**나** 성실하게 일했다.
The person worked hard, rain or shine.

Unlike connective endings of serial relationship, using both '-거나' and
'-든지' in a single sentence is a grammatical error.

버스를 타고 가**거나** 비행기를 타고 가**거나** 늦기는 마찬가지다.

Whether you take the bus or airplane, you'll be late anyway.

버스를 타고 가<u>든지</u> 비행기를 타고 가<u>든지</u> 늦기는 마찬가지다.

Whether you take the bus or airplane, you'll be late anyway.

*버스를 타고 가<u>거나</u> 비행기를 타고 가<u>든지</u> 늦기는 마찬가지다.

*버스를 타고 가<u>든지</u> 비행기를 타고 가<u>거나</u> 늦기는 마찬가지다.

● **Use of subject**: There are no constraints for subjects, so the same subject may be applied to both the preceding and following clause, or a different subject may be applied to both clauses.

<u>나는</u> 슬플 때면 늘 피아노를 {치<u>건</u>/치<u>든</u>} 노래를 {듣<u>건</u>/듣<u>든</u>} 했다.
When I feel sad, I tried to do something, whether it's playing the piano or singing a song.

<u>준서가</u> {오<u>거나</u>/오<u>든지</u>} <u>민서가</u> {오<u>거나</u>/오<u>든지</u>} 결과는 마찬가지다.
Whether Jun-Seo or Min-Seo comes, things will be just the same.

● **Use of prefinal endings**: When it comes to prefinal endings such as '-았/었-, -았/었었-, -겠-', the same ending must be used in both the preceding and following clause. Otherwise, it would be a grammatical error. Prefinal ending '-더-' cannot be used in conjunction with endings that convey selection.

그가 일을 {끝<u>냈건</u>/끝<u>냈든</u>} 못 {끝<u>냈건</u>/끝<u>냈든</u>} 내가 알 바가 아니다.
Whether he finished the work or not, it is none of my business.

그가 일을 {끝<u>냈었건</u>/끝<u>냈었든</u>} 못 {끝<u>냈었건</u>/끝<u>냈었든</u>} 내가 알 바가 아니다.

그가 일을 {끝내<u>겠건</u>/끝내<u>겠든</u>} 못 {끝내<u>겠건</u>/끝내<u>겠든</u>} 내가 알 바가 아니다.

*그가 일을 {끝<u>냈건</u>/끝<u>냈든</u>} 못 {끝내<u>건</u>/끝내<u>든</u>} 내가 알 바가 아니다.

*비가 {오<u>더건</u>/오<u>더든</u>} 바람이 {불<u>더건</u>/불<u>더든</u>} 그 일은 계획대로 진행이 된다. / Whether it is rainy or windy, things will go as planned.

- **Use of predicates**: Since there are no constraints for predicates, verbs, adjectives, '이다, 있다' may be used freely.

공부를 {하건/하든} 일을 {하건/하든} 열심히 해야 인생에 성공할 수 있다.
Whether you study or work, you have to do it hard to be successful in life.
그녀가 {뚱뚱하건/뚱뚱하든} {날씬하건/날씬하든} 나는 상관없다.
Whether she is fat or slim, I do not care.

그 사람이 {동양인이건/동양인이든} {서양인이건/서양인이든} 인격을 가진 인간임에는 틀림이 없다.
Whether the person is an Asian or a Westerner, it is certain that he is a man of noble character.
돈이 많이 {있건/있든} {없건/없든} 차별 대우를 받아서는 안 된다.
Whether you have lots of money or not, you should not be discriminated.

- **Use of sentence endings**: Since there are no special constraints for sentence endings, it is possible to use all sort of sentence endings, from declarative, interrogative, imperative, propositive to exclamatory endings.

준서가 음악을 {듣건/듣든} 그림을 {그리건/그리든} 꾸준히 {한다/하니?}
Whether Jun-Seo is listening to music or drawing a picture, he does it steadily.
Whether Jun-Seo is listening to music or drawing a picture, does he do it steadily?
공부를 {하건/하든} 운동을 {하건/하든} 열심히 {해라/하자}
Whatever you do, whether it be studying or playing sports, do it hard.
Whatever you do, whether it be studying or playing sports, let us do it hard.
비가 오나 눈이 오나 열심히 {공부했다/공부했니?/공부해라/공부하자/공부하는구나!}
I studied hard, whether it rained or snowed.

Did you study hard whether it rained or snow?

Study hard whether it rains or snows.

Let us study hard whether it rains or snows.

You are studying hard whether it rains or snows!

● **Use of negation**: There are no special constraints for negation. However, if there is a choice between positive and negative, the positive statement generally comes before the negative one.

나는 민서가 서울에 **오건 안 오건** 상관하지 않는다.
Whether Min-Seo comes to Seoul or not, I don't care.
[?]나는 민서가 서울에 **안 오건 오건** 상관하지 않는다.

민서는 그 사과가 맛이 **있든 없든** 불평을 하지 않았다.
Min-Seo did not complain about the taste of the apple.
[?]민서는 그 사과가 맛이 **없든 있든** 불평을 하지 않았다.

● **Common use**: Original forms such as '-거나, -든지' are mainly used in written language, whereas condensed forms such as '-건, -든' are mainly used in spoken language.

{오**거나**/오**건**} {말**거나**/말**건**} 네 마음대로 해도 된다.
It's up to you whether you come or not.
그 일을 {잘하**든지**/잘하**든**} {못하**든지**/못하**든**} 관계없으니까 최선을 다해라.
It does not matter whether you are good at it or not, so just do your best.

If there should be at least two '-거나' or '-든지' in a single sentence, they are generally used in the form of '··· -거나 ··· -거나 하다' or '··· -든지 ···-든지 하다'.

그는 한가할 때면 늘 음악을 {듣든지/듣거나} 노래를 {부르든지/부르거나}
한다. / When he is free, he listens to music or sings a song.
맛있는 음식을 {먹든지/먹거나} 친구와 이야기를 {먹든지/먹거나} 하면
기분이 좋아진다.
If (I) have tasty food or chat with your friends, I feel better.

In other words, it is very awkward or even ungrammatical to mix '-거나'
and '-든지' in a single sentence.

^{?*}그는 한가할 때면 늘 음악을 듣든지 노래를 부르거나 한다.
^{?*}맛있는 음식을 먹거나 친구와 이야기를 하든지 하면 기분이 좋아진다.

22.2.1.3 Contrast

Connective endings for **contrast**(대립 · 대조), which include '-아/어도,
-지만, -(으)나, etc'. form a contrastive relationship between the preceding
and following clause, and act almost the same as 'but'. Thus, these endings
have the meaning of 'contrast' or 'while'.

● **Meaning**: '-아/어도, -지만, -(으)나' can connect two clauses whose
meanings run counter to, or conflict with each other.

준서는 축구는 {잘해도/잘하지만/[?]잘하나} 야구는 잘 못한다.
Jun-Seo is good at football, but not good at baseball.
인생은 {짧아도/짧지만/[?]짧으나} 예술은 길다.
Life is short, (but) art is long.
그는 돈이 {많아도/많지만/[?]많으나} 그녀는 지식이 많다.
He has lots of money, but she has lots of knowledge.
민서는 춤은 잘 {춰도/추지만/[?]추나} 노래는 못한다.
Min-Seo is good at dancing, but not good at singing.

In the sentences above, '-(으)나' sounds very awkward. However, combination of '-(으)나' with prefinal ending '-았/었-' makes a natural sentence, which means that '-(으)나' acts to connect semantically confirmed propositions to form a contrastive relationship.

준서는 축구는 잘**했으나** 야구는 잘 못했다.
Jun-Seo was good at football but not good at baseball.
인생은 짧**았으나** 예술은 길었다. / Life was short, but art was long.
그는 돈이 많**았으나** 그녀는 지식이 많았다.
He had lots of money, but she had lots of knowledge.
민서는 춤은 잘 추**었으나** 노래는 못했다.
Min-Seo was good at dancing, but not good at singing.

Contrast endings may be used to form a concessional relationship to act almost the same as 'though' or 'although'. In other words, contrast endings convey the meaning of '-(으)ㄴ/는데 반해' 'in contrast to something' in a contrastive relationship, but they convey the meaning of '(비록) ⋯ -(으)ㄹ지라도, ⋯ -(으)ㅁ에도 불구하고' 'although', 'though' in a concessional relationship.

준서는 키가 작**아도** 농구를 잘한다. [Concessional]
Jun-Seo, though short, is good at basketball.
→ **비록** 준서는 키가 작**을지라도** 농구를 잘한다.
Although Jun-Seo is short, he is good at basketball.
→ 준서는 키가 작**음에도 불구하고** 농구를 잘한다.
Even though Jun-Seo is short, he is good at basketball.

준서는 축구는 잘**해도** 야구는 잘 못한다. [Contrast]
Jun-Seo is good at football, but not good at baseball.
→ 준서는 축구는 잘하**는데 반해** 야구는 잘 못한다.
Jun-Seo is good at football. On the contrary, he is not good at baseball.

- **Order of the preceding and following clause**: Even if the order of the preceding and following clauses should change, the meaning of the whole sentence does not change in a contrastive sentence.

준서는 야구는 잘 못**해도** 축구는 잘한다.
Although Jun-Seo is poor at baseball, he is good at football.
예술은 길**지만** 인생은 짧다. / Life is short but art is long.
그녀는 지식이 많**으나** 그는 돈이 많다.
Although she has lots of knowledge, he has lots of money.

- **Use of subject**: Since there are no special constraints for subjects, the same subject can be applied to both the preceding and following clause, or different subjects can be applied for both. Usually, when it comes to contrastive sentences, two clauses conflict with each other under the same topic.

준서는 한국 사람이**지만**, 토마스는 미국 사람이다.
Jun-Seo is Korean, but Thomas is American.
민서는 공부는 잘**해도** 운동은 잘 못한다.
Min-Seo is good at studying, but poor at sports.
한국 사람은 성격이 좀 급하**나** 솔직한 편이다.
Koreans are somewhat impulsive, but outspoken.

- **Use of prefinal endings**: If one intends to convey such meanings as past perfect or past-experience with prefinal endings like '-았/었-, -았/었었-', the prefinal endings should be applied to both the preceding and following clauses.

준서는 농구를 {잘**했으나**/잘**했어도**/잘**했지만**} 민서는 배구를 잘했다.
Jun-Seo was good at basketball, but Min-Seo was good at volleyball.
준서는 농구를 {^{?*}잘하**나**/[?]잘**해도**/^{?*}잘하**지만**} 민서는 배구를 잘했다.

준서는 노래를 {불렀으나/불렀어도/불렀지만} 민서는 춤을 추었었다.
Jun-Seo sang, but Min-Seo danced.
?*준서는 노래를 {부르나/불러도/부르지만} 민서는 춤을 추었었다.

However, if the preceding clause denotes the past and the following clause the present, '-았/었-, -았/었었-' may be used only in the preceding clause.

준서는 예전에는 농구를 {잘했으나/잘했어도/잘했지만} 이제는 야구를 잘한다. / Jun-Seo was good at basketball, but is now good at baseball.
준서는 예전에는 기타를 즐겨 {연주했었으나/연주했었어도/연주했었지만} 요즘은 피아노를 자주 치는 편이다. / Jun-Seo enjoyed playing the guitar, but he often plays the piano these days.

Sometimes, if one wishes to use '-겠-' to represent future-volition or future-surmise, '-겠-' can be combined with '-(으)나, -지만' without particular restrictions, but '-겠-' cannot be combined with '-아/어도'. However, '-겠-' can be employed in the following clause of '-아/어도'.

준서는 고국으로 {돌아가겠으나/*돌아가겠어도/돌아가겠지만} 민서는 결국 돌아가지 않을 것이다.
Jun-Seo will return to his home country, but Min-Seo will not.
그녀를 내일 만나기는 {하나/해도/하지만} 차마 그 일을 그만두라는 말은 못 하겠다.
I will meet her tomorrow, but I can't bring myself to tell her to stop the work.

Prefinal ending '-더-' can come only in the following clause. If used in the preceding clause, or both clauses, the sentence becomes ungrammatical.

준서는 서울에 {가나/가도/가지만} 민서는 부산에 가더라.

Jun-Seo is going to Seoul, but Min-Seo is going to Busan.

*준서는 한국 음악을 {듣더나/듣더도/듣더지만} 민서는 중국 음악을 듣더라.

*준서는 사과를 {먹더나/먹더도/먹더지만} 민서는 파인애플을 먹는다.

● **Use of predicates**: Verbs, adjectives, 이다 and 있다 can be used freely without particular constraints.

준서는 노래를 {부르나/불러도/부르지만} 민서는 춤을 춘다.

Jun-Seo is singing, but Min-Seo is dancing.

그 사람은 {용감하나/용감해도/용감하지만} 부정직하다.

The person is brave, but dishonest.

준서는 {여행가이나/여행가여도/여행가이지만} 민서는 무용가이다.

Jun-Seo is a traveler, but Min-Seo is a dancer.

민서는 돈은 많이 {있으나/있어도/있지만} 교양이 없다.

Min-Seo has lots of money, but no culture.

● **Use of sentence endings**: '-(으)나, -아/어도, -지만' impose no particular constraints on the use of sentence endings, so sentences with '-(으)나, -아/어도, -지만' can end in an declarative, interrogative, imperative, propositive or exclamatory manner. However, if the preceding clause ends in '-(으)ㄴ/는데', the following clause cannot end in imperative or propositive tones.

시험은 {끝났으나/끝났어도/끝났지만} 그래도 열심히 {공부한다/공부하니?/공부해라/공부하자/공부하는구나!}

The exam has ended, but (I) study hard.

The exam has ended, but are you studying hard?

The exam has ended, but study hard.

The exam has ended, but let us study hard.

The exam has ended, but you are studying hard!

준서는 맥주를 {마시나/마셔도/마시지만} 민서는 콜라를 {마신다/마시니?/마셔라/마시자/마시는구나!}

Jun-Seo is drinking beer, but Min-Seo is drinking coke.

Jun-Seo is drinking beer, but is Min-Seo drinking coke?

Jun-Seo is drinking beer, but Min-Seo, drink coke.

Jun-Seo is drinking beer, but let us drink coke.

Jun-Seo is drinking beer, but Min-Seo is drinking coke!

준서는 미국으로 유학을 갔는데 민서는 영국으로 유학을 {갔다/갔니?/*가라/*가자/가는구나!}

Jun-Seo is going to America to study, but Min-Seo is going to the UK to study.

Jun-Seo is going to America to study, but is Min-Seo going to the UK to study?

Jun-Seo is going America to study, but Min-Seo is going to the UK to study!

- **Use of negation**: There are no particular constraints in the use of negation.

준서는 유학을 {가나/가도/가지만} 민서는 유학을 가지 않았다.
Jun-Seo went abroad to study, but Min-Seo did not.
준서는 유학을 안 {가나/가도/가지만} 민서는 유학을 갔다.
Jun-Seo did not go abroad to study, but Min-Seo did.

- **Common use**: Using contrast endings in conjunction with contrastive auxiliary particle '-은/는' emphasizes the contrast or conflict.

준서는 축구는 {좋아하나/좋아해도/좋아하지만} 야구는 좋아하지 않는다.
Jun-Seo likes football, but not baseball.
민서는 뉴욕에는 가 {보았으나/보았어도/보았지만} 런던에는 가 보지 못했다. / Min-Seo has been to New York, but not London.

22.2.2 Subordinate connection

Subordinate connection(종속적 연결) connects the preceding and following clause to form a semantically subordinate relationship. Generally, the preceding clause is the subordinate to the following clause. Subordinate connection has 14 semantic functions, and the meaning of the sentence depends on the order of the clauses, so the preceding and following clause cannot change their position. Also, the preceding and following clause cannot constitute a contrastive relationship.

	Semantic relationship	Connective endings
1	Simultaneity	-(으)며, -(으)면서, -고, -자
2	Sequence	-고(서), -아/어서, -자, -자마자
3	Interruption, Conversion	-다가
4	Concession	-(으)ㄴ/는데도, -(으)ㄴ들, -(으)나마, -(으)ㄹ망정, -(으)ㄹ지라도, -(으)ㄹ지언정, -건만, -기로서니, -더라도, -아/어도, -았/었자
5	Condition	-(ㄴ/는)다면, -(으)면, -거든, -거들랑, -아/어야, -았/었던들
6	Cause, Reason	-(으)ㄴ/는지라, -(으)니까, -(으)ㄹ세라, -(으)므로, -(으/느)니만큼, -기에, -길래, -느라(고), -아/어서
7	Purpose, Intention	-(으)러, -(으)려(고), -고자
8	Result	-도록
9	Circumstance	-(으)ㄴ/는데, -(으)니(까), -다시피
10	Comparison	-느니
11	Simile, figure	-듯(이)
12	Proportion	-(으)ㄹ수록
13	Degree	-(으)리만치, -(으)리만큼
14	Addition	-(으)ㄹ뿐더러, -(으)려니와, -거니와
15	Habit, Repetition	-고는

22.2.2.1 Simultaneity

Connective endings for **simultaneity**(동시) are '-(으)며, -(으)면서, -고, -자' and these connect the preceding and following clause so that what is said in the preceding clause happens at the same time as the following clause. These endings have almost the same function as 'as soon as', which refers to 'simultaneous, at the same time', etc.

- **Meaning**

① '-(으)면서' is the representative connective ending for simultaneity, which can be combined with verbs, adjectives, 이다 and 있다 to form simultaneity. Also, '-(으)며' may be used to form simultaneity even though it usually forms a serial relationship.

준서는 텔레비전을 {보**면서**/보**며**} 아침을 먹었다.
Jun-Seo had breakfast while watching TV.
이 노트북은 성능이 {좋**으면서**/좋**으며**} 값이 싼 편이다.
This laptop has good performance and cheap price.
그는 {의사이**면서**/의사이**며**} 화가이다. / He is a doctor and painter.
그녀는 뉴욕에 {있**으면서**/있**으며**} 사업을 하고 있다.
She is doing business while living in New York.

② '-고' usually represents completion when combined with verbs, but represents simultaneity when combined with verbs that refer to continuity of actions such as 맞다 'to be drenched in (water)', 입다 'to wear', 신다 'to put on'. When combined with 이다, '-고' also represents simultaneity.

준서가 비를 맞**고** 길을 걸어가고 있다.
Jun-Seo, drenched in rain, is walking on the road.
민서는 드레스를 입**고** 춤을 추고 있다. / Min-Seo, clad in a dress, is dancing.
그는 피아니스트이**고** 교수이다. / He is a pianist and professor.

③ '-자' conveys simultaneity only when combined with copula 이다.

그녀는 디자이너이**자** 영화평론가이다. / She is a designer and film critic.
우리 아버지는 은행원이**자** 소설가입니다.
My father is a banker and novelist.

● **Use of subject**: There is a particular restriction for subject. If people or animals are subjects, the subject of both the preceding and following clause must be the same.

*<u>준서</u>가 텔레비전을 보**면서** <u>민서</u>가 아침을 먹었다.
*<u>민서</u>는 피아노를 치**며** <u>준서</u>가 노래를 불렀다.
*<u>준서</u>가 비를 맞**고** <u>민서</u>가 걸어가고 있다.

However, if things become the subject, the subject of the preceding clause may be different from that of the following clause, provided however that the preceding and the following clause must have a coherent topic. In other words, the sentences below describe one single topic (yesterday, Hanbok) with the preceding and following clause forming a simultaneous relationship.

<u>어제</u>는 바람이 많이 불**면서** 눈이 내렸다.
Yesterday, it was very windy and snowy at the same time.
이 <u>한복</u>은 맵시가 있**으면서** 실용적이다.
This Hanbok looks stylish and practical at the same time.

● **Use of prefinal endings**: All prefinal endings, ranging from '-았/었-, -겠-, -았/었었-' to '-더-', cannot be combined with connective endings which form simultaneity. Therefore, prefinal endings must be put in the following clause.

*민서는 노래를 {부르<u>었면서</u>/부르<u>겠면서</u>/부르<u>었었면서</u>/부르<u>더면서</u>} 춤을 추었다.

민서는 노래를 부르<u>면서</u> 춤을 {추었다/추<u>겠</u>다/추<u>었었</u>다}

Min-Seo, while singing, danced.

준서는 성격이 좀 급하<u>면서</u> 솔직한 편이<u>더</u>라.

Jun-Seo, while being impulsive, seemed to be quite outspoken.

● **Use of predicates**: Even though there are no constraints in use of predicates, '-(으)면서' is usually combined with verbs, adjectives or 있다, while '-(으)며' and '-고' are attached to adjectives or 이다. '-자' can be combined with 이다 only.

준서는 부모님들의 사랑을 많이 {<u>받으면서</u>/<u>받으며</u>/<u>받고</u>} 살아왔다.

Jun-Seo was beloved by his parents.

그 사람은 성격이 {<u>쾌활하면서</u>/<u>쾌활하며</u>/<u>쾌활하고</u>} 상냥하다.

That man is pleasant and nice.

준서는 {음악가<u>이면서</u>/음악가<u>이며</u>/음악가<u>이고</u>/음악가<u>이자</u>} 칼럼니스트 이다. / Jun-Seo is a musician and columnist.

민서는 미국 뉴욕에 가 <u>있으면서</u> 계속 사업을 확장해 갔다.

Min-Seo, while in New York, has continued to expand her business.

However, there are hardly a few cases where combination of '-고' and verbs form simultaneity. Such a combination is limited to cases where the sentence has a repetitive and habitual meaning and the meaning of the verb in the preceding clause extends to the following clause.

한국에는 여름에 늘 장마가 {<u>오면서</u>/오<u>며</u>/오<u>고</u>} 바람이 많이 분다.

In Korea, the summer is always rainy and windy.

어머니는 나의 손을 꼭 {잡<u>으면서</u>/잡<u>으며</u>/잡<u>고</u>} 건강을 늘 조심하라고 당부 하셨다. / Mother held my hand tightly, telling me to take care of myself.

그 사람만은 나를 인정해 주리라 {생각하<u>면서</u>/생각하<u>며</u>/생각하<u>고</u>} 열심히 일을 하고 있다.

Believing that he will definitely recognize me, I am working very hard.

Moreover, combination of '-(으)며' or '-고' with adjectives or 이다 may sometimes form a serial relationship.

민서는 마음씨도 {착하며/착하고} 공부도 잘한다.

Min-Seo is kind and even a good student.

준서는 야구 {선수이며/선수이고} 축구 선수이다.

Jun-Seo is a baseball player and football player.

- **Use of sentence endings**: All sentence endings, such as declarative, interrogative, imperative, propositive and exclamatory endings, may be used without any restrictions.

춤을 {추면서/추며} 노래를 {했다/했니?/해라/하자/하는구나!}

While dancing, (we) sang.

While dancing, did you sing?

While dancing, sing.

While dancing, let us sing.

While dancing, you are singing!

우리 점심을 {먹으면서/먹으며} 회의를 {할까?/하자}

While having lunch, shall we have a meeting?

While having lunch, let us have a meeting.

- **Use of negation**: There are no particular restriction to the use of negation, but careful attention is needed to interpret the meaning of the sentence. The sentences below are one way to emphasize the preceding clause rather than to form a simultaneous relationship. They mean 'he studied, refraining from listening to music; she lacks effort even though she is even worse at cooking; and she is definitely not a doctor even though she is a musician'.

그는 음악을 **안** 들**으면서** 공부했다.
He studied while not listening to music.
민서는 요리 솜씨가 **안** 좋**으면서** 그나마 성의도 없다.
Min-Seo is not good at cooking, and she does not even make effort.
민서는 의사가 **아니면서** 음악가이다.
Min-Seo is not a doctor, but a musician.

If the preceding clause uses a negative expression 아니 and the following clause negates what is said in preceding clause, the sentence may convey a contrastive or concessional relationship, meaning '아니 + (verb/adjective/copula)-지만 ; 아니 + (verb/adjective/copula)-(으)ㅁ에도 불구하고'.

그는 음악을 **안** 들**으면서** (음악을) 듣는 척했다.
He was not listening to music, but pretended to do so.
민서는 요리 솜씨가 **안** 좋**으면서** (요리 솜씨가) 좋은 척했다.
Min-Seo was not good at cooking, but pretended that she was.
민서는 의사가 **아니면서** 의사인 척했다.
Min-Seo was not a doctor, but pretended that she was.

Furthermore, the use of negative expressions in the following clause may generate several different meanings. In other words, it can negate only the preceding clause, or both the preceding and following clause. For example, the sentences below can be interpreted as 'he studied while refraining from music' or 'he neither listened to music nor studied'.

그는 음악을 들**으면서** 공부하**지 않**았다.
He studied, not listening to music though.
He neither studied nor listened to music.

오늘은 날씨가 좋<u>으면서</u> 바람이 불<u>지 않</u>았다.

Today, the weather was nice, and not windy.

Today, the weather was neither nice nor windy.

민서는 의사이<u>면서</u> 변호사<u>가 아니</u>다.

Min-Seo is a doctor, but not a lawyer.

Min-Seo is neither a doctor nor a lawyer.

22.2.2.2 Completion

Connective endings for **sequence**(계기), which include '-고(서), -아/어서, -자, -자마자', connect clauses so as to make the preceding clause happen before the following clause. These connective endings act almost the same as 'and then'.

- **Meaning**:

① '-아/어서' connect the preceding and following clause in the order of time, provided that they describe what is said in the following clause on the assumption of what is told in the preceding clause. In other words, the preceding clause becomes the essential background for the following clause, and the following clause is established on the assumption of the preceding clause; as a result, the preceding and following clause have a close coherence.

For example, in the sentences below, 'Jun-Seo's visit to Seoul' and 'Min-Seo's drawing a picture' become the essential background and premise for 'Jun-Seo's meeting with friends in Seoul' and 'Min-Seo's giving the drawing to Yun-Seo' respectively, and they also precede the following clause in terms of time. In other words, if Jun-Seo didn't go to Seoul and Min-Seo didn't draw a picture, Jun-Seo couldn't have met his friends and Min-Seo couldn't have given the picture to Yun-Seo.

준서는 서울에 {가서/*가고(서)} (서울에서) 친구를 만났다.
Jun-Seo went to Seoul and met his friends.
민서는 그림을 {그려서/*그리고(서)}, (그 그림을) 윤서에게 주었다.
Min-Seo drew a picture and gave it to Yun-Seo.

② '-고(서)', which connects the preceding and following clause in the order of time, emphasizes the fact that the front clause precedes the following clause. In this case, the preceding clause does not need to be the prerequisite for the following clause. The preceding clause definitely precedes the following clause in terms of time, and is the circumstantial background for the following clause, but the two clauses are only loosely linked to one another.

For example, the sentences below stress that 'eating breakfast' happened before 'going to the library' and 'watching movies' happened before 'going home': the two clauses are not inevitably linked together in semantic terms.

준서는 아침을 {*먹어서/먹고(서)} 도서관에 공부하러 갔다.
Jun-Seo had breakfast and then went to the library to study.
민서는 영화를 {*봐서/보고(서)} 집으로 돌아갔다.
Min-Seo watched the movie and then went home.

③ '-자' and '-자마자', which connect the preceding and following clause in the order of time, express that the following clause happens as soon as the preceding clause happens. In particular, '-자마자' means 'as soon as what happened in the first clause', while '-자' simply means 'after what happened in the first clause'.

민서는 어머니를 만나자마자 (곧장) 고향으로 돌아가자고 했다.
Min-Seo, as soon as she met her mother, suggested that they go back

to the hometown immediately.

형은 나를 만나자 (1년 후에는 꼭) 고향으로 돌아가자고 했다.

My elder brother, when he met me, suggested that they go back to the
hometown (no matter what, after one year).

● **Use of subject**: The use of subject depends on connective endings.
Subjects must be the same with '-아/어서', but they do not have to be
the same with '-고(서), -자마자'. However, clause connection for completion
usually represents something in the order of time, so the subject of the
preceding clause is usually the same as that of the following clause.

준서가 은행에서 돈을 찾아서 {준서가/*민서가} 등록금을 냈다.
Jun-Seo withdrew some money from bank and paid the tuition fee.
날이 밝아지자(마자) 모두들 잠에서 깨어났다.
As soon as the day broke, everyone woke up from sleep.
그녀는 숙제를 끝내고서 공원에 놀러 갔다.
She, after finishing her homework, went out to the park.

● **Use of prefinal endings**: None of the prefinal endings, ranging from
'-았/었-, -겠-, -았/었었었-', to '-더-', cannot be directly combined with
connective endings that form simultaneity. Thus, they should come only
in the following clause.

*준서는 서울에 갔어서, (서울에서) 친구를 만났다.
Jun-Seo went to Seoul and met his friends.
*준서는 아침을 먹었고(서) 도서관에 공부하러 갔다.
Jun-Seo had breakfast and then went to the library to study.
*민서는 어머니를 만났자(마자) 고향으로 돌아가자고 했다.
Min-Seo, as soon as she met her mother, suggested that they go back
to the hometown.

- **Use of predicates**: There are many restrictions on the use of predicates. Predicates can be used only in combination with verbs, because completion represents certain things or action in the order of time.

범인을 **잡아서** 경찰서로 넘겼다.
The criminal was arrested and handed over to the police station.
눈을 **감고(서)** 걸어 보세요.
Close your eyes and walk. (Walk with your eyes closed).
길을 **나서자(마자)** 눈이 내리기 시작했다.
As soon as I hit the road, it started snowing.

However, predicates can be combined with adjectives, 이다 or 있다 to express cause/reason or simultaneity instead of completion.

그는 키가 너무 **작아서** 농구 선수가 될 수 없었다. [Cause/Reason]
He was too short to become a basketball player.
그 사람은 한 아이의 {엄마**이고(서)**/엄마**이자**} 예술가이다.
The person is mother of a child and an artist. [Simultaneity]
그녀는 교양이 많이 **있어서** 친구들과 잘 사귀는 편이다. [Cause/Reason]
She is highly cultivated, so she makes friends easily.

- **Use of sentence endings**: '-아/어서, -고(서), -자마자' have no restrictions in terms of sentence endings, so it can come with all kinds of sentence endings, from declarative, interrogative, imperative, propositive to exclamatory endings. However, '-자' cannot be used in conjunction with imperative or propositive endings.

물고기를 잡**아서** 구워 {먹었**다**/먹었**니**?/먹**어라**/먹**자**/먹**는구나**!}
(I) caught some fish and roasted them.
Did you catch some fish and roast them?
Catch some fish and roast them.

Let us catch some fish and roast them.

You caught some fish and are eating them!

소설 '소나기'를 읽고(서) 독후감을 {썼다/썼니?/써라/쓰자/쓰는구나!}

(I) read the novel Sonagi and wrote a book report.

Did you read the novel Sonagi and wrote a book report?

Read the novel Sonagi and write a book report.

Let us read the novel Sonagi and write a book report.

You are reading the novel Sonagi and writing a book report!

서울에 도착하자마자 곧바로 친구를 {만났다/만났니?/만나라/만나자/만나는구나!}

As soon as I arrived in Seoul, I met my friends.

As soon as you arrived in Seoul, did you meet your friends?

As soon as you arrive in Seoul, meet your friends.

As soon as we arrive in Seoul, let us meet friends.

As soon as you arrive in Seoul, you are meeting your friends!

그녀는 남편이 죽자 (3년 후에) 재혼을 {했다/했니?/*해라/*하자/하는구나!}

She, after the death of her husband, remarried (three years after).

Did she, after the death of her husband, get remarried (three years after)?

진실이 드러나자 준서는 변명을 {했다/했니?/*해라/*하자/하는구나!}

As the truth was uncovered, Jun-Seo made excuses.

As the truth was uncovered, did Jun-Seo make excuses?

• **Use of negation**: There are no restrictions for '-고(서), -자' in the use of negation. However, with '-아/어서, -자마자', negative elements cannot be put to the preceding clause. Negative elements should be used only in the following clause.

아침도 안 먹고서 학교에 가면 어떡하니?

How could you go to school without having breakfast?

아무도 그 일을 하려고 하지 **않자** 선생님께서는 화를 많이 내셨다.

As nobody seemed to be willing to do the work, the teacher got very angry.

*해열제를 **안** 먹**자마자** 열이 내리기 시작했다.

The fever started to mitigate as soon as I didn't take a fever reducer.

*고향 친구를 **안** 만나**서** 돈을 좀 빌려 달라고 했다.

I did not meet my homie, and I asked my homie to lend me some money.

However, special attention needs to be paid when interpreting the meaning of the sentence. Even if negative expressions are used in the following clause, the preceding clause may also be negated. The sentences below mean 'I took cold medication, and my fever was eased after a very long period of time; I asked my friends to lend me some money, but I didn't do that to my friends from hometown'. Auxiliary particle '-은/는' which represents difference, emphasizes the negation.

감기약을 먹**자마자** 열이 내리**지는** **않**았다.

The fever did not subside right after taking the cold medicine.

고향 친구를 만**나서는** 돈을 좀 빌려 달라고 하**지 않**았다.

When I met my friends from hometown, I did not ask them to lend me some money. (even though I asked others to lend me some money)

The following clause can also be negated to mean 'there was no change immediately after taking the medication; I didn't ask my friends to lend me some money'.

22.2.2.3 Interruption or Conversion

Connective ending for **interruption**(중단) or **conversion**(전환) is '-다가'. It shows that an ongoing or finished action or status in the preceding clause changes into a new action or status in the following clause.

• **Meaning**: '-다가' connects the preceding and following clause to form a relationship of conversion, but has secondary meanings such as interruption, completion, progression, cause/reason, condition and repetition of an action.

> 그는 학교에 가**다가** 왔다. [Suspension]
> He stopped on his way to school and came back.
> 그는 학교에 갔**다가** 왔다. [Completion]
> He went to school and came back.
> 그는 학교에 가**다가** 친구를 만났다. [In progress]
> On his way to school, he met his friends.
> 과속을 하**다가** 결국 사고를 냈다. [Cause/Reason]
> (I), while speeding up, ended up causing an accident.
> 그렇게 하**다가(는)** 쪽박 차기 십상이다. [Condition]
> If you do that, you are bound to go bankrupt.
> 준서는 일을 하**다가** 말다가 했다. [Repetition of an action]
> Jun-Seo was always on and off the work.

• **Use of subjects**: Subjects can be the same or different in both the preceding and following clause.

> 준서는 고향에 가**다가** 돌아왔다.
> Jun-Seo, on his way to hometown, came back.
> 비가 오**다가** 지금은 눈이 오고 있다. / It was rainy, but now it's snowy.

• **Use of prefinal endings**: '-았/었-' can be attached to the clause, and the meaning of the sentence changes according to the presence of '-았/었-'. In other words, '-았/었다가' means that the subject goes on to do something new after he completes the action in the preceding clause, while '-다가' means the subject suspends doing something midway in the preceding clause and then goes on to do something new in the following clause, even if it is something of the past.

그는 서울에 가**다가** 고향으로 돌아왔다. [Suspension]
On his way to Seoul, he came back to his hometown.
그는 서울에 갔**다가** 고향으로 돌아왔다. [Completion]
He went to Seoul, but came back to hometown.

'-겠-, -았/었었-, -더-' cannot be attached to '-다가'. They must come in the following clause.

준서는 서울에 {*가**겠다가**/*갔었**다가**/*가**더다가**} 민서를 만났다.
Jun-Seo, on his way to Seoul, met Min-Seo.
준서는 서울에 가**다가** 민서를 {만나**겠**다/만났었다/만나**더**라}
Jun-Seo, on his way to Seoul, will meet Min-Seo.

However, '-겠-, -았/었었-' can be affixed to '… -다가 … -다가'.

준서는 유학을 가**겠**다고 하**다가** 안 가**겠**다고 하**다가** 변덕이 심하더라.
Jun-Seo kept changing his mind, saying he will go abroad to study and the next minute he won't. He is so fickle.

기상청에서는 날씨가 좋**겠**다고 하**다가** 안 좋**겠**다고 하니 무엇이 사실인지 알 수가 없다. / The Meteorological Administration says that the weather is going to be good and then the weather is going to be bad, so it's impossible to know which is the truth.

할머니께서는 점심을 먹**었었**다고 하**다가** 안 먹**었었**다고 했다.
Grandmother said that she had lunch, and then she said she didn't have lunch.

● **Use of predicates**: There are restrictions on the use of predicates. In the preceding clause, verbs, adjectives, 이다 and 있다 may all be used as predicates.

그는 텔레비전을 **고치다가** 손을 다쳤다.
While fixing the TV, his hands got hurt.
민서는 **뚱뚱하다가** 요즘은 많이 날씬해졌다.
Min-Seo was fat, but got much slimmer these days.
준서는 그동안 계장**이다가** 이제 과장이 되었다.
Jun-Seo was a subsection chief, but he is now a manager.
민서는 서울에 조금 **있다가** 런던으로 떠났다.
Min-Seo stayed in Seoul for a while and left for London.

However, in the following clause, only verbs can be employed as predicate.

민서가 명랑하**다가** 나중에는 {*울적하다/울적해졌다}
Min-Seo was cheerful, but became melancholy later on.
그는 음악가이**다가** 이제는 {*조각가이다/조각가가 **되었다**}
He was musician, but he is now a sculptor.

● **Use of sentence endings**: There are no restrictions, so all kinds of endings, from declarative, interrogative, imperative, propositive to exclamatory endings, can be used.

금강산 구경을 좀 하**다가** {갔다/갔니?/가거라/가자/가는구나!}
(I) went to see Mountain Geumgang.
Did you go to see Mountain Geumgang?
Go to see Mountain Geumgang.
Let us go to see Mountain Geumgang.
You are going to see Mountain Geumgang!

뉴욕에 10년쯤 살**다가** 서울로 {왔다/왔니?/오너라/오자/오는구나!}
After living in New York for roughly ten years, (I) came to Seoul.

After living in New York for roughly ten years, did you come to Seoul?

After living in New York for roughly ten years, come to Seoul.

After living in New York for roughly ten years, let us come to Seoul.

After living in New York for roughly ten years, you are coming to Seoul!

- **Use of negation**: '-다가' imposes no restrictions on negation.

그녀는 다이어트를 **안** 하**다가** 뚱보가 되었다.

She became fat as she had not been on a diet.

예전에는 그렇게 빨리 **못** 걷**다가** 요즘은 아주 잘 걷는다.

In the past, [I] was not able to walk that fast, but these days, [I] can walk very well.

아프면 약을 먹**다가** 말**다가** 하지 말고 계속 먹어야 한다.

If [you] are sick, you should take pills consistently rather than stopping in between.

22.2.2.4 Concession

'-아/어도, -건만' are connective endings for **concession**(양보). The sentences with these connective endings indicate that even though the speaker acknowledge the situation in the preceding clause, expected situation does not appear in the following clause. These endings are similar to 'although' in English.

- **Meaning**:

① '-아/어도, -더라도, -(으)ㄹ지라도' are typical connective endings that form concession. These negate what has been anticipated in the preceding clause, but they always imply what has been negated, thereby stressing the following clause. The meaning of concession is stronger in '-더라도' than '-아/어도' and '-(으)ㄹ지라도' than '-더라도'.

비록 비가 많이 {**와도**/오더라도/**올지라도**} 우리는 소풍을 간다.

Even though it may rain a lot, we will go on a picnic.

→ Expectation: If it rains a lot, we will not be able to go on a picnic.

→ Negation of the expectation: Despite that, we will go on a picnic.

→ Implication: If it does not rain, we will definitely go on a picnic.

준서가 거짓말을 {**해도**/하더라도/**할지라도**} 그는 준서를 믿었다.

Even if Jun-Seo may lie, he trusted Jun-Seo.

→ Expectation: If Jun-Seo lies, he would not be able to trust him.

→ Negation of the expectation: Even though Jun-Seo lied, he trusted Jun-Seo.

→ Implication: If Jun-Seo does not lie, I would definitely trust him.

Also, in a concessional sentence, the more extreme the preceding clause is, the more emphasis the following clause is given, as demonstrated by Korean old sayings.

하늘이 무너**져도** 솟아날 구멍이 있다.

Even if the sky falls down, there is a silver lining.

처녀가 아이를 낳**아도** 할 말이 있다.

Even single mothers have something to say. (= Every evil-doer has his reasons.)

호랑이에게 물려 가**도** 정신만 차리면 산다.

Even if you are caught by a tiger, you will survive if you keep yourself alert.

② '-(으)ㄹ지언정' approves what has been said in the preceding clause while carrying the meaning of 'nevertheless'. In other words, it assumes or acknowledges the extreme incident stated in the preceding clause, but shows that the following clause is not bound by what is said in the preceding clause, thereby highlighting the following clause. The following

.clause tends to use negative expressions such as '않다, 없다, 못하다' and prefinal ending '-겠-' which implies volition.

굶어 죽<u>을지언정</u> 너의 도움을 받지 않겠다.
Even if I die from starvation, I will not receive your help.
시험에 떨어<u>질지언정</u> 부정행위는 절대로 하지 않겠다.
Even if I fail the exam, I will never cheat.

③ '-(으)나마' means that the subject is not fully satisfied with something, but the subject shall nevertheless be happy with what is available. The preceding clause suggests a substandard case and the following clause shows that the subject is not fully happy with it but accepts it anyway.

비록 돈이 적<u>으나마</u> 받으세요.
Please keep the money, though it is not much.
잠자리가 변변치 못하<u>나마</u> 편히 쉴 수 있었다.
Even though the room was not decent, (I) was able to sleep comfortably.

④ '-았/었자' shows that even though the event in the preceding clause may be realized, it is negligible since it falls short of the speaker's expectations. It has a derogative nuance of the action or status of the preceding clause, and is mainly used in the form of '-아/어 보았자'.

그 사람이 돈이 있<u>어 보았자</u> 얼마나 있겠습니까?
How much money would he have even if he did have any?
네가 아무리 발버둥 <u>쳐 보았자</u> 도망갈 수 없다.
Even if you try, you cannot run away.

⑤ '-기로서니' means that the speaker may approve what is said in the preceding clause, but he/she strongly disapproves of the action in the following clause.

아무리 거짓말을 하<u>기로서니</u> 그렇게 왕따를 시켜서야 되겠는가?
He/she may be a liar, but do you think it is right to ostracize him/her like that?
→ Implication: Even if he/she may lie a lot, it is not right to ostracize him/her.

밥을 한 끼 굶었<u>기로서니</u> 도둑질을 해서야 되나.
You may have skipped a meal, but do you think it is right to steal things?
→ Implication: Even if you skipped a meal, you should not steal.

⑥ '-(으)ㄴ/는들' is the same as '-(으)ㄴ/는다고 할지라도'. It means the subject may approve the preceding clause, but does not believe that the resultant event in the following clause can be realized. Sentences with '-(으)ㄴ/는들' usually end with rhetorical interrogative expressions.

고추가 맵다 **한들** 시집살이보다야 맵**겠어요**?
Chilli peppers may be hot, but can they be more burning than living with in-laws?
→ Implication: Living with in-laws is much more burning than chilli peppers

아무리 이번 폭풍이 거**센들** 지난번 카트리나만 하**겠습니까**?
Even if the storm is so strong this time, can it be stronger than Katrina?
→ Implication: The magnitude of Katrina is much higher than that of the storm this time.

• **Use of subject**: Since there are no constraints for the use of subject, the preceding and following clause may have identical or different subjects.

<u>준서</u>가 민서를 {사랑**해도**/사랑하**더라도**/사랑**할지라도**} 민서와 결혼은 하지 못할 것이다.

Even though Jun-Seo loves Min-Seo, he will not be able to marry her.

아무리 **날씨**가 {추**워도**/춥**더라도**/추**울지라도**} 나는 민서를 만나러 가겠다.

No matter how cold it is, I will go see Min-Seo.

● **Use of prefinal endings**: '-아/어도' can be combined with '-았/었-, -았/었었-, -겠-' without particular restrictions, but it can never be combined with '-더-'. Moreover, combining '-아/어도' with '-겠-' can make an awkward sentence.

아무리 일이 {어려**웠어도**/어려**웠었어도**/어렵**겠어도**/[*]어렵**더도**} 그는 결코 포기하지 않았다.

No matter how hard the work was, he never gave up.

아무리 재능이 {**있었어도**/**있었었어도**/[?]**있겠어도**/[*]**있더도**} 노력하지 않았더라면 성공하지 못했을 것이다.

No matter how talented he was, he would not have been successful had he not made strenuous efforts.

However, '-더라도' and '-(으)ㄹ지라도' can be attached to '-았/었-, -았/었었-'. Yet, they cannot be combined with '-겠-, -더-'.

민서가 일을 잘 {**못했더라도**/**못했었더라도**/[*]**못하겠더라도**/[*]못하<u>더</u>**더라도**} 나는 용서하겠다.

Even if Min-Seo may not be good at it, I will forgive her.

너와 {**헤어졌을지라도**/**헤어졌었을지라도**/[*]**헤어지겠을지라도**/[*]헤어지<u>더</u>**지라도**} 결코 사랑은 변하지 않을 것이다.

Even if I may be away from you, my love will never change.

● **Use of predicates**: Since there are no restrictions on the use of predicates, verbs, adjectives, 이다 and 있다 can be the predicate of the preceding clause.

> 준서는 스트레스가 {쌓<u>여도</u>/쌓<u>이더라도</u>/쌓<u>일지라도</u>} 잘 참는다.
> Jun-Seo, even if stress builds up, can put up with it very well.
> 아무리 배가 {고<u>파도</u>/고<u>프더라도</u>/고<u>플지라도</u>} 구걸해서 먹어서는 안 된다.
> No matter how hungry you are, you should not beg for food.
> 아무리 그가 {바보<u>여도</u>/바보<u>이더라도</u>/바보<u>일지라도</u>} 그런 짓은 안 할 것이다. / No matter how foolish he is, he would not have done such a thing.
> 돈이 아무리 많이 {<u>있어도</u>/<u>있더라도</u>/<u>있을지라도</u>} 교양이 없으면 사람답게 살 수 없다. / No matter how much money one has, one cannot live decently if he is not cultured.

● **Use of sentence endings**: '-아/어도, -더라도, -(으)ㄹ지라도' impose no restrictions on sentence endings, so all types of endings such as declarative, interrogative, imperative, propositive and exclamatory endings can be used.

> 시험 결과가 좋지 않아도 실망하지 {않았<u>다</u>/않았<u>니</u>?/<u>마라</u>/<u>말자</u>/않<u>는구나</u>!}
> I was not disappointed with the result of the exam.
> Were you not disappointed with the result of the exam?
> Do not be disappointed with the result of the exam.
> Let us not be disappointed with the result of the exam.
> You are not disappointed with the result of the exam!

> 밥맛이 없더라도 많이 먹어 {두었<u>다</u>/두었<u>니</u>?/두<u>어라</u>/두<u>자</u>/두<u>는구나</u>!}
> Even if I didn't feel like eating, I ate a lot.
> Did you eat a lot even if you don't feel like eating?
> Eat a lot even if you don't feel like eating.
> Let us eat a lot even if we don't feel like eating.
> You are eating a lot even if you don't feel like eating!

하늘이 두 쪽이 날지라도 변명하지 {않겠**다**/않겠**니**?/마**라**/말**자**/않는**구나**!}

I shall never justify myself even if the sky tears down in half.

Will you never justify yourself even if the sky tears down in half?

Never justify yourself even if the sky tears down in half.

Let us not justify ourselves even if the sky tears down in half.

You are not justifying yourself even if the sky is tearing down in half!

However, '-(으)ㄴ들' should always come with rhetorical interrogative endings. '-기로서니' should come with interrogative and exclamatory endings only.

민서가 런던에 **간들** 너를 {*잊는**다**/잊겠**니**?/*잊어**라**/*잊**자**/*잊는**구나**!}

Even if Min-Seo goes to London, do you think she will forget you?

아무리 공부를 시켜 **본들** 사람 구실 {못한**다**/못하겠**니**?/*못해**라**/*못하**자**/못하는**구나**!}

No matter how much he is forced to study, he does not behave as a person should.

Even though he is forced to study, doesn't he behave as a person should?

No matter how much he is forced to study, he still does not behave as a person should!

아무리 도둑질을 했**기로서니** 사형까지 {*시켰**다**/시킬 필요가 있는**가**?/*시키지 마**라**/*시키지 말**자**/사형까지 시키**다니**!}

Even though he stole things, was it necessary to have him executed?

Even though he stole things, how could they have him executed!

'-았/었자' can be used in declarative, interrogative and exclamatory sentences.

비가 많이 와 **봤자** {얼마 오지 않을 거**야**/얼마나 오겠**어요**?/*얼마나 와**라**/*얼마나 오**자**/얼마 오지 못하는**구나**!}

Even though it rains a lot, it won't last long.

Even though it rains a lot, for how long would it rain?

Even though it is raining, it does not last long!

민서가 공부를 잘해 **봤자** {소용없**다**/소용없**지**?}

Even if Min-Seo gets high scores, it is useless.

Even if Min-Seo gets high scores, it is useless, isn't it?

- **Use of negation**: There are no restrictions on the use of negation.

그녀는 다이어트를 **안** {**해도**/하더**라도**/**할지라도**} 요즘 날씬하다.

Even though she is not on a diet, she is slim these days.

준서는 아무리 {아**파도**/아프더**라도**/아플**지라도**} 약을 먹**지 않**는다.

Jun-Seo, no matter how sick he may be, does not take medication.

아무리 돈을 많이 {벌**어도**/벌더**라도**/벌**지라도**} 교만해지**지 마**라.

No matter how much you earn, do not become arrogant.

- **Common use**: '··· 아/어도 ··· 아/어도' help emphasize the verb.

먹**어도** 먹**어도** 배가 부르지 않다.

No matter how much I eat, I don't feel full.

예**뻐도** 예**뻐도** 그렇게 예쁠 수가 없다.

(She) is very pretty.

22.2.2.5 Condition

Connective endings for **condition**(조건 · 가정), which include '(ㄴ/는)다면/다면, (으)면, 거든, 거들랑, 아/어야, 았/었던들', connect the preceding and following clause so as to make the preceding clause the condition or assumption to constitute the following clause, and to make the following clause the outcome of the preceding clause. These connective endings act almost the same as 'if'.

● **Meaning**:

① '-(으)면, -거든, -아/어야' usually act as conditional connective endings. '-(으)면' in particular, is most common since it represents conventional conditions with the least grammatical restrictions.

서울에 가게 되**면**, 경복궁을 꼭 구경해 보세요.
If you go to Seoul, do visit Gyeongbokgung Palace.
내일 날씨가 좋<u>으면</u> 함께 소풍 갑시다.
If the weather is fine tomorrow, let's go on a picnic.
3에다 5를 더하**면** 8이 된다. / If you add 5 to 3, it becomes 8.

'-거든' represents a factual condition which stresses what is said in the preceding clause is true. It can come with executional sentence endings such as interrogative, imperative and propositive endings. Thus, it is fair to say that '-거든' signifies a conditional relationship which implies execution of a fact.

봄이 {오**면**/*오**거든**} 진달래꽃이 핀다.
When the spring comes, azaleas blossom.

봄이 오거든 꼭 놀러 {*<u>온다</u>/오겠니?/<u>오너라</u>/오자/*<u>오는구나!</u>}
When the spring comes, will you come visit me?
When the spring comes, do come visit me.
When the spring comes, let us visit (the place).

'-아/어야' represents not only inevitable conditions but also non-execution, thus, it can come with only declarative, interrogative and exclamatory sentence endings. For example, in sentences below with '-아/어야', 'the only and inevitable way to resolve the issue is to meet Jun-Seo', and 'the only way to catch a tiger is to go to the mountain'. However, in sentences with '-(으)면', 'there are several ways to resolve the issue, and one of them is to meet Jun-Seo', and 'there are several ways to catch a tiger, and one of them is to go to the mountain'.

준서를 {만나**면**/만나**야**} 그 일을 해결할 수 있다.
If we meet Jun-Seo, the issue can be resolved.
The issue can be resolved only if we meet Jun-Seo.

산에 {가**면**/가**야**} 범을 {잡**는다**/잡**니**?/*잡**아라**/*잡**자**/잡**는구나**!}
If we go to the mountain, we can catch a tiger./We can catch a tiger only if we go to the mountain.
Can we catch a tiger if we do not go to the mountain?/Can we catch a tiger only if we do not go to the mountain?
If we go to the mountain, we can catch a tiger!/We can catch a tiger only if we go to the mountain!

'-(으)면' and '-거든' can be connective endings for assumptional sentences, yet, their assumption is much weaker than '-(ㄴ/는)다면'.

해가 서쪽에서 {뜨**면**/뜬**다면**} 네 말을 믿어 주겠다.
If the Sun rises from the West, I will trust your words.
혹시 네가 아들을 낳게 {되**거든**/된**다면**} 내게 연락해 다오.
If you give birth to a son, please contact me.

② '-(ㄴ/는)다면' usually acts as a clause ending for a suppositional sentence, which represents an assumption of something uncertain, not true or impossible. In such a sentence, '-ㄴ/는다면' is attached to verbs, '-다면' to adjectives and '-라면' to 이다.

네가 진정으로 민서를 사랑**한다면** 제발 민서 곁을 떠나 다오.
If you truly love Min-Seo, please leave Min-Seo.

민서가 준서만큼만 키가 **크다면** 농구를 잘할 수 있었을 텐데.
Min-Seo, if she were as tall as Jun-Seo, would have been able to play
basketball well.
내일이 공휴일이**라면** 얼마나 좋을까?
How I wish it is holiday?
(= I would be so happy if tomorrow were a holiday.)

However, if the preceding clause is true, '-(ㄴ/는)다면' can be the clause
ending for a conditional relationship.

그 사람이 범인임이 {확실하**면**/확실하**다면**} 곧 체포하세요.
If it is certain that the man is the criminal, arrest him immediately.
민서가 {아프**면**/아프**다면**} 굳이 여기에 데려올 필요가 없다.
If Min-Seo is ill, you do not have to bring her here.

③ '-던들' can be a clause ending for concessional assumptions, and
is always combined with prefinal ending '-았/었-'. '-던들' is an assumption
of something that lies contradictory to what happened in the past, so
it can be used interchangeably with '-았/었다면'. The sentences below
mean that 'the accident took place because you dozed off' and 'the farmers
had a row because it didn't rain at all'.

네가 졸지만 {않**았던들**/않**았다면**} 자동차 사고는 나지 않았을 것이다.
If you had not doze off, the car accident would not have taken place.
비가 조금이라도 {**왔던들**/**왔다면**} 농부들이 그렇게 싸우지 않았을 텐데.
Had it rained even just a little, the farmers would not have had a row
like that.

• **Use of subjective**: There are no particular restrictions on the use
of subjects, so identical or different subjects can be used for the preceding
and following clause. Also, '-거든' has implications of 'execution', so

the subject of the following clause in sentences with '-거든' can be first person or second person, but not third person.

(네가) 뉴욕에 {도착하**면**/도착하**거든**} 꼭 연락해라.
If you arrive in New York, please do contact me.
가을이 {오**면**/오**거든**} **우리** 함께 세계 여행을 떠납시다.
When the autumn comes, let us travel the world together.
준서가 대학 시험에 합격하**거든**, **네**가 나에게 꼭 연락해 다오.
If Jun-Seo passes the college entrance exam, please do contact me.
날이 새**거든** {**나는**/*그는} 고향을 떠나겠다.
When the day breaks, I shall leave my hometown.

준서는 야구 경기에 나가**야** **힘**이 솟는다.
Jun-Seo feels reinvigorated when he plays the baseball game.
한국에서는 **12월**이 되**어야** **눈**이 내린다.
In Korea, it snows from December.

네가 민서를 만나지 않았**다면** 그런 오해를 사지 않았을 텐데.
If you did not meet Min-Seo, you wouldn't have invited such misunderstanding.
그 사람이 이미 잘못을 빌었**다면** (**우리**는) 더 이상 그를 비난하지 말자.
If the person apologized for his fault, do not criticize him any more.

그가 조금만 참았**던들** 이혼은 당하지 않았을 것이다.
Had he put up with it just a little longer, he would not have been divorced.
엄마가 아이를 조금만 더 잘 돌보았**던들** **아이**가 다치지는 않았을 텐데.
Had the mother taken care of the child just a little bit better, the child would not have been hurt.

• **Use of prefinal endings**: '-(으)면, -거든, -아/어야, -(ㄴ/는)다면' can be combined with '-았/었-, -았/었었-, -겠-' without any restriction, but never with '-더-'. However, the connective endings can be combined with

'-았/었더-' to form '-았/었더면, -았/었더라면'. However, there is no such combination as '-았/었더야'.

고향으로 {돌아**왔으면**/돌아**왔었으면**} 당연히 나를 찾아와야지.
If you had come back to the hometown, you should have sought me.
고향으로 돌아오**겠으면** 가능한 한 빨리 돌아오세요.
If you have made up your mind to come back to the hometown, come as soon as possible.
고향으로 빨리 {*돌아오**더면**/돌아**왔더면**} 얼마나 좋았을까.
It would have been so good if you had come back to the home town early.

'-던들' can be affixed to '-았/었-, -았/었었-' but not with '-겠-, -더-, -았/었더-'.

그가 고향으로 좀 더 빨리 {돌아**왔던들**/돌아**왔었던들**/*돌아오**겠던들**/*돌아오**더던들**/*돌아**왔더던들**}, 생전에 어머니를 만날 수 있었을 텐데.
Had he returned back to the hometown just a little earlier, he would have been able to meet his mother before her death.
그 시험 문제를 잘 {풀**었던들**/풀**었었던들**/*풀**겠던들**/*풀**더던들**/*풀**었더던들**} 대학 입시에서 떨어지지는 않았을 것이다. / Had he done well on his test, he would not have failed entering university.

● **Use of predicates**: '-(으)면, -아/어야' impose no restriction for the use of predicates, so they can come with verbs, adjectives, 이다 and 있다.

숙제를 다 {**끝마치면**/**끝마치거든**} 내게 연락해 다오.
When/If you finish the homework, contact me.
날씨가 {**좋으면**/**좋아야**} 항해를 시작할 수 있다.
When/If the weather is fine, we can start sailing.
그 사람이 {변호사**이면**/변호사**이어야**} 우리를 변호해 줄 수 있겠지.
If he is a lawyer, he will be able to represent us.

(He has to be a lawyer to be able to represent us.)

시간이 {있으면/있거든} 놀러 오세요. / If you have time, come visit me.

'-거든' can be combined with verbs or 이다 in the preceding clause, but it can become very awkward if combined with adjectives. The following clause of '-거든' cannot use adjectives, because the following clause must have executional expressions.

> 네가 민서를 **사랑하거든** 사랑한다고 고백해라.
> If you love Min-Seo, tell her that you love her.
> 그것이 사실<u>이거든</u>, 솔직하게 잘못을 인정해라.
> If it is true, admit your faults frankly.
> 몸이 좀 더 {[?]**날씬하거든**/**날씬해지거든**} 치마를 입고 다녀라.
> If you become slimmer, wear skirts.

'-았/었던들' has no restrictions on the use of predicates, so it can be combined with verbs, adjectives, 이다 and 있다.

> 조금만 더 일찍 회의장에 **갔던들** 네가 그런 오해를 받지는 않았을 텐데.
> Had I gone to the conference hall just a little earlier, you would not have been misunderstood.
> 네가 좀 더 **겸손했던들** 네 운명이 달라졌을 것이다. / Had you been just a little more humble, your destiny would have changed.
> 그가 억만장자**였던들** 그 사태를 막을 수 있었겠니? / Even if he had been a millionaire, would he have been able to prevent the situation?
> 준서가 그곳에 **있었던들** 그런 사고를 방지할 수 있었을 텐데.
> Even if Jun-Seo had been there, the accident could have been prevented.

● **Use of sentence endings**: '-(으)면' imposes no restrictions on the use of sentence endings, so it can come with all types of sentence endings, from declarative, interrogative, imperative, propositive to exclamatory endings.

눈이 너무 많이 오면 학교에 가지 {않는다/않니?/마라/말자/않는구나!}
If it snows too heavily, we do not go to school.
If it snows too heavily, do you not go to school?
If it snows too heavily, do not go to school.
If it snows too heavily, let us not go to school.
If it snows too heavily, you are going to the school!

좋은 생각이 떠오르면 항상 메모를 해 {두었다/두었니?/두어라/두자/두는
구나!}
If I came across a good idea, I always made a memo.
If you came across a good idea, did you always make a memo?
If you come across a good idea, make a memo always.
If we come across a good idea, let us make a memo always.
If you come across a good idea, you are making a memo always!

'-거든' can come with interrogative, imperative and propositive endings
but not with declarative sentence endings, since its following clause should
be executional. On the other hand, '-아/어야' can come with declarative
and interrogative endings but not with imperative or propositive endings,
since it is non-executional.

서울에 가거든 항상 민서를 {*만난다/만나니?/만나라/만나자/*만나는구나!}
When you go to Seoul, do you always meet Min-Seo?
When you go to Seoul, always meet Min-Seo.
When we go to Seoul, let us always meet Min-Seo.

서울에 가야 항상 민서를 {만난다/만나니?/*만나라/*만나자/만나는구나!}
When I go to Seoul, I always meet Min-Seo.
When you go to Seoul, do you always meet Min-Seo?
When you go to Seoul, you are always meeting Min-Seo!

'-던들' can come with declarative and interrogative endings only that imply presumptions.

5분만 늦었던들 그녀를 만나지 {못했겠다/못했겠니?/*못해라/*못하자/*못하는구나!}

If I had been late by five minutes, I would not have been able to meet her.

If you had been late by five minutes, would you not have been able to meet her?

사랑만 안 했던들 울지는 {않았겠다/않았겠니?/*마라/*말자/*않는구나!}

Hadn't I loved him, I would not have cried.

Hadn't you loved him, would you not have cried?

비행기가 고장만 나지 않았던들 벌써 서울에 도착을 {했겠다/했겠지?/*해라/*하자/*하는구나!}

If the airplane had not gone out of order, I would have arrived in Seoul already.

If the airplane had not gone out of order, you would have arrived in Seoul already, wouldn't you?

- **Use of negation**: There are no restrictions on the use of negation.

그녀는 다이어트를 **안** 하**면** 곧 몸무게가 늘어난다.

When she is not on a diet, she gains weight immediately.

몸이 **안** 아프**거든** 일찍 학교에 가거라.

If you are not sick, go to school early.

돈이 아무리 많아도 교만해지**지 않아야** 존경을 받는다.

Even if you are wealthy, you should not become arrogant to be respected by others.

조금만 더 비가 **오지 않았던들** 그렇게 큰 홍수는 나지 않았을 거야.

If it rained just a little less, such a big flood would have taken place.

- **Common use**: Conditional connective endings tend to be combined with connective ending that form intentions, '-(으)려', as in the case of '-(으)려면(◁-(으)려 (하)면), -(으)려거든(◁-(으)려 (하)거든), -(으)려야(◁-(으)려 (해)야)'. They represent intended conditions.

한국으로 유학을 가려면 어떤 것을 준비해야 합니까?
If I am to go to Korea to study, what should I prepare?
네가 한국으로 유학을 가려거든 우선 한국어 공부부터 해 두어라.
If you are to go to Korea to study, study Korean first.
나의 고향은 이미 가려야 갈 수 없는 곳이 되어 버렸다.
My hometown has already become an unaccessible place even if I wanted to.

22.2.2.6 Cause and Reason

Connective endings which maker **cause**(원인) and **reason**(이유) are '-(으)니/는지라, -(으)니까, -(으)ㄹ세라, -(으)므로, -(으/느)니만큼, -기에, -길래, -느라(고), -아/어서'. The preceding clause of these connective endings serves as the cause or reason for the following clause, while the following clause is the result or outcome of the preceding clause. These connective endings act almost the same as 'because'.

- **Meaning**:
① '-아/어서' connect the preceding and following clause so that the preceding clause can be the cause and the following clause the result. In other words, what comes before '-아/어서' is the cause and what comes after is the result. Therefore, the preceding clause of '-아/어서' puts forth an objective event that already happened or is currently happening, and the following clause shows a natural and obvious result of the event.

For example, in the sentences below, 'Min-Seo's pain in her legs; too much rain; a passenger ship's drowning' are the natural and obvious cause behind 'not being able to stand up; not being able to go to school; death of every passenger'. In other words, '-아/어서' is used if the event described in the preceding clause results in the following clause so naturally that the reader does not need to make assumptions to fully understand the sentence.

민서는 다리가 너무 {아**파서**/$^?$아프**니까**} 일어서지도 못한다.
Min-Seo has a serious pain in her legs that she cannot even stand up.
비가 너무 많이 {**와서**/*오**니까**} 학교에 갈 수 없었다.
It rained so much that I was not able to go to school.
여객선이 바다에 {가라앉<u>**아서**</u>/$^?$가라앉<u>**으니까**</u>} 승객 전원이 사망했다.
The passenger ship drowned in the sea, so every passenger died.

'-아/어서' not only describe the objective and phenomenal cause behind certain events, but also have characteristics of non-execution, thus, they usually come with declarative or interrogative endings.

눈이 많이 <u>**와서**</u> 결석을 {했**다**/했**니**?/***해라**/*하**자**/*하**마**/하**는구나**!}
It snowed a lot, so I was absent.
It snowed a lot, so were you absent?
It snowed a lot, so you are absent!

회사에 일이 많<u>**아서**</u> 집에 늦게 {들어갔**다**/들어갔**니**?/*들어가**거라**/*들어가**자**/*들어가**마**/들어가**는구나**!}
There was so much work at the office, so I went home late.
There was so much work at the office, so did you go home late?
There was so much work at the office, so you are going home late!

② '-(으)니까' connects the preceding and following clause so as to form a relationship of reason and end/conclusion. In other words, the preceding clause becomes the reason and the following clause the end or conclusion of the reason. What comes before '-(으)니까' puts forth certain events which involve the speaker's subjective and emotional judgment as the reason behind the following clause, and what comes after '-(으)니까' shows the end or conclusion that is derived from such judgment.

For example, 'Jun-Seo's becoming a high school student; the advent of spring; being able to meet Min-Seo if one stays here' do not naturally result in 'Jun-Seo's looking like a grown-up; Jun-Seo's feeling very lonely; and waiting just a little bit more'. Rather, the preceding clause is just a particular reason made by the speaker's subjective judgment.

In other words, '-(으)니까' is used if the reader has to make assumptions to fully understand the sentence and the relationship between the preceding and following clause. The reason behind 'looking like a grown-up; Jun-Seo's feeling lonely; waiting just a little bit more' may not necessarily be what is stated in the preceding clause, but at least the speaker personally believes that the reason for the following clause is the preceding clause, in which case '-(으)니까' comes into use.

준서가 고등학생이 {?*되어서/되니까} 좀 더 의젓해 보인다.
As Jun-Seo became a high school student, he looks more like a grown-up.
봄이 {?*되어서/되니까} 준서가 많이 외로워한다.
As spring came, Jun-Seo feels quite lonely.
여기 있으면 민서를 만날 수 {?*있어서/있으니까} 조금만 기다리자.
If we wait here, we can meet Min-Seo, so let's wait just a little longer.

'-(으)니까' not only demonstrates the reason based on the speaker' subjective judgment on certain events but also has characteristics of execution, thus, it usually ends the sentence in declarative or propositive forms.

눈이 많이 오니까 결석을 {ᵖ했다/ᵖ했니?/**해라/하자/하는구나!**}
As it snows a lot, do not go to school.
As it snows a lot, let us not go to school.
As it snows a lot, you are not going to school!

회사에 일이 많<u>으니까</u> 집에 늦게 들어{ᵖ갔다/ᵖ갔니?/**가거라/가자/가마/가**
는구나!}
As there is so much work at the office, go home late.
As there is so much work at the office, let us go home late.
As there is so much work at the office, I shall go home late.
As there is so much work at the office, you are going home late!

While '-아/어서' represent general and objective description of a cause, '-(으)니까' represents emotional and subjective questioning of the reason. For example, the sentences below are the answer to 'why did you leave the hospital?' The sentence with '-아/어서' means 'I naturally left the hospital because I got well', whereas the sentence with '-(으)니까' means 'I left the hospital because I got well, but since you know all about it, why are you asking?'

병이 다 나<u>아서</u> 퇴원했습니다. / I got well, so I left the hospital.
병이 다 나았<u>으니까</u> {ᵖ퇴원했습니다/퇴원했지요}
I got well, so [obviously enough,] I left the hospital.

③ '-(으)므로' shows that the preceding clause serves as the reason, cause or ground for the following clause. It also helps make a logical description of such grounds, so it carries a logical causal relationship. Therefore, '-(으)므로' is mainly used in such sentences as syllogism. '-(으)므로' is hardly employed in spoken language.

사람은 모두 죽는다. / All human beings die.

소크라테스는 사람이다. / Socrates is a human being.

따라서 소크라테스는 사람이<u>므로</u> 죽는다.

Henceforth, since Socrates is a human being, he will die.

④ '-느라(고)' not only shows that the action described in the preceding clause is the cause for the following clause, but also that the action in the preceding clause happens at the same time as that of the following clause; thus, it implies a simultaneous causal relationship. For example, in the sentences below, 'not being able to sleep a wink' is because of 'studying for exams', and 'not being able to sleep a wink' happens at the same time as 'studying for exams'.

시험공부를 하<u>느라고</u> 한잠도 못 잤다.

I was studying for exams, so I was not able to sleep a wink.

민서는 외국인들에게 한국어를 가르치<u>느라고</u> 고생이 많았다.

Min-Seo made strenuous efforts to teach Korean to foreigners.

준서는 울음을 참<u>느라고</u> 눈을 꼭 감고 있었다.

Jun-Seo, to suppress his tears, had his eyes closed.

'-느라(고)' also has intentional causal relationship, in which case it can be converted into '-기 위하여'.

유관순은 나라를 {구하<u>느라고</u>/구하<u>기 위하여</u>} 온갖 고생을 다했다.

Gwan-Sun Yu, to save the country, suffered a lot.

그는 딸을 {시집보내<u>느라고</u>/시집보내<u>기 위해</u>} 아파트마저 팔았다.

He, to have his daughter married, even sold his apartment unit.

● **Use of subject**: '-아/어서, -(으)니까, -(으)므로' impose no restrictions on the use of subjects, so identical or different subjects can be used in the preceding and following clause.

날씨가 추워**져서** 얼음이 꽁꽁 얼었다.

The weather got very cold, so water froze into ice.

눈이 많이 왔**으니까** 우리 스키 타러 가자.

As it snowed a lot, let's go skiing.

나는 공부해야 할 것이 많**으므로** 도서관으로 가야겠다.

Because I have a lot to study, I have to go to the library.

However, with '-느라(고)', the subject in both the preceding and following clause must be an identical person or animal.

나는 오늘 자전거를 고치**느라고** {**나는**/***그는**} 많이 바빴다.

I fixed the bike today so I was very busy.

다람쥐가 쳇바퀴를 돌리**느라** {**다람쥐**가/***토끼**가} 정신이 없는 것 같다.

The squirrel was running on the wheels so it seemed preoccupied.

There are some exceptions as below. Still, it is difficult to see the subjects in the preceding and following clause as totally separate entities, since 'fan → noise made by the fan, monsoon → cloud caused by the monsoon, Jun-Seo's height → Jun-Seo's body' are semantically related to each other.

고장 난 **선풍기**가 돌아가**느라고** 삐걱거리는 **소리**가 많이 난다.

The broken fan was turned on, so it made a lot of noise.

장마가 오**느라고** **먹구름**이 끼었다.

The monsoon is coming, so it is cloudy.

준서가 **키**가 크**느라고** **몸**이 많이 말랐다.

Since Jun-Seo is getting taller, he has become very thin.

* **Use of prefinal endings**: '-아/어서' and '-느라(고)' cannot be combined with '-았/었-, -겠-', but '-(으)니까, -(으)므로' can be combined with '-았/었-, -겠-'.

그들이 파티에 너무 일찍 {*왔어서/**와서**} 당황스러웠다.
They came to the party too early, so it embarrassed me.
그림을 {*그렸느라고/**그리느라고**} 그의 말을 잘 알아듣지 못했다.
I was painting a picture, so I did not understand him very well.
시험 준비를 많이 {**했으니까**/하니까} 걱정하지 마세요.
Because you studied a lot for the exam, do not be worried.
민서가 충고를 자주 {**했으므로**/하므로} 상황이 좋아질 것이다.
Because Min-Seo gave advice quite often, things will get better.

However, no connective endings that form cause and reason can be combined with '-더-, -았/었더-, or -겠더-'.

*바람이 너무 세게 {불더서/불었더서/불겠더서} 비닐하우스가 모두 날아가 버렸다.
*바람이 너무 세게 {불더니까/불었더니까/불겠더니까} 오늘은 집에서 쉬자.
*바람이 너무 세게 {불더므로/불었더므로/불겠더므로} 오늘은 집에서 쉬자.
*태풍이 {오더느라(고)/왔더느라(고)/오겠더느라(고)} 서쪽 하늘이 캄캄해 온다.

● **Use of predicates**: There are no restrictions on the use of predicates, so verbs, adjectives, 이다 and 있다 can be used as predicates.

준서는 키가 **작아서** 농구를 잘 못한다.
Jun-Seo is short, so he does not play basketball well.
그는 능력 있는 프로그래머**이니까** 앞으로 크게 성공할 수 있을 것이다.
He is a capable programmer, so he will be able to reap much success in the future.
연봉이 3억에다 보너스 1억까지 총 4억이 **되므로** 노후 준비는 걱정이 없다.
(His) annual salary is 300 million won, plus a bonus of 100 million won, so (he) has no worries about his life after retirement.
그는 돈이 많이 **있으니까** 노후에 대한 걱정이 없을 것 같다.
He has a lot of money, so I don't think he is worried about his life

after retirement.

Nonetheless, '-느라(고)' can be affixed to verbs only, since it constitutes a simultaneous causal relationship. 크다 'to get bigger' is a verb.

일을 빨리 **하느라고** 많이 바빴었다.
Because I was trying to rush things, I was very busy.
오늘은 날씨가 {**좋아서**/*좋느라고} 놀러 가기 알맞다.
The weather was fine today, so it is a good day for a picnic.
그는 {변호사<u>이니까</u>/*변호사<u>이느라고</u>} 우리를 변호해 줄 수 있겠지.
Because he is a lawyer, he will be able to represent us.
준서의 키가 {크느라고/커지느라고} 몸이 많이 말랐다.
Since Jun-Seo was getting taller, he became vary thin.

● **Use of sentence endings**: '-(으)니까' and '-(으)므로' impose no restrictions on the use of sentence endings, so all kinds of endings from declarative, interrogative, imperative, propositive to exclamatory endings can be used.

날씨가 {더<u>우니까</u>/더<u>우므로</u>} 학교에 가지 {않았<u>다</u>/않았<u>니</u>?/마<u>라</u>/말<u>자</u>/않
<u>으마</u>/않<u>는구나</u>!}
Since the weather is hot, I did not go to school.
Since the weather is hot, did you not go to school?
Since the weather is hot, do not go to school.
Since the weather is hot, let us not go to school.
Since the weather is hot, I shall not go to school.
Since the weather is hot, you are not going to school!

눈이 많이 {오<u>니까</u>/오<u>므로</u>} 밖에 나가지 {말**까요**?/말<u>자</u>/않<u>으마</u>}
Since it is snowing heavily, shall we not go outside?
Since it is snowing heavily, let us not go outside.
Since it is snowing heavily, I shall not go outside.

Sentences with '-아/어서' and '-느라(고)' may end in declarative and interrogative forms but not in imperative, propositive, pledging or interrogative forms that demand permission of the hearer, due to their non-executional aspects.

그는 죄를 지<u>어서</u> 벌을 {받았<u>다</u>/받았<u>니</u>?/*받<u>아라</u>/*받<u>자</u>/*받<u>으마</u>/받<u>는구나</u>!}
He committed a crime, so he was punished.
He committed a crime, so was he punished?
He committed a crime, so he is getting punished!

한국어 공부를 하<u>느라고</u> 고생을 {했<u>다</u>/했<u>니</u>?/*<u>해라</u>/*하<u>자</u>/*하<u>마</u>/하<u>는구나</u>!}
I am learning Korean, so I am studying so hard.
You are learning Korean, so did you study so hard?
You are learning Korean, so you are studying so hard!

- **Use of negation**: There are no restrictions.

비가 조금밖에 오<u>지</u> {<u>않아서</u>/<u>않으니까</u>/<u>않으므로</u>} 농사짓기가 쉽<u>지 않</u>다.
It rained only a little, so it is not easy to farm.
오늘은 몸이 <u>안</u> {아프<u>니까</u>/아프<u>므로</u>} 도서관에서 계속 공부를 하자.
Since I am not sick today, let us continue to study in the library.
돈이 그다지 많<u>지</u> {<u>않아서</u>/<u>않으니까</u>/<u>않으므로</u>} 다른 사람을 도와주기 어렵다.
Since I don't have a lot of money, it is difficult for me to help others.
그녀는 다이어트를 <u>안</u> {<u>해서</u>/하<u>니까</u>/하<u>므로</u>} 몸무게가 부쩍 늘어났다.
She had not been on a diet, so she gained a lot of weight.

It is possible for the preceding clause of '-느라(고)' to describe something negative, but it only results in a very awkward sentence. This is because having something negative in the preceding clause of '-느라(고)', which implies simultaneity of actions, negates the simultaneity of actions.

[?]숙제를 <u>안</u> <u>하느라고</u> 요리조리 엄마를 피해 다녔다.

In order not to do the homework, I tried to avoid my mom.

[?]그 당시에는 거짓말을 <u>안</u> <u>하느라고</u> 얼마나 고생했는지 모른다.

At that time, I struggled so much not to lie.

22.2.2.7 Intention

Connective endings that form **intention**(의도), which include '-(으)러, -(으)려(고), -고자', express purpose or intention of the subject in the preceding clause, and detailed measures to fulfil such purpose or intention in the following clause. They act almost the same as 'in order to'.

- **Meaning**:

① '-(으)러' represents intentions, especially **purpose**(목적), makes the preceding clause the aim or purpose and the following clause the method and manner. In other words, the preceding clause is the purpose the subject seeks to fulfil, whereas the following clause is the method to fulfil the purpose.

For example, in the sentences below, 'studying business administration; having dinner' are the purpose of the subject, and the method to fulfil the purpose is to 'go to the US; go to a Korean restaurant'.

> 준서는 경영학을 공부하<u>러</u> 미국으로 유학을 갔다.
> Jun-Seo, in order to study business administration, went to the US to study.
> 그는 저녁을 먹<u>으러</u> 한국 식당으로 갔다.
> He, in order to have dinner, went to a Korean restaurant.

② '-(으)려(고)' is the most general connective ending that forms intention, which makes the preceding clause the intention and the following clause the method and manner to achieve the intention. In other words, the preceding clause serves as the intention of the subject, and the following clause the detailed method to achieve the intention.

For example, in the sentences below, 'playing football; learning Korean' is the intention that the subject wishes to fulfil, and 'going to the playground; going to great lengths' is the method of fulfilling that intention.

준서는 축구를 하**려고** 운동장으로 나갔다.
Jun-Seo, in order to play football, went to the playground.
→ Jun-Seo's going to the playground was to play the football.

그는 한국어를 배우**려고** 온갖 노력을 했다.
He, in order to learn Korean, went to great lengths.
→ His going to great lengths was to learn Korean.

'-(으)려고' sometimes implies the speaker's prediction. It makes the preceding clause the forecast/conjecture and the following clause the present condition.

비가 오**려고** 먹구름이 몰려온다. / To rain, the dark clouds are gathering.
→ As dark clouds are gathering, it looks like it will rain.

다리가 무너지**려고** 기우뚱거린다. / For the bridge to collapse, it is swaying.
→ As the bridge is swaying, it looks like it will collapse.

③ '-고자' especially represents wishes out of intentions by making the preceding clause the **wish/hope/desire**(희망) and the following clause the method/manner. In other words, the preceding clause becomes the wish of the subject and the following clause the detailed method to fulfil the wish. '-고자' is mainly used in the form of '-고자 하다', and tends to mean '-기(를) 원하다/바라다' 'to wish for something to'.

나는 약속을 꼭 지키<u>고자</u> 한다. / I seek to keep promises.

→ 나는 약속을 꼭 지키<u>기</u>를 {<u>**원한**</u>다/<u>**바란**</u>다}

　I want to keep promises. / I hope I will keep promises.

나는 어머님을 만나<u>고자</u> 고향을 찾아왔습니다.

To meet mother, I visited the hometown.

→ 나는 어머님을 만나<u>기</u>를 {<u>**원해**</u>서/<u>**바라**</u>서} 고향을 찾아왔습니다.

Because I wished to meet my mother, I visited the hometown.

● **Use of subject**: Connective endings that form intentions require the preceding and following clause to have the identical animate subject, because inanimate entities cannot have intentions or purposes.

<u>준서</u>가 사과를 사<u>러</u> {<u>**준서**</u>가/[*]<u>**민서**</u>가} 과일 가게에 갔다.

Jun-Seo, to buy apples, went to the grocery store.

<u>민서</u>가 친구를 {만나<u>려고</u>/만나<u>고자</u>} {<u>**민서**</u>가/[*]<u>**준서**</u>가} 서울에 갔다.

Min-Seo, to meet friends, went to Seoul.

<u>호랑이</u>가 토끼를 {잡아먹<u>으려고</u>/잡아먹<u>고자</u>} {<u>**호랑이**</u>가/[*]<u>**사자**</u>가} 으르렁 거리고 있다. / The tiger, to catch and eat up the rabbit, is growling.

[*]<u>텔레비전</u>이 뉴스를 보도하<u>러</u> 방송실로 들어갔다.

[*]Television, to air the news, went into the broadcasting room.

[*]<u>자전거</u>가 학교에 {가<u>려고</u>/가<u>고자</u>} 자전거가 길을 나섰다.

[*]The bicycle, to go to school, hit the road.

Nonetheless, connective endings that form intentions can have inanimate subjects if the subjects are metaphorical.

<u>앰뷸런스</u>가 환자를 {실<u>으러</u>/실<u>으려고</u>/싣<u>고자</u>} 우리 집에 왔다.

The ambulance, to carry the patient, came to our house.

<u>해님</u>이 새 친구를 {사귀<u>러</u>/사귀<u>려고</u>/사귀<u>고자</u>} 달님을 찾아왔다.

The Sun, to make new friends, came to see the Moon.

Also, inanimate entities can become the subject if the connective ending '-(으)려고' implies the speaker's prediction.

버스가 넘어지려고 기우뚱거린다. / The bus, to fall down, is swaying.
→ As the bus is swaying, it looks like it will fall down.

비가 오려고 달무리가 끼었다. / To rain, there is a ring around the moon.
→ As there is a ring around the moon, it looks like it will rain.

● **Use of prefinal endings**: No prefinal endings, from '-았/었-, -겠-, -았/었었-', to '-더-' can be directly combined with intentional connective endings; instead, prefinal endings must come in the following clause.

*그는 한국 역사책을 {샀으러/사겠으러/샀었으러/사더러} 종로서점에 갔다.
→ 그는 한국 역사책을 사러 종로서점에 {갔다/가겠다/갔었다/가더라}
He, to buy a Korean history book, went to a book store in Jongno.

*준서는 자기 아들을 뉴욕으로 유학을 {보냈으려고/보내겠으려고/보냈었으려고/보내더려고} 준비한다.
→ 준서는 자기 아들을 뉴욕으로 유학을 보내려고 {준비했다/준비하겠다/준비했었다/준비하더라}
Jun-Seo, to send his son to New York, is making preparations.

*민서는 한 번만이라도 준서를 {만났고자/만나겠고자/만났었고자/만나더고자} 한다.
→ 민서는 한 번만이라도 준서를 만나고자 {했다/하겠다/했었다/하더라}
Min-Seo wants to meet Jun-Seo even just for once.

● **Use of predicates**: It is impossible to use adjectives in both the preceding and following clause of a sentence which has intentional connective endings, because the preceding clause has to put forward the subject's volition to do or change something, while the following clause has to show an action based on that volition.

> *민서는 {<u>예쁘러</u>/<u>예쁘려고</u>/<u>예쁘고자</u>} 미장원으로 갔다.
> *그녀는 {<u>날씬하려고</u>/<u>날씬하고자</u>} 헬스클럽에 등록했다.

However, adjectives can be combined with intentional connective endings if they are verbalized in combination with '-아/어지다, -게 되다'.

> 민서는 {예뻐지러/예뻐지려고/예뻐지고자} 미장원으로 갔다.
> To become pretty, Min-Seo went to a hairdresser's.
> 그녀는 날씬하게 {되려고/되고자} 헬스클럽에 등록했다.
> To become slim, she registered for a fitness center.

As for '-(으)러', the preceding clause cannot have motional verbs such as 가다 'to go', 오다 'to come', 들어가다 'to enter', 나오다 'to come out', 나서다 'to set off', 돌아오다 'to return', 떠나다 'to leave', 도착하다 'to arrive', 내려오다 'to come down', 올라가다 'to go up', whereas the following clause always has to have motional verbs.

> 민서는 클라리넷 연습실에 {*<u>가러</u>/<u>가려고</u>/<u>가고자</u>} 집을 나섰다.
> Min-Seo, to go to the clarinet practice room, left home.
> 그녀는 빨리 집에 {*<u>도착하러</u>/<u>도착하려고</u>/<u>도착하고자</u>} 비행기를 타고 왔다.
> She, to arrive home quickly, took the airplane.
> 준서는 물고기를 {*<u>잡으러</u>/<u>잡으려고</u>/<u>잡고자</u>} 그물을 냇가에 쳤다.
> Jun-Seo, to catch some fish, cast a net on the stream.
> 그는 한국 민요를 {*<u>들으러</u>/<u>들으려고</u>/<u>듣고자</u>} 라디오를 켰다.
> He, to listen to Korean folk songs, turned the radio on.

● **Use of sentence endings**: '-(으)러' imposes no restrictions on the use of sentence endings, so it can come with declarative, interrogative, imperative, propositive and exclamatory endings. However, '-(으)려고' and '-고자' cannot come with imperative or propositive endings.

내일 골프를 치러 경주에 {간다/가니?/가거라/가자/가는구나!}
To play golf tomorrow, I am going to Gyeongju.
To play golf tomorrow, are you going to Gyeongju?
To play golf tomorrow, go to Gyeongju.
To play golf tomorrow, let's go to Gyeongju.
To play golf tomorrow, you are going to Gyeongju!

한국으로 유학을 {가려고/가고자} 계획을 {세웠다/세웠니?/*세워라/*세우자/세우는구나!}
To go to Korea to study, I set up a plan.
To go to Korea to study, did you set up a plan?
To go to Korea to study, you are setting up a plan!

● **Use of negation**: '-(으)려고' and '-고자' impose no restrictions on the use of negation. However, with '-(으)러', only the following clause may have negative expressions. Negative expressions can be put in the following clause to negate the preceding clause, or the following clause itself.

*그는 공부를 안 하러 학교에는 갔다.
그는 공부를 하러는 학교에 안 갔다.
He did not go to school to study.
→ He did go to school, but not to study. In other words, he went to school for something else.

그는 공부를 하러 학교에는 안 갔다.
He did not go to school to study.
→ He went somewhere to study, but not school.

민서는 준서와 더 이상 싸우지 {않으려고/않고자} 최선의 노력을 다했다.

Min-Seo, to fight with Jun-Seo any longer, made her best efforts.

준서는 민서와 사이좋게 {지내**려고**/지내**고자**} 조금도 노력하**지 않**았다.

Jun-Seo, to get along with Min-Seo, made no efforts.

● **Common use**: '‑(으)려(고)' is usually combined with other connective endings, as in the case of '‑(으)려거든(◁‑(으)려(고) (하)거든), ‑(으)려니(◁ ‑(으)려(고) (하)니), ‑(으)려면(◁‑(으)려(고) (하)면), ‑(으)려야(◁‑(으)려(고) (해)야)'.

한국어를 제대로 배우**려거든** 한국으로 유학을 가라.
To learn Korean properly, go to Korea.
이제 졸업을 하**려니** 시원섭섭하다.
As I am to graduate now, I get mixed feelings.
민서를 만나**려면** 음악실에 가 보세요.
To meet Min-Seo, go to the music room.

22.2.2.8 Result

There is one connective ending that form **result**(결과), '‑도록', which means that the action or status in the following clause reaches the status mentioned in the preceding clause. There are three types of results represented by '‑도록'.

● **Meaning**: First, combination of '‑도록' with verbs implies an intentioned result. In other words, the action in the following clause is intended to bring about what is said in the preceding clause. The preceding clause may or may not be true.

그가 사업을 잘하**도록**, 준서는 그를 도와주었다.
For him to run his business well, Jun-Seo helped him.
→ Jun-Seo's helping him was intended to make him run his business

well.

자동차 사고가 나지 않**도록**, 민서는 교통법규를 잘 지켰다.
To prevent car accidents, Min-Seo observed traffic rules strictly.
→ Min-Seo's observing traffic rules was intended to prevent car accidents.

Combination of '-도록' with adjectives implies results to a certain degree. In other words, the subject engages in the action stated in the following clause, but only up to the degree stated in the preceding clause.

준서는 그녀를 죽**도록** 사랑했다.
Jun-Seo loved her madly.
가슴이 아프**도록** 준서는 그녀의 처지를 불쌍해했다.
Jun-Seo had pity on her circumstances by heart.

Finally, '-도록' implies progressive results, which means the action of the following clause takes place until what is said in the preceding clause comes true. In this case, the preceding clause must be a fact.

밤이 이슥하**도록**, 그녀는 이리저리 돌아다녔다.
Until the evening wore on, she wandered from here to there.
→ Her wondering from here to there was until the evening wore on.

1년이 다 가**도록**, 준서에게서 아무런 소식이 없었다.
Until one year has passed, we did not hear from Jun-Seo.
→ Not hearing from Jun-Seo was until one year has passed.

- **Use of subject**: '-도록' imposes no restrictions on the use of subjects, so an identical or different subject can be used in the preceding and following clause.

민서는 내년에 한국으로 유학을 갈 수 있<u>도록</u> 준비를 철저히 했다.
Min-Seo, to go to Korea to study next year, made thorough preparations.
어머님의 **건강**이 좋아지<u>도록</u> <u>그</u>는 하나님께 정성껏 기도했다.
For his mother to get well, he prayed to God wholeheartedly.

- **Use of prefinal endings**: No prefinal endings, from '-았/었-, -겠-, -았/었었-', to '-더-' can be affixed to resultant connective endings. Instead, prefinal endings should come only in the following clause.

   *내가 잘살 수 {있<u>었도록</u>/있<u>겠도록</u>/있<u>었었도록</u>/있<u>더도록</u>} 친구가 많이 도와준다.
   → 내가 잘살 수 있도록 친구가 많이 {도와**줬**다/도와주**겠**다/도와**줬었**다/도와주**더**라} / For I to thrive, my friend is helping a lot.

- **Use of predicates**: '-도록' cannot be combined with 이다, if it represents intended results or results to a certain degree. However, '-도록' can be combined with other verbs without restrictions.

   준서가 정답을 **말하도록** 선생님이 기회를 주었다.
   For Jun-Seo to say the correct the answer, the teacher gave him a chance.
   방이 **깨끗하도록** 청소를 해 다오.
   To make the room clean, please clean up.
   민서가 좋은 {*음악가<u>이도록</u>/음악가<u>가 되도록</u>} 그녀의 어머니를 도와주었다. / For Min-Seo to become a good musician, I helped her mother.

However, '-도록' is generally combined with verbs if it signifies progressive results, because progression of time requires change of action or status.

   한 해가 다 **가도록** 편지 한 장 없었다.
   Until one year has passed, I did not get a letter.

마술을 통해 거인이 {*작도록/작아지도록} 우리는 하루를 기다렸다.
For the giant to become small by magic, we waited for one day.
그녀는 유명한 {*피아니스트이도록/피아니스트가 되도록} 10년을 노력해
왔다. / She, to become a renowned pianist, strove for 10 years.

● **Use of sentence endings**: '-도록' imposes no restrictions on the use of sentence endings, so all types of sentence endings, from declarative, interrogative, imperative, propositive to exclamatory endings can be used.

범인이 스스로 자백을 하도록 경찰은 끝까지 {기다렸다/기다렸니?/기다려
라/기다리자/기다리는구나!}
For the criminal to confess his crime voluntarily, the police waited patiently.
For the criminal to confess his crime voluntarily, did the police wait patiently?
For the criminal to confess his crime voluntarily, wait patiently.
For the criminal to confess his crime voluntarily, let's wait patiently.
For the criminal to confess his crime voluntarily, you are waiting patiently!

가슴이 터지도록 승리의 기쁨을 {누렸다/누렸니?/누려라/누리자/누리는구나!}
I enjoyed the victory to the point that my heart nearly bursted.
Did you enjoy the victory to the point that your heart nearly bursted?
Enjoy the victory to the point of bursting your heart.
Let's enjoy the victory to the point of bursting our hearts.
You are enjoying the victory to the point that your heart will nearly burst!

밤이 이슥하도록 오랫동안 {공부했다/공부했니?/공부해라/공부하자/공부
하는구나!}
Until the evening deepened, I studied for a long time.
Until the evening deepened, did you study for a long time?
Until the evening deepens, study for a long time.
Until the evening deepens, let's study for a long time.
Until the evening deepened, you are studying for a long time!

- **Use of negation**: There is no restrictions on the use of negation if '-도록' signifies intentions or degrees.

준서가 실수하<u>지 않도록</u> 잘 설명해 주세요.
For Jun-Seo not to make any mistake, please give him a good explanation.
범인이 도망가<u>지 못하도록</u> 경찰이 잘 감시했다.
To prevent the criminal from running away, the police kept an eye on him.

However, negative expressions cannot be used in the preceding clause if '-도록' implies progression of time.

*밤이 안 이슥하<u>도록</u> 오랫동안 공부했다.
For the evening not to deepen, I studied for a long time.
*1년이 다 안 가<u>도록</u>, 준서에게서 아무런 소식이 없었다.
Until one year has not passed, I did not hear from Jun-Seo.

22.2.2.9 Circumstance

Connective endings that form **circumstances**(상황 제시), which include '-(으)ㄴ/는데, -(으)니(까), -다시피', put forward an adequate situation in the preceding clause to deliver the message of the following clause effectively.

- **Meaning**:
① '-(으)ㄴ/는데' especially represents the background among circumstances. In other words, it puts forward a particular situation in the preceding clause, which serves as the background for the event/news stated in the following clause. Such backgrounds can be time, space, people, events, etc.

오후 3시경에 인천 공항에 도착했<u>는데</u>, 뉴욕으로 가는 비행기가 출발하고 없었다. / I arrived at Incheon Airport at around 3pm, but the plane bounded for New York has already taken off.

오랜만에 죽도시장에 갔었**는데**, 거기서 고향 친구를 만났어.

I went to Jukdo Market after a long time, and I met my hometown friends there.

옛날 옛적에 한 할아버지와 할머니가 살았**는데**, 그들에게는 아들이 하나 있었다. / Once upon a time, there was an old man and an old woman, and they had a son.

경부고속도로에서 교통사고가 났**는데**, 두 사람이 사망하고 열 사람이 다쳤대.

There was a car accident on the Gyeongbu Expressway, and two people died and ten people were injured.

② '-(으)니' implies amplification among circumstances. In other words, the preceding clause puts forward a certain fact that the subject has newly realized while the following clause amplifies the fact in detail.

그 문제를 자세히 살펴보**니** 해결책이 있더라.

Having observed the problem, there seemed to be a solution.

지난번 화재 때 나를 구해 준 분이 누구였나 했더**니** 바로 고향 친구인 준서였다.

I was wondering who rescued me from the fire, and it turned out to be my friend Jun-Seo from hometown.

약속 장소에 도착을 해 보**니** 이미 많은 사람들이 와 있었다.

As I arrived at the place, many people had already arrived there.

아침 일찍 일어나 보**니** 내가 이미 유명인이 되어 있었다.

I woke up early in the morning, to find that I had become famous.

③ '-다시피' represents a fait accompli among circumstances. It is usually combined with perceptive verbs such as 알다 'to know', 보다 'to see', 느끼다 'to feel' and 짐작하다 'to estimate'. The preceding clause puts forward a fact that the hearer is already aware of and makes it a fair accompli. Based on the established fact, the following clause conveys what the hearer intends to say. '-다시피' is the same as '-(으)ㄴ/는 바와 같이'.

> 너도 알**다시피** 내가 지난번 마라톤 대회에서 우승을 했잖니?
> As you know, I won the marathon last time.
> 보시**다시피** 지금 제가 가지고 있는 것은 아무것도 없습니다.
> As you can see, I have nothing at the moment.
> 고객께서도 짐작하시**다시피** 우리 회사는 이미 파산했습니다.
> As you might have guessed, our company has already gone bankrupt.

● **Use of subject**: '-(으)ㄴ/는데' and '-(으)니(까)' impose no particular restrictions on the use of subjects, so an identical or different subject can be used in the preceding and following clause.

> 민서가 지난달에 수술을 했**는데** 수술 경과가 매우 좋다.
> Min-Seo had an operation last month, and the result of the operation is very good.
> 내가 커피를 마시고 있**는데** 민서가 말을 걸어왔다.
> While I was drinking coffee, Min-Seo started a conversation with me.
> 민서가 내게 메모지를 내밀더**니** 사인을 해 달라고 했다.
> Min-Seo pushed a memo pad to me and asked me for an autograph.
> 매장 안에 가 보**니** 이미 손님들이 많이 들어와 있었다.
> I went inside the store and there were already many customers in the store.

● **Use of prefinal endings**: '-(으)ㄴ/는데' can be combined with prefinal endings '-았/었-' and '-았/었었-', but this combination usually appears in the following clause.

> 기차가 막 {출발**했는데**/출발**했었는데**} 준서가 세워 달라며 {달려**왔**다/달려**왔었**다}

기차가 막 출발하**는데** 준서가 세워 달라며 {달려**왔**다/달려**왔**었다}

As the train was about to depart, Jun-Seo came running, telling them to stop.

If the chronological order of the preceding and following clause needs to be made clear, these prefinal endings should be inserted in both clauses.

의상 전시회를 {열**었는데**/열**었었는데**} 관람객이 매우 {많**았**다/많**았었**다}

A clothes exhibition was held, and there were a lot of visitors.

?*의상 전시회를 여**는데** 관람객이 매우 {많**았**다/많**았었**다}

'-(으)ㄴ/는데' cannot be combined with future prefinal ending '-겠-'. Instead, '-겠-' is generally put in the following clause.

?*내일 너를 만나러 가**겠는데** 무엇을 준비해야 할지 모르**겠**다.

내일 너를 만나러 가**는데** 무엇을 준비해야 할지 모르**겠**다.

Tomorrow, I am going to see you, and I don't know what to prepare.

Nonetheless, '-겠-' can be affixed to '-(으)ㄴ/는데' if it implies conjecture or volition, not the future.

정답을 도저히 모르**겠는데** 어떡하지?

I have absolutely no idea what the correct answer is, so what shall I do?

사랑한다고 고백해야**겠는데** 언제쯤이 좋을까?

I have to tell him that I love him, and when will be the right time?

Yet, '-(으)니' cannot be combined with '-았/었-, -겠-, -았/었었-'. These prefinal endings must come in the following clause. However, '-(으)니' can be combined with '-더-' and '-았/었더-'.

민서가 어디에 있느냐고 {*물어**봤**으니/*물어보**겠**으니/물어**봤더**니} 다들 모른다고 했다. / I asked where Min-Seo was, and nobody said he/she knew where Min-Seo was.

그가 준서의 얼굴을 한번 {*쳐다**봤으니**/*쳐다보**겠으니**/쳐다**보더니**} 함께 일해 보자고 했다.
He looked at Jun-Seo's face and suggested Jun-Seo work with him.

- **Use of predicates**: '-(으)ㄴ/는데' can be combined with verbs, adjectives, 이다 and 있다 without restrictions.

일을 막 끝내고 **나가는데** 손님이 찾아왔다.
I was about to leave after finishing the work, and a customer came.
키가 그렇게 **작은데** 농구를 잘 해낼 수 있겠니?
You are so short, so will you be able to play basketball well?
저 분은 우리 학교 선생님**이신데** 덕망이 매우 높으십니다.
He is one of the teachers in my school, and he is a man of excellent qualities.
친구와 이야기를 하고 **있는데** 전화가 왔다.
I was talking with my friend, and the phone rang.

Nonetheless, '-(으)니' can be attached to verbs only. If '-(으)니' is combined with adjectives or 이다, it represents a causal relationship instead of circumstantial relationship.

큰딸은 가만히 아빠를 **올려다보더니** 한참 뒤에야 말을 꺼냈다. / The eldest daughter looked up at her dad and began speaking after a long time.
오늘은 날씨가 **좋으니** 우리 나들이 갈까?
The weather is lovely, so shall we go on a picnic?
너도 이제 어른**이니** 어른답게 행동해야지.
You are an adult now, so you should behave like an adult.

- **Use of sentence endings**: '-(으)ㄴ/는데' imposes no restrictions on the use of sentence endings, so all types of sentence endings, from declarative, interrogative, imperative, propositive to exclamatory endings, can be used.

퇴근하면서 코코아를 사 왔는데 아이들이 무척 {좋아했다/좋아했니?/좋아하더구나!}

I bought hot chocolate on my way home from work, and children were very happy with it.

You bought hot chocolate on my way home from work, and were children very happy with it?

I bought hot chocolate on my way home from work, and children were very happy with it!

김 선생이 할 말이 많은 것 같은데 이야기를 좀 들어 {주어라/주자}

Mr Kim seems to have a lot to say, so listen to him.

Mr Kim seems to have a lot to say, so let's listen to him.

Yet, '-(으)니' cannot end the sentence in propositive or imperative forms.

서울에 도착을 하니 눈이 내리고 {있었다/있었니?}

As I arrived in Seoul, it was snowy.

As you arrived at Seoul, was it snowy?

한국 음식을 먹어 보더니 잘 먹었다고 {했다/했니?/*해라/*하자/하더구나!}

He had Korean food, and said he enjoyed it.

He had Korean food, and did he say he enjoyed it?

He had Korean food, and said he enjoyed it!

- **Use of negation**: '-(으)ㄴ/는데' imposes no restrictions on the use of negation.

아이들 선물을 안 사 왔는데 어떻게 하지?

I did not buy any present for children, so what shall I do?
친구의 부탁을 <u>안</u> 들어 주었<u>는데</u> 욕을 <u>안</u> 할지 모르겠다.
I did not do my friend a favor, so he may or may not speak ill of me.

Nonetheless, the preceding clause of '-(으)니' cannot have negative expressions, because the preceding clause should be based on something that has already been realized.

*편지를 <u>안</u> 읽어 보았<u>더니</u> 네가 잘못한 것이 많더구나.
I did not read the letter, and found that you made lots of blunders.
*낚시를 <u>안</u> 해 보았<u>더니</u> 낚시하는 게 얼마나 재미있는 것인지 알겠더라.
I have never done fishing, so I realized how fun it is.

22.2.2.10 Comparison

There is one connective ending that forms **comparison**(비교) '-느니'. '-느니' implies that it is better to choose what is suggested in the following clause than what is suggested in the preceding clause. If '-느니' is combined with comparative particle '보다' and adverb '차라리' to form '-느니보다 차라리', it can stress the comparison even more.

- **Meaning**: '-느니' implies that it is better to choose something in the following clause than the preceding clause. It is often used in the form of '-느니보다', in combination with comparative particle '-보다'.

그렇게 가만히 있<u>느니</u> 제게 옛날 얘기나 좀 해 주세요.
Instead of doing nothing like that, tell me some good-night stories.
준서의 뜻을 따르<u>느니</u> 민서의 뜻을 따르는 것이 좋겠다.
I would rather go for Min-Seo's idea than go for Jun-Seo's idea.
한국 문화를 알려면 백화점에 가<u>느니보다</u> 재래시장에 가는 것이 더 낫다.
To understand the Korean culture, it is better to go to the marketplace

than department stores.

If '-느니' is attached to auxiliary particle '-만' to form '-느니만', the combination has to be accompanied with 못하다 to form '-느니만 못하다', which means the preceding clause is no better than the following clause.

이렇게 구차하게 사는 것은 **차라리 죽느니만 못하다**.
It is better to die than living in poverty.
나라 없이 사는 삶은 노예로 사**느니만** (**차라리**) **못하다**.
Living without a country is no better than a life of slavery.

● **Use of subject**: '-느니' imposes no restrictions on the use of subjects, so an identical or different subject can be used in the preceding and following clause.

나는 오래된 아파트에 사**느니** (**나는**) 차라리 한옥에 살겠다.
I would rather live in Han-ok than live in an old apartment unit.
민서는 검은색 부츠를 신**느니** (**민서는**) 흰색 운동화를 신으려 했다.
Min-Seo would rather put on the white shoes than black boots.
우리가 그 일을 하**느니**(보다) **그들**이 그 일을 하는 것이 더 낫다.
It would be better for them than us to do the work.

● **Use of prefinal endings**: No prefinal endings, from '-았/었-, -겠-, -았/었었-', to '-더-', can be combined with '-느니'. Instead, these prefinal endings should come in the following clause.

*잘못을 {꾸짖**었느니**(보다)/꾸짖**었었느니**(보다)/꾸짖**겠느니**(보다)/꾸짖**더느니**(보다)} 칭찬을 하는 것이 훨씬 교육적이다.
잘못을 꾸짖**느니**(보다) 칭찬을 하는 것이 훨씬 교육적{**이었**다/**이었었**다/**이겠**다/**이더**라}
It is much more educational to compliment than reprimand.

- **Use of predicates**: '-느니' can be combined with verbs only, because it is supposed to convey the progression of an action.

오늘은 요리를 <u>하느니</u>(보다) 나는 청소를 하겠다.
I would rather clean up than cook today.
*그녀는 <u>예쁘느니</u>(보다) 아름다운 편이다.
*그는 사장<u>이느니</u>(보다) 예술가라고 하는 것이 더 정확한 표현이다.

- **Use of sentence endings**: '-느니' imposes no restrictions on sentence endings, so all types of endings, from declarative, interrogative, imperative, propositive to exclamatory forms, can be used.

자전거를 타고 가<u>느니</u>(보다) 걸어서 {가겠<u>다</u>/가겠<u>니</u>?/가<u>거라</u>/가<u>자</u>/가<u>는구나</u>!}
I would rather walk than take the bicycle.
Would you rather walk than take the bicycle?
Walk instead of taking the bicycle.
Let's rather walk than take the bicycle.
You would rather walk than take the bicycle!

빵을 먹느니(보다) 비빔밥을 {먹겠<u>다</u>/먹겠<u>니</u>?/먹<u>어라</u>/먹<u>자</u>/먹<u>는구나</u>!}
I would rather have bibimbap than bread.
Would you rather have bibimbap than bread?
Have bibimbap instead of bread.
Let's rather have bibimbap than bread.
You would rather have bibimbap than bread!

- **Use of negation**: '-느니' imposes no restrictions on the use of negation.

서울에 <u>안</u> 가<u>느니보다</u> 서울에 가서 직접 문제를 해결하는 것이 좋다.
It would be better to go to Seoul and solve the problem firsthand than not going to Seoul.

자녀에게 관심을 **안** **두느니보다** 관심을 많이 두고 조언을 해 주어라.
Rather than paying no attention to children, pay a lot of attention and give them advice.
그런 폭력 영화는 **안** **보느니만** **못한** 것 같다.
It would be better not to see such a violent movie at all.
그렇게 하려면 **안** 하느니만 **못하**다.
It would be better not to do it at all.

22.2.2.11 Simile or Figure

Connective endings that form **simile** or **figure**(비유), which include '-듯 (이)', put forward figurative words in the preceding clause and corresponding words in the following clause, so that what comes in the following clause is almost the same as the preceding clause.

● **Meaning**: '-듯(이)' puts forward in the preceding clause something similar to the following clause to deliver the following clause more effectively. It is mostly found in literary works. There are various metaphors, from imaginative metaphors to factual metaphors.

구름에 달 가**듯이** 잘도 가는구나!
As clouds overshadow the moon, it moves so fast!
마파람에 게 눈 감추**듯이** 행동이 빠르구나!
As crabs hide their eyes to the south wind, it is so agile!
나비가 봄바람을 타고 날아가**듯이** 민서가 춤을 잘 추는구나!
As butterflies fly on the spring breeze, Min-Seo is dancing so well!
내가 그 어려움을 극복했**듯이** 너도 그 어려움을 잘 극복해야 한다.
As I overcame the difficulty, you must overcome that difficulty well.

● **Use of subject**: '-듯(이)' imposes no particular restrictions on the use of subjects, so an identical of different subject can be used in the preceding and following clause. However, the preceding and following clause tend to have different subjects in general.

거대한 **파도**가 밀려오**듯이 슬픔**이 내게 밀려왔다.
As a great wave comes into the shore, sorrow came in droves.
네가 서울에 가 보았**듯이 서울**은 매우 아름다운 도시다.
As you have been to Seoul, Seoul is a very beautiful city.
그는 피아노 연주를 잘하**듯이** 클라리넷 연주도 잘할 것이다.
As he plays the piano well, he would be also good at clarinet.

● **Use of prefinal endings**: '-았/었-' and '-았/었었-' can be combined with '-듯(이)', but '-겠-' and '-더-' cannot. Instead, they can come in the following clause.

네가 외교관이 되기를 {꿈꾸**었듯이**/꿈꾸**었었듯이**}, 나도 외교관이 되기를 원했다.
As you dreamed of becoming a diplomat, I also wanted to become a diplomat.

*어머니가 민서를 {사랑하**겠듯이**/사랑하**더듯이**} 민서도 아이들을 사랑하겠다.
→ 어머니가 민서를 사랑하**듯이** 민서도 아이들을 {사랑하**겠다**/사랑하**더라**}
As mother loves Min-Seo, Min-Seo would love the children.

● **Use of predicates**: '-듯(이)' can be combined with verbs, adjectives, 이다 and 있다 without restrictions.

눈이 **녹듯이** 걱정거리가 사라졌다.
Just like snow melting down, my concerns have subsided.
민서는 준서와 생김새가 **다르듯이** 생각 또한 많이 다르다.
As Min-Seo looks different from Jun-Seo, her ideas are very different

from Jun-Seo's.

사자의 이빨이 무기<u>이듯이</u> 그 사람의 무기는 바로 튼튼한 발이란다.

As a lion's teeth are his weapon, humans' weapon is strong feet.

누구에게나 꿈이 **있듯이** 그도 큰 꿈을 가지고 있다.

As everyone has a dream, he also has a big dream.

● **Use of sentence endings**: '-듯(이)' imposes no restrictions on the use of sentence endings, so all types of endings, from declarative, interrogative, imperative, propositive to exclamatory forms, can be used.

{너는/그는/우리는} 원수를 대하**듯이** 준서를 {대했**다**/대했**니**?/대**해라**/대하**자**/대하**는구나**!}

You/he/we treated Jun-Seo as if he was an enemy.

Did you/he/we treat Jun-Seo as if he was an enemy?

Treat Jun-Seo as if he is an enemy.

Let's treat Jun-Seo as if he is an enemy.

You are treating Jun-Seo as if he is an enemy!

그가 우리의 의견에 동의해 주었**듯이** {우리도/너도/그녀도} 그의 의견에 동의해 {주어야 **한다**/하**니**?/주**자**/주**어라**/주**는구나**!}

As he agreed with our idea, we/you/she should also agree with his idea.

As he agreed our idea, should we/you/she also agree with his idea?

As he agreed with our idea, let's also agree with his idea.

As he agreed with our idea, agree with his idea also.

As he agreed with your idea, you are also agreeing with his idea!

● **Use of negation**: '-듯(이)' imposes no restrictions on the use of negation.

너도 그 의견에 동의 **안** 하**듯이** 나도 동의하**지 않**는다.

As you do not agree with the opinion, I do not agree with it either.

그녀도 진실을 고백 **못 했듯이** 우리도 고백하기가 어렵다.

As she could not tell the truth, it is also difficult for us to tell the truth.

22.2.2.12 Proportion

Connective ending '-(으)ㄹ수록' presents **proportion**(비례) between the preceding and following clause. Sentences with these connective endings implies that the degree of the situation in the preceding clause affects that of following clause.

- **Meaning**: '-(으)ㄹ수록' means that the details of the following clause add up or deduct from itself in proportion to the preceding clause, and details of the following clause is highlighted according to the magnitude of the preceding clause.

머리가 좋**을수록** 노력도 많이 해야 한다.

The smarter you are, the more you should strive.

문화재는 세월이 **갈수록** 그 가치가 높아진다.

The older the cultural assets get, the more valuable they become.

'-(으)ㄹ수록' is mainly used in the form of '… -(으)면 … -(으)ㄹ수록'. Using the same verbs repeatedly in front of '… -(으)면 … -(으)ㄹ수록' underlines the meaning of the verb.

한국어 공부는 하**면** **할수록** 재미가 있다.

The more you study Korean, the more fun it gets.

추억이 많**으면** **많을수록** 삶은 행복해진다.

The more memories you have, the happier you become.

- **Use of subject**: '-(으)ㄹ수록' imposes no particular restrictions on the use of subjects, so an identical or different subject can be used in the preceding and following clause.

세월이 가면 <u>갈수록</u> 아내 <u>사랑</u>이 깊어졌다.
With time, his love for his wife deepened.
<u>그</u>는 민서를 만나면 만<u>날수록</u> 행복해 했다.
The more he met Min-Seo, the happier he got.

● **Use of prefinal endings**: No prefinal endings, from '-았/었-, -겠-, -았/었었-', to '-더-', can be combined with '-(으)ㄹ수록'. Instead, they should be put in the following clause.

[*]한국은 세월이 가면 {<u>갔</u>을수록/가겠을수록/<u>갔었</u>을수록/가더수록} 발전해 갔다.
→ 한국은 세월이 가면 갈수록 발전해 {<u>갔</u>다/가겠다/<u>갔었</u>다/가더라}
　 Over the years, Korea made more and more developments.

[*]권위를 내세우면 {내세<u>웠</u>을수록/내세우겠을수록/내세<u>웠었</u>을수록/내세우더수록} 사람과의 관계는 나빠진다.
→ 권위를 내세우면 내세울수록 사람과의 관계는 {나빠졌다/나빠지겠다/나빠졌었다/나빠지더라} / The more you try to be authoritative, the worse the relationship will get.

● **Use of predicates**: '-(으)ㄹ수록' can be combined with verbs, adjectives, 이다 and 있다 without restrictions.

많이 웃으면 <u>웃을수록</u> 건강해진다.
The more you laugh, the healthier you become.
과자는 달면 달수록 맛있는 법이다.
The sweeter the snack, the better it tastes.
어른일수록 말조심을 해야 한다.
The older you are, the more you should be careful with what you say.

학식이 많이 **있을수록** 겸손해야 한다.

The more educated you are, the humbler you should be.

● **Use of sentence endings**: '-(으)ㄹ수록' imposes no restrictions on the use of sentence endings, so it can come with all types of endings from declarative, interrogative, imperative, propositive to exclamatory forms.

{너는/그는/우리는} 민서가 미**울수록** 더 잘 대해 {주었**다**/주었**니**?/주**어라**/주**자**/주**는구나**!}

The more you/he/we hated Min-Seo, the kinder you/he/we were/was to Min-Seo.

The more you/he/we hated Min-Seo, were you (was he) kinder to Min-Seo?

The more you/he/we hate Min-Seo, the kinder you/he/we should be to Min-Seo.

The more we hate Min-Seo, let's be kinder to Min-Seo.

The more you hate Min-Seo, the kinder you are to Min-Seo!

그가 우리에게 잘해 **줄수록** {우리도/너도/그녀도} 그에게 잘해 {주어야 **한다**/주어야 하**니**?/주**자**/주**어라**/주**는구나**!}

The kinder he is to us, the more we/you/she should be kind to him.

The kinder he is to us, should we/you/she be kind to him?

The kinder he is to us, let's be kind to him.

The kinder he is to us, be kind to him.

The kinder he is to us, the kinder to him!

● **Use of negation**: '-(으)ㄹ수록' imposes no restrictions on the use of negation.

잠이 **안** **올수록** 마음은 더 불안해졌다.

The more I became sleepless, the more I became anxious.

이상이 높지 않을수록 삶에 대한 적극성도 떨어질 수밖에 없다.

The lower the ideals, the less the drive.

범죄는 저지르지 않을수록 좋다. / The less the crime, the better it gets.

22.2.2.13 Degree

Connective endings that form **degree**(정도), which include '-(으)리만큼' and '-(으)리만치', put forward an extreme degree of a certain event or action in the preceding clause, and a similar degree of action or status in the following clause.

● **Meaning**: '-(으)리만큼' and '-(으)리만치' have common semantic and grammatical functions, meaning that the action or status in the following clause is up to the degree stated in the preceding clause.

그는 번갯불에 콩 구워 {먹으리만큼/먹으리만치} 재빨리 일을 처리했다.
He, as if cooking beans with a flash of lightning, completed the work quickly. (= He completed the work as quickly as cooking beans with a flash of lightning.)

거짓말을 한 마디도 {못하리만큼/못하리만치} 그는 정직한 사람이다.
To the degree of not being able to tell a lie, he is honest. (= He is too honest to tell a lie.)

● **Use of subject**: '-(으)리만큼' and '-(으)리만치' impose no particular restrictions on the use of subjects, so an identical or different subject can be used in the preceding and following clause. However, the same subject is generally used in both clauses.

민서는 물 한 모금도 마시지 {못하리만큼/못하리만치} 몸이 약해져 있었다.

Min-Seo, to the point of not being able to take a sip of water, got weak. (= Min-Seo got so weak that she was not even able to take a sip of water.)

그는 콧바람에도 {날아가**리만큼**/날아가**리만치**} 몸이 약했다.
He, to the point of being blown away by a snort, was weak. (= He was so weak that he could be blown away by a snort.)

우리가 축구를 해도 {되**리만큼**/되**리만치**} 방이 넓고 좋았다.
The room, to the point of letting us play football, was large and comfortable. (= The room was so large and comfortable that we could play football.)

● **Use of prefinal endings**: '-았/었-' and '-았/었었-' may be combined with '-(으)리만큼' and '-(으)리만치', but '-겠-, -더-' cannot; instead, they should come in the following clause.

뇌물과 선물을 구별하지 {못**했으리만큼**/못**했으리만치**} 나는 바보가 아니다.
뇌물과 선물을 구별하지 {못**했었으리만큼**/못**했었으리만치**} 나는 바보가 아니다. / I am not too foolish to tell apart bribes and gifts.
  → 뇌물과 선물을 구별하지 {못하**리만큼**/못하**리만치**} 나는 바보가 {아니**었**다/아니**었었**다}
  To the extent that I cannot tell apart bribes and gifts, I am not foolish.

*그녀의 자존심을 {버리**겠으리만큼**/버리**겠으리만치**} 그녀는 준서를 설득했다.
*그녀의 자존심을 {버리**더리만큼**/버리**더리만치**} 그녀는 준서를 설득했다.
  → 그녀의 자존심을 {버리**리만큼**/버리**리만치**} 그녀는 준서를 {설득하**겠**다/설득하**더**라}
  To the extent of giving up her pride, she persuaded Jun-Seo.

● **Use of predicates**: '-(으)리만큼' and '-(으)리만치' may be combined with verbs, adjectives and 있다, but not 이다.

합격 소식에 하늘을 {날아가리만큼/날아가리만치} 너무나 기뻤다.

I was so happy with the news that I passed the exam that I could even fly.

준서는 이번 선행으로 {과분하리만큼/과분하리만치} 칭찬을 받았다.

Jun-Seo, due to his good deed, was commended rather generously.

그는 저 빌딩을 살 수 {있으리만큼/있으리만치} 돈이 많지는 않다.

He does not have as much money as to afford that building.

^{?*}그는 살인자{이리만큼/이리만치} 악하지 않다.

^{?*}He is not so bad as much as a murderer.

● **Use of sentence endings**: '-(으)리만큼' and '-(으)리만치' impose no restrictions on the use of sentence endings, so they may come with all types of endings from declarative, interrogative, imperative, propositive to exclamatory forms.

{그는/너는/우리는} 청백리라고 {불리리만큼/불리리만치} 욕심 없이 {살았다/살았니?/살아라/살자/사는구나!}

He/you/we lived so frugally that he/you/we was/were called an upright man.

Did he/you live so frugally that he/you was/were called an upright man?

Live so frugally as to be called an upright man.

Let's live so frugally as to be called an upright man.

He/you are living so frugally that he/you is/are called an upright man!

{그는/너는/우리는} 굴러오는 복을 차 {버리리만큼/버리리만치} 바보이지는 {않다/않니?/마라/말자/않구나!}

He/you/we are not so foolish as to kick away good fortune.

Are you/is he/are we not so foolish as to kick away good fortune?

Don't be so foolish as to kick away good fortune.

Let's not be so foolish as to kick away good fortune.

He is/you are not so foolish as to kick away good fortune!

● **Use of negation**: '-(으)리만큼' and '-(으)리만치' impose no restrictions on the use of negation.

그녀는 꼼짝 **못** {하리**만큼**/하리**만치**} 피곤하<u>지는 않</u>다.

She is not so tired that she cannot move an inch. (= She is not too tired to be unable to move an inch.)

나는 아무런 잘못도 **안** {하리**만큼**/하리**만치**} 선량한 사람<u>이 아닙</u>니다.

I am not so righteous that I do nothing wrong. (= I am not as righteous as to do nothing wrong.)

22.2.2.14 Addition

Connective endings that form **addition**(첨가) include '-(으)ㄹ뿐더러, -(으)려니와, -거니와'. They mean that there is something in the following clause in addition to something in the preceding clause. Inserting an adverb '게다가' at the beginning of the following clause while using these connective endings, stresses the meaning of the sentence.

- **Meaning**:

① '-(으)ㄹ뿐더러' means that a certain event or action is introduced in the preceding clause and an additional fact or action relevant to the preceding clause is introduced in the following clause.

준서는 공부도 잘**할뿐더러** 운동도 잘한다.

Jun-Seo is not only a good student but also a good sports player.

그분은 정직**할뿐더러** 선량하다. / He is not only honest but also kind.

② '-거니와' acknowledges that a certain event or action in the preceding clause is true, but suggests that there is additional action or event relevant to the preceding clause in the following clause.

민서는 노래도 잘하**거니와** 피아노도 잘 친다.

Min-Seo is good at not only singing but also playing the piano.

오늘은 날씨도 덥**거니와** 비까지 내린다.

Today, it is not only hot but also rainy.

③ '-(으)려니와' acknowledges a certain event or action in the preceding clause as true based on the speaker's conjecture, while suggesting that there is additional action or event relevant to the preceding clause in the following clause.

그는 테니스도 잘 치**려니와** 골프는 더 잘한다.

He is good at tennis, and even better at golf.

한국은 봄도 좋으**려니와** 가을은 더욱 좋다.

In Korea, spring is lovely, and autumn is even more lovely.

'-(으)려니와' reveals a volition to do something in the preceding clause and also reveals a volition do something more in the following clause.

나는 서울에도 안 가**려니와** 부산에도 안 가려고 한다.

I will neither go to Seoul nor go to Busan.

나는 너의 부탁도 안 들어주**려니와** 어느 누구의 청탁도 거절하겠다.

I will do a favor for neither you nor anyone else.

● **Use of subject**: '-(으)ㄹ뿐더러, -거니와' and '-(으)려니와' impose no restrictions on the use of subjects, so an identical or different subject can be used in the preceding and following clause. However, the same topic or subject is used for both clauses most of the time.

민서는 인정이 많**을뿐더러** 순박하다.

Min-Seo is not only compassionate but also naive.

민서와 윤서는 성격도 비슷하**거니와** 행동까지도 비슷하다. / Min-Seo and Yun-Seo are similar in not only character but also the way they act.

한국의 **김치**는 맛도 좋**으려니와** **영양**도 만점이다.

Korea's Kimchi is not only tasty but also highly nutritious.

나도 그 일을 안 하**려니와** **준서**도 그 일을 안 하려 하더라.

I myself wouldn't do the work and Jun-Seo wouldn't do the work either.

- **Use of prefinal endings**: '-았/었-, -았/었었-' and '-겠-' can be combined with '-(으)ㄹ뿐더러, -거니와, -(으)려니와'. However, '-더-' cannot. Instead, '-더-' should be put in the following clause.

그는 며칠째 밥을 안 먹**었을뿐더러** 물 한 모금도 마시지 않았다.

He, for days, has neither eaten any meals nor taken a sip of water.

민서는 수영도 못 **했었거니와** 스케이트도 못 탔다.

Min-Seo was neither good at swimming nor skating.

그 영화는 재미도 **없겠으려니와** 관람료 또한 너무 비쌀 것 같다.

I think the movie would be boring and the ticket so expensive.

- **Use of predicates**: '-(으)ㄹ뿐더러, -거니와, -(으)려니와' can be combined with verbs, adjectives, 이다 and 있다 without any restrictions.

그는 대학에 **합격했을뿐더러** 장학금까지 받게 되었다.

He not only passed the college entrance exam but also won a scholarship.

이 노트북은 성능도 **좋거니와** 가격 또한 싸다.

This laptop has not only good performance but also cheap price.

숭례문은 국보**이려니와** 천금을 줘도 살 수 없는 건축물이다.

Sungryemun Gate is not only a national treasure but also an invaluable architecture.

그녀는 학식도 많이 가지고 {**있거니와/있으려니와**} 돈도 많이 가지고 있다.

She is not only highly educated but also very wealthy.

- **Use of sentence endings**: '-(으)ㄹ뿐더러, -거니와' and '-(으)려니와' can end the sentence in declarative, interrogative, imperative, propositive and exclamatory forms.

{그는/너는/우리는} 이번에 자동차를 새로 {샀**을뿐더러**/샀**거니와**/샀**으려 니와**} 별장까지 {샀**다**/샀**니**?/사**라**/사**자**/사**는구나**!}

He/you/we bought not only a new car but also a villa.
Did he/you buy not only a new car but also a villa?
Buy not only a new car but also a villa.
Let's buy not only a new car but also a villa.
He is/you are buying not only a new car but also a villa!

{그는/너는/우리는} 영국에도 가 {보았**을뿐더러**/보았**거니와**/보았**으려니 와**} 미국에도 물론 가 {보았**다**/보았**니**?/보**아라**/보**자**/보**는구나**!}

He/you/we has/have been to not only Great Britain but also America.
Has/have he/you been to not only Great Britain but also America?
Go to not only Great Britain but also America.
Let's go to not only Great Britain but also America.
He/you is/are going to not only Great Britain but also America!

● **Use of negation**: '-(으)ㄹ뿐더러, -거니와' and '-(으)려니와' impose no restrictions on the use of negation.

나는 그녀와 결혼을 <u>안</u> 했**을뿐더러** 그녀를 한 번도 만난 적이 <u>없</u>다.
I and she were not married, and I have never even seen her.
그녀는 얼굴도 <u>안</u> 예쁘**거니와** 마음씨도 고약하다.
She is not only not pretty but also nasty.
그는 굽실대지도 <u>안</u> 하**려니와** 그렇다고 건방지<u>지도</u> <u>않</u>다.
He does not grovel, but it doesn't mean that he is cocky.

22.2.2.15 Habit and repetition

Connective ending for **habit**(습관) and **repetition**(반복) are '-고는'. '-고 는' must be used as a '-고는 하다' form. It represents the behavior in preceding clause appears habitually or same thing happening repeatedly. Meaning of 'habit' and 'repetition' comes clear when '-고는 하다' is used with adverb '늘, 항상' in the preceding clause. '-고는' is only used in 'phrase connection' and never used in 'clause connection'. In modern Korean language '-곤' which is contraction of '-고는' is often used.

그는 토요일에는 늘 등산을 가고는 했다.
He used to go hiking on every Saturday.
태풍이 불면 항상 산사태가 나곤 했다.
Everytime a typhoon comes, landslide occurred.

● **Meaning:** Preceding clause of '-고는' represents certain behavior or event and '하다' is used in following clause for ending. In this case, '하다' has a function of substituting the content of preceding clause. '-곤 하다' indicates a meaning of 'habit' that is a certain behavior regularly happens. In addition, it has a meaning of 'repetition' which indicates a same event occur recurrently.

Habit : 준서는 시간이 나면 테니스를 치곤 했다.
　　　　Jun-Seo used to play tennis whenever he had time.
　　　　그분은 명절에는 고국을 방문하곤 했다.
　　　　He used to visit his native country during national holidays.
Repetition : 한국은 늦여름에 태풍이 자주 오곤 했다.
　　　　Typhoons often used to come at the late summer in Korea.
　　　　이 지역에서는 지진이 가끔 일어나곤 한다.
　　　　Earthquake sometimes occurs in this region.

● **Use of subject:** Connective endings for habit and repetition has no particular limitation except that the subject of preceding clause and following clause should be identical. When a subject is animate[+animate] such as 'person, animal, insect', '-곤 하다' represents habit. On contrary if the subject is in animate[-animate] like 'storm, earthquake, car accident, cold wave, war' and so on, it represents simple 'repetition'.

Habit : <u>민서</u>는 엄마가 보고 싶을 때면 늘 칠포해변에 가곤 했다.
Min-Seo used to go to Chilpo beach whenever she missed her mother.
<u>그분</u>은 화가 나면 종종 목소리를 높이곤 했다.
He often raised his voice when he was upset.

Repetition : 이곳은 한파가 몰아치면 교통이 두절되곤 했다.
Whenever cold wave came over in this region, the traffic tied up.
그는 <u>가뭄</u>이 자주 들곤 하는 지역을 피해서 이사를 했다.
He moved away form the drought.

● **Use of prefinal ending :** No prefinal endings, from '-았/었-, -겠-, -았/었었-', to '-더-', can be combined '-고는'. Instead they should be put in the following clause.

*그녀는 파티에 자주 {늦었곤/늦었었곤/늦었겠곤/늦겠곤} 했다.
→ 그녀는 파티에 자주 늦곤 {<u>한다</u>/했다/했었다/하겠다/하<u>더</u>라}.
She used to be late at the parties.

*요즘은 살인 사건이 종종 {났곤/났었곤/나겠곤/나더곤} 했다.
→ 요즘은 살인 사건이 종종 나곤 {<u>한다</u>/했다/했었다/하겠다/하<u>더</u>라}.
Murder incidents often happen in these days.

● **Use of predicates:** '-고는' can be combined with verbs, most adjectives, 이다 and 있다.

그녀는 내 도움이 필요하면 늘 나를 찾아오곤 했다.

She used to come and see me whenever she needed help.

예전에는 여윳돈이 많이 **있곤** 했다.

I used to have a lot of spare money.

민서가 제 자리에 **없곤** 하면 그는 불안해했다.

He felt anxious when Min-Seo is not in her position.

그녀가 예전에는 콧대가 **높곤** 했다.

She used to be a toffee-nosed girl.

예전에는 그가 **싫곤** 했는데 요즘은 괜찮아졌다.

I used to hate him but now I can cope with him.

내가 전화를 했을 때는 공부 중**이곤** 했다.

When I call, he/she used to be studying.

However, '-곤는' has a limitation in combination with adjectives and 이다 used in sentences representing non-habitual or non-repeatable.

*민서는 키가 **작곤** 했다.

*Min-Seo used to be short.

*이것이 **책상이곤** 했다.

*This used to be a desk.

→ 이것이 책상으로 **사용되곤** 했다.

This thing was used as a desk.

● **Use of sentence endings:** When '-곤는' is used as a meaning of 'habit', it imposes no restrictions on the use of sentence endings, so it may come with all types of endings from declarative, interrogative, imperative, propositive to exclamatory forms.

고향에 자주 가곤 {했**다**/했**니**?/**해라**/하**자**/하**는구나**!}

I used to go to hometown often.

시간이 날 때면 소설을 읽곤 {한**다**/하**니**?/**해라**/하**자**/하**는구나**!}

I used to read novels whenever I have time.

However, when used as a meaning of 'repetition', there are limitation in using imperative and propositive forms. In case of 'repetition', inanimate[-animate] nouns come as a subject of a sentence, therefore, it is impossible to co-occur with imperative or propositive form which represents performance of behavior.

<u>항공기 사고</u>가 최근에 자주 일어나<u>곤</u> {한다/하니?/*해라/*하자/하는구나!}
Air crashes occur frequently these days.

치안이 잘 안 되면 <u>폭행사건</u>이 생기<u>곤</u> {한다/하니?/*해라/*하자/하는구나!}
Scanty public security leads to assault incident.

● **Use of negation:** Negation expressions cannot be used in the following clause.

민서는 가끔 학교에 가<u>지 않곤</u> 했다.
Min-Seo sometimes did not go to school.
→ ^{?*}민서는 가끔 학교에 가<u>곤</u> 하<u>지 않</u>았다.
     *Min-Seo sometimes did go not to school.

^{?*}준서는 자주 아침밥을 먹<u>곤</u> 하<u>지 않</u>았다.
*Jun-Seo usually eat not breakfast.
→ 준서는 자주 아침밥을 <u>안</u> 먹<u>곤</u> 했다.
     Jun-Seo seldom ate breakfast.

■ Connective expressions

It is possible to connect sentences without connective endings. There are several forms of sentence connections as follows:

● Contrast: '-(으)ㄴ/는 반면'
준서는 서울에 {가지만/가는 반면} 나는 부산에 간다.
Jun-Seo is going to Seoul, but on the other hand, I am going to Busan.
민서는 그 의견에 {동의하지만/동의하는 반면} 준서는 동의하지 않는다.
Min-Seo agrees with the opinion, but on the other hand, Jun-Seo does not.

● Simultaneity: '-(으)ㄴ/는 동시에'
그는 노래를 {들으면서/듣는 동시에} 공부를 한다.
He is listening to songs while studying at the same time.
그녀는 일을 {하면서/하는 동시에} 재미있는 얘기를 많이 한다.
She, while doing her work, tells a lot of interesting things at the same time.

● Completion: '-고 나서', '-(으)ㄴ 뒤에', '-(으)ㄴ 후에', '-(으)ㄴ 다음에'
준서는 숙제를 다 {하고 나서/한 뒤에} 놀러 나갔다.
Jun-Seo, having completed his homework, went out to play.
민서가 서울을 {떠나고 나서/떠난 후에} 준서도 서울을 떠났다.
After Min-Seo left Seoul, Jun-Seo also left Seoul.
민서를 {만나고 나서/만난 다음에} 미국으로 출발하자.
After meeting Min-Seo, let's leave for America.

● Conversion: '-는 도중에'
그는 서울에 {가다가/가는 도중에} 집으로 다시 돌아왔다.
On his way to Seoul, he came back home.
준서는 잠을 {자다가/자는 도중에} 꿈을 많이 꾼다.
Jun-Seo dreams a lot in the middle of sleeping.

● Concession: '-(ㄴ/는)다 해도'
아무리 눈이 많이 {와도/온다 해도} 우리는 여행을 가려고 한다.
Even if it snows heavily, we plan to start travelling.
수학 문제를 풀기가 {어려워도/어렵다 해도} 포기하지 마세요.
Even though it is difficult to solve maths questions, don't give up.

- **Condition**: '-(으)ㄴ/는/(으)ㄹ 경우에는', '-(으)ㄴ/는 날에는'

내일 비가 많이 {오면/올 경우에는} 운동 경기를 취소합시다.

If it rains a lot, let's cancel the sports game.

그가 우리의 비밀을 {알면/아는 날에는} 정말 큰일이 날 거야.

If he finds out our secret, we will be in great trouble.

- **Cause/Reason**: '-기 때문에', '-는 바람에', '-(으)ㄴ/는 통에', '-(으)ㄴ/는 고(故)로', '-(으)ㄴ/는 탓에', '-(으)ㄴ/는 관계로', '-(으)ㄴ/는 까닭에', '-(으)ㄴ/는 터라', '-(으)ㄴ/는 만큼', '-(으)ㄴ/는 이상'

너무 오랫동안 비가 안 {와서/왔기 때문에} 저수지가 다 말라 버렸다.

It has not rained for too long, so the reservoir showed its bottom.

준서와 민서가 {싸워서/싸우는 바람에} 회의가 제대로 되지 않았다.

Because Jun-Seo and Min-Seo had a row, the meeting did not proceed smoothly.

칭찬을 너무 많이 {해서/하는 통에} 다들 쑥스러워했다.

Because they received too many compliments, they all became red-faced.

그녀가 잘못을 {빌어서/비는 고로} 용서를 해 주었다.

Because she apologized for her fault, I forgave her.

민서가 나를 자꾸 {비난해서/비난하는 탓에} 나는 속이 많이 상했다.

Because Min-Seo kept criticizing me repeatedly, I was very upset.

배가 너무 {불러서/부른 관계로} 더 이상 아무 것도 먹고 싶지 않다.

Because I am too full, I don't feel like eating any more.

그가 자꾸 거짓말을 {해서/하는 까닭에} 모두들 화가 많이 났다.

Because he kept on lying, everyone got quite mad.

그가 교통사고를 당한 사실을 알고 {있어서/있던 터라} 아무도 놀라지 않았다.

Since they knew about his accident, nobody was surprised.

이미 경기가 {끝났으니까/끝난 만큼} 이제 후회는 하지 말자.

Since the game is over, let's not feel regret.

그 사건의 진실을 알고 {있으니까/있는 이상} 입을 다물고 있을 수가 없다.

Since I know the truth about the incident, I cannot stay tight-lipped.

- **Purpose/Intention**: '-기 위하여'

민서는 공부를 {하려고/하기 위하여} 도서관에 갔다.

Min-Seo, to study, went to the library.

그는 점심을 {먹으러/먹기 위해} 식당으로 향했다.

He, to have lunch, headed to the cafeteria.

- **Result: '-기까지'**

  민서는 유명한 디자이너가 {되도록/되기까지} 한 평생 노력해 왔다.

  Min-Seo, until she became a renowned designer, strived throughout her life.

  준서가 교수가 {되도록/되기까지} 그의 아버지가 많이 도와주었다.

  Until Jun-Seo became a professor, his father helped him a lot.

- **Circumstance: '-(으)ㄴ/는 마당에', '-(으)ㄴ/는 터에', '-(으)ㄴ/는 판에'**

  이미 게임이 {끝났는데/끝난 마당에} 후회해야 무슨 소용이 있나?

  Once the game is over, what is the use of regret?

  준서가 이미 런던으로 {갔는데/간 터에} 지금 와서 무슨 말을 하겠니?

  Now that Jun-Seo has already gone to London, what can we say about it now?

  목구멍에 풀칠을 하기도 {어려운데/어려운 판에} 세계 여행이 웬 말이야?

  When it is difficult to even live from hand to mouth, how can we travel the world?

- **Comparison: '-(으)ㄴ/는/(으)ㄹ 것보다', '-기보다', '-(으)ㄴ/는/(으)ㄹ 바에야', '-(으)ㄴ/는/(으)ㄹ 바에는'**

  {앓느니/앓는 것보다} 차라리 죽는 것이 낫다.

  It is better to die than suffer.

  그녀와 {결혼하느니/결혼하기보다} 나는 차라리 혼자 살겠다.

  It is better to live alone than marry her.

  밥 대신 빵을 {먹느니/먹을 바에야} 나는 차라리 굶겠다.

  I would rather starve than eat bread instead of rice.

- **Simile/Figure: '-(으)ㄴ/는/(으)ㄹ 것처럼', '-(으)ㄴ/는/(으)ㄹ 양'**

  구름에 달 {가듯이/가는 것처럼} 잘도 간다.

  As clouds overshadow the moon, it moves fast!

  음악이 사람을 행복하게 {하듯이/하는 것처럼} 그림도 사람을 행복하게 한다.

  As music brings happiness to people, pictures also bring happiness to people.

  대마도가 한국 땅이 {아니듯이/아닌 것처럼} 독도도 일본 땅이 아니다.

  As Taemado is not Korean territory, Dokdo is not Japan's territory.

  그 살인범은 아무렇지도 {않듯이/않은 양} 태연하게 행동을 재연했다.

  The murderer reenacted his action as if he doesn't give a damn.

- **Proportion: '-에 따라서'**

  자주 {만날수록/만남에 따라서} 정도 깊어지는 법이다.

  The more they meet, the closer they get.

  한국 인삼은 많이 {먹을수록/먹음에 따라서} 몸에 좋다.

  The more we eat Korean ginseng, the healthier we will be.

- **Degree**: '-(으)ㄹ 정도로', '-(으)ㄹ 때까지'
  그는 민서에게 귀가 {아프도록/아플 정도로} 잔소리를 했다.
  He nagged Min-Seo to the point of hurting Min-Seo's ears.
  그는 {밤새도록/밤샐 때까지} 한국어 공부를 했다.
  He studied so much to stay awake throughout the night.

- **Addition**: '-(으)ㄹ 뿐만 아니라'
  한국 고추는 {매울뿐더러/매울 뿐만 아니라} 맛도 좋다.
  Korean chilli peppers are not only pungent but also tasty.
  한국은 볼거리도 {많을뿐더러/많을 뿐만 아니라} 먹을거리도 많다.
  Korea has not only many tourist destinations but also many delicacies.

22.3 Korean cultural aspects as reflected in sentence connection

First, Koreans love using connective expressions. In fact, several connective endings can be often found in a single sentence. There are five to six connective endings in the following sentences.

물건을 잃**으면** 적게 잃는 것이**고**, 신용을 잃**으면** 크게 잃는 것이**며**, 용기를 잃**으면** 모든 것을 잃는 것이다.
Losing a thing is a small loss, and losing credibility is a big loss, and losing courage is a loss of everything.

그런데 갑자기 그 집 막내아들이 내 손을 잡**고** 집으로 데려 가더**니** 형수를 나무라**면서** 젖은 내 머리를 닦아 주었**는데**, 그때부터 나는 그를 삼촌이라 부르**며** 의지했**고** 삼촌도 나를 아껴 주었다.
By the way, all of a sudden, the youngest son of that family grabbed my hand and took me into the house and dried my wet hair while scolding

his sister-in-law. From that time, I called him Uncle and relied on him, and Uncle also loved me dearly.

Second, it is important for the reader to understand the semantic function of connective endings in consideration of the context and circumstances, since most of the connective endings have several semantic functions. For example, '-고' has following semantic functions:

[Serial] 바람이 불고 비가 온다. / It is windy and rainy.
[Simultaneity] 그는 온종일 우산을 쓰고 다녔다.
He held an umbrella all day long.
[Completion] 민서는 옷을 잘 차려입고 나들이를 갔다.
Min-Seo wore nice clothes and went on a picnic.

[Cause/Reason] 그는 상한 음식을 먹고 배탈이 났다.
He got a stomachache after having stale food.
[Emphasis] 멀고 먼 고향, 언제 한 번 찾아가려나.
When will I ever go back to my hometown that is far, far away.

Third, there are various forms of connections, such as connection of words, phrases and clauses.

[Word connection] 우리 아버지는 30년 전에 돌아가셨다.
My father passed away 30 years ago.
나뭇잎이 벌써 다 떨어졌다.
Leaves have all fallen off already.

[Phrase connection] 나는 빨리 고향으로 돌아가고 싶다.
I want to go back to my hometown as soon as possible.

한국 김치를 먹<u>어</u> 봤어요?

Have you ever tasted Korean Kimchi?

나는 그녀에게 큰 박수를 **쳐** 주<u>**려고**</u> 해요.

I would like to give her a big hand.

[Clause connection] 한국에는 봄이 오<u>**면**</u> 꽃이 많이 핀다.

In Korea, when spring comes, flowers blossom a lot.

그는 하버드 대학에 유학을 가<u>서</u> 역사학을 공부하고 있다.

He entered Harvard University and is studying history

민서는 책을 빌리<u>**려고**</u> 도서관에 갔다.

Min-Seo, to borrow some books, went to the library.

23 Sentence embedding

23.1 What is sentence embedding?

Sentence embedding(내포) is one way of expanding a sentence, by using the end of the embedded sentence so that one sentence can be embedded in another sentence. When a sentence is embedded, the sentence becomes a clause. The embedded clause is divided into noun clause, adnominal clause, adverbial clause, predicate clause and quotative clause.

23.2 Types and characteristics of sentence embedding

23.2.1 Embedding noun clauses

Noun clauses(명사절) are generally created by predicates that take the form of '-(으)ㅁ, -기, -(으)ㄴ/는 것'. However, sentence endings like '-(으)/느냐, -(으)ㄴ/는가, -(으)ㄴ/는지' can be used in a noun clause without any changes. The noun clause can act as subject, object or adverb in the sentence.

- First, noun clauses can act as a **subject**

[준서가 범죄를 {했음/한 것}]이 사실로 드러났다.
Jun-Seo's committing a crime turned out to be a fact.
[외국인들이 1년 안에 한국 문화를 모두 이해하기]가 힘들다.
It is hard for foreigners to fully understand the Korean culture within one year.
[얼마나 효과적으로 한국어 공부를 {하느냐/하는가/하는지}]가 중요하다.
How effectively you study Korean is important.

- Second, noun clauses can act as an **object**

나는 [민서가 {피아니스트임/피아니스트인 것}]을 최근에 알았다.
I recently realized that Min-Seo was a pianist.
우리는 [네가 내년에 꼭 한국으로 유학을 갈 수 있기]를 바란다.
We hope that you will definitely go to Korea to study next year.
[우리가 얼마나 성실하게 공부했는가]를 생각해 보자.
Let's think about how hard we studied.

- Third, noun clauses can act as an **adverb**

[이 짧은 말이 다른 사람의 마음을 {움직임/움직이는 것}]에 주목해 주세요.
Please pay attention to how this short word can change the minds of others.
이곳의 기온은 [우리가 노후를 보내기]에 아주 적당하다.
The temperature here is very adequate for us to spend our latter years.
준서의 의견은 [민서가 며칠 전에 제안했던 것]과 매우 비슷하다.
Jun-Seo's opinion is very similar to what Min-Seo suggested a few days ago.
그는 [고흐가 이 그림을 어떻게 그렸는가]에 관심을 가지고 있다.
He is interested in how Van Gogh painted this picture.

23.2.2 Embedding adnominal clauses

Adnominal clauses(관형절) are generally created by predicates that take the form of adnominal endings such as '-는, -(으)ㄴ, -(으)ㄹ'. However, sentence endings like '-(으)ㄴ/는다, -(으)/느냐, -(아/어)라, -자' can be attached to '-(고 하)는' to create an adnominal clause. Adnominal clauses are divided into relative adnominal clause and appositional adnominal clause.

23.2.2.1 Relative adnominal clause

Relative adnominal clause(관계관형절) refers to clauses where common elements of the embedded sentence and the matrix sentence have a modifying relationship. In other words, in a relative adnominal clause, the common element (present in both embedded and matrix sentences) is deleted in the embedded sentence, the sentence ending of the embedded sentence is changed into '-는[present], -(으)ㄴ[past], -(으)ㄹ[future]' and then is embedded into the matrix sentence.

For example, if sentence① (embedded sentence) is embedded into sentence② (matrix sentence), find the element present in both sentences (i.e. 나, 준서), delete 나 and 준서 in sentence①, and replace the prefinal ending '-았-' and sentence ending '-다' with adnominal ending '-ㄴ'.

> Sentence①: (나)는 어제 (준서)를 만났다. / I met Jun-Seo yesterday.
> Sentence②: 나는 준서에게 선물을 주었다. / I gave Jun-Seo a present.
> → 나는 <u>**어제 만난 준서**</u>에게 선물을 주었다.
>
> I gave a present to Jun-Seo whom I met yesterday.

Adnominal endings can be categorized as below according to the tense.

	Present progressive	Past perfect	Past-retrospective	Past perfect-retrospective	Future-surmise/volition
Verb	-는	-(으)ㄴ	-던	-았/었던	-(으)ㄹ
Adjective	-(으)ㄴ	-(으)ㄴ	-던	-았/었던	
이다	-ㄴ		-던	-었던	-ㄹ
있다	-는		-던	-었던	-을

● **Verbs** come with following adnominal endings. Use '-는' for present progressive verbs, '-(으)ㄴ' for past perfect verbs and '-(으)ㄹ' for future-surmise or future-volition verbs. Use '-던' for past-retrospective, which is a combination of past-retrospective prefinal ending '-더-' and adnominal ending '-ㄴ'. Use '-았/었던-' for past perfect-retrospective, which is a combination of past perfect prefinal ending '-았/었-', recollective prefinal ending '-더-' and adnominal ending '-ㄴ'.

준서가 {만나는/만난/만나던/만났던/만날} 사람이 바로 민서다.
The person that Jun-Seo sees is Min-Seo.
민서가 {읽는/읽은/읽던/읽었던/읽을} 책이 소설 '춘향전'이다.
The book Min-Seo read is Chunhyang Story.

● **Adjectives** come with following adnominal endings. Use '-(으)ㄴ' for present progressive and past perfect, '-던' for past-retrospective and '-았/었던' for past perfect-retrospective.

민서는 디자인이 예쁜 차를 {산다/샀다}
Min-Seo {purchases/purchased} a car with a pretty design.
민서는 건강이 안 {좋던/좋았던} 때가 있었다.
Min-Seo {was/had been} once unhealthy.

There are no certain adnominal endings for future-surmise/volition adjectives. Yet, '-(으)ㄹ 것', which is a combination of adnominal ending '-(으)ㄹ' and dependent noun '것/거', can convey surmise regardless of the tense and form.

> 나는 마음씨가 {착한/*착할} 사람을 좋아한다.
> I like people who are good in nature.
> 이 옷은 네게는 좀 작을 거야.
> I guess this outfit would be a little small for you.
> 예전에는 이 강이 꽤 넓었을 것 같다.
> In the past, I guess this river would be very wide.

● 이다 comes with following adnominal endings. Use '-ㄴ' for present progressive, '-던' for past-retrospective, '-었던' for past perfect-retrospective and '-ㄹ' for future-surmise.

> 그 사람에게는 야구 선수인 아들이 있다.
> He has a son who is a baseball player.
> 신문 기자이던 애인이 갑자기 나를 찾아왔다. / My boyfriend(girlfriend) who was a newspaper reporter suddenly came to see me.
> 예전에 성당이었던 건물이 요즘은 박물관으로 쓰이고 있다. / The building, which had been a cathedral in the past, is now being used as a museum.
> 민서와 결혼할 사람이 반드시 은행원일 필요는 없다.
> Min-Seo does not necessarily need to marry a banker.

● 있다 comes with following adnominal endings. Use '-는' for present progressive, '-던' for past-retrospective, '-었던' for past perfect-retrospective and '-을' for future-surmise.

> 지금까지 서울 광장에 모여 있는 사람이 몇 명이나 되지?
> How many have gathered in Seoul Plaza till now?
> 그 당시 교통사고 현장에 있던 사람을 찾아보자.

Let's find people who were at the site of the car accident at that time.

10년 전 준서가 머물고 있었던 곳이 바로 뉴욕이었다.

The place where Jun-Seo had been staying ten years ago was New York.

한국 김치가 맛이 있을 것 같아요.

I guess Korea's Kimchi would be tasty.

23.2.2.2 Appositional adnominal clause

Appositional adnominal clause(동격관형절) refers to adnominal clauses where the contents of the embedded sentence has an identical meaning to a noun in the matrix sentence. In other words, in an appositional adnominal clause, the matrix and the embedded sentence do not share any common element, so there is no need to delete a certain element in the embedded sentence.

Appositional adnominal clauses are divided into long appositional adnominal clause which affixes '-(고 하)는' to the sentence ending and short appositional adnominal clause which affixes '-ㄴ/는' instead of the ending of the embedded sentence.

- **Long appositional adnominal clause**

In a **long appositional adnominal clause**(긴 동격관형절), adnominal ending '-는' is attached to the end of the embedded sentence to modify the appositional verb that follows. Attach '-(ㄴ/는)다는, -(이)라는' if the embedded sentence is an declarative sentence, '-(으/느)냐는' if it is an interrogative sentence, '-라는' if it is an imperative sentence, '-자는' if a propositional sentence and '-(ㄴ/는)다는' if an exclamatory sentence.

For instance, in order to embed sentence① (the embedded sentence) into sentence② (the matrix sentence) as a Long appositional adnominal clause, attach adnominal ending '-는' to the ending of sentence①, '-다',

and insert the clause in the place of 그 in sentence②.

Sentence①: 준서는 매우 정직하다. / Jun-Seo is very honest.
Sentence②: 나는 그 사실을 알고 있다. / I am aware of the fact.
→ 나는 <u>준서가 매우 정직하다는</u> 사실을 알고 있다.
        └─── (=) ───↑

I am aware that Jun-Seo is very honest.

- **Short appositional adnominal clause**

In a **Short appositional adnominal clause**(짧은 동격관형절), the ending of the embedded sentence is replaced with adnominal ending '-ㄴ/는' to modify the appositional noun that follows.

For example, in order to embed sentence① (the embedded sentence) into sentence② (the matrix sentence), attach adnominal ending '-ㄴ/는' to the end of sentence①, '-다', and insert the clause in the place of 그 in sentence②.

Sentence①: 준서가 나의 부탁을 거절했다. / Jun-Seo refused my request.
Sentence②: 나는 그 이유를 잘 모르겠다. / I don't know why.
→ 나는 <u>준서가 나의 부탁을 거절한</u> 이유를 모르겠다.
        └─── (=) ───↑

I don't know why Jun-Seo refused my request.

- **Appositional noun**

Appositional noun(동격명사) can either: come with Long appositional adnominal clause only; or come with Short appositional adnominal clause only; or come with both Long and Short appositional adnominal clauses.

Adnominal clause	Appositional noun	
Long appositional adnominal clause	Independent noun	고백 'confession', 낭설 'canard', 느낌 'feeling', 독촉 'urging', 명령 'command', 보고/보도 'report', 소문 'rumors', 소식 'news', 정보 'information', etc.
Short appositional adnominal clause	Independent noun	가능성 'possibility', 경험 'experience', 경우 'case', 기억 'memory', 사건 'event', 예정 'schedule', 용기 'courage', 까닭 'reason', etc.
	Dependent noun	데, 리, 바, 수, 적, 줄, 듯, 양, 체, 만, 법, 성
Long or Short appositional adnominal clause	Independent noun	견해 'opinion', 결심 'resolution', 목적 'purpose', 사실 'fact', 생각 'thinking', 약점 'weakness', 연락 'contact', 요청 'request', 욕심 'greed', 이론 'theory', 질문 'question', etc.
	Dependent noun	것

23.2.2.3 Characteristics of adnominal clauses

Koreans in general use adnominal ending '-는' in following cases even though they are supposed to use adnominal ending '-(으)ㄴ' to convey the past tense.

① Use present-tense adnominal endings to represent habitual behavior, since habitual behavior is not a one-off event but the result of a certain event that had continued from a certain point in the past. In other words, they represent the 'then-present' based on that time of the sentence.

*그는 평생 동안 학생들을 가르<u>친</u> 직업에 종사했다.
→ 그는 평생 동안 학생들을 가르<u>치는</u> 직업에 종사했다.
    He dedicated his life to teaching students.
*제 아버지께서는 작년까지만 해도 농사지<u>은</u> 일을 해 오셨어요.

→ 제 아버지께서는 작년까지만 해도 농사짓<u>는</u> 일을 해 오셨어요.

My father, until last year, had been engaged in farming.

② Use present-tense adnominal ending '-는' or future-tense adnominal ending '-(으)ㄹ' in front of nouns representing the process of a behavior, '중, 도중, 동안, 과정', because the process of a behavior implies that the behavior is ongoing at the moment.

*고향에 간 동안 차 안에서 책을 읽었다.

→ 고향에 가<u>는</u> 동안 차 안에서 책을 읽었다.

On my way to hometown, I read books in the car.

*그 일을 한 과정에 많은 시행착오를 겪었습니다.

→ 그 일을 하<u>는</u> 과정에 많은 시행착오를 겪었습니다.

In the process of doing the work, I experienced many trials and errors.

③ Verbs related to attire, such as (옷을) 입다 'to wear', (안경을, 모자를) 쓰다 'to put on glasses or hats', (구두를, 양말을) 신다 'to put on shoes or socks', (넥타이를) 매다 'to wear a tie', (시계를, 허리띠를) 차다 'to put on a watch', (귀걸이를) 걸다 'to put on earrings', (스카프를) 두르다 'to wear a scarf', (목걸이를) 하다 'to put on a necklace', (메달을) 달다 'to drape someone with medals', (양말을) 벗다 'to take off socks' should come with past-tense adnominal ending '-(으)ㄴ' even though it signifies the present, because the action has been completed a long time ago. These verbs may also come with '-는', but this can change the meaning of the sentence.

In the sentences below, '안경을 낀, 모자를 쓴' used the past-tense expression '-ㄴ', but they mean present-status, i.e. currently in the state of wearing glasses, currently in the state of wearing a hat. Yet, '안경을 끼는' and '모자를 쓰는', which uses the present-tense expression '-는',

imply a habitual behavior. If combined with such adverbs as 항상 'always', 늘 'at all times', 매일 'every day', 매주 'every week', 매년 'every year' and 날마다 'on a daily basis', the meaning becomes even more clear. Moreover, the present-tense '-는' may sometimes convey present progressive.

안경을 **낀** 사람은 손을 들어 주세요.
Those of you wearing glasses, please put your hands up.
안경을 **항상** 끼**는** 사람은 손을 들어 주세요.
Those of you who always wear glasses, please put your hands up.
모자를 **쓴** 저 신사는 누구예요?
Who is that gentleman wearing a hat?
모자를 **늘** 쓰**는** 저 신사는 누구예요?
Who is that gentleman who always wears a hat?

However, even verbs related to attire should come with present-tense '-는' if combined with '-고 있-'.

안경을 끼**고 있는** 사람은 손을 들어 주세요.
Those of you wearing glasses, please put your hands up.
모자를 쓰**고 있는** 저 신사는 누구예요?
Who is that gentleman wearing a hat?

■ Adnominal clause and connective ending

First, it is very difficult to understand a sentence if adnominal clauses continue in series. Therefore, to make the sentence much easier to understand, adnominal endings can be connected into a clause with a connective ending.

안경을 **낀**, 키가 작은 한 여자가 나를 쏘아 보고 있다.
A woman wearing glasses who is short was giving me a hostile glare.
→ 안경을 끼고 키가 작은 한 여자가 나를 쏘아 보고 있다.
    A woman wearing glasses who is short was giving me a hostile glare.

나는 미국으로 이민을 가서 **산** 한 여자에 대**한** 일생을 소설로 썼다.
I wrote a novel about the life of a woman who emigrated to the US.
→ 한 여자가 미국으로 이민을 갔**는데**, 나는 그녀의 일생을 소설로 썼다.
    A woman emigrated to the US, and I wrote a novel about her life.

서민들의 쉬**운** '내 집 마련'을 돕기 위**한** 연금 저축이 만들어졌다.
Pension savings were created to help ordinary citizens to buy their own home
more easily.
→ 서민들이 '내 집'을 쉽게 마련할 수 있**도록** 도와주려고 연금 저축이 만들어졌다.
    Pension savings were created to help ordinary citizens to buy their own home
    more easily.

Second, making modifiers into adverbial clauses or connective clauses
instead of adnominal clauses, can make the sentence easier and more precise.

시청자 여러분의 많**은** 참여가 있기를 바랍니다.
→ 시청자 여러분께서 참여를 많**이** 해 주시기 바랍니다.
    We are looking forward to your active participation.

앞으로의 교육은 학생들의 특성을 잘 개발할 수 있**는** 교육이 되어야 한다.
→ 앞으로는 학생들이 자신의 특성을 잘 개발할 수 있**도록** 교육해야 한다.
    Going forward, students need to be educated such so that they can develop
    their talents well.

빈곤층 아동들의 학자금 마련을 위**한** 바자회를 열었다.
→ 빈곤층 아동들의 학자금을 마련하**려고** 바자회를 열었다.
    A charity bazaar was held to provide underprivileged children with educational
    expenses.

23.2.3 Embedding adverbial clauses

In **adverbial clauses**(부사절), the predicate of the sentence is represented by '-이, -게, etc', modifying the predicate that follows.

For example, in order to embed sentence① (the embedded sentence) into sentence② (the matrix sentence) as an adverbial clause, attach adverbial ending '-이' after the ending of sentence①, '-다', and insert this expression in front of the predicate of sentence②.

Sentence①: 준서^{i}가 도시에서 자란 아이들과 다르다.
            Jun-Seo is different from children grown up in cities.
Sentence②: 준서^{i}는 매우 순수하다. / Jun-Seo is very naive.
→ 준서^{i}는 도시에서 자란 아이들과 달리 순수하다.

Jun-Seo is naive, unlike children grown up in cities.

It is disputed whether the following sentences should be considered as an adverbial clause or a preceding clause of a dominant-subordinate sentence. However, it is true that they modify the predicate that follows.

Sentence①: 무궁화 꽃^{i}이 아주 예쁘다. / Mugunghwa is very beautiful.
Sentence②: 무궁화 꽃^{i}이 뜰에 피어 있다.
            Mugunghwa has blossomed in the garden.
→ 무궁화 꽃^{i}이 뜰에 아주 예쁘게 피어 있다.

Mugunghwa has blossomed very beautifully in the garden.

Sentence①: 준서^{i}가 한국어 공부를 잘할 수 있다.
            Jun-Seo can study Korean well.
Sentence②: 나는 준서^{i}를 도와주었다. / I helped Jun-Seo.
→ 나는 준서^{i}가 한국어 공부를 잘할 수 있도록 도와주었다.

I helped Jun-Seo so that he can study Korean well.

23.2.4 Embedding predicate clauses

Predicate clauses(서술절) refer to sentences being embedded in another sentence without any changes in form, acting as the predicate of the matrix sentence. They do not take the form of a certain ending.

For example, in order to embed sentence① (the embedded sentence) into sentence② as a predicate clause, replace the predicate of sentence② with sentence①.

> Sentence①: **(토끼ⁱ의)** 앞발이 짧다. / A rabbit's foreleg is short.
> Sentence②: 토끼ⁱ가/는 있다. / A rabbit has.
> → 토끼ⁱ가/는 앞발이 짧다. / A rabbit's foreleg is short.

However, it is disputed whether to consider the following sentences as an embedded predicate clause or a sentence with double subjects, or a composition of topic-comment.

> Sentence①: **(남대문시장ⁱ의)** 옷값이 매우 싸다.
> Clothes in Namdaemun Market are very cheap.
> Sentence②: 남대문시장ⁱ이/은 있다. / Namdaemun Market has.
> → 남대문시장ⁱ이/은 옷값이 매우 싸다.
>
> Clothes in Namdaemun Market are very cheap.

> Sentence①: **(준서ⁱ의)** 아들이 유명한 변호사이다.
> Jun-Seo's son is a renowned lawyer.
> Sentence②: 준서ⁱ가/는 있다. / Jun-Seo has.
> → 준서ⁱ가/는 아들이 유명한 변호사이다.
>
> Jun-Seo has a son who is a renowned lawyer.

23.2.5 Embedding quotative clauses

Quotative clauses(인용절) refer to quotation of speech, writing, thoughts, etc. of others or oneself. The embedded sentence complements the meaning of the predicate of the matrix sentence. Quotative clauses are divided into direct quotative clauses and indirect quotative clauses.

23.2.5.1 Direct quotative clauses

Direct quotative clauses(직접 인용절) refer to verbatim quotation of speech, writing, thoughts, etc. of others or oneself, and are expressed with double quotation marks ["…"], quotative particle '-(이)라고' or quotative verb '하다'.

- **Direct quotation by quotative particle**

This refers to verbatim quotation plus quotative particle '-(이)라고'. Since it is a literary style, direct quotation is hardly ever used in everyday speech.

For example, when 'I' below wants to quote 'Jun-Seo's speech' by adding quotative particle '-(이)라고', insert double quotation marks to Jun-Seo's speech and add quotative particle '-(이)라고' thereafter.

> Jun-Seo: 한국어 공부하러 학교에 가자.
>   Let's go to school to study Korean.
> I : 준서가 나에게 "한국어 공부하러 학교에 가자."**라고** 말했다.
>   Jun-Seo said to me, "let's go to school to study Korea."

Direct quotative clauses with '-(이)라고' can use declarative, interrogative, imperative, propositive and exclamatory endings. They are embedded into the matrix sentence without any modification.

준서는 나에게 "너를 지금도 믿**는다**."**라고** 말했다.

Jun-Seo said to me, "I still trust you."

민서는 "언제 고국으로 돌아가**니?**"**라고** 했다.

Min-Seo said, "When are you going back to your home country?"

나는 민서에게 "빨리 고향으로 돌아가**라**."**라고** 말했다.

I said to Min-Seo, "Go back to your hometown ASAP."

그는 "올해는 책을 많이 읽**자**."**라고** 했다.

He said, "Let's read books a lot this year."

어머니께서는 "야! 벌써 봄이 왔**구나!**"**라고** 말씀하셨다.

Mother said, "Hey! It's already spring!"

Following verbs are frequently used in matrix sentences.

[Question and answer]

하다 'to do'   말하다 'to speak'

말씀하다 'to speak'   소리치다 'to shout'

꾸짖다 'to scold'   비난하다 'to criticize'

칭찬하다 'to commend'   격려하다 'to encourage'

묻다 'to ask'   대답하다 'to answer'

[Thoughts]

결심하다 'to make up one's mind'   느끼다 'to feel'

믿다 'to believe'   상상하다 'to imagine'

생각하다 'to think'   추측하다 'to predict'

판단하다 'to judge'   확신하다 'to be convinced'

[Writing]

쓰다 'to write'   적다 'to jot down'

- **Expressions by quotative verb 하다**

This refers to verbatim quotation plus quotative verb '-하고'(◁하[verb stem]-고[quotative ending]). It is very frequently used in everyday speech.

For example, when 'I' want to quote the speech of '준서' by using quotative verb 하다, insert double quotation marks around 준서's speech and add quotative verb '-하고' thereafter.

Jun-Seo: 나는 행복하다. / I am happy.

I: 준서가 나에게 "나는 행복하다." <u>하고</u> 말했다.

Jun-Seo said to me, "I am happy."

Direct quotative clauses with 하다 can use declarative, interrogative, imperative, propositive and exclamatory endings. They are embedded into the matrix sentence without any modification.

그는 "한국말을 잘하고 싶<u>다</u>." <u>하고</u> 말했다.

He said, "I want to speak Korean well."

준서는 내게 "오늘 왜 학교에 가지 않<u>니</u>?" <u>하고</u> 물었다.

Jun-Seo asked me, "Why are you not going to school today?"

아저씨는 "어려움이 와도 절대 용기를 잃지 마<u>라</u>." <u>하고</u> 격려해 주셨다.

He encouraged me, saying "Do not lose courage even if you face adversities."

어머니는 우리에게 "좀 더 넓은 아파트로 이사를 가<u>자</u>." <u>하고</u> 제안하셨다.

Mother suggested to us, "Let's move to a larger apartment."

- ● **Quotation of words or phrases**

Not only sentences but also words or phrases can be quoted. In general, words can be quoted by using quotative particle '-(이)라고' and quotative verb 하다.

준서가 {"오! 하나님"<u>이라고</u>/"오! 하나님" <u>하고</u>} 소리를 질렀다.

Jun-Seo shouted, "Oh! God".

선생님께서 {"김준서"<u>라고</u>/"김준서" <u>하고</u>} 이름을 불렀다.

Sir called his name, "Jun-Seo Kim."

However, onomatopoeia and exclamations can be quoted by quotative verb 하다 only. In particular, direct quotation by 하다 can quote even the emotional state of the speaker, so it can deliver the feeling of the speaker more realistically than (이)라고-quotation.

갑자기 {*"멍멍! 멍멍!"**이라고**/"멍멍! 멍멍!" **하고**} 개가 짖기 시작했다.
Suddenly, the dog started barking, "woof! woof!"
멀리 산 너머에서 {*"펑! 펑! 펑!"**이라고**/"펑! 펑! 펑!" **하고**} 축포가 터졌다.
There were cannon salute beyond the mountain, "pop! pop! pop!"
준서는 주사를 맞자 {*"아야!"**라고**/"아야!" **하고**} 고통스러워했다.
Jun-Seo was suffering after he got a shop, "ouch! ouch!"

23.2.5.2 Indirect quotative clause

Indirect quotative clause(간접 인용절) refers to quotation of others' or one's speech, writing, thoughts, etc. that is expressed from the speaker's perspective. Indirect quotative clause modifies the sentence structure radically, which undermines the vitality that could be felt in direct quotative clauses.

Unlike direct quotative clauses, indirect quotative clauses do not use such punctuation marks as full stop[.], exclamation mark[!], question mark[?], double quotation mark[" "], single quotation mark[' '], or double corner brackets [『 』] and corner brackets [「 」].

① Indirect quotative clause is made by combining the sentence ending of the embedded clause with quotative particle -고. In **declarative sentences**, indirect quotative clauses end with '-ㄴ/는다고[verb], -다고[adjective], or -라고[이다]'.

준서는 "할아버지께서 서울에서 살고 계십니다."라고 말했다.
Jun-Seo said, "Grandfather is living in Seoul."
→ 준서는 할아버지께서 서울에 살고 계**신다고** 말했다.
　 Jun-Seo said that his grandfather is living in Seoul.

준서는 민서에게 "나는 너무 행복해." 하고 말했다.

Jun-Seo said to Min-Seo, "I am very happy."

→ 준서는 민서에게 행복하**다고** 말했다.

  Jun-Seo said to Min-Seo that he was very happy.

그는 나에게 "저 동물의 이름은 코끼리예요."라고 말했다.

He said to me, "The name of that animal is elephant."

→ 그는 나에게 저 동물의 이름을 코끼리**라고** 말했다.

  He said to me that the name of that animal was elephant.

② In **interrogative** sentences, indirect quotative clauses end with '-(느)냐고[verb], -(으)냐고[adjective], -냐고[이다]'.

그는 외국인들에게 "경주에 가 보았습니까?"라고 물었다.

He asked the foreigners, "Have you been to Gyeongju?"

→ 그는 외국인들에게 경주에 가 보았**느냐고** 물었다.

  He asked the foreigners whether they have been to Gyeongju.

준서는 존에게 "옷이 너무 작아?" 하고 물었다.

Jun-Seo asked John, "Are these clothes too small for me?"

→ 준서는 존에게 옷이 너무 작**으냐고** 물었다.

  Jun-Seo asked John whether the clothes are too small for him.

필립은 민서에게 "이것이 바로 김치예요?"라고 물었다.

Philip asked Min-Seo, "Is this Kimchi?"

→ 필립은 민서에게 이것이 바로 김치**냐고** 물었다.

  Philip asked Min-Seo whether it was Kimchi.

③ In **imperative** sentences, indirect quotative clauses end with '-(으)라고[verb], -으라고[있다]'. Adjectives and 이다 do not have imperative forms, so they cannot make indirect quotations.

어머니께서는 나에게 "공부 좀 열심히 해." 하고 말씀하셨다.

Mother told me, "Study hard."
→ 어머니께서는 나에게 공부 좀 열심히 하**라고** 말씀하셨다.
　　Mother told me to study hard.

선생님은 민서에게 "좀 더 큰 꿈을 가져라."라고 하셨다.
Sir told Min-Seo, "Have a bigger dream."
→ 선생님은 민서에게 좀 더 큰 꿈을 가지**라고** 하셨다.
　　Sir told Min-Seo to have a bigger dream.

간호사가 준서에게 "이쪽으로 오세요." 하고 말했다.
Nurse said to Jun-Seo, "Come this way."
→ 간호사가 준서에게 이쪽으로 오**라고** 말했다.
　　Nurse said to Jun-Seo to come that way.

형이 동생에게 "다른 데 가지 말고 여기 있어."라고 충고했다.
Elder brother advised younger brother, "Don't go anywhere but stay here."
→ 형이 동생에게 다른 데 가지 말고 여기 있**으라고** 충고했다.
　　Elder brother advised younger brother not to go anywhere but stay there.

④ In **propositive sentences**, indirect quotative clauses end with '-자고 [verb], -자고[있다]'. Adjectives and 이다 do not have propositive forms, so they cannot make indirect quotations.

선생님께서는 "이만 수업을 끝냅시다." 하고 말씀하셨다.
Teacher said, "Wrap up."
→ 선생님께서는 이만 수업을 끝내**자고** 말했다. / Teacher said to wrap up.

팀장은 "이제 새로운 프로젝트를 시작하지."라고 말했다.
Team head said, "Let's start a new project now."
→ 팀장은 이제 새로운 프로젝트를 시작하**자고** 말했다.
　　Team head suggested that we start a new project now.

소대장은 "여기에 조용히 숨어 있자." 하고 말했다.

The platoon leader said, "Let's hide here quietly."

→ 소대장은 여기에 조용히 숨어 있**자고** 말했다.

　　The platoon leader suggested that we hide there quietly.

⑤ In exclamatory sentences, indirect quotative clauses end with '-ㄴ/는 다고[verb], -다고[adjective], -다고[있다], -라고[이다]' as in the case of declarative clauses. Exclamations in the embedded sentence are omitted.

민서는 "이야, 벌써 봄이 왔네!" 하고 말했다.

Min-Seo said, "Wow, it's already spring!"

→ 민서는 벌써 봄이 왔**다고** 말했다.

　　Min-Seo said that it was already spring.

그는 "와, 바람이 너무 많이 부는구나!" 하고 말했다.

He said, "Wow, it's too windy!"

→ 그는 바람이 너무 많이 **분다고** 말했다. / He said that it was too windy.

민서는 "아, 이 꽃이 정말 예쁘구나!"라고 말했다.

Min-Seo said, "Wow, these flowers are really beautiful!"

→ 민서는 이 꽃이 정말 예쁘**다고** 말했다.

　　Min-Seo said that the flowers were really beautiful.

여행객들이 "여기가 바로 금강산이로구나!"라고 말했다.

The tourists said, "This is the Mountain Geumgang!"

→ 여행객들이 여기가 바로 금강산**이라고** 말했다.

　　The tourists said that it was the Mountain Geumgang.

● **Omission and change of components of quotative clauses**

First, the subject of the quotative clause can be omitted regardless of who the person is (first/second/third person) if the subject of the matrix sentence, the quoter, is the same person as the subject of the quotative clause. If the subject is third person, it is better to change the subject of the quotative clause into reflexive pronoun 자기 to clarify who it is.

나ⁱ는 어머니께 "나ⁱ는 민서와 결혼하겠어요." 하고 말했다.
I said to Mother, "I will marry Min-Seo."
→ 나ⁱ는 어머니께 (Øⁱ) 민서와 결혼하겠다고 말했다.
   I said to Mother that I will marry Min-Seo.

준서ⁱ는 친구들에게 "나ⁱ는 거짓말을 못해."라고 말했다.
Jun-Seo said to friends, "I cannot lie."
→ 준서ⁱ는 친구들에게 {Øⁱ, 자기ⁱ는} 거짓말을 못한다고 말했다.
   Jun-Seo said to friends that he could not lie.

Second, both the subject and the object of the quotative clause can be omitted if: ⓐ the subject of the matrix sentence is the same as the subject of the quotative clause; and ⓑ the hearer of the matrix sentence is the same as the object of the quotative clause. However, they should not be submitted if the hearer needs emphasis.

나ⁱ는 준서ʲ에게 "나ⁱ는 너ʲ를 사랑해."라고 말했다.
I said to Jun-Seo, "I love you."
→ 나ⁱ는 준서에게 (Øⁱ) 너ʲ를 사랑한다고 말했다.
   I said to Jun-Seo that I loved him.
→ 나ⁱ는 준서에게 (Øⁱ) (Øʲ) 사랑한다고 말했다.
   I said to Jun-Seo (that I) loved him.

Moreover, the subject of the quotative clause can be omitted if the subject of the matrix sentence is third person, but the object of the quotative clause cannot be omitted, otherwise it becomes uncertain who is being indicated.

준서ⁱ는 민서ʲ에게 "나ⁱ는 너ʲ를 닮고 싶어." 하고 말했다.
Jun-Seo said to Min-Seo, "I want to be like you."
→ 준서ⁱ는 민서ʲ에게 (Øⁱ) 너ʲ를 닮고 싶다고 말했다.

Jun-Seo said to Min-Seo that he wanted to be like her.

→ *준서ⁱ는 민서^j에게 (Øⁱ) (Ø^j) 닮고 싶다고 말했다.

Jun-Seo said to Min-Seo that he wanted to be like (Ø^j).

If the subject of the matrix sentence is third person and the hearer first person, both the subject and the object of the quotative clause can be omitted. If 너 in the quotative clause is replaced with 나, the sentence becomes even more clear.

민서ⁱ는 나^j에게 "나ⁱ는 너^j를 사랑해." 하고 말했다.

Min-Seo said to me, "I love you."

→ 민서ⁱ는 나^j에게 (Øⁱ) (Ø^j) 사랑한다고 말했다.

Min-Seo said to me that (she) loved (me).

→ 민서ⁱ는 나^j에게 (Øⁱ) 너^j를 사랑한다고 말했다.

Min-Seo said to me that (she) loved me.

Third, if the hearer of the matrix sentence and the subject of the quotative clause are the same, the subject of the quotative clause can be omitted as long as the quotative clause is an interrogative, imperative or propositive clause, since the entity and subject of the interrogation, command and proposition are clear.

나는 준서ⁱ에게 "너ⁱ는 한국어 숙제를 했니?" 하고 물었다.

I asked Jun-Seo, "Did you do your Korean homework?"

→ 나는 준서ⁱ에게 (Øⁱ) 한국어 숙제를 했느냐고 물었다.

I asked Jun-Seo whether (he) did his Korean homework.

준서는 민서ⁱ에게 "너ⁱ 경주로 여행을 가 봐." 하고 말했다.

Jun-Seo said to Min-Seo, "Why don't you travel to Gyeongju."

→ 준서는 민서ⁱ에게 (Øⁱ) 경주로 여행을 가 보라고 말했다.

Jun-Seo suggested to Min-Seo that (Min-Seo) travel to Gyeongju.

나ⁱ는 준서ʲ에게 "우리ⁱʲ 함께 한국어를 공부하자."라고 제안했다.

I suggested to Jun-Seo, "Let's study Korean together."

→ 나ⁱ는 준서ʲ에게 (Øⁱʲ) 함께 한국어를 공부하자고 제안했다.

I suggested to Jun-Seo that (we) study Korean together.

However, it is impossible to omit the subject of the quotative clause if the clause is declarative or exclamatory, because the person being indicated becomes uncertain if omitted.

나는 민서ⁱ에게 "너ⁱ의 한국어 시험 점수가 A야." 하고 말했다.

I said to Min-Seo, "Your Korean score is A."

→ *나는 민서ⁱ에게 (Øⁱ) 한국어 시험 점수가 A라고 말했다.

(I) said to Min-Seo that her Korean score was A.

민서는 준서ⁱ에게 "너ⁱ는 농구를 매우 잘하는구나!" 하고 말했다.

Min-Seo said to Jun-Seo, "You are very good at basketball!"

→ 민서는 준서ⁱ에게 (Øⁱ) 농구를 매우 잘한다고 말했다.

Min-Seo said to Jun-Seo that (he) was very good at basketball.

Fourth, if the subject of the matrix sentence is the same as the object of the quotative clause, the object of the quotative clause cannot be omitted as long as the quotative clause is declarative. Instead, the object of the quotative clause is changed into reflective noun, 자기.

준서ⁱ는 민서에게 "민서가 나ⁱ를 미워해."라고 말했다.

Jun-Seo said to Min-Seo, "Min-Seo hates me."

→ 준서ⁱ는 민서에게 민서가 자기ⁱ를 미워한다고 말했다.

Jun-Seo said to Min-Seo that Min-Seo hated him.

However, if the quotative clause is interrogative, it is impossible to omit the object of the quotative clause, even though it is possible to omit the subject of the interrogative clause or change the subject into reflexive noun 자기.

나는 민서에게 "너는 나를 좋아하니?" 하고 물었다.
I asked Min-Seo, "Do you like me?"
→ 나는 민서에게 (Ø) 나를 좋아하느냐고 물었다.
I asked Min-Seo whether (she) liked me.
→ 나는 민서에게 자기가 나를 좋아하느냐고 물었다.
I asked Min-Seo whether she liked me.

23.3 Korean cultural aspects as reflected in sentence embedding

First, Koreans prefer indirect quotation to direct quotation. Direct quotation is hardly ever used in everyday speech.

선생님께서는 내게 "민서야 사랑한다." 하고 말씀하셨다.
Teacher said to me, "Min-Seo, I love you."
→ 선생님께서는 내게 사랑한다고 말씀하셨다.
Teacher said to me that he loved me.

Second, noun ending '-(으)ㅁ' is hardly ever spoken in everyday speech. Instead, '-(으)ㄴ/는 것' is mainly spoken.

고향에 오심을 환영합니다. / Welcome to hometown.
→ 고향에 오신 것을 환영합니다. / Welcome to hometown.

제가 어제 성냄을 용서해 주세요. / Forgive me for getting angry yesterday.
→ 제가 어제 성낸 것을 용서해 주세요.
Forgive me for getting angry yesterday.

Section 5

Special
Expressions

Standard Korean Grammar
for Foreigners

24 Classifier

24.1 What is a classifier?

Koreans have a highly sophisticated level of **classifiers**(분류사), which refer to units and measurements of people, animals and objects.

24.2 Types and characteristics of classifiers

24.2.1 People

① 사람, 명(名): The most general classifier used to count the number of men. Applicable to men, women, adults, children, Korean, foreigners, etc.

남자 한 사람/명 'one man'
여자 두 사람/명 'two women'
어린이 세 사람/명 'three children'
어른 네 사람/명 'four adults'
노인 다섯 사람/명 'five senior people'
노약자 여섯 사람/명 'six elderly and weak people'
학생 일곱 사람/명 'seven students'

② 분: An elevated form of 사람. Applied to those older or at a higher social status than the speaker.

선생님 한 분 'one teacher'   목사님 두 분 'two reverends'
학부형 세 분 'three parents'   장관 네 분 'four ministers'
교수 다섯 분 'five professors'   판사 여섯 분 'six judges'
변호사 일곱 분 'seven lawyers'   음악가 여덟 분 'eight musicians'
조각가 아홉 분 'nine sculptors

③ 구(具): Applied to the dead.

시체 한 구 'two corpses'
어른 시체 두 구 'two adult corpses'
어린이 시체 세 구 'three children corpses'
한국인 시체 네 구 'four Korean corpses'

24.2.2 Animals, fishes and insects

① 마리: Applied to animals, birds, fishes, insects, etc.

강아지 한 마리 'one puppy'   소 두 마리 'two cows'
고양이 세 마리 'three cats'   제비 한 마리 'one swallow'
비둘기 두 마리 'two doves'   독수리 세 마리 'three eagles'
금붕어 한 마리 'one goldfish'   고등어 두 마리 'two mackerels'
갈치 세 마리 'three cutlassfishes'   개미 한 마리 'one ant'
매미 두 마리 'two cicadas'   잠자리 세 마리 'three dragonflies'

24.2.3 Objects

① 개(個): For objects in general.

사과 한 개 'one apple'   귤 두 개 'two tangerines'
접시 세 개 'three dishes'

② 장(張): For thin and flat objects.

종이 한 장 'one piece of paper'
영화 티켓 두 장 'two movie tickets'
수표 세 장 'three cheques'
전표 네 장 'four statements'
만 원짜리 다섯 장 'five 10,000 wons'
복사 용지 여섯 장 'six pieces of copy paper'
사진 일곱 장 'seven photos'
통유리 여덟 장 'eight pieces of float glass'

③ 권(眷): For books or notebooks.

한국어 책 한 권 'one Korean Language book'
수필집 두 권 'two essay books'
학급 문집 세 권 'three collections of the class' literary works'
노트 네 권 'four notebooks'
잡지 다섯 권 'five magazines'

④ 대(臺): For cars, airplanes and machines.

자가용 한 대 'one car'   트럭 두 대 'two trucks'
버스 세 대 'three buses'   비행기 네 대 'four airplanes'
여객기 다섯 대 'five passenger planes' 전투기 여섯 대 'six fighter planes'
복사기 일곱 대 'seven photocopy machines'
프린터 여덟 대 'eight printers'   텔레비전 아홉 대 'nine TVs'
냉장고 열 대 'ten refrigerators'
에어컨 열한 대 'eleven air conditioners'

세탁기 열두 대 'twelve washing machines'
건조기 열세 대 'thirteen drying machines'
피아노 열네 대 'fourteen pianos'   오디오 열다섯 대 'fifteen stereos'

⑤ 채, 동(棟): For houses or buildings.

집 한 채/동 'one house'
한옥 두 채/동 'two Korean-style houses'
양옥 세 채/동 'three Western-style houses'
주상복합 네 채/동 'four multipurpose buildings'
빌딩 다섯 동 'five buildings'

⑥ 척: For ships and vessels. Interchangeable with 대(臺).

배 한 척/대 'one ship'   여객선 두 척/대 'two passenger ships'
전함 세 척/대 'three warships'   잠수함 네 척/대 'four submarines'
항공모함 다섯 척/대 'five aircraft carriers'

⑦ 그루: For trees.

사과나무 한 그루 'one apple tree'   배나무 두 그루 'two pear trees'
귤나무 세 그루 'three mandarine trees'
대추나무 네 그루 'four jujube trees'

⑧ 알: For little and round objects.

감기약 한 알 'one pill of cold medicine'
완두콩 두 알 'two peas'   밤 세 알 'three chestnuts'
사탕 네 알 'four candies'   보석 다섯 알 'five jewel beads'
진주 여섯 알 'six pearl beads'
다이아몬드 일곱 알 'seven diamond beads'

⑨ 개비: For thin and long stick-like objects.

담배 한 개비 'one cigarette'   성냥 두 개비 'two matches'
장작 세 개비 'three pieces of split firewood'

⑩ 박스(container): For boxes.

사과 한 박스 'one box of apples'   배 두 박스 'two boxes of pears'
물 세 박스 'three boxes of water'   콜라 네 박스 'four boxes of coke'
맥주 다섯 박스 'five boxes of beer'   책 여섯 박스 'six boxes of books'
노트 일곱 박스 'seven boxes of notebooks'
옷 여덟 박스 'eight boxes of clothes'
원피스 아홉 박스 'nine boxes of dresses'

⑪ 송이: For flowers.

무궁화 한 송이 'one rose of Sharon'
진달래 두 송이 'two azaleas'
국화 세 송이 'three chrysanthemums'
벚꽃 네 송이 'four cherry blossoms'
매화 다섯 송이 'five Japanese apricot flowers'

⑫ 원: For Korean money.

이백오십 원 '250 won'   삼천사백이십 원 '3,420 won'
사만 오천육백 원 '45,600 won'   십만 팔천 원 '108,000 won'
이백육십오만 원 '2,650,000 won'
칠천사백구십팔만 원 '74,980,000 won'
일억 원 'one hundred million won'   일조 원 'one trillion won'

⑬ 층: To count the floors bottom-up, or just to count the number of floors.

일 층 'first floor' 이 층 'second floor/two-storey'
삼 층 'third floor/three-storey' 사 층 'fourth floor/four-storey'
오 층 'fifth floor/five-storey' 십 층 'tenth floor/ten-storey'
이십 층 'twentieth floor/twenty-storey'
삼십 층 'thirtieth floor/thirty-storey'
사십 층 'fortieth floor/forty-storey'
오십 층 'fiftieth floor/fifty-storey'
백 층 'hundredth floor/hundred-storey'

한 층 'one floor' 두 층 'two floors'
세 층 'three floors' 네 층 'four floors'
다섯 층 'five floors' 열 층 'ten floors'
스무 층 'twenty floors' 서른 층 'thirty floors'
마흔 층 'forty floors' 쉰 층 'fifty floors'

몇 층 'some floor' 어느 층 'which floor'
무슨 층 'what floor' 아무 층 'whichever floor'
어떤 층 'which floor'

⑭ 자루, 다스: 자루 is for pencils, knives or guns, while 다스 refers to a dozen of pencils.

연필 한 자루 'one pencil'
HB 연필 두 자루 'two HB pencils'
제도용 연필 세 자루 'three drawing pencils'
칼 한 자루 'one knife'
식칼 두 자루 'two kitchen knives'
총 한 자루 'one gun'
권총 두 자루 'two pistols'
M1 소총 세 자루 'three M1 rifles'
연필 한 다스 'one dozen of pencils'
HB 연필 두 다스 'two dozens of HB pencils'

제도용 연필 세 다스 'three dozens of drawing pencils'

⑮ 켤레: For shoes or socks.

　신 한 켤레 'one pair of shoes'
　운동화 두 켤레 'two pairs of sneakers'
　구두 세 켤레 'three pairs of shoes'
　장화 네 켤레 'four pairs of high boots'
　양말 한 켤레 'one pair of socks'
　스타킹 두 켤레 'two pairs of stockings'
　버선 세 켤레 'three pairs of traditional Korean socks'

⑯ 끼: For the number of meals.

한 끼 'one meal'		두 끼 'two meals'	
세 끼 'three meals'		여러 끼 'many meals'	
이번 끼 'this meal'		저번 끼 'last meal'	

⑰ 벌: For a set of clothes or tableware.

　양복 한 벌 'a suit of clothes'　　한복 두 벌 'two hanboks'
　트레이닝복 세 벌 'three sweatsuits'　등산복 네 벌 'four hiking outfits'
　운동복 다섯 벌 'five jogging suits'
　웨딩드레스 여섯 벌 'six wedding dresses'
　나들이복 일곱 벌 'seven outfits'
　하복 열 벌 'ten pieces of summer clothes'
　동복 열한 벌 'eleven pieces of winter clothes'
　춘추복 열세 벌 'thirteen suits for spring and autumn'
　접시 세 벌 'three sets of dishes'
　식기류 네 벌 'four sets of tablewear'

24.2.4 Weight, length and width

① **Weight:** 그램 'gram/g', 킬로그램 'kilogram/kg' and 근(斤) 'geun'

쇠고기 100그램 '100 grams of beef'
돼지고기 150그램 '150 grams of pork'
쇠고기 3킬로그램 'three kilos of beef'
돼지고기 4킬로그램 'four kilos of pork'
몸무게 60킬로그램 '60 kilos of weight'
쇠고기 한 근 'one geun of beef'
돼지고기 두 근 'two geuns of pork'

② **Length:** 밀리미터/밀리 'millimeter/mm', 센티미터/센티 'centimeter/cm', 미터 'meter/m', 킬로미터 'kilometer/km', 자 'ja' and 길 'gil'

0.5밀리미터 샤프심 '0.5mm leads'
0.7밀리미터 볼펜 '0.7mm ball-point pens'
0.9밀리미터 철판 '0.9mm thick iron plate'
30센티미터 자 '30cm ruler'
175센티미터의 키 'height of 175cm'
50미터의 폭포 '50 meter-high waterfall'
500미터 길이의 조깅 트랙 '500 meter-long jogging track'
높이 한 자의 탑 'a tower one-ja high'
깊이 열 자의 웅덩이 'a pond ten-ja deep'
길이 세 자의 고무줄 'three-ja long rubber bands'
열 길 깊이의 샘 'a spring ten-gil deep'

③ **Width:** 제곱미터 'Square meter/m^2', and 평(坪) 'pyeong'

10제곱미터의 방 'a 10m^2 room'
50제곱미터의 아파트 'a 50m^2 apartment unit'
100제곱미터의 밭 'a 100m^2 field'

1,000제곱미터의 운동장 'a 1,000m^2 playground'
논 천 평 'a 1,000 pyeong rice paddy'
밭 이천백 평 'a 2,100 pyeong field'
과수원 삼천 평 'a 3,000 pyeong orchard'
삼십이 평짜리 아파트 'a 32-pyeong apartment'
오십 평짜리 상가 'a 50-pyeong store'
백 평짜리 공장 부지 'a 100-pyeong factory site'
일만 평짜리 공원 'a 10,000-pyeong park'

24.2.5 Quantity

① 잔(盞), 컵 'cup', 병(瓶) 'bottle': For liquid.

술 한 잔/컵/병 'one glass/cup/bottle of alcohol'
맥주 두 잔/컵/병 'two glasses/cups/bottles of beer'
소주 세 잔/컵/병 'three glasses/cups/bottles of soju'
양주 네 잔/컵/병 'four glasses/cups/bottles of hard liquor'
물 다섯 잔/컵/병 'five glasses/cups/bottles of water'

② 되, 말: For grains or cereals.

쌀 한 되/말 'one doe/mal of rice'
보리쌀 두 되/말 'two does/mals of barley corns'
콩 세 되/말 'three does/mals of beans'
밀가루 네 되/말 'four does/mals of flours'

25 Dependent noun

25.1 What is a dependent noun?

Dependent nouns(의존명사) cannot be used alone, always require preceding adnominal phrases. They can be used various sentence components.

25.2 Types and characteristics of dependent nouns

① 것

ⓐ It is used in the form of '-(으)ㄴ/는 것' and has the meaning of thing, affair or phenomenon. It can be used with verbs, adjectives, or copula.

너는 **웃는 것**이 예쁘다. / Your smile is so pretty.
욕심이 지나치게 **많은 것**은 좋지 않다. / Excessive greed brings no good.
위의 명제 가운데 **참인 것**을 고르시오.
Choose the true thesis of the above sentences.

ⓑ It is also used in the form of '-(으)ㄹ 것(이다)' and it implies speaker's prospect, conjecture or subjective belief.

그렇게 놀다가는 분명히 성적이 떨어**질 것이다**.
Surely your grades will drop, if you play all the time.
올해 여름은 매우 무더**울 것이다**. / This summer will be very hot.

② 겸: It is used in the form of '-(으)ㄹ 겸' and can be combined with verbs only. It implies two or more movements or actions that take place simultaneously.

세상 돌아가는 얘기도 듣고 네 얼굴도 **볼 겸** 해서 서울에 왔다.
I have come to Seoul to listen what's going on in the world and see you, too.
김치도 사고 한국 사람도 만**날 겸** 한국 식품점에 갔었다.
I went to Korean grocery to buy Kimchi and see Korean people, too.

③ 김: It is always used in the form of '-(으)ㄴ/는 김에' and can be combined with verbs only. It implies an opportunity or occasion.

이왕 만**난 김에** 함께 점심이나 먹읍시다.
While we are meeting, why don't you have lunch with me?
서울에 **온 김에** 김 선생님을 만나고 싶습니다.
While I am in Seoul, I want to meet teacher Kim.

④ 따름: It is mainly used in the form of '-(으)ㄹ 따름이다' and has the meaning of 'only' and 'no more'.

나는 그저 사실대로 말했**을 따름입니다**. / I just told the truth.
네가 살아 있다니 고마**울 따름이다**. / I am just thankful you are alive.

⑤ 대로: It is always used in the form of '-(으)ㄴ/는/(으)ㄹ 대로' and can be combined with verbs and adjectives but not 이다. It has the meaning of 'in accordance with'.

생각나는 대로 말해 보세요. / Speak off the top of your head.

키가 작으면 작은 대로 할 일이 있습니다.

Short people has his/her duty as he/she is short.

쉴 대로 쉬어 버린 밥을 먹었으니 탈이 날 수밖에 없다.

I must have stomach trouble because I ate rice just as spoiled as can be.

⑥ 데: It is used in the form of '-(으)ㄴ/는 데' and implies place, affair, thing or case.

그는 안 가 본 데가 없다. / He has been everywhere.

그 책을 다 읽는 데 이틀이 걸렸다. / It took two days to finish that book.

머리 아픈 데 먹는 약 좀 주세요. / Give me the medicine for headache.

⑦ 동안: It is always used in the form of '-는 동안' and can be combined with verbs only. It implies the time during which it happens or exists.

서울에 가는 동안 네 생각만 했다.

I was thinking of you alone while going to Seoul.

잠을 자는 동안 꿈을 많이 꾸었다.

While I was sleeping, I dreamed too much.

⑧ 듯(이): It is used in the form of '-(으)ㄴ/는/(으)ㄹ 듯(이)' and has the meaning of guess or conjecture.

그는 한국에 대해 잘 아는 듯(이) 말했다.

He spoke as though he is very much aware of Korea.

대학 입학시험에 합격하자 뛸 듯(이) 기뻤다.

I jumped for joy when I pass my college entrance exam.

⑨ 때문: It is used in the form of 'nouns, pronouns, -기 때문, -(으)ㄴ/는/던 때문' and implies the reason for or cause of the situation.

그는 **빚 때문**에 고생을 했다.

He had a terrible time on account of the debts.

오늘은 일이 많**기 때문**에 집에 일찍 들어갈 수가 없다.

I can't come home earlier today because of the work load.

두 사람이 사이가 좋은 것은 욕심이 없**는 때문**이 아닐까? / The two get along well with each other because they're not greedy, I think.

⑩ **리:** It is used in the form of '-(으)ㄹ 리가 있다/없다' and has the meaning of reasons or grounds.

그는 정직한 사람이기 때문에 부정을 저지**를 리**가 없다. / There is no way that he would have done wrong things because he is honest.

이렇게 입단속을 하는데 비밀이 새 나**갈 리**가 있겠니?

We don't let it out, is it really possible that the secret could leak out?

⑪ **마련:** It is used in the form of '-기/게 마련이다' and has the meaning of the occurrence of something is natural or can be generally expected.

겨울이 아무리 추워도 봄은 **오기 마련이다**.

No matter how cold winter is, spring is bound to come.

물건이란 오래 쓰면 닳**게 마련이다**.

It's normal for things to wear out with long use.

⑫ **만:** It is used in the form of '-(으)ㄹ 만' and implies justification or possibility of actions.

그가 화를 **낼 만**도 하다. / No wonder he got angry.

비록 한약이 쓰기는 하지만 먹**을 만**은 합니다.

Herbal medicine is bitter, but edible.

⑬ **만큼**

ⓐ It is mainly used in the form of '-(으)ㄴ/는/(으)ㄹ 만큼' and implies that preceding and following clauses are equal or have reached the same extent.

그는 노력**한 만큼** 좋은 성적을 받았다.
He got a good grade as much as he makes an effort.
주**는 만큼** 너도 받을 수 있을 거야.
You can get as much as you give.

ⓑ It is used in the form of '-(으)ㄴ/는/던 만큼' and has the meaning of reason for a certain action or state of affairs.

네가 잘못**한 만큼** 벌을 받아야 한다.
Because you did the wrong thing, you should be punished.
많이 혼을 **낸 만큼** 이제는 그가 어른들의 말에 순종할 것이다.
Because I scolded him, for now he will obey elders.

⑭ 망정: It is mainly used in the form of '-기에/(으)니(까)/아서/어서 망정이지' and has the meaning of good luck or fortune.

엄마가 바로 옆에 있었**으니까 망정이지** 하마터면 아기가 크게 다칠 뻔했다.
It is good luck that his/her mother was there when it happened; otherwise, the baby would have got badly hurt.
여럿이 있었**기에 망정이지** 혼자였더라면 누명을 썼을 거예요. / It was good that there were a lot of people; otherwise, I would have been framed.

⑮ 모양: It is mainly used in the form of '-(으)ㄴ/는/(으)ㄹ 모양' and has the meaning of guess or conjecture.

먹구름이 몰려오는 것을 보니 소나기가 **올 모양**입니다.
Seeing dark clouds are moving in now, it looks like a shower.
그는 암만해도 미심쩍은 것이 풀리지 **않은 모양**으로 질문을 계속했다.
He repeated his question with a doubtful look on his face.

⑯ 바: It is used in the form of '-(으)ㄴ/는/(으)ㄹ/던 바' and can be combined with verbs only. It implies the immediately preceding content, thing, or method.

평소에 느**낀 바**를 말씀해 주세요. / Tell me what you usually feel.
나는 어찌**할 바**를 모르겠다. / I'm at my wits' end.

⑰ 바람: It is used in the form of '-는 바람에' and can be combined with verbs only. It implies the cause or reason for the statement in the following clause.

급히 먹**는 바람에** 체했다. / Because I ate too quickly, I had upset stomach.
비가 많이 오**는 바람에** 소풍이 취소됐다.
On account of rain, the school outing was cancelled.

⑱ 법: It is used in the form of '-는/(으)ㄹ 법' and has the meaning of duty, reasons or habit. It also implies that some action or state of affair is only natural that it will be come so.

갑자기 약속을 취소하**는 법**이 어디 있어요?
How can you cancel the appointment so suddenly?
그녀는 아무리 바빠도 저녁을 거르**는 법**이 없다.
No matter how busy she is, she never skips dinner.
죄를 지으면 당연히 벌을 받**는 법**입니다.
One should be punished for his/her crimes.

⑲ 뿐: It is used in the form of '-(으)ㄹ/았다/었다 뿐(이지)' and has the meaning of only just nothing but.

모두들 구경만 **할 뿐(이지)** 경찰에 신고하지 않았다.
Everyone was just looking without getting to report it to the police.

그녀는 웃고만 있**을 뿐(이지)** 아무 말도 하지 않았다.
She was just smiling without saying anything.
그는 시간만 보**냈다 뿐(이지)** 한 일이 아무것도 없다.
He hasn't done anything, just spent time.

⑳ 셈

ⓐ It is mainly used in the form of '-(으)ㄴ 셈(이다)' and has the meaning of circumstances or results.

어찌 **된 셈**이냐? / Tell me why.
이 정도면 잘**한 셈**이다. / I think you've done well.

ⓑ It is mainly used in the form of '-(으)ㄹ 셈(이다)' and has the meaning of the thought of what someone is going to do.

앞으로 어**쩔 셈**이냐? / What are you planning to do now?
남의 돈을 떼어 먹**을 셈**이니? / Won't you pay up?

ⓒ It is mainly used in the form of '-(으)ㄴ/는 셈 치다' and has the meaning of supposition.

속**은 셈 칩**시다. / Let us suppose that we made nothing to lose.
너 같은 친구는 없**는 셈 치**겠다.
I will suppose that there is no friend like you.

㉑ 수: It is mainly used in the form of '-(으)ㄴ/는/(으)ㄹ 수 있다/없다' and implies a possibility or general abilities.

잘못하다가는 죽**는 수(가) 있다**. / If things go wrong, you can die.
나는 그 일을 잘 **해낼 수 있다**. / I can achieve that.

㉒ 양

ⓐ It is used in the form of '-(으)ㄴ/는 양' and implies the appearance of doing.

그녀는 얼이 **빠진 양** 우두커니 서 있었다.
She stood around as if her mind were some-where else.
그가 폐병에라도 **걸린 양** 기침을 심하게 하고 있다.
She is coughing hard as if she had a chest trouble.

ⓑ It is also used in the form of '-(으)ㄹ 양' and implies the intention or will.

사법고시 시험을 **칠 양**이면 제대로 공부해라.
Study hard if you want to take bar examination
아기의 잠을 깨우지 **않을 양**으로 조심스럽게 얘기를 했다.
We talked carefully so as not to wake the baby.

㉓ 이: It is used in the form of '-(으)ㄴ/는/(으)ㄹ/던 이' and has the meaning of a person.

저기에 서 있**는 이**가 누구냐? / Who is that standing there?
이 일을 잘 해**낼 이**가 여기에는 아무도 없다.
There's no one who can do it.

㉔ 자: It is used in the form of '-(으)ㄴ/는/(으)ㄹ/던 자' and has the meaning of a guy or a person. it is used to look down on the other routinely.

낯**선 자**가 대문 앞에 서성인다.
There is a stranger pacing around at the gate.
그녀는 말솜씨가 뛰어나 맞**설 자**가 없다. / Because she is an excellent speaker, there is no one who can match for her.

죽<u>은 자</u>가 <u>산 자</u>를 오히려 위로하고 있다.
The dead are consoling the living.

㉕ 적: It is mainly used in the form of '-(으)ㄴ/(으)ㄹ 적' and implies a time when something happens, or a case of it happening.

나는 한 번도 서울에 가 <u>본 적</u>이 없다. / I have never been to Seoul.
한국 김치를 먹어 <u>본 적</u>이 있어요? / Have you ever tried Kimchi?
정글에서 사자를 만<u>난 적</u>이 있으면 말씀해 주세요.
If you have met a lion in the jungle, please tell me about it.

㉖ 줄

ⓐ It is used in the form of '-는/(으)ㄹ 줄' and has the meaning of the way or abilities(be able to, knowing how to do something).

나는 자전거를 <u>탈 줄</u> 모른다. / I don't know how to ride the bicycle.
그는 실력이 모자라서 그 문제를 어떻게 <u>푸는 줄</u>을 모른다.
He does not know how to solve that problem of his poor skills.

ⓑ It is also used in the form of '-(으)ㄴ/는/(으)ㄹ 줄' and has the meaning of the thing, fact or circumstance.

그 목걸이가 도둑질한 <u>것인 줄</u> 몰랐다.
I didn't know that it's a stolen necklace.
다리가 아<u>픈 줄</u> 모르고 열심히 달렸다.
I ran without even knowing that my leg hurt.

㉗ 중: It is mainly used in the form of '-는/던 중' and can be combined with verbs only. It has the meaning of 'in the middle of doing something'.

공부를 하<u>는 중</u>에는 전화를 받지 마라.
While you are studying, don't answer the phone.

그때는 내가 영국에서 유학하고 있**는 중**이었다.

I was studying abroad in Britain at the time.

민서와 얘기하**던 중**에 새로운 사실을 많이 알게 되었다.

I learned something new more while I was talking to Min-Seo.

㉘ 지: It is used in the form of '-(으)ㄴ 지' and implies the amount of time that has elapsed since an event occurred.

그녀를 만**난 지**도 꽤 오래 되었다.

It's a very long time since I've met her.

집 떠**난 지** 3년 만에 돌아왔다. / I returned home three years after I left.

㉙ 지경: It is used in the form of '-(으)ㄴ/는/(으)ㄹ 지경' and implies the case, circumstances or degree.

어쩌다가 이**런 지경**에 처했니?

What happened that caused matters to come to this?

병세가 악화되어 더 이상 손을 쓸 수 없**는 지경**이다.

The condition has worsened, so it is getting totally out of hand.

매일 웃음을 참느라 죽**을 지경**이다.

I'm dying to hold back a laugh every day.

㉚ 차: It is used in the form of '-던 차' and can be combined with verbs only. It implies an opportunity or moment of doing something.

잠이 막 들려고 하**던 차**에 전화가 왔다.

When I was just about to fall asleep the phone rang.

배고프**던 차**에 빵을 잘 얻어먹었다.

I was treated to bread when I was really hungry.

너를 만나러 가**던 차**였는데 마침 잘 왔구나.

You've come at just the right time. I was just about to leave to see you.

③① 참

ⓐ It is used in the form of '-(으)ㄴ/던 참' and implies the case or time of doing something.

그녀는 직장에서 막 돌아**온 참**인 듯 화장도 지우지 않은 얼굴이었다.
She was still in make-up, as if she just came back home from work.
이제 막 떠나려**던 참**이다. / I am about to leave.

ⓑ It is also used in the form of '-는/(으)ㄹ 참' and implies the thought or intention of what someone is going to do.

도대체 어떻게 **할 참**이냐? / What do you intend to do?
그렇지 않아도 막 이야기를 하려**는 참**이다.
The thing is I am about to tell you.

③② 채: It is used in the form of '-(으)ㄴ/는 채(로)' and has the meaning of just as it is or did.

그녀는 옷을 입**은 채로** 수영을 했다. / She swam with her clothes on.
토끼를 **산 채로** 잡았다. / I caught a rabbit alive.
그는 이미 감각을 잃고 통증도 모르**는 채** 침대에 누워 있다.
He is lying in his bed without feeling.

③③ 척: It is used in the form of '-(으)ㄴ/는 척' and implies an action or way of behaving that is intended to make people believe something that is not true.

자**는 척**하지 마세요. / Don't pretend to be asleep.
그는 애써 태연**한 척**을 했다. / He struggled to seem cool.
그녀는 내 말을 들**은 척**도 안 했다.
She acted like she didn't even hear me.

㉞ 체: It is used in the form of '-(으)ㄴ/는 체' and implies an action or way of behaving that is intended to make people believe something that is not true.

그는 나를 보고도 못 **본 체** 딴전을 부렸다.
He affected not to see me and keep on looking elsewhere.
잘 알지도 못하면서 왜 아**는 체**를 했니?
Why did you pretend to know without the least knowledge of it?
내가 아무리 설득해도 그는 들**은 체**도 안 했다. / No matter how much I tried to persuade him, he didn't care for what I said.

㉟ 축: It is used in the form of '-(으)ㄴ/는 축' and implies the category that is classified by certain characteristics.

나에 비하면 너는 젊**은 축**이다.
You are one of the young ones compared to me.
그는 노래를 잘하**는 축**에 든다. / He ranks among the good singers.
그녀는 한국 음식을 잘 먹**는 축**에 든다.
She is part of the group that eats Korean food well.

㊱ 탓: It is mainly used in the form of '-(으)ㄴ/는 탓' and has the meaning or the cause or reason why something bad is occurring.

그는 성격이 급**한 탓**에 실수를 많이 한다.
He is so impetuous that he makes many mistakes.
네가 고자질**한 탓**에 선생님께 혼났다.
I was scolded because you squealed on me.
네 건강이 나빠진 것은 술을 너무 많이 마**신 탓**이다.
Your health failed from drinking too much.

㊲ 터

ⓐ It is used in the form of '-(으)ㄹ 터' and has the meaning of schedule, conjecture or will.

내일 네 집에 **갈 터**이니 그리 알아라. / I am going to your house tomorrow.
시장**할 터**이니 어서 먹기나 해라. / You must be hungry. Help yourself.

ⓑ It is also used in the form of '-(으)ㄴ/는/던 터' and has the meaning of conditions or circumstances.

사나흘을 굶**은 터**에 찬밥 더운밥을 가릴 수가 없었다.
I could not choose a cold or hot meal because I hadn't eaten three or four days.
그때는 마침 그들이 서울을 떠나려**는 터**였다.
They were just about to leave Seoul at that time.

㊳ 통: It is used in the form of '-(으)ㄴ/는 통(에)' and implies the situation or circumstances of something.

친구들이 교실에서 떠드**는 통에** 공부를 제대로 할 수 없었다.
With my friends making such an uproar, I was unable to study.
장마가 길어지**는 통에** 손해가 많다.
The longer monsoon caused much damage.
네가 잔소리를 하**는 통에** 머리가 아프다.
Your nagging gives me a headache.

㊴ 편: It is mainly used in the form of '-(으)ㄴ/는 편(이다)' and has the meaning of 'belonging to the side of'.

그녀는 말이 좀 많**은 편이다**. / She is a woman of many words.
아직은 시간적 여유가 좀 있**는 편이다**. / I still have time on my side.
그는 운동을 잘하**는 편이다**. / He is good at sports.

26 Co-occurrence

26.1 What is co-occurrence?

Co-occurrence(공기) refers to the limited usage that a particular word comes after another particular word in a sentence. This idiomatic use of two words helps to clear the meaning of the sentence. Particular adverbs can be often co-occurred with sentential or connective endings in Korean.

26.2 Types and characteristics of co-occurrence

26.2.1 co-occurrence of adverbs and sentence endings

① 과연[1], 정말(로), 참말(로) … -다, -구나, -군

'과연[1], 정말(로)' and '참말(로)' which have the meaning of 'indeed; really' use when thought and reality are same. They can come with assertive, interrogative and exclamatory endings.

> **과연** 소문대로 민서가 **예쁘다**. / Indeed, Min-Seo is as pretty as they say.
> 민서가 결혼한다는 소문이 **정말(로)** 사실이**니?**
> Is the rumor really true that Min-Seo is getting married?

참말(로) 준서는 한국말을 잘하<u>는**구나!**</u> / Indeed, Jun-Seo is good at Korean!

② 도대체(대관절), 과연[2] … -(으)ㄹ까?

'도대체' means '(how/what/why) on earth (in the world)' and '과연[2]' has the meaning of 'indeed or really'. They are used in combination with words representing question.

<u>도대체</u> 그 사람의 정체는 무엇<u>**일까?**</u> / Who on earth is he?
<u>과연</u> 그녀는 여기에 왜 왔<u>**을까?**</u> / Indeed, why did she came here?

③ 드디어 … -고야 말았다

'드디어' means 'finally, eventually or at last'. It is used in combination with words representing something happens as wanted or expected.

<u>드디어</u> 내 꿈을 이루어 내<u>**고야 말았다**</u>. / I finally realize my dream.
<u>드디어</u> 모든 시험이 끝났다. / All of my examinations are finally over.
<u>드디어</u> 밀린 숙제를 다 <u>**해 버렸다**</u>.
I finally did all of the delayed homeworks.

④ 마치 … -듯(이)/처럼, 같다/양하다/듯하다

'마치' has the meaning of 'about the same', and it is usually used with the words '처럼 or 듯이' is added and adjectives such as '같다, 양하다, 듯하다'.

민서는 <u>**마치**</u> 천사<u>**처럼**</u> 마음씨가 착하다.
Min-Seo is good-hearted like an angel.
그녀의 목소리는 <u>**마치**</u> 하늘에서 들려오는 음악 소리 <u>**같다**</u>.
Her voice is like the sound of music from the heaven.
<u>**마치**</u> 천국에 와 있는 <u>**듯하다**</u>. / It is just like I am in the heaven.

⑤ 부디, 아무쪼록/모쪼록, 제발 … -기 바라다/기원하다/희망하다/빌다/기대하다

'부디, 아무쪼록/모쪼록, 제발' have the meaning of 'please; I implore you; I beg; for goodness sake', and imply one's earnest desire or hope.

부디 건강하시**기 바랍니다**. / I hope you are healthy.
어머님, **아무쪼록** 몸조심하십시오.
Mom, I hope you will take good care of yourself.
제발 살아서 돌아오**기를 기원한다**.
I really hope you can come back alive.

⑥ 하물며, 설마 … -(으)랴, -는가? -(으)ㄹ까? -겠느냐?

'하물며' which means 'much more' and '설마' which means 'on no account' express strong affirmation of the following fact compared to the preceding fact. They can come with interrogative and exclamatory endings.

내 자식도 어찌 못하는데 **하물며** 남의 자식을 어찌할 수 있**겠는가?**
I don't have a clue how to deal with my children, much less other children.
동물도 제 새끼는 귀한 줄 아는데 **하물며** 사람이 제 자식 귀한 줄 모르**랴!**
If a beast knows how to care for its young ones, how much more would human beings!
아무리 돈이 궁해도 **설마** 도둑질이야 했**으랴!**
No matter how poor, indeed, did he steal?

26.2.2 co-occurrence of adverbs and connective expressions

① 마땅히, 무릇, 모름지기 … -아/어야 한다
'마땅히' means 'deservedly', '무릇' means 'generally speaking', 모름지

기 means 'by all means; necessarily'. They used in combination with words representing obligation.

> 죄를 지었으면 **마땅히** 벌을 받**아야 한다**.
> It's only natural for one to be punished for his/her crime.
> **무릇** 법도는 누구나 잘 지**켜야 한다**.
> In general, everyone must obey the law.
> **모름지기** 학생은 공부를 열심히 해**야 한다**.
> Students should by all means bend to studying.

② 만약, 만일, 가령, 혹시 … -(으)면, -(ㄴ/는)다면, -거든, -아/어도, -더라도, -(으)ㄹ지라도

'만약, 만일' mean 'hypothetically, suppose that', '가령' means 'suppose that' and '혹시' means 'by any chance'. They used with connective endings for condition.

> **만약/만일** 내일 비가 **온다면** 소풍을 갈 수 없을 것이다.
> If it should rain tomorrow, we wouldn't go on a picnic.
> **만약/만일** 내가 새**라면** 하늘을 날아다닐 수 있을 텐데.
> If I were a bird, I could fly in the sky.
> **가령** 누가 너에게 거짓말을 했**다면** 너는 어떻게 하겠니?
> Suppose that someone told a lie to you, what would you do?
> **혹시** 내일 죽게 **된다면** 무엇을 하고 싶니?
> If you were destined to die tomorrow, what would you like to do?

③ 비록 … -더라도, -(으)ㄹ지라도

'비록', which has the meaning of 'although; even though; despite the fact that', used with connective endings for contrast or concession.

> **비록** 사소한 것이라 하**더라도** 나와 의논하도록 해라.
> Discuss with me anything even though it is trivial.

비록 가난할지라도 기죽지 마라.

Even though they are poor, don't feel small.

비록 미물이지만 함부로 죽이지 마라.

Although it is small and insignificant a creature, don't kill it.

④ 설령, 설사, 아무리 ... -아/어도, -더라도, -(으)ㄹ지라도, -(으)ㄹ망정, -(으)ㄹ지언정, -았/었자, -기로서니

'설령, 설사' which mean 'even though; even supposing that' and '아무리' which means 'no matter how' used with connective endings for concession.

설령/설사 장마가 온다 하더라도 비가 그리 많이 오지는 않을 것이다.

Even though the rainy season is here, it will not rain too much.

아무리 시험에 실패했을지라도 결코 실망하지 마라.

No matter how many you failed in the examination, never be disappointed.

⑤ 아마(도) ... -(으)ㄹ 것이-, -겠-

'아마' means 'probably; perhaps', and used with conjecture expressions.

아마(도) 아직도 너를 기다리고 있을 거야.

He is probably still waiting for you.

아마 지금쯤 수업이 끝났을 것 같아. / Class is probably over by now.

아마 그곳엔 눈이 내리고 있겠지? / Maybe it is snowing there.

⑥ 하도 ... -아/어서, -아/어 가지고, -(으)니(까)

'하도' has the meaning of 'very much indeed; ever so (hard)' and used with connective endings for cause or reason.

하도 기가 막혀서 말을 못 하겠다. / I was so shocked I am speechless.

하도 길이 넓어 가지고 교통사고가 날 일은 없어요.

The road is so broad that traffic accidents will never occur.

제 아들이 **하도** 밥을 적게 먹**으니까** 걱정이 많죠.

I have many worries about my son, because he eats to little.

⑦ 혹시 ... ㅡ(으)면, -거든, -더라도

'혹시', which means 'by any chance; in case', used with connective
endings for condition or concession.

혹시 내일 지구에 종말이 온다**면** 뭘 하고 싶니? / If by any chance the
earth is coming to an end tomorrow, what do you want to do?
혹시 민서를 만나**거든** 내가 사랑한다고 꼭 전해 주세요.
If you meet Min-Seo, please tell her I love her.
혹시 실패하**더라도** 실망하지 마라.
Even if you fail, don't be disappointed.

26.2.3 co-occurrence of adverbs and negative forms

① 결코, 전혀, 절대로, 도무지, 도저히, (도)통, 조금도 ... 않다/없다/아니
다/못하다/모르다

'결코, 전혀' mean 'never; at all', '절대로' means 'never; absolutely',
'도무지, 도저히, (도)통' mean 'at all; simply' and '조금도' means 'in the
least, in any degree'. They always have to occur with negative expressions.

너를 만난 것은 **결코/전혀/절대로** 우연이 **아니다**.
It is surely no accident that I met you.
도무지/도저히/도통 정답을 **모르겠다**.
I don't know the correct answer at all.
준서는 민서보다 음식 솜씨가 **조금도** 나을 것이 **없다**.
Jun-Seo had nothing on Min-Seo when it comes to cook.

② 그다지 ... 않다/못하다/없다

'그다지' means 'that (much)', and mainly used with negative expressions.

그녀는 <u>그다지</u> 예쁘지 <u>않</u>아요. / She is not that pretty.

나는 한국 음식을 <u>그다지</u> 잘 만들지 <u>못하</u>는 편이에요.

I can't cook Korean food very well.

이 스파게티는 <u>그다지</u> 맛이 <u>없</u>네요.

This spaghetti doesn't taste that good.

③ 다시는 … 않다/못하다, -나 봐라

When '다시', which means 'again', combines with auxiliary particle '-는', it used with negative expressions.

<u>다시는</u> 너와 만나지 <u>않</u>겠다. / I will never meet you again.

건강이 안 좋아서 <u>다시는</u> 외국 여행을 가지 <u>못하</u>게 되었다.

I was never to travel abroad on account of ill health.

<u>다시는</u> 너와 함께 일하<u>나 봐라</u>. / See if I ever work with you again.

④ 도대체(대관절) … 없다/않다/못하다, -(으)ㄹ까?

'도대체' means 'at all', and used with negative expressions.

그 사람은 <u>도대체</u> 이해할 수가 <u>없</u>다. / I can't understand him at all.

그녀는 <u>도대체</u> 다른 사람의 말은 들으려 하지 <u>않</u>는다.

She doesn't listen to other at all.

⑤ 별로 … 않다/못하다/없다/모르다

'별로' means 'particularly', and is mainly used with negative expressions.

오늘은 <u>별로</u> 기분이 좋지 <u>않</u>아요. / I'm not particularly feeling well today.

그는 공부를 <u>별로</u> 잘 <u>못한</u>다. / He is not very good at his studies.

사업은 <u>별로</u> 생각해 본 적이 <u>없</u>습니다.

I haven't really thought about business.

요즘은 <u>별로</u> 더운 줄 <u>모르</u>겠다.

Nowadays I don't particularly feel the heat.

⑥ 비단 ... 뿐 아니라, 아니다

'비단' means 'only', and is used with words that have a negative meaning such as 아니다.

이런 일은 **비단** 어제오늘의 일이 **아니**다.
This is not something that started just yesterday.
그 사고를 목격한 사람은 **비단** 준서뿐만 **아니**라 다른 사람도 많았다.
Many people not only Jun-Seo witnessed the accident.

⑦ 차마 ... 못하다/없다

'차마' means 'bear; most pitiful', and is mainly used with negative expressions.

그가 사람이라면 **차마** 그런 짓은 **못할** 거예요.
If he is a person, he couldn't do such a thing.
차마 그녀의 부탁을 거절할 수 **없**었다.
I didn't have the heart to refuse her request.

27 Korean grammatical pattern

27.1 What is a grammatical pattern?

Particles and verb endings are the function word in Korean. In addition, when two or more grammar elements or vocabulary elements combined, it can have new meaning and roles as a function word. It is expressed in the form of 'ending+particle, particle+ending, ending+ending, particle+ predicate, ending+noun, particle, etc.' and called a grammatical pattern. The following are grammatical patters classified by their meanings.

27.2 Types and characteristics of grammatical pattern

27.2.1 Possibility

Expressions of **possibility**(가능), which include '-(으)ㄹ 리가 없다/있다, -(으)ㄹ 만하다, -(으)ㄹ 법하다, -(으)ㄹ 뻔하다, -(으)ㄹ 수 없다/있다, -(으)ㄹ 수 있는 대로, -(으)ㄹ 줄 알다/모르다, -(으)ㄹ래야 -(으)ㄹ 수가 없다, -겠-, -기 십상이다', express an ability or possibility.

그걸 내가 몰랐을 리가 없지.

There is no way I couldn't have known that.

그는 집을 살 만한 형편이 못 된다. / He can't afford to buy a house.

그녀로서는 그럴 법하지요.

It was only natural that she should have done so.

그 아이는 하마터면 차에 치일 뻔했다.

The child almost got hit by a car.

비가 너무 많이 와서 학교에 갈 수 없었다.

It rained so much that I was not able to go to school.

될 수 있는 대로 많이 주무세요. / Sleep as much as possible.

테니스를 칠 줄 알지만 시간이 없어서 오늘은 칠 수 없어요. / I know how to play tennis, but I cannot play today because I don't have time.

북한은 갈래야 갈 수가 없어요.

I cannot go to North Korea no matter how much I want to.

힘이 없기 때문에 더 이상은 걷지 못하겠다.

With no strength left, no more can I walk.

그렇게 하다가는 쪽박을 차기 십상이다.

If you do that, you are bound to go bankrupt.

27.2.2 Condition

Expressions of **condition**(조건·가정), which include '-(ㄴ/는)다고/라고 치다, -(ㄴ/는)다면/라면, -(느/으)냐에 달려 있다, -(으)니는 날에는, -(으)니/는 셈 치다, -(으)니는/(으)ㄹ 경우에, -(으)되, -(으)ㄹ라치면, -(으)려(고) 하면, -(으)려면, -(으)면, -(으)면 되다, -거든(=거들랑), -고서야, -고야, -기 나름이다, -노라면, -는 한, -아/어야, -았/었더라면, -았/었던들', express supposition or condition.

내가 지금 비행기를 탄다고 쳐도 오늘 밤까지 거기에 못 가.

I couldn't get there by tonight even if I were to go by plane.

길에서 넘어진다면 창피할 거예요.

I would get embarrassed if I got tripped over on the road.

모든 일은 어떻게 마음먹**느냐에 달려 있다**.

Everything depends on the way you look at things.

그가 우리의 비밀을 아**는 날에는** 정말 큰일이 날 거야.

If he finds out our secret, we will be in great trouble.

이제부터 그 아들 하나 없**는 셈 치고** 살 거야.

I'm going to live from now on as if I never had that son.

내일 비가 많이 **올 경우에**는 운동 경기를 취소합시다.

If it rains a lot tomorrow, let's cancel the sports game.

아침을 먹기는 먹**되** 빨리 서둘러라.

You may have breakfast, but hurry over.

밥 좀 먹**을라치면** 손님들이 갑자기 잇따라서 오는 거 있지?

Whenever I try to eat, customers come in one after another, you know?

모처럼 날 잡아서 소풍을 가**려고 하면** 비가 오네.

Whenever I choose a day to go on a picnic, it rains.

김 선생님을 만나**려면** 내일 오후에 오세요.

If you want to meet Mr. Kim, please come tomorrow afternoon.

돈이 많**으면** 뭘 하고 싶어요?

If you had a lot of money, what would you like to do?

집 앞에서 버스를 타**면 돼요**.

It is okay if I take a but in front of the house.

신발이 잘 안 맞**거든**(=맞**거들랑**) 반품하세요.

If the shoes do not fit well, take it back.

나는 선생님의 설명을 듣**고서야** 이해했다.

I understood after hearing the explanation from my teacher.

이래 가지**고야** 어디 해외에 나갈 수 있겠어?

With the way things stand at the moment, I can´t go abroad.

인간이란 습관들이**기 나름인가** 보다! (윌리엄 셰익스피어)

How use doth breed a habit in a man! (William Shakespeare)

규칙적인 운동을 하**노라면** 건강이 좋아질 거예요.

If you exercise regularly, your health can be better.

계획을 바꾸지 않**는 한** 실패할 수밖에 없어요.

There is no choice but to fail unless we change the plan.

날씨가 **좋아야** 항해를 시작할 수 있다.

When/If the weather is fine, we can start sailing.

그가 아무리 재능이 있어도 노력하지 **않았더라면** 성공하지 못했을 것이다.

No matter how talented he was, he would not have been successful had he not made strenuous efforts.

엄마가 아이를 조금만 더 잘 돌보**았던들** 아이가 다치지는 않았을 텐데.

Had the mother taken care of the child just a little bit better, the child would not have been hurt.

27.2.3 Emphasis

Expressions of **emphasis**(강조), which include '-(ㄴ/는)다고(요)/라고 (요), -(ㄴ/는)다니까(는)/라니까(는), -(으)ㄹ/는 수밖에 없다, -(이)라고는/(이) 라곤, -(이)야, -(이)야말로, -고말고(요), -고서는, -기(가) 그지없다, -기(가) 이를 데 없다, -기(가) 짝이 없다, -기도 하다, -기만 하다, -만 아니면, -아/어(서) 죽겠다, 얼마나 -(으)ㄴ/는지 모르다, 여간 -지 않다', is used when indicate that it is particularly important or true, or to draw special attention to it.

아무리 배가 고파도 그건 먹지 마. 먹지 말**라고**.

However hungry you may be, do not eat it.

그 사람은 술만 마시면 난폭해**진다니까**. / He gets violent when he is drunk.

이상이 높지 않을수록 삶에 대한 적극성도 떨어**질 수밖에 없다**.

The lower the ideals, the less the drive.

내가 가진 돈**이라고는** 이게 전부야. / This is all the money I have on me.

준서**야** 당연히 여기 오겠지요. / Jun-Seo will definitely come here.

이번에**야말로** 꼭 가야 한다. / I must go this time or never.

정말 좋은 사람들인 것 같아요. - 그렇**고말고요**.

They must be very nice men. - Yes, they are.

한쪽 말만 듣**고서는** 결정할 수가 없어요.

I can't judge fairly by hearing only one side of the story.

할머니가 내 눈 앞에서 돌아가셨어요. 슬프<u>기가 그지없네요</u>.

My grandmother died on me. Nothing could make me sadder.

아내가 임신했다는 소식을 듣고 기쁘<u>기가 이를 데 없었어요</u>.

I was overjoyed to hear that my wife was pregnant.

멍청하<u>기(가) 짝이 없구나</u>. / You are extremely stupid.

그 사람은 키가 참으로 크<u>기도 하다</u>. / I think he is indeed very tall.

나는 하루 종일 울<u>기만 했어요</u>. / I did nothing but cry all day.

시험<u>만 아니면</u> 당장 집에 갈 텐데.

If I didn't have a quiz, I would come home right now.

요즘 같은 날은 아이스크림이 먹고 싶<u>어서 죽겠어</u>.

On days like this, I'm dying for some ice cream.

그 아기가 <u>얼마나 귀여운지 몰라요</u>. / The baby is indescribably cute.

그 학생 <u>여간</u> 똑똑하<u>지 않다</u>. / The student is remarkably clever.

27.2.4 Result

Expressions of **result**(결과), which include '-(으)ㄴ 결과, -(으)ㄴ 끝에, N 끝에, -(으)ㄴ 나머지, -(으)니/는 셈, -게 되다, -고 말다, -고야 말다, -다(가) 보니(까), -다(가) 보면, -다가는, -아/어 내다', express something that happens or exists because of something else that has happened.

열심히 노력<u>한 결과</u> 내 꿈은 실현되었다.

With hard work, my dream finally came true.

수년 간 열심히 노력<u>한 끝에</u> 나는 결국 꿈을 이루었어요.

After years of hard work, I have finally achieved my dream.

그는 서두<u>른 나머지</u> 지갑을 가져오는 것을 잊어버렸다.

He forgot to bring his purse in his haste.

자기가 자기 발등을 찍<u>은 셈</u>이다. / It's like cutting his or her own throat.

이번에 한국에 가서 한국 문화를 좋아하<u>게 됐어요</u>.

I have been to Korea lately, and I fell in love with Korean culture.

늦잠을 자서 셔틀버스를 놓치고 **말았어요**.

I overslept and missed shuttle bus.

그것은 결국 큰 문제를 일으키**고야 말았다**.

It eventually caused a great trouble.

연습을 많이 하**다가 보니까** 요령이 생기네요.

I'm getting the hang of it after practicing it a lot.

이 길을 따라 쭉 가**다가 보면** 병원이 나올 거예요.

Go straight ahead down this street and you'll come across the hospital.

내일 오전까지 날씨가 맑**다가는** 오후부터 흐려지겠다.

We will have a sunny start, with clouds developing in the afternoon.

그는 매우 아팠지만 결국 강인한 정신력으로 그 병을 이**겨 냈어요**. / He was very sick, but finally he overcame his sickness with strong will power.

27.2.5 Listing, contrast

Expressions of **listing**(나열) or **contrast**(대립·대조), which include '-(느/으)니 -(느/으)니, -(으)ㄴ/는 반면(에), -(으)ㄴ/는가 하면, -(으)나, -(으)되, -(으)랴 -(으)랴, -(으)며, -(으)면서, -(이)며 -(이)며, -고, -고도, -더니, -아/어도, -지만', connect the first and the second clauses symmetrically or express the difference between two clauses.

> 그녀는 시장은 복잡하**니** 환불이 안 되**느니** 하면서 마트만 간다.
> She only goes to large stores, saying that traditional markets are too crowded and that they don't accept returns.
> 민서는 그 의견에 동의하**는 반면** 준서는 동의하지 않는다. / Min-Seo agrees with the opinion, but on the other hand, Jun-Seo does not.
> 우리 중에 몇 명은 준비가 되었**는가 하면**, 몇 명은 준비가 안 되었다.
> Some of us are ready and some of us are not.
> 준서는 예전에는 기타를 즐겨 연주했었**으나**, 요즈음은 피아노를 자주 치는 편이다.
> Jun-Seo enjoyed playing the guitar, but now he plays the piano often.

나도 가고 싶기는 하**되** 시간이 없다.

I should like to come, but I haven't time.

낮에는 학교에서 공부하**랴** 저녁에는 서점에서 아르바이트 하**랴** 쉴 틈이

없다. / I am so busy studying during the day and working part-time

at a bookstore in the evening.

5월 5일은 어린이날**이며**, 5월 15일은 스승의 날이다.

May 5th is Children's day, and May 15th is teachers' day.

그는 음악을 안 들**으면서** (음악을) 듣는 척했다.

He was not listening to music, but pretended to do so.

준서는 음악**이며**, 수학**이며**, 운동**이며**, 모두 다 잘한다.

Jun-Seo is good at everything, from music, maths to sports.

이 치마는 싸**고** 예뻐요. / This skirt is cheap and pretty.

저는 이제 사전을 찾아보지 않**고도** 한국어 신문을 읽을 수 있어요.

Now I can read a Korean newspaper without recourse to the dictionary.

준서가 어제는 학교에 가**더니** 오늘은 집에 있다.

Jun-Seo went to school yesterday, but stays at home today.

준서는 축구는 잘**해도** 야구는 잘 못한다.

Jun-Seo is good at football, but not good at baseball.

제 할머니께서 연세는 많으시**지만** 아주 건강하세요.

My grandmother is very healthy for her age.

27.2.6 Obligation

Expressions of **obligation**(당위), which include '-(으)ㄴ/는 법이다, -게
마련이다, -기 마련이다, -은/는 물론(이고)', express right things to do or
to be.

자주 만날수록 정도 깊어지**는 법이다**.

The more they meet, the closer they get.

사람마다 장점과 단점이 있**게 마련이다**.

Each person has his or her strong and weak points.

살아 있는 것은 죽기 마련이다. / Life is subject to decay.

그녀는 영어는 물론이고 한국어도 할 줄 안다.

She speaks Korean, not to mention English.

27.2.7 Command, duty, permission, prohibition

Expressions of **command**(명령), **duty**(의무), **permission**(허락) or **prohibition**(금지) include '-(으)ㄹ 것, -(으)면 안 되다, -(으)세요, -아/어도 되다, -아/어야 되다/하다, -지 말다, -지 않아도 되다(안 -아/어도 되다), -지 않으면 안 되다'.

쓰레기를 함부로 버리지 **말 것**. / Do Not Litter.

집에 가**면 안 돼요**. / You may not go home.

여기에 이름을 **쓰세요**. / Put your name here.

오늘 밤에 영화 보러 가**도 돼**. / I can go to the movies tonight.

학생은 열심히 공부**해야 돼요/해요**. / Students must study hard.

길이 복잡하니까 마중 나오**지 마**.

It's too crowded, so please don't come out to meet me.

이 병원은 예약하**지 않아도 돼**.

We don't need a reservation for this hospital.

오늘 당장 하**지 않으면 안 돼**. / You must do it this very day.

27.2.8 Purpose, intention

Expressions of **purpose**(목적) or **intention**(의도), which include '-ㄴ/는다는 것이, -(으)ㄹ 셈, -(으)ㄹ 터(이다)/테다, -(으)ㄹ 테야, -(으)ㄹ까 하다, -(으)라고, -(으)러 가다/오다, -(으)려(고) 들다, -(으)려(고) 하다, -(으)려(고), -(으)려다가, -(으)려던 참(에/이다), -게(끔), -고 들다, -고 말겠다, -고자, -기 위한, -기 위해(서)/위하여, -을/를 위해(서)/위하여, -기로 들다, -기로 하다, -느라(고), -도록, -아/어야지, -자고', express purpose or intention of the subject.

커피에 설탕을 넣**는다는 것이** 소금을 넣었어요.
I inadvertently put salt into the coffee instead of sugar.
그래서 어떻게 **할 셈**이니? / So how are you gonna do it?
이번에는 성공**할 테다**. / I hope to succeed this time.
이제부터 나는 매일 한 시간씩 운동**할 테야**!
From now on, I'll work out for an hour every day.
저녁에 가족들과 외식을 **할까 해요**.
I am thinking of eating out with my family for dinner.
언니가 시험에 붙**으라고** 찹쌀떡을 사 줬어요.
My sister gave me chapsalttock to pass through the exam.
일요일에 저녁 드시**러 오세요**. / Come over for dinner on Sunday.
걔네들은 만나기만 하면 항상 싸우**려고 든다**.
Whenever they meet, they are always looking for a fight.
담배를 끊**으려고 해요**. / I am planning to quit smoking.
주말에 읽**으려고** 책을 한 권 샀어요.
I bought a book to read during the weekend.
뒤차가 눈길에 미끄러지는 바람에 피하**려다가** 벽을 받았어요.
Because the car behind slipped on the snowy road, I tried to avoid it
and (then) hit a wall.
막 전화하**려던 참이었어요**. / I was about to call you.
사람들은 구급차가 지나가**게** 한쪽으로 비켜서 주었다.
People stood aside to let the ambulance pass.
너는 왜 항상 모든 일에 그렇게 따지**고 드니**?
Why do you always have to be so argumentative about everything?
주말까지 꼭 이 일을 끝내**고 말겠습니다**.
I'm going to finish this job by the end of the week no matter what.
나는 어머님을 만나**고자** 고향을 찾아왔습니다.
To meet my mother, I visited the hometown.
그는 대학에 들어가**기 위한** 시험을 준비하고 있다.
He is preparing for the test to enter the university.

한국에 대해 배우**기 위해서** 한국에 왔어요.

I came to Korea (in order) to learn about Korea.

그녀가 일단 하**기로 들면** 아무도 그녀의 마음을 못 바꾼다.

If she once decides to do something, no one can change her mind.

친구와 같이 제주도에 가**기로 했어요**.

I have decided to go to Jeju Island with my friend.

그녀는 아이들을 학교에 보내**느라** 아침 일찍 일어났어요.

She woke up early in the morning to get the kids ready for school.

자동차 사고가 나지 않**도록**, 민서는 교통법규를 잘 지켰다.

To prevent car accidents, Min-Seo observed traffic rules strictly.

캠핑을 간다면 텐트를 가지고 가**야지**.

You should take a tent along if you are going camping.

그냥 웃**자고** 한 말이야. 너무 심각하게 생각하지 마.

I just did it for a laugh. Don't think so seriously.

27.2.9 Comparison, selection

Expressions of **comparison**(비교) or **selection**(선택) include '-(ㄴ/는)다기보다는/라기보다는, -(으)ㄴ/는 대신(에), N 대신(에), -(으)ㄴ/는/(으)ㄹ 것보다, -(으)ㄴ/는/(으)ㄹ 바에, -(으)나, -(이)나, -(이)라도, -거나 -거나/-건 -건, -기보다, -느니 (차라리), -느니만 못하다, -은/는 고사하고, -든가, -든(지) -든(지), -만 같아도/해도/하더라도, 아무 + -(이)나, 아무 + -도, -에 비하면/비하여/비해(서)'.

이 고양이는 애완동물이**라기보다는** 제 가족이에요.

This cat is my family rather than a pet.

일부 아이들은 밖에 나가서 **노는 대신에** 컴퓨터 앞에 앉아 있고 싶어 한다. / Some children want to sit in front of a computer instead of going out to play.

앓는 것보다 차라리 죽는 것이 낫다. / It is better to die than suffer.

도둑질을 **할 바에야** 차라리 굶어 죽겠다.

I had rather starve to death than steal.

그 사람은 비가 오나 눈이 오나 성실하게 일했다.

The person worked hard, come rain or come snow.

월요일이나 화요일에 시간이 있어요?

Do you have time on Monday or Tuesday?

밥이 없다면, 빵이라도 먹고 가자.

If there is no rice, let's just eat some bread.

네가 서울에 오거나 말거나 나는 상관하지 않겠다.

Whether you come to Seoul or not, I will not care.

그 사람과 결혼하기보다 나는 차라리 혼자 살겠다.

It is better to live alone than marry him.

친구를 잃느니 차라리 돈을 잃겠어요. / I'd rather lose money than a friend.

일하는 것이 공부하느니만 못한 것 같아요.

It seems that working is worse than studying.

반에서 일등은 고사하고 꼴찌나 면해라.

Come out on the bottom, let alone trying for the top in your class.

무슨 말이든가 해 보세요. / Please say anything, whatever that may be.

귤을 먹든지 사과를 먹든지 하자.

Let's eat something, whether tangerines or apples.

어제까지만 해도 날씨가 대단히 좋았다.

The weather was amazing until yesterday.

저는 오후에는 아무 때나 괜찮아요. / In the afternoon anytime is okay.

그녀는 많이 먹는 데에 비해 날씬해.

She is pretty slim considering she eats so much.

27.2.10 Proportion

Expressions of **proportion**(비례), which include '-(으)면) -(으)ㄹ수록, -에 따라서', express increases or decreases of one thing in proportion to another thing.

한국어는 하**면 할수록** 어려운 것 같아요.

The more I speak Korean, the more difficult it seems.

자주 만남**에 따라서** 정도 깊어지는 법이다.

The more they meet, the closer they get.

27.2.11 Metaphor

Expressions of **metaphor**(비유), which include '-(으)ㄴ/는/(으)ㄹ 것처럼, -(으)ㄴ/는/(으)ㄹ 양, -다시피, -듯(이)', is used when speak figuratively.

음악이 사람을 행복하게 하**는 것처럼** 그림도 사람을 행복하게 한다.

As music brings happiness to people, pictures also bring happiness to people.

그 범인은 아무렇지도 않**은 양** 태연하게 행동을 재연했다.

The criminal reenacted his action as if he doesn't give a damn.

그는 연구실에서 살**다시피** 했어요.

He spent most of his time in the laboratory.

눈이 녹**듯이** 걱정거리가 사라졌다. / Tears pour down like rain.

27.2.12 Status

Expression of **status**(상태), which include '-(으)ㄴ/는 대로, -(으)ㄴ/는 채(로), -(으)ㄴ/는 편이다, -(으)려(고) 하다, -고, -고 있다, -아/어 놓다, -아/어 두다, -아/어 있다, -아/어지다', express the state of affairs or events at a particular time.

내가 하**는 대로** 해 보세요. / Do it as I do it.

한국에서는 신발을 신**은 채(로)** 집에 들어가면 안 돼요.

In Korea, you cannot enter the house with your shoes on.

저는 테니스를 자주 치**는 편이에요**. / I tend to play tennis often.

서두르세요. 지하철이 떠나**려고 해요**.

Hurry up. The subway is about to leave.

어머니는 나를 업**고** 병원까지 가셨다.

My mother took me to hospital on her back.

어머니는 책을 읽**고** 계세요. / My mother is reading the book.

나는 서울행 비행기 표를 예매**해 놓았다**.

I reserved a ticket for Seoul.

문을 항상 잠**가 두세요**. / Always lock your door.

벽에 시계가 걸**려 있어요**. / The clock is on the wall.

봄에는 날씨가 따뜻**해져요**. / In spring, the weather becomes warmer.

27.2.13 Circumstance, criterion

Expressions of **circumstance**(상황) or **criteria**(기준), which include '-(으)ㄴ/는 가운데, -(으)ㄴ/는데, -(으)ㄴ/는 마당에, -(으)ㄴ/는 터, -(으)ㄴ/는/(으)ㄹ 판, -(으)니, -다시피, -에 따라, -치고', express situations or criteria.

그는 자식들이 지켜보**는 가운데** 숨을 거두었다.

He passed away with his children at his side.

오랜만에 동대문시장에 갔**는데**, 거기서 고향 친구를 만났어.

I went to Dongdaemun Market after a long time, and I met my hometown friends there.

이미 게임이 끝**난 마당에** 후회해야 무슨 소용이 있나?

Once the game is over, what is the use of regret?

준서가 이미 런던으로 **간 터에** 지금 와서 무슨 말을 하겠니? / Now that Jun-Seo has already gone to London, what can we say about it now?

목구멍에 풀칠을 하기도 어려**운 판에** 세계 여행이 웬 말이야?

When it is difficult to even live from hand to mouth, how can we travel the world?

매장 안에 가 보**니** 이미 손님들이 많이 들어와 있었다. / I went inside the store and there were already many customers in the store.

보시**다시피** 지금 제가 가지고 있는 것은 아무것도 없습니다.

As you can see, I have nothing at the moment.

휴대전화 사용자 수가 증가함**에 따라** 공중전화가 사라지고 있다.

Along with the increase in users of mobile phone, public phone booths are disappearing.

신입 사원**치고는** 일을 잘하네요.

For a new employee, he works quite well.

27.2.14 Habit, attitude

Expressions of **habit**(습관) or **attitude**(태도), which include '-(으)ㄴ/는 법이 없다/있다, -(으)ㄴ/는 척하다, -(으)ㄴ/는 체하다, -고는 하다/-곤 하다, -기(가) 일쑤이다, -기는(요), -는 둥 마는 둥/-(으)ㄹ 둥 말 둥/-(으)ㄴ 둥 만 둥, -아/어 대다', express repeated action or subject's stance.

그는 약속 시간을 지키**는 법이 없어요**. / He is never on time.

나는 잠자**는 척/체하고** 있었다. / I was pretending like I was sleeping.

우리는 주말마다 낚시하러 가**곤 했다**.

We used to go fishing every weekend.

우리 아들은 울**기 일쑤였어요**. / My son was a constant crybaby.

재미있**기는**. 지루해서 중간에 잠들어 버렸어. / Interesting? No way. It was boring and I fell asleep in the middle of it.

나는 늦잠을 자서 아침을 먹**는 둥 마는 둥** 하고 출근했다.

I overslept and left for work after barely eating breakfast.

아기가 밤새도록 울**어 대서** 잘 수가 없었어요.

I couldn't easily sleep because the baby was crying all night long.

27.2.15 Time(simultaneity, completion, conversion, etc.)

Expressions of **time**(시간), which include '-ㄴ/는 동시에, -(으)ㄴ 뒤에/N

다음에, -(으)ㄴ 지, -(으)ㄴ 후에/N 후에, -(으)ㄴ/는 김에, -(으)ㄴ/는 다음(에), -(으)ㄴ/는 대로, -(으)ㄴ/는 사이(에), -(으)ㄹ 때/N 때, -(으)며, -(으)면서, -고 나다, -고서, -기 전에/N 전에, -기(가) 무섭게, -기(가) 바쁘게, -기에 앞서 (서), -는 길에, -는 도중에, -는 동안/N 동안, -는 중/N 중, -는 한편, -다(가), N 만에, -아/어 가지고, -아/어다가, -아/어서, -자, -자마자', express process, time or relationship of events.

그는 노래를 듣는 **동시에** 공부를 한다.
He is listening to songs while studying at the same time.
어린이들은 어른들에게 절을 **한 뒤에** 세뱃돈을 받는다.
Children get cash gifts from adults after bowing to them.
한국에 **온 지** 3년이 됐어요. / It has been three years since I came to Korea.
대학을 졸업**한 후에** 뭐 할 거예요?
What are you going to do after graduating from college?
쇠뿔도 **단김에** 빼라. / Pull out the horn at a stretch. (Strike the iron while it is hot. If you are determined to do something, do it immediately.)
대학을 졸업**한 다음(에)** 뭐 할 거예요?
What are you going to do after graduating from college?
도착하**는 대로** 전화 드릴게요. / As soon as I arrive, I'll give you a call.
내가 없**는 사이에** 무슨 일이 있었어요? / What has passed in my absence?
저는 어렸**을 때** 가수가 되고 싶었어요.
When I was a child, I wanted to be a singer.
어머니는 나의 손을 꼭 잡**으며**, 건강을 늘 조심하라고 당부하셨다.
Mother held my hand tightly, telling me to take care of myself.
운전하**면서** 휴대전화를 사용하지 마세요.
Do not use a cell phone while driving a car.
어제 영화를 **보고 나서** 뭐 했어?
What did you do after you saw the movie yesterday?
아침도 안 먹**고서** 학교에 가면 어떡하니?
How could you go to school without having breakfast?
저녁 먹**기 전에** 빨리 좀 씻을게요.

I will just have a quick wash before dinner.

그녀는 수업이 끝나**기가 무섭게** 집으로 쏜살같이 달려갔다.

She ran home at a great bat after the class.

우리가 도착하**기가 바쁘게** 그 문제가 발생했다.

Hardly had we arrived than the problem come up.

공연을 시작하**기에 앞서** 몇 가지 간단한 주의 사항을 말씀드리겠습니다.

Before the show begins, I want to remind you of a few simple rules.

거기에 가**는 길에** 간단한 스낵을 살게요.

I'm going to grab a quick snack on my way over.

옮기**는 도중에** 접시가 깨졌어요.

The dish was broken in the process of moving.

모두가 잠자**는 동안** 도둑이 집에 들어왔어요.

While everybody was sleeping, a thief came into the house.

선생님은 회의하시**는 중**이에요. / He is in a meeting right now.

나는 대학교에 다니**는 한편**, 집에서 개인 과외도 한다.

While I attend university, I also do private tutoring at home.

그는 학교에 가**다가** 친구를 만났다.

On his way to school, he met his friends.

하루 **만에** 거기에 갔다 올 수 있나요? / Can I get there and back in a day?

내가 **사 가지고** 갈게요. / I will buy one (and take it to the party).

민서는 그림을 **그려다가** 준서에게 주었다.

Min-Seo drew a picture and gave it to Jun-Seo.

친구를 만나**서** 영화를 보러 갔어요.

I met my friend, and (then) we went to see a movie.

아무도 그 일을 하려고 하지 않**자** 선생님께서는 화를 많이 내셨다. / As nobody seemed to be willing to do the work, the teacher got very angry.

너무 피곤해서 집에 들어가**자마자** 잤어.

I was so tired that I fell asleep as soon as I got home.

27.2.16 Attempt, experience

Expressions of **attempt**(시도) or **experience**(경험) include '-(으)ㄴ/는

적이 있다/없다, -고 보다, -아/어 보다'.

한국에서 운전<u>해 본 적이 있어요</u>? / Have you ever driven in Korea?
실제 만나<u>고 보니</u> 그는 내가 상상했던 그런 사람이 아니었다.
In real life he was not how I had imagined him.
김치를 먹<u>어 봤어요</u>? - 아니요, 안 먹<u>어 봤어요</u>.
Have you eaten Kimchi? - No, I have not.

27.2.17 Concession

Expression of **concession**(양보), which include '-((으)ㅁ)에도 불구하고, -(ㄴ/는)다 해도, -(으)ㄴ/는데(도), -(으)ㄴ/는들, -(으)나마, -(으)ㄹ망정, -(으)ㄹ지라도, -(으)ㄹ지언정, -건마는/건만, -기로서니, -는 한이 있어도/있더라도, -더라도, -아/어도, -았/었자', express concession.

노력을 했<u>음에도 불구하고</u> 결과가 좋지 않았다.
The result wasn't good, in spite of the effort.
수학 문제를 풀기가 어렵<u>다 해도</u> 포기하지 마세요.
Even though it is difficult to solve maths questions, don't give up.
이 옷은 비<u>싼데</u> 별로 예쁘지 않아요.
This cloth is expensive but not so pretty.
고추가 맵다 <u>한들</u> 시집살이보다야 맵겠어요? / Chilli peppers may be hot, but can they be more burning than living with in-laws?
비록 돈이 적<u>으나마</u> 받으세요.
Please keep the money, though it is not much.
굶어 죽<u>을망정</u> 도둑질은 못하겠다.
I would rather starve to death than steal from others.
준서는 비록 키가 작<u>을지라도</u> 농구를 잘한다.
Although Jun-Seo is short, he is good at basketball.
굶어 죽<u>을지언정</u> 너의 도움을 받지 않겠다.
Even if I die from starvation, I will not receive your help.

기다리고 또 기다렸<u>건만</u> 그녀는 오지 않았어요.

I waited and waited, but she didn't come.

그가 아무리 부자이<u>기로서니</u> 영원한 젊음은 살 수 없다.

No matter how rich he may be, he cannot buy eternal youth.

내가 죽<u>는 한이 있더라도</u> 그것은 안 하겠다.

I will not do it if it kills me.

비록 비가 많이 오<u>더라도</u> 우리는 소풍을 간다.

Even though it may rain a lot, we will go on a picnic.

아무리 일이 어려웠<u>어도</u> 그는 결코 포기하지 않았다.

No matter how hard the work was, he never gave up.

그 사람이 돈이 있어 보<u>았자</u> 얼마나 있겠습니까?

How much money would he have even if he did have any?

27.2.18 Completion

Expression of **completion**(완료) include '-(으)ㄴ/는 다음에야, -아/어 버리다, -아/어 치우다, -았/었다(가), -았/었던'.

사랑이란 떠나고 **난 다음에야** 깨닫는 것이다.

Love is only realizing what you had when it's gone.

강아지가 죽<u>어 버려서</u> 나는 너무 슬펐다.

I was so sad because my puppy was dead for ado.

내가 그 비스킷을 다 먹<u>어 치웠어</u>! / I eaten all the biscuits!

집에 오는 길에 슈퍼에 좀 들<u>렀다(가)</u> 오세요.

On your way home, please stop at the supermarket.

지난번에 우리가 같이 **봤던** 영화 제목이 뭐예요?

What is the name of the movie we saw together?

27.2.19 Cause, reason

Expressions which used when express **cause**(원인) or **reason**(이유) are

'-(ㄴ/는)다고/라고, -(ㄴ/는)답시고/랍시고, -(느/으)니만큼, -(느/으)니만치, -(으)ㄴ/는 고로, -(으)ㄴ/는 관계로, -(으)ㄴ/는 까닭에, -(으)ㄴ/는 만큼, -(으)ㄴ/는 이상, -(으)ㄴ/는 탓/N 탓, -(으)ㄴ/는 터라, -(으)ㄴ/는 통에, -(으)ㄴ/는지라, -(으)니까, -(으)ㄹ세라, -(으)로 말미암다, -(으)로 인하다, -(으)로 해서, -(으)ㅁ으로써, -(으)므로, -거든(요), -고 해서, -기 때문/N 때문, -기에, -기에 망정이지, -길래, -느라(고), -는 바람에, -다(가), -더니, -아/어 가지고, -아/어서, -았/었더니, -잖아(요)'.

어떤 것이 당신의 계획대로 되지 않**는다고** 그것이 불필요한 것은 아니다. (토마스 A. 에디슨) / Just because something doesn't do what you planned it to do doesn't mean it's useless. (Thomas A. Edison)

그녀는 요리를 한**답시고** 수선을 떨었다.
She made a big fuss about doing some cooking.

그는 돈이 많이 {있**으니만큼**/있**으니만치**} 노후에 대한 걱정이 없을 것 같다. / He has a lot of money, so I don't think he is worried about his life after retirement.

그녀가 잘못을 비**는 고로** 용서를 해 주었다.
Because she apologized for her fault, I forgave her.

배가 너무 부**른 관계로** 더 이상 아무 것도 먹고 싶지 않다.
Because I am too full, I don't feel like eating any more.

그가 자꾸 거짓말을 하**는 까닭에** 모두들 화가 많이 났다.
Because he kept on lying, everyone got quite mad.

이미 경기가 끝**난 만큼** 이제 후회는 하지 말자.
Since the game is over, let's not feel regret.

당신이 여기에 있**는 이상** 한국어를 배워야 해요.
You are here, you must learn Korean.

어젯밤에 과음**한 탓에** 머리가 너무 아파요.
I have a horrible headache from drinking too much last night.

그가 교통사고를 당한 사실을 알고 있**던 터라** 아무도 놀라지 않았다.
Since they knew about his accident, nobody was surprised.

칭찬을 너무 많이 하**는 통에** 다들 쑥스러워했다.

Because they received too many compliments, they all became red-faced.

자네가 묻는 것인지라, 내가 가르쳐 주지. / Since you ask, I will teach you.

오늘은 바쁘니까 내일 오세요.

Since I am busy today, please come tomorrow.

늦게 들어온 것을 엄마에게 들킬세라 살금살금 방으로 들어갔다.

I crept into my room, for fear of coming back home late.

만물이 그로 말미암아 지은 바 되었으니 지은 것이 하나도 그가 없이는 된 것이 없느니라. (성경) / Through him all things were made; without him nothing was made that has been made. (The Bible)

폭설로 인하여 비행기가 연착되었어요.

Owing to a heavy snowfall, the airplane was delayed.

그 사람으로 해서 우리 회사가 유명해졌다.

Because of him, our company became famous.

열심히 공부함으로써 영어를 잘할 수 있게 되었어요.

I became fluent in English by studying hard.

민서가 충고를 자주 했으므로 상황이 좋아질 것이다.

Because Min-Seo gave advice quite often, things will get better.

선생님 전화번호를 가르쳐 드릴게요. 제가 알거든요.

I will tell you teacher's phone number. It is because I know it.

그가 이 자리에 없다고 해서 그렇게 말하지 마.

Don't talk like that because he isn't here.

비가 왔기 때문에 집에 있었어. 비 때문에 집에 있었어.

I stayed at home because it rained.

책이 싸기에 한 권 샀어요. / As the book was cheap, I bought a copy.

네가 전화했기에 망정이지 약속을 깜빡 잊어버릴 뻔했어요. / It is good luck that you called me; otherwise, I would have forgotten the appointment.

책이 싸길래 한 권 샀어요. / As the book was cheap, I bought a copy.

시험이 있어서 공부하느라 어제 모임에 못 갔어요.

I couldn't go to yesterday's gathering because I had to study for a test.

미안해요. 급히 나오는 바람에 잊어 버렸어요.

I am sorry. Because I came out in a hurry, I forgot it.

어제 농구를 하다가 다쳤어요. / I hurt it while playing basketball yesterday.

그는 열심히 공부하**더니** 수석으로 학교를 졸업했다.

He studied so hard that he graduated as the top student of his school.

어제 잠을 못 **자 가지고** 피곤해요.

I am tired because I couldn't sleep yesterday.

저는 한국어를 배우고 싶**어서** 서울에 왔습니다.

I came to Seoul because I wanted to learn Korean.

오랜만에 테니스를 **쳤더니** 굉장히 피곤해요. / As I (just) played tennis for the first time in a long time, I am very tired.

날씨도 따뜻해지고, 꽃도 많이 피**잖아요**.

You know, the weather becomes warmer and many flowers bloom, too.

27.2.20 Opinion, suggestion, recommendation, help

Expressions which used when ask **opinion**(의견 묻기), **suggest**(제안), **recommend**(추천) or **help**(도움) are '-(으)ㄹ까(요)? -(으)ㄹ래(요)? -(으)ㅂ시다, -겠-, -도록 하다, -아/어 주다, -자, -지(그래(요))?'

같이 춤추러 **갈까요?** / Shall we go dancing?

제 차로 모셔 **드릴까요?** / Can I offer you a ride?

커피 한 잔 하**실래요?** / Would you like a cup of coffee?

퇴근하고 뭐 좀 먹**읍시다**/먹**자**. / Let's get something to eat after work.

커피 한 잔 더 드시**겠**어요? / Would you like another cup of coffee?

휴대 전화를 너무 오래 사용하지 않**도록 하세요**.

Don't use mobile phone too long.

이메일 주소 좀 가르**쳐 주세요**. / Please let me have your e-mail address.

목이 마르면 물을 마시**지그래**?

Why don't you drink water if you're thirsty?

27.2.21 Intention, will

Expressions of **intention**(의향) or **will**(의지) include '-(으)ㄹ 것(이다),

-(으)ㄹ 참(이다), -(으)ㄹ 테냐, -(으)ㄹ 테니(까), -(으)ㄹ게(요), -(으)ㄹ까 보다, -(으)ㄹ래(요), -겠'.

나는 담배를 끊고 술을 줄**일 거야**.
I'm quitting smoking cigarettes and cutting down on drinking.
오늘 점심은 안 먹**을 참이야**. / I am going to skip lunch today.
너는 언제 결혼**할 테냐**? / When are you going to get married?
내가 저녁을 **살 테니까** 같이 식당에 갑시다.
I will buy dinner. Let's go to the restaurant together.
제가 책을 읽**을게요**. / I will read the book.
오늘 저녁은 가족과 함께 저녁을 먹**을까 보다**.
I guess I shall have dinner with my family this evening.
저는 불고기를 먹**을래요**. / I would like to eat Bulgogi.
누가 책을 읽**겠**어요? - 제가 읽**겠**습니다.
Who will read the book? - I will read it.

27.2.22 Degree

Expressions of **degree**(정도), which include '-(으)ㄴ/는/(으)ㄹ 만큼, -(으)ㄴ/는/(으)ㄹ 지경, -(으)ㄹ 때까지, -(으)ㄹ 만하다, -(으)ㄹ 정도로, -(으)로까지, -(으)리만큼, -(으)리만치, -기까지, -다(가) 못하여, -도록, -에 불과하다', express amount or level of something.

먹**을 만큼**만 덜어 가세요. / Take only as much as you can eat.
실업 문제가 손을 쓸 수 없**을 지경**이 되어 가고 있어요.
Unemployment is getting out of hand.
물을 붓고, 반 정도 익**을 때까지** 끓이세요.
Cover with water, simmer until half done.
인사동은 전통적인 물건이 많아서 정말 구경**할 만해요**.
Insadong has a lot of traditional things, so it is worth visiting.
그는 민서에게 귀가 아**플 정도로** 잔소리를 했다.

He nagged Min-Seo to the point of hurting Min-Seo's ears.

아이들 싸움이 어른들 싸움**으로까지** 번져 버렸어요.

The fight between the children turned into a big fight between the parents.

거짓말을 한 마디도 못하**리만큼** 그는 정직한 사람이다.

To the degree of not being able to tell a lie, he is honest.

합격 소식에 하늘을 날아가**리만치** 너무나 기뻤다. / I was so happy with the news that I passed the exam that I could even fly.

민서는 유명한 디자이너가 되**기까지** 한평생 노력해 왔다. / Min-Seo, until she became a renowned designer, strived throughout her life.

배가 고프**다 못해** 속이 쓰리네요. / I am so hungry that I have heartburn.

그는 밤이 새**도록** 한국어 공부를 했다.

He studied so much to stay awake throughout the night.

우리 학교 학생은 20명**에 불과하다**.

Students in our school consisted of only twenty.

27.2.23 Addition

Expressions of **addition**(첨가), which include '-(으)ㄴ/는 데다가, -(으)되, -(으)ㄹ 뿐(만) 아니라/N뿐만 아니라, -(으)ㄹ뿐더러, -(으)려니와, -거니와, -은/는커녕, -을/를 비롯해서(비롯한), -마저, -조차', express adding to something else.

나는 배고**픈 데다가** 목도 말라요. / I am hungry and thirsty too.

보기는 하**되** 만져서는 안 된다.

It is okay to look at it, but you must not touch it.

그분은 작가**일 뿐만 아니라** 화가이기도 하다.

He is a painter as well as a writer.

그는 대학에 합격했**을뿐더러** 장학금까지 받게 되었다.

He not only passed the college entrance exam but also won a scholarship.

한국의 김치는 맛도 좋**으려니와** 영양도 만점이다.

Korea's Kimchi is not only tasty but also highly nutritious.

이 노트북은 성능도 좋**거니와** 가격 또한 싸다.

This laptop has not only good performance but also cheap price.

그는 사과를 하기**는커녕** 오히려 내게 화를 냈어요.

He got mad at me, let alone apologize.

조종사**를 비롯해서** 승객 전원이 비행기에서 탈출했습니다.

The whole passengers, including the pilot, escaped from the plane.

너**마저** 나를 믿지 못하는구나. / Even you are distrustful of me.

선생님**조차** 그 문제를 해결하지 못했어요.

Even the teacher could not solve the problem.

27.2.24 Conjecture

Expressions of **conjecture**(추측) include '-(으)ㄴ/는/(으)ㄹ 것 같다, -(으)ㄴ/는/(으)ㄹ 듯(이), -(으)ㄴ/는/(으)ㄹ 듯싶다, -(으)ㄴ/는/(으)ㄹ 듯하다, -(으)ㄴ/는/(으)ㄹ 모양이다, -(으)ㄴ/는/(으)ㄹ 줄 알다/모르다, -(으)ㄴ/는/(으)ㄹ지도 모르다, -(으)ㄴ/는가 보다/나 보다, -(으)ㄴ/는가 싶다/나 싶다, -(으)ㄴ/는가 하다/나 하다, -(으)ㄹ 것(이다), -(으)ㄹ 테니(까)(요), -(으)ㄹ 텐데(요), -(으)ㄹ 걸(요), -(으)ㄹ까 보다, -(으)ㄹ까(요)?, -(으)랴마는, -겠-, -아/어 보이다'.

지금 밖에 비가 **오는 것 같아요**. / I think it's raining outside.

휴대전화가 날개 돋**친 듯이** 팔린다.

Mobile phones are selling like hotcakes.

저녁에는 비가 **올 듯싶어요**. / It may rain in the evening.

선생님께서는 아무래도 편찮**으신 듯해**. / The teacher seems to be ill.

아버지가 기분이 좋**으신 모양이에요**.

My father looks like he is in a good mood.

날씨가 이렇게 더**울 줄 몰랐어**.

I didn't know the weather would be this hot.

곧 교황이 한국을 방문**할지도 모르겠다**. / Soon the Pope may visit Korea.

저 식당에는 항상 손님이 많네. 음식이 맛있**나 봐**.

That restaurant is always full of people. I guess the food tastes good.

제 인생에서 가장 좋았던 때가 그때가 아니었**나 싶네요**.

I think that they were the best times of my life.

왜 이렇게 추**운가 했지요**. / I thought about why it is so cold.

약 5분 후면 도착**할 거예요**. / I should be there in about five minutes.

민준 씨는 또 1시간 늦**을 테니까** 우리 먼저 가요.

Because Min-Jun will be an hour late again, let's go ahead.

조금만 기다리면 **올 텐데**, 조금만 더 기다리지요.

If we wait just a little, she will come, so let's wait just a little more.

교실에는 아직 아무도 없**을걸요**.

I don't think there will be anybody in the classroom yet.

기차를 놓쳤**을까 봐** 불안해. / I am afraid lest I should miss the train.

내일 날씨가 좋**을까요?** / Do you think tomorrow's weather will be good?

준서가 도서관에서 공부하**랴마는** 그래도 한번 믿어 보자.

Jun-Seo may not study in the library, but let's trust him.

구름 좀 봐요. 비가 오**겠**네요. / Look at the clouds. It's going to rain.

구두가 멋있**어 보여요**. / Those shoes look cool.

27.2.25 Limitation

Expressions of **limitation**(한정), which include '-(으)ㄹ 따름이다, -(으)ㄹ 뿐이다, -만 -아/어도', express limited things.

우리는 다만 추측**할 따름입니다**. / We can only conjecture.

5년 전**만 해도** 우리 집은 잘 살았는데….

My family was really well-off only 5 years ago.

27.2.26 Retrospection

Expressions of **retrospection**(회상), which include '-더라고(요), -던, -던데(요), -데(요)', express the act of recalling things past.

한 모금 먹어 봤는데 맛있**더라고요**! / I took a sip and it was so good!

이것이 제가 쓰**던** 노트북이에요. / This is the laptop I used to use.

며칠 전에 가서 먹었는데 맛있**던데요**.

A few days ago I went there and then ate; I thought it was good.

우리 딸이 피아노를 배운 지 얼마 안 됐는데 잘 치**데요**.

My daughter had only been learning the piano for a little while, but she plays the piano very well.

27.2.27 Regret

Expression of **regret**(후회) include '-(으)ㄹ걸 (그랬다), -았/었어야 했는데'.

지난주에 산 옷이 마음에 안 들어. 사지 **말걸 그랬어**.

I don't like the clothes I bought last week. I shouldn't have bought them.

시험이 너무 어려웠어요. 더 많이 공부**했어야 했는데**….

The test was so difficult. I should have studied more.

27.2.28 Hope

Expressions of **hope**(희망) include '-(으)면 좋겠다, -고 싶다, -고 싶어 하다, -기나 하다, -았/었으면 좋겠다/하다/싶다'.

이번 주말에는 날씨가 따뜻하**면 좋겠어요**.

I hope it will be warm this weekend.

저는 영화를 **보고 싶어요**. / I want to watch a movie.

준서도 영화를 **보고 싶어 해요**. / Jun-Seo also wants to watch a movie.

(다른 건 잊고) 술을 마시**기나 합시다**.

Let's just drink some wine (forgetting about other things).

빨리 일요일이 **왔으면 좋겠다**. / I wish Sunday would come soon.

28 Verbal conjugation charts

It is very important to learn how Korean verbs are used, since there is a broad range of verbal endings and irregular verbs in Korea. The verbal conjugation charts below show basic facts about Korean verbal conjugation.

28.1 Verb

28.1.1 Regular verb

Let's take an example of 읽다 'to read', with a focus on hearer-honorific verbal endings, classified by formal honorific, ordinary honorific, ordinary non-honorific and formal non-honorific style.

[Sentence endings]

High honorific style		Indicative style	Retrospective style
Declarative	Present progressive	읽습니다	읽습디다
	Past perfect	읽었습니다	읽었습디다
	Future-surmise/volition	읽겠습니다, 읽을 겁니다.	읽겠습디다
Interrogative	Present	읽습니까?	읽습디까?
	Past	읽었습니까?	읽었습디까?
	Future	읽겠습니까?	읽겠습디까?
Imperative		읽으시오	-
Propositive		읽읍시다	-
Exclamatory		읽으시는구나!	-

Ordinary honorific style		'-아/어요' form	'-(으)오' form
Declarative	Present progressive	읽어요, 읽지요, 읽으세요	읽으오
	Past perfect	읽었어요, 읽었지요, 읽었으세요	읽었소
	Future-surmise/ volition	읽겠어요, 읽겠지요, 읽겠으세요	읽겠소
Interrogative	Present	읽어요? 읽지요? 읽으세요?	읽소?
	Past	읽었어요? 읽었지요? 읽었으세요?	읽었소?
	Future	읽겠어요? 읽겠지요? 읽겠으세요? 읽을 거예요? 읽을 거지요?	읽겠소?
Imperative		읽어요, 읽지요, 읽으세요	읽으오, 읽구려
Propositive		읽어요, 읽지요, 읽으세요	읽으오
Exclamatory		읽는군요! 읽으리요!	읽으오!

Ordinary non-honorific style		'-아/어' form	'-네' form
Declarative	Present progressive	읽어, 읽지	읽네
	Past perfect	읽었어, 읽었지	읽었네
	Future-surmise/ volition	읽겠어, 읽겠지	읽겠네
Interrogative	Present	읽어? 읽지? 읽니?	읽는가?
	Past	읽었어? 읽었지? 읽었니?	읽었는가?
	Future	읽겠어? 읽겠지? 읽겠니? 읽을 거야? 읽을 거지? 읽을 거니?	읽겠는가? 읽을 건가?
Imperative		읽어, 읽지	읽게
Propositive		읽어, 읽지	읽세
Exclamatory		읽어! 읽지! 읽으리!	읽네!

Low non-honorific style		Indicative style	Retrospective style
Declarative	Present progressive	읽는다	읽더라
	Past perfect	읽었다	읽었더라
	Future-surmise/ volition	읽겠다, 읽을 거다	읽겠더라, *읽을 거더라
Interrogative	Present	읽느냐?	읽더냐?
	Past	읽었느냐?	읽었더냐?
	Future	읽겠느냐?	읽겠더냐?
Imperative		읽어라	-
Propositive		읽자	-
Exclamatory		읽는구나! 읽는다! 읽는도다!	읽더구나!

[Connective endings]

Connective	Endings	Connective	Endings
Serial	읽고, 읽으며	Comparison	읽느니
Selection	읽거나, 읽든지	Degree	읽으리만큼

Contrast	읽어도, 읽지만, 읽는데, 읽으면서도	Condition	읽으면, 읽거든, 읽어야, 읽는다면
Simultaneity	읽으면서	Circumstance	읽는데
Completion	읽고서, 읽자	Comparison	읽듯이
Conversion	읽다가	Proportion	읽을수록
Concession	읽어도, 읽더라도, 읽었자, 읽은들, 읽는데도	Cause/Reason	읽어서, 읽으니까, 읽느라고
Result	읽도록	Habit/Repetition	읽곤
Purpose/Intention	읽으러, 읽으려고, 읽고자	Addition	읽거니와, 읽을뿐더러

28.1.2 Irregular verb

Let's take an example of 짓다 'to make', with a focus on hearer-honorific verbal endings, classified by formal honorific, ordinary honorific, ordinary non-honorific and formal non-honorific style.

[Sentence endings]

High honorific style		Indicative style	Retrospective style
Declarative	Present progressive	짓습니다	짓습디다
	Past perfect	지었습니다	지었습디다
	Future-surmise/volition	짓겠습니다, 지을 겁니다.	짓겠습디다
Interrogative	Present	짓습니까?	짓습디까?
	Past	지었습니까?	지었습디까?
	Future	짓겠습니까?	짓겠습디까?
Imperative		지으시오	-
Propositive		지읍시다	-
Exclamatory		지으시는구나!	-

Ordinary honorific style		'-아/어요' form	'-(으)오' form
Declarative	Present progressive	지어요, 짓지요, 지으세요	지으오
	Past perfect	지었어요, 지었지요	지었소
	Future-surmise/ volition	짓겠어요, 짓겠지요	짓겠소
Interrogative	Present	지어요? 짓지요? 지으세요?	짓소?
	Past	지었어요? 지었지요?	지었소?
	Future	짓겠어요? 짓겠지요? 짓겠으세요? 지을 거예요? 지을 거지요?	짓겠소?
Imperative		지어요, 짓지요, 지으세요	지으오
Propositive		지어요, 짓지요, 지으세요	지으오, 짓구려
Exclamatory		짓는군요! 지으리요!	지으오!

Ordinary non-honorific style		'-아/어' form	'-네' form
Declarative	Present progressive	지어, 짓지	짓네
	Past perfect	지었어, 지었지	지었네
	Future-surmise/ volition	짓겠어, 짓겠지	짓겠네
Interrogative	Present	지어? 짓지? 짓니?	짓는가?
	Past	지었어? 지었지? 지었니?	지었는가?
	Future	짓겠어? 짓겠지? 짓겠니? 지을 거야? 지을 거지? 지을 거니?	짓겠는가? 지을 건가?
Imperative		지어, 짓지	짓게
Propositive		지어, 짓지	짓세
Exclamatory		지어! 짓지! 지으리!	짓네!

Low non-honorific style		Indicative style	Retrospective style
Declarative	Present progressive	짓는다	짓더라
	Past perfect	지었다	지었더라
	Future-surmise/volition	짓겠다, 지을 거다	짓겠더라, *지을 거더라
Interrogative	Present	짓느냐?	짓더냐?
	Past	지었느냐?	지었더냐?
	Future	짓겠느냐?	짓겠더냐?
Imperative		지으라	-
Propositive		짓자	-
Exclamatory		짓는구나! 짓는다! 짓는도다!	짓더구나!

[Connective endings]

Connective	Endings	Connective	Endings
Serial	짓고, 지으며	Comparison	짓느니
Selection	짓거나, 짓든지	Degree	지으리만큼
Contrast	지어도, 짓지만, 짓는데, 지으면서도	Condition	지으면, 짓거든, 지어야, 짓는다면
Simultaneity	지으면서, 지으며	Circumstance	짓는데
Completion	짓고서, 짓자	Comparison	짓듯이
Conversion	짓다가	Proportion	지을수록
Concession	지어도, 짓더라도, 지었자, 지은들, 짓는데도	Cause/Reason	지어서, 지으니까, 짓느라고
Result	짓도록	Habit/Repetition	짓곤
Purpose/Intention	지으러, 지으려고, 짓고자	Addition	짓거니와, 지을뿐더러

28.2 Adjective

28.2.1 Regular adjective

Adjectives cannot be made into imperative or propositive forms. Let's take an example of 작다 'to be small'.

[Sentence endings]

High honorific style		Indicative style	Retrospective style
Declarative	Present progressive	작습니다	작습디다
	Past perfect	작았습니다	작았습디다
	Future-surmise/volition	작겠습니다, 작을 겁니다	작겠습디다
Interrogative	Present	작습니까?	작습디까?
	Past	작았습니까?	작았습디까?
	Future	작겠습니까?	작겠습디까?
Imperative		-	-
Propositive		-	-
Exclamatory		작으시구나!	-

Ordinary honorific style		'-아/어요' form	'-(으)오' form
Declarative	Present progressive	작아요, 작지요, 작으세요	작으오
	Past perfect	작았어요, 작았지요	작았소
	Future-surmise/ volition	작겠어요, 작겠지요, 작을 거예요	작겠소
Interrogative	Present	작아요? 작지요? 작으세요?	작소?
	Past	작았어요? 작았지요? 작았으세요?	작았소?
	Future	작겠어요? 작겠지요? 작겠으세요?	작겠소?
Imperative		-	-

Propositive	-	-
Exclamatory	작군요! 작으리요!	작으오!

Ordinary non-honorific style		'-아/어' form	'-네' form
Declarative	Present progressive	작아, 작지	작네
	Past perfect	작았어, 작았지	작았네
	Future-surmise/volition	작겠어, 작겠지, 작을 거야	작겠네
Interrogative	Present	작아? 작지? 작니?	작은가?
	Past	작았어? 작았지? 작았니?	작았는가?
	Future	작겠어? 작겠지? 작겠니?	작겠는가?
Imperative		-	-
Propositive		-	-
Exclamatory		작아! 작지! 작으리!	작네!

Low non-honorific style		Indicative style	Retrospective style
Declarative	Present progressive	작다	작더라
	Past perfect	작았다	작았더라
	Future-surmise/volition	작겠다, 작을 거다	작겠더라
Interrogative	Present	작으냐?	작더냐?
	Past	작았느냐?	작았더냐?
	Future	작겠느냐?	작겠더냐?
Imperative		-	-
Propositive		-	-
Exclamatory		작구나! 작다! 작도다!	작더구나!

[Connective endings]

Connective	Endings	Connective	Endings
Serial	작고, 작으며	Comparison	*작느니
Selection	작거나, 작든지	Degree	작으리만큼
Contrast	작아도, 작지만, 작은데, 작으면서도	Condition	작으면, 작거든, 작아야, 작다면
Simultaneity	작으면서, 작으며	Circumstance	작은데
Completion	*작고서, 작아서, *작자	Comparison	작듯이
Conversion	작다가	Proportion	작을수록
Concession	작아도, 작더라도, 작았자, 작은들, 작은데도	Cause/ Reason	작아서, 작으니까, *작느라고
Result	작도록	Habit/ Repetition	작곤
Purpose/ Intention	*작으러, *작으려고, *작고자	Addition	작거니와, 작을뿐더러

28.2.2 Irregular adjective

Adjectives cannot be converted into imperative or propositive forms. Let's take an example of 춥다 'to be cold'.

[Sentence endings]

High honorific style		Indicative style	Retrospective style
Declarative	Present progressive	춥습니다	춥습디다
	Past perfect	추웠습니다	추웠습디다
	Future-surmise/volition	춥겠습니다 추울 겁니다	춥겠습디다
Interrogative	Present	춥습니까?	춥습디까?
	Past	추웠습니까?	추웠습디까?
	Future	춥겠습니까?	춥겠습디까?

Imperative		-	-
Propositive		-	-
Exclamatory		추우시구나!	-

Ordinary honorific style		'-아/어요' form	'-(으)오' form
Declarative	Present progressive	추워요, 춥지요, 추우세요	추우오
	Past perfect	추웠어요, 추웠지요, 추웠으세요	추웠소
	Future-surmise/volition	춥겠어요, 춥겠지요, 춥겠으세요, 추울 거예요	춥겠소
Interrogative	Present	추워요? 춥지요? 추우세요?	춥소?
	Past	추웠어요? 추웠지요? 추웠으세요?	추웠소?
	Future	춥겠어요? 춥겠지요? 춥겠으세요?	춥겠소?
Imperative		-	-
Propositive		-	-
Exclamatory		춥군요! 추우리요!	추우오!

Ordinary non-honorific style		'-아/어' form	'-네' form
Declarative	Present progressive	추워, 춥지	춥네
	Past perfect	추웠어, 추웠지	추웠네
	Future-surmise/volition	춥겠어, 춥겠지, 추울 거야	춥겠네
Interrogative	Present	추워? 춥지? 춥니?	추운가?
	Past	추웠어? 추웠지? 추웠니?	추웠는가?
	Future	춥겠어? 춥겠지? 춥겠니?	춥겠는가?
Imperative		-	-
Propositive		-	-
Exclamatory		추워! 춥지! 추우리!	춥네!

Low non-honorific style		Indicative style	Retrospective style
Declarative	Present progressive	춥다	춥더라
	Past perfect	추웠다	추웠더라
	Future-surmise/ volition	춥겠다, 추울 거다	춥겠더라
Interrogative	Present	추우냐?	춥더냐?
	Past	추웠느냐?	추웠더냐?
	Future	춥겠느냐?	춥겠더냐?
Imperative		-	-
Propositive		-	-
Exclamatory		춥구나! 춥다! 춥도다!	춥더구나!

[Connective endings]

Connective	Endings	Connective	Endings
Serial	춥고, 추우며	Comparison	*춥느니
Selection	춥거나, 춥든지	Degree	추우리만큼
Contrast	추워도, 춥지만, 추운데, 추우면서도	Condition	추우면, 춥거든, 추워야, 춥다면
Simultaneity	추우면서, 추우며	Circumstance	추운데
Completion	*춥고서, 추워서, *춥자	Comparison	춥듯이
Conversion	춥다가	Proportion	추울수록
Concession	추워도, 춥더라도, 추웠자, 추운들, 추운데도	Cause/ Reason	추워서, 추우니까, *춥느라고
Result	춥도록	Habit/ Repetition	춥곤
Purpose/ Intention	*추우러, *추우려고, *춥고자	Addition	춥거니와, 추울뿐더러

28.3 이다

As in the case of adjectives, 이다 cannot be turned into imperative or propositive forms.

[Sentence endings]

High honorific style		Indicative style	Retrospective style
Declarative	Present progressive	입니다	입디다
	Past perfect	이었습니다	이었습디다
	Future-surmise/volition	이겠습니다, 일 겁니다	이겠습디다
Interrogative	Present	입니까?	입디까?
	Past	이었습니까?	이었습디까?
	Future	이겠습니까?	이겠습디까?
Imperative		-	-
Propositive		-	-
Exclamatory		이시구나!	-

Ordinary honorific style		'-아/어요' form	'-(으)오' form
Declarative	Present progressive	이에요, 이지요, 이세요	이오
	Past perfect	이었어요, 이었지요, *이었으세요	이었소
	Future-surmise/ volition	이겠어요, 이겠지요, *이겠으세요, 일 거예요	이겠소
Interrogative	Present	이에요? 이지요? 이세요?	*이소? 이오?
	Past	이었어요? 이었지요? *이었으세요?	이었소?
	Future	이겠어요? 이겠지요? 이겠으세요?	이겠소?
Imperative		-	-

Propositive	-	-
Exclamatory	이군요! 이리요!	이오!

Ordinary non-honorific style		'-아/어' form	'-네' form
Declarative	Present progressive	이야, 이지	이네
	Past perfect	이었어, 이었지	이었네
	Future-surmise/volition	이겠어, 이겠지, 일 거야	이겠네
Interrogative	Present	이야? 이지? 이니?	인가?
	Past	이었어? 이었지? 이었니?	이었는가?
	Future	이겠어? 이겠지? 이겠니?	이겠는가?
Imperative		-	-
Propositive		-	-
Exclamatory		이어! 이지! 이리!	이네!

Low non-honorific style		Indicative style	Retrospective style
Declarative	Present progressive	이다	이더라
	Past perfect	이었다	이었더라
	Future-surmise/volition	이겠다, 일 거다	이겠더라
Interrogative	Present	이냐?	이더냐?
	Past	이었느냐?	이었더냐?
	Future	이겠느냐?	이겠더냐?
Imperative		-	-
Propositive		-	-
Exclamatory		이구나! 이다! 이로다!	이더구나!

[Connective endings]

Connective	Endings	Connective	Endings
Serial	이고, 이며	Comparison	*이느니
Selection	이거나, 이든지	Degree	이리만큼
Contrast	이어도, 이지만, 인데, 이면서도	Condition	이면, 이거든, 이어야, 이라면
Simultaneity	이면서, 이며, 이자	Circumstance	인데
Completion	*이고서, *이어서, *이자	Comparison	이듯이
Conversion	이다가	Proportion	일수록
Concession	이어도, 이더라도, 이었자, 인들, 인데도	Cause/Reason	이어서, 이니까, *이느라고
Result	*이도록	Habit/Repetition	*이곤
Purpose/Intention	*이러, *이려고, *고자	Addition	이거니와, 일뿐더러

28.4 있다

있다 'to be' has similar conjugations to verbs.

[Sentence endings]

High honorific style		Indicative style	Retrospective style
Declarative	Present progressive	있습니다	있습디다
	Past perfect	있었습니다	있었습디다
	Future-surmise/volition	있겠습니다, 있을 겁니다	있겠습디다
Interrogative	Present	있습니까?	있습디까?
	Past	있었습니까?	있었습디까?
	Future	있겠습니까?	있겠습디까?
Imperative		있어라	-

Propositive		있자	-
Exclamatory		있으시구나!	-

Ordinary honorific style		'-아/어요' form	'-(으)오' form
Declarative	Present progressive	있어요, 있지요, 있으세요	있으오
	Past perfect	있었어요, 있었지요	있었소
	Future-surmise/ volition	있겠어요, 있겠지요, 있을 거예요	있겠소
Interrogative	Present	있어요? 있지요? 있으세요?	있소?
	Past	있었어요? 있었지요?	있었소?
	Future	있겠어요? 있겠지요? 있겠으세요?	있겠소?
Imperative		있어요, 있지요	있으오, 있으소
Propositive		있었요, 있지요	있으오
Exclamatory		있군요! 있으리요!	있으오!

Ordinary non-honorific style		'-아/어' form	'-네' form
Declarative	Present progressive	있어, 있지	있네
	Past perfect	있었어, 있었지	있었네
	Future-surmise/ volition	있겠어, 있겠지, 있을 거야	있겠네
Interrogative	Present	있어? 있지? 있니?	있는가?
	Past	있었어? 있었지? 있었니?	있었는가?
	Future	있겠어? 있겠지? 있겠니?	있겠는가?
Imperative		있어	있게
Propositive		있자	있자
Exclamatory		있어! 있지! 있으리!	있네!

Low non-honorific style		Indicative style	Retrospective style
Declarative	Present progressive	있다	있더라
	Past perfect	있었다	있었더라
	Future-surmise/ volition	있겠다, 있을 거다	있겠더라
Interrogative	Present	있느냐?	있더냐?
	Past	있었느냐?	있었더냐?
	Future	있겠느냐?	있겠더냐?
Imperative		있어라	-
Propositive		있자	-
Exclamatory		있구나! 있다! 있도다!	있더구나!

[Connective endings]

Connective	Endings	Connective	Endings
Serial	있고, 있으며	Comparison	있느니
Selection	있거나, 있든지	Degree	있으리만큼
Contrast	있어도, 있지만, 있는데, 있으면서도	Condition	있으면, 있거든, 있어야, 있다면
Simultaneity	있으면서, 있으며, 있자	Circumstance	있는데
Completion	있고서, 있어서, 있자	Comparison	있듯이
Conversion	있다가	Proportion	있을수록
Concession	있어도, 있더라도, 있었자, 있은들, 있는데도	Cause/ Reason	있어서, 있으니까, 있느라고
Result	*있도록	Habit/ Repetition	있곤
Purpose/ Intention	있으러, 있으려고, 있고자	Addition	있거니와, 있을뿐더러

[References]

Alexander Arguelles & Jong Rok Kim(2004) *A Handbook of Korean Verbal Conjugation*. Dunwoody Press.

Bong Ja Baek(1999), *Korean Grammar Dictionary for Foreigners*, Yonsei University Press.

Chang Gyun Yu(1992), *Translation and Footnote of Hunminjeongeum*, Hyeoseol Press.

Cheol Eui Song(1992), *A Study of Korean Word Formation*, Taehaksa Press.

Dong So Kim(2002), *Introduction to Middle Korean*, Daegu Catholic University Press.

Hangeulhakhoe(1991), *Great Korean Dictionary*, Eumungak Press.

Ho Bin Ihm, Kyung Pyo Hong & Suk In Chang(1988), *Korean Grammar for International Learners*, Yonsei University Press.

Ho Min Sohn(1999), *The Korean Language*, Cambridge: Cambridge University Press.

Hong Bin Lim(1987), *A Study of Korean Reflexives*, Singumunhwasa Press.

Ho Yeong Lee(1996), *Korean Phonetics*, Thaehaksa Press.

Hyeon Bae Choi(1937=1980), *Korean Grammar*, 8th edition, Jeongeumsa Press.

Ik Seop Lee(2012), *Korean Grammar*, Seoul National University Press

Jae Hoon Yeon & Lucien Brown (2011). *Korean : A Comprehensive Grammar*. London and New York: Routledge.

Jae Hui Choe(2004), *Korean Syntax*, Taehaksa Press.

Jae Il Kwon(1992), *Korean Syntax*, Minumsa.

Jae Seong Hong et al.(1997), *Dictionary of Modern Korean Verbal Structure*, Doosandong Press, Inc.

Jeong Su Seo(1994), *Korean Grammar*, Ppurigipeunnamu Press.

Jin U Kim(1985), Language : *The Theory and Application*, Thap Press.

Ji Ryong Lim & Jong Rok Kim et al.(2005), *Korean School Grammar and Grammar Education*, Pagijong Press.

Ji Ryong Lim(2003) *Korean Semantics*, Thap Press.

Jong Rok Kim(2005), A Basic Study to develop a Dictionary of Korean Verbal Conjunction for Foreigners, *Hangeul*, vol. 270, The Korean Language Society(Hangulhakhoi).

Jong Rok Kim(2012), *Korean Verbal Conjunction Dictionary for Foreigners*, Pagijong Press.

Jong Rok Kim(2012), Reflective Study of Korean Verbal Conjunction Dictionary for Foreigners, *Hangeul*, vol. 295, The Korean Language Society(Hangeulhakhoe).

Jong Taek Kim(1992), *Korean Lexis*, Thap Press.

Ju Won Kim(1993), *A Study of Korean Vowel Harmony*, Yeungnam University Press.

KBS(1993), *Great Korean Pronunciation Dictionary*, Eumungak Press.

Kil Han(1999), *A Study of Korean Sentential Ending*, Kangwon University Press.

Ki Sim Nam & Yeong Keun Ko(1993), *A Study of Standard Korean Grammar*, Thap Press.

Korea University Research Institute of Korean Studies(2009), *Korea University Korean Dictionary*, Research Institute of Korean Studies Press.

Kyeong Hui Jang(1985), *A Study of Modern Korean Modality*, Thap Press.

Min Su Kim et al.(1991), *Great Korean Dictionary*, Geumseongsa Press.

Mungyobu(1988), *Rule Book of Korean Orthography*, Korea Textbook Press.

Mun Kyu Lee(2004), *Contemporary Korean Phonology for Korean Language education*, Hankukmunhwasa.

Pil Yeong Lee(1993), *A Study of Korean Quotation Structure*, Thap Press.

Pyeong Hyeon Yun(2005), *A Study of Modern Korean Connective Endings*, Pagijong Press.

Sang Tae Lee(1995), *A Syntecto-semantic study of Korean Connective endings*,

Hyungseul Press.

Semodol Son(1996), *A Study of Korean Auxiliary Verb*, Hangukmunhwasa Press.

Seok Choong Song(1988), *201 KOREAN VERBS*, Barron's Educational Series, Inc.

Seoul National Univ. Korean Language Education Research Institute(2002), *Korean Grammar for highschool students*, The Ministry of Education and Human Resources Development.

Tae Ryong Seo(1988), *Form and Meaning of Korean Conjugation Ending*, Thap Press.

The National Institute of Korean Language(1999), *Standard Korean Dictionary*, Doosandong Press, Inc.

The National Institute of Korean Language(2005), *Korean Grammar II for Foreigners*, Communication Books.

The National Institute of Korean Language(2006), *Korean Grammar for Foreigners*, Communication Books.

Ung Heo(1985), *Korean Phonology : Yesterday and today of Korean sound*, Saemmunwhasa.

Ung Heo(1995), *20th century Korean Morphology*, Saemmunwhasa Press.

Yeong Keun Ko(1989), *A Study of Korean Morphology*, Seoul National University Press.

Yonsei University Institute of Language and Information Studies(1998), *Yunsei Korean Dictionary*, Doosandonga Press, Inc.

[Index]